MANLY FERRIES
OF SYDNEY HARBOUR

One of the most graphic pictures of the Manly ferries ever taken. This drama, captured by a Sydney Daily Telegraph *photographer, shows a deckhand grasping for support as the steam ferry* South Steyne *lurches into a big head sea, battling across The Heads on a trip from Manly to the city. Weather like this, of course, is all in a day's work for the crews of these gallant ships and it has to become really bad before the ferry service is suspended.*

OTHER BOOKS
BY TOM MEAD

In print, available from major bookstores. If they do not have them the bookstore can order them from Tower Books, who distribute nationally to bookshops. Tower (02) 975 5566:

Empire of Straw *The rise and fall of colonial tycoon Benjamin Boyd* (Dolphin Books 1994) RRP $29.95. A quality production book of 288 pages with many illustrations, including 8 pages of color pictures and paintings by Oswald Brierly. ISBN 0 909089 04 3.

Killers of Eden *The killer whales of Twofold Bay* (Angus & Robertson 1961-1991. Hardcover and seven paperback editions). Dolphin Books 1992 (enlarged soft cover edition), re-printed 1994. RRP $16.95. Sales more than 64,000 copies. ISBN 0 909089 02 7.

The Fatal Lights (Dolphin Books 1993). *Two strange tragedies of the sea*——the Dunbar (1857) and the Ly-ee-Moon (1886)—drawn to their destruction under lighthouses. RRP $14.95. SBN 0 909089 03 5.

A Few Words (Newspaper & Media Services 1990). *Simple English and sensible grammar for journalists, authors and publicity people.* Used for journalism courses at University of Technology Sydney; University of Western Sydney; Edith Cowan University, Perth WA. ISBN 0 7316 89 X. Available from Dolphin Books, 13/1 Addison Road, Manly 2095, $8.50 posted.

MANLY
FERRIES
OF SYDNEY HARBOUR

THE · SEVEN · MILE · SHIPS

TOM MEAD

DOLPHIN BOOKS

Sydney, Australia.

To the men
of the
Port Jackson & Manly
Steamship Company,
who left
a tradition.

Revised, updated edition published August 1994 by Dolphin Books, 13/1 Addison Road, Manly, 2095, Australia. Printed and bound in Australia by McPhersons Printing Group, Maryborough Victoria. Distributed nationally by Tower Books, Sydney (02) 975 5566.

Published originally by Child & Associates Publishing Pty Ltd, Sydney in February 1988. Reprinted April 1988.

ISBN 0 909089 12 4.

Captain Harold Gibson in full uniform as captain for the Port Jackson & Manly Steamship Company.

Front cover: The SS Barrenjoey *crossing The Heads during a 60-mph south-east gale on Easter Sunday, 16 April 1927. (Fred Elliott)*

Back cover: PS The Brothers. *The first Manly ferry. (John Allcot)*

CONTENTS

This view of Manly shows St Patrick's College as a landmark with new wharves and a good deal of local building.

PART I
EARLY DAYS

1. Prelude

This is a story that should have been told long ago. Much of it has—in the news of the day, in newspaper and magazine articles and in various small historical publications. But nobody previously has put all the pieces together. Two very good books on the ferries of Sydney deal mainly with the inner harbour ferries, allotting only a part to the major Manly service, of which there is a tale to be told, quite different from that of ferries plodding the quiet waters of similar ports all over the world. The Manly ferries and the Port Jackson & Manly Steamship Company are the central characters in a romantic saga of the sea, which, although it embraces more than a century of time, covers mainly only seven miles of water inside what is recognised internationally as probably the finest harbour on earth, Port Jackson, better known as Sydney Harbour. When this manuscript was finished, in 1987, the Manly ferries had been around in one form or another for 140 years; and 67 of those years were under the direction of the Port Jackson & Manly Steamship Company.

Most Australians and many people of other countries know of Manly and the Manly ferries. For those who don't know, Manly is a very beautiful seaside suburb at the northern tip of Sydney Harbour, built on a sandy isthmus with a long ocean surf beach on one side and quiet harbour beaches on the other side. The ferries, and nowadays hydrofoils, are an important link between that end of the harbour and the City of Sydney, where they berth at a terminal near the Opera House, known as Circular Quay. The Manly ferries are stout little ships, usually about 61 metres long—double-enders with propellers and rudders at each end so that they can be driven in and out of the wharves without having to be turned around. Their seven-mile, non-stop journey traverses about one mile of open sea across the majestic entrance to Sydney Harbour known as The Heads. Usually quiet, in bad weather that mile across The Heads can be one of the roughest stretches of estuary water to be encountered anywhere. Because of the big beam swell and lumpy seas they have to ride, often side on, the Manly ferries have traditionally been designed to cope with these conditions. Some were built in Scotland and steamed to Australia under their own power, assisted in earlier days by sails. Contrary to popular belief, however, not all were built abroad and made their way to Sydney over some 12 000 miles of ocean. Most of them were built in Sydney.

Perhaps it is appropriate that this story is told now, when the service has become government-operated and vessels of a different design have taken over from famous names like *Baragoola* and *Bellubera*. Ironically, the State Government of New South Wales, which was largely responsible for the decline of the Manly ferry service after World War II by putting buses into competition with the ferries, has in recent years been building it up again with new ferries and hydrofoils which have attracted growing patronage. The Manly service is unique in being both a commuter service and a tourist attraction, patronised heavily by weekday commuters who work in the city and at weekends by tourists and trippers.

In modern times, when those who are in a hurry can travel the seven miles in 12 minutes on new 40-knot hydrofoils, it is hard to realise that the early settlers of Manly were 112 kilometres from Sydney by rough road or bush track. Before the advent of the ferries, when no bridges crossed the harbour or its upper reaches, commonly known as the Parramatta River, they faced a journey which could take days rather than minutes, involving horse and cart travel over rough tracks around the shores of the whole huge estuary through what are now Narrabeen, Lane Cove, Hunters Hill and Parramatta. Until the first ferry arrived in 1848, a mere 12 families lived in isolation at Manly, now home for nearly a quarter of a million and the holiday resort for about five million tourists a year.

A man named Henry Gilbert Smith first saw the possibilities of Manly back in the early part of the last century. He bought land there and when it was ready for subdivision in 1853 he had built a hotel and a wharf and went into the business of ferrying people to Manly to view what he saw as a magnificent seaside playground of the future. He chartered from John and Joseph Gerard their little paddle-wheel boat, *The Brothers*, with which the Gerard brothers had inaugurated the first ferry service in 1848.

Surfing first became popular at Manly at the beginning of this century, when William Henry Gocher, proprietor and editor of the weekly *Manly and North Sydney News*, forerunner of the *Manly Daily*, defied the police and surfed in the forbidden hours of daylight. In 1902, under the Police Offences Act, it was unlawful to bathe in any waters exposed to view from any wharf, street or dwelling house after 7.30 am and before 8 pm. Gocher's daylight swims attracted police attention to his third attempt, but he exposed the absurdity of the law and in no time surf bathing was allowed, provided men wore neck-to-knee costumes and ladies did not expose their breasts. Five years later, grateful local citizens rewarded him with a purse of 50 sovereigns and a gold watch, and when he died in August 1921, the *Manly Daily* said of his first daring swim: 'That one action of Gocher's has added pounds to every foot of land in Manly, for that was the start of the increase in land values.'

The business centre of Manly fronts The Corso, stretching from the ferry wharf to the ocean beach at South Steyne, a distance of less than half a kilometre. It includes some very valuable property, all of which was given originally as a land grant by Governor Macquarie in 1810 to Gilbert Baker. Henry Gilbert Smith acquired much of this land later, and cleared the place he named The Corso after a street he had known in Rome. Smith was the father of Manly and left to its people most of its important reserves, including the East and West Esplanades fronting the harbour beach. He was also the father of the ferries.

One of the company's proudest achievements was its safety record, despite the sometimes hazardous conditions in which it operated. Former traffic manager, George Marshall, in an address at the 25th anniversary dinner of the World Ship Society in Sydney in April 1982, said:

> It was a wonderful service, world-renowned in the ferry sphere, and it is a pity that such a company should have been allowed to disappear so quietly. The company carried millions of passengers over a period of 100 years without a single loss of life. People have been killed in railway and road accidents, there have been ferry accidents on Sydney Harbour in which lives have been lost, but the Port Jackson & Manly Steamship Company never had a loss of life other than when people jumped overboard deliberately or attempted to board or leave a vessel before it was properly moored.

That good safety record has been carried on by the Urban Transit Authority.

This photograph, taken for the Manly Daily *in May 1983, shows how Manly has grown. The headland beyond Eastern Hill, used for many years as Sydney's quarantine station, is now part of the Sydney Harbour National Park and will be preserved as open park space.*

The Manly ferries have been one of the loves of my life—not unusual for many who have lived in Sydney. John Darroch, a collaborator in this book, also loves them. He has spent 30 years photographing and collecting photographs of the ferries. Many people have helped with their memories of the past. Several were employees of the Port Jackson & Manly Steamship Company, whose slogan, 'Seven miles from Sydney and a thousand miles from care', made Manly like the pot of gold at the foot of the rainbow.

2. The End of an Era

When the *Baragoola* tied up at Circular Quay around 6.40 pm on Saturday, 8 January 1983, and the gangways thudded on to her decks to disembark the passengers, a romantic chapter of maritime history was nearing its end. It was the *Baragoola's* last trip after 60 years in the Manly ferry fleet and far more than a peak-hour load of people had crowded aboard at Manly to have the last ride up the harbour the 'old girl' had tramped so long and so faithfully since her builders delivered her in 1922 to the Port Jackson & Manly Steamship Company. Since then, she had covered nearly 100 miles a day—just on 30 000 miles a year—allowing for time out on refits and overhauls, and she had totalled up 1 763 580 miles during her long working life. Normally, *Baragoola*'s peak-hour commuter load was about 1200 passengers, but on this emotional occasion nobody took any notice of the regulations. They crammed into both decks and overflowed on to the roof and into both wheelhouses.

For *Baragoola* it was all over. She had been on borrowed time with more than one extension of her Maritime Services Board certificate while the Public Transport Commission of the New South Wales Government, which had taken over the ferries nearly 10 years previously, waited for the first of the 'new look' ferries being built to replace the two ageing warriors—*Baragoola* and *North Head*—the last remnants of the once great fleet of seven mighty ships operated by the private company. Up on the bridge, Captain Ron Hart, one of *Baragoola*'s masters for 14 years, saw the last of the huge load of well-wishers ashore, and as the deckhands took in fore and aft mooring lines he pushed the engine control handle to put the ship ahead, then, sadly, turned to the wheelhouse and the man at the wheel. 'Starboard,' he called—the usual instruction for the helmsman to put the wheel to starboard when leaving a wharf on the starboard side—and when he saw the ship's stern was clear of the Quay's No. 3 wharf, Ron went inside and took the wheel himself. It was a strange coincidence that he should be taking the *Baragoola* to be tied up for the last time in active service. When she entered service in 1922 her first master had been Captain John Hart—no relation to Ron—one of the famous old skippers with service dating back to the paddle-wheel days of the 1890s. Out from the Quay, Ron put the wheel slightly to port to turn upstream under the Harbour Bridge and head for the ferry depot at Balmain where it arrived after a detour into the Lane Cove River. The 'old girl' had become part of him. She had been a member of his family, all of whom went with Ron on that last trip.

So did many others with close attachments to the *Baragoola*. One elderly gentleman had come up to the wheelhouse and said to Ron Hart: 'I bet you don't remember me.' Usually the victim of such a greeting doesn't. But Ron said: 'I sure do. I remember when you used to travel with us.' The man had been a commuter. He started as a brass boy in the *Baragoola* in 1923, a year after she was launched. In those days there was plenty of brass for a boy to polish. But Ron remembered him when he worked at Garden Island Naval Depot later and travelled to work from Manly in the ferries. The old fellow looked very ill, as if he had struggled out of a sick bed to go on that last trip,

as indeed he had. The man died a few days later.

Trails of streamers which the well-wishers had brought aboard flopped over the side as the *Baragoola* slowed, stopped and was tied up at Balmain.

Baragoola was being replaced by MV *Freshwater*, an $8.5 million, modern vessel—bigger, faster and promising more comforts—and in less than a year, when another of these new ships was due, *Baragoola* was to have been joined in retirement by an even older companion, the MV *North Head,* formerly the SS *Barrenjoey*, whose travels between Sydney and Manly covered 70 years. This did not happen, however. Two and a half years later the ferry traffic had increased so much that four vessels were really needed instead of three and the *North Head* was being done up to give her another one or two years of life as a spare boat to relieve the three Freshwater class ships when they needed a refit or were out of action for some other reason. The question of building a fourth new vessel was being considered. The service was going through a new boom in patronage which warranted building the new ships. For years a big sign slung across the entrance to the Port Jackson company's Circular Quay wharf had proclaimed 'Seven miles from Sydney and a thousand miles from care.' It had been painted with a background of Manly's Norfolk Island pines and featured the greatest and most famous ferry of them all, the SS *South Steyne*, which had steamed its own way out from Scotland in 1938 and dominated the harbour until a tragic fire ended its reign in 1974. She could have been salvaged and kept running for a fraction of what it was costing to build the new ships and many people had given time and money to prevent her loss, but the *South Steyne* was abandoned because she was the last of the steamships, and because they said she was too big and too costly to operate.

The South Steyne *when she was undisputed Queen of the Harbour, crowded with Sunday-trippers steaming down harbour to Manly.*

The *South Steyne* is a very important part of this story. But not yet. Its saga is to come. Here we are concerned with the general picture of what has made the Manly ferry service unique in a world full of ferry services, what has drawn the people of Sydney to it and, in Sydney, has provided a lifelong attraction for country folk as well as city dwellers.

There are, of course, some who could not be induced aboard the ferries for any consideration when bad south-east or north-east weather propels those long rolling seas in through The Heads. That ride on the roll, on the other hand, is part of the thrill for those who love ships and the sea. It is what has distinguished the Manly ships from the smaller, inner harbour ferry boats which ply between Circular Quay and the quieter waters of Neutral Bay, Cremorne, Mosman, Taronga Park Zoo and the even more sheltered up-river wharves at Balmain, Cockatoo Island, Drummoyne, Greenwich, Gladesville and Meadowbank. Coming up from Manly the ferries thrash into the chop and the swell, hurling walls of water and white spray out from under the sponson, the stout buffer around the hull like a car's bumper bar to protect the sides when bumping against the wharves. Although the ferries are designed to ride beam seas, which means running side on to the swell, some of them do roll considerably. To counter this, going into the seas the captains try to make the ride more comfortable by quartering the swell at an angle instead of taking it head on, which causes a ship to pitch and toss. With the sea behind them it is easier, so, going to Manly, they steer out between The Heads until they turn and ride the waves in, sometimes like a surf boat. At weekends and holidays there are squeals from children and a few screams from women tourists, but on weekdays the commuters never turn a hair. They rarely ever look up from the *Manly Daily* or whatever else they are reading.

At times of gale weather, conditions have forced suspension of the service until the sea settles down from wild to being merely rough. That does not happen very often. It has to be very bad indeed to stop the Manly ferries. Once, in recent years, they continued operating through vile weather in which the Port of Sydney was closed to big shipping. The *Baragoola* and *North Head* climbed mountainous grey peaks, then slid down the backs of the rollers with their propellers racing.

The ferries were stopped after I had travelled to Manly in the *South Steyne* one day in 1974. Surge was so bad at Manly wharf that heavy mooring ropes were snapped, and when they did get the ship tied up it was difficult to keep the gangways in position. When services are suspended, buses are provided to take passengers around the north shore by road. These conditions do not happen often, however, and months can pass with fairly flat seas.

Much has been written in the news of recent times about the decline of the Manly ferry service. True, it did decline for some years because of various factors. But a different situation has applied since January 1978, when the Public Transport Commission brought the inner harbour ferry *Lady Wakehurst* back from Hobart, where she had been on loan as a Derwent River ferry during repairs to the bridge which crashed into the river when struck by a ship.

Withdrawal of the *South Steyne* four years earlier had left only the *Baragoola* and *North Head,* and Manly, once served by a fleet of seven large vessels, had to make do with just two. The government transport authorities told the State Government at the time that two would be sufficient. They said the future lay in hydrofoils, not ferries. Eight hydrofoils had been acquired since 1964. They were twice as fast, covering the seven miles in 15 minutes or less compared with the 33-minute ferry trip, although their maximum carrying capacity was only about one-tenth that of the ferries.

In 1977-78, the Manly ferries carried 3 037 000 passengers and the hydrofoils took 1 985 000. In 1978-79 the hydrofoils increased their loading to 2 066 000, showing a growth rate of 4.08 per cent. But the ferries had a growth rate more than double—3 298 000 passengers, an 8.5 per cent increase. In 1979-80, with the addition of the third ferry to the timetable, the ferry growth rate was quite spectacular. It rose by nearly a million passengers to 4 222 000—up 28 per cent. The hydrofoils took 2 169 000 people, showing about the same growth rate as the previous year—5 per cent. This all proved that a better service would attract better patronage.

At its peak, the Port Jackson & Manly Steamship Company had seven ferries carrying capacity commuter loading as well as heavy weekend and holiday tourist business. The *South Steyne* was licensed to carry 1781, *Dee Why* and *Curl Curl* more than 1500 each, *North Head*, *Bellubera* and *Baragoola* about 1300 each. Between them, they were transporting 14 million passengers a year. They were fed these passengers by the Manly-Warringah tramway system, which brought people to Manly wharf from as far north as Narrabeen. The ferries were so packed in peak hours that people sat on the stairs, despite notices prohibiting this.

But the ferry patronage eventually fell away, Manly's trams were among the first to be scrapped when the Labor State Government decided that buses would supersede them. No doubt there were political considerations. The buses were government-operated and the ferries were private enterprise. In any case, the buses, instead of feeding the ferries as the trams had done for so many years, began to take trade away with direct routes to the city from all the northern beach suburbs. Another big factor in the decline of the ferries was the increased use of private cars with the end of petrol rationing after the war. Whatever the reasons, the ferry patronage fell away and so did the revenue necessary to maintain the service and replace the older ships. Operating costs were rising, too, and in an effort to achieve more economical working, three of the remaining six ferries were converted from steam to diesel-electric power. *Dee Why* and *Curl Curl*, both steamers, were taken off the run and scrapped, the

Bellubera did her last trip in 1973, and a year later the fire that finished the *South Steyne* left only the *Baragoola* and *North Head*.

The Port Jackson company had fallen on hard times long before and in 1972 had sold out to Brambles Industries Ltd, a large transport group which was more interested in acquiring Port Jackson's oil rig supply subsidiary than in taking over the Manly ferries. Brambles fared no better with the ferries and eventually dumped the problem on the State Government, of which I was then a member and chairman of the Government Transport Committee. I had told the Minister for Transport, Mr Milton Morris, some time previously that the Manly ferries were deteriorating as ships and as a service, and we would soon be forced to assume responsibility if the service was to continue. To abandon the service would, of course, be unthinkable. But how much longer would the old vessels last? I suggested that the government should begin to think about building two, if not three, new Manly ferries. That was back in 1972. The Transport Committee held an inquiry into Sydney Harbour ferry services generally and recommended that two new vessels being built for the Mosman and inner harbour routes should be modified with higher bows and upstairs gangway gates so that they could be used in an emergency for Manly. This was a bit of forward thinking that did pay off. The *Lady Wakehurst* and *Lady Northcott*, never intended as Manly ferries, spent much of their time filling in as the third ship during refits of the others before the three Freshwater class vessels came on the scene.

It was 10 years later—December 1982—before the first new Manly ferry built in 45 years, the *Freshwater*, arrived. By then, the government, having realised that three new ships was the minimum requirement, had launched the *Queenscliff* and had let a contract for a third of similar type, the *Narrabeen*. One reason for abandoning the *South Steyne* had been that she was too big, yet these three new vessels were slightly bigger. They had to be to cater for the growing passenger traffic and provide crew accommodation and amenities demanded by the unions. They were comfortable and clean and they had such modern marvels as self-loading gangways which folded up on board and were let down hydraulically, like the drawbridges of old castles, on to wharf landings which could be adjusted to the rise and fall of the tide.

But the young folk who travelled in them would never know the ocean liner feel of the *South Steyne*, the tall funnels of the *Dee Why* and *Curl Curl* belching black smoke, or the clang of the engine room telegraphs. No more would winter travellers sit around the open engine bays to absorb the warmth from the cylinder heads and the exciting smell of those massive steam engines. For boys—even old ones—it was a never-ending thrill when

the bell rang down below and the engineer in his white overalls rose from his rest bench to 'stand by'. Then another clang clang for 'full ahead' and he would begin turning wheels, pulling levers and doing all those things that made the sleeping giants come to life and pulsate their rhythmic beat through the ship.

With the disappearance of the steam engines went part of the soul of the great ferries. The diesels of the new age were hidden below deck and you knew they were there only because of the noise and vibration. The telegraphs and their bells were replaced by controls operating the engines direct from the bridge. Then, with the Freshwater class of vessels, things became even more sophisticated—too much so for a while. The *Freshwater*'s computerised systems were a Frankenstein feature of her first few months in service, causing the ship, amongst other things, to run up on the harbour beach at Manly and on another occasion to drop anchors halfway up to town.

There was a time when weekend trips to Manly had another special feature. Every ferry had a piano and groups of musicians provided enter-tainment, usually adding a banjo and a saxophone to the piano. Percussion was provided by a colleague shaking a collection box as he walked around the decks.

It is easy to be very sentimental about the old days and the old ships. Times change and we must move on. But it is important that those who come after know what went before, even if the older ones insist that 'they don't build things today like they used to build them'. Perhaps. Apart from their antique value, who would prefer to drive a 1910 model car instead of a current model? It might be different with ships, although most people, if they had to go around Cape Horn, would surely prefer the *QE2* to the *Cutty Sark*. The *Freshwater*, *Queenscliff* and the *Narrabeen* are continuing the Manly tradition in a new way, in a new era, but it is fairly safe to forecast that long after they are scrapped, less will have been written about them than the grand old ladies who preceded them.

3. In the Beginning

The first white men who went to Manly nearly 200 years ago sailed or rowed there in ships' boats. Contrary to what most people believe, Manly, not Sydney, was the first landing place in Sydney Harbour. Commander of the First Fleet and Governor of the colony of New South Wales, Captain Arthur Phillip, found not long after arriving at Botany Bay that the bay was not suitable for settlement because every anchorage was exposed to strong winds. He decided, therefore, to explore the possible harbour some miles north which Captain James Cook had passed by without entering 18 years before.

Cook, sailing away from Botany Bay on 6 May 1770, sighted Sydney Heads, but was too far out to sea to notice more than the possible entrance to a port and, strange for one so thorough and inquisitive as Cook, he missed what would have been one of his most exciting discoveries, described later to the British Admiralty by Governor Phillip as 'The finest harbour in the world, in which a thousand sail of the line might ride in the most perfect security'. On those shores was to rise in less than 200 years the great metropolis of Sydney, home of more than three million people and one of the world's great ports and centres of commerce. The sheltered tidal waters of the harbour cover more than 57 square kilometres, bounded by 240 kilometres of foreshores. The depth of water in the one-mile opening across The Heads is 24.4 metres, and the greatest depth inside the harbour, near Balls Head, upriver of the Harbour Bridge, is 49 metres.

The Pier, Manly, NSW.

Cook named the magnificent harbour he never saw, Port Jackson, after the Secretary of the British Admiralty, George Jackson, who probably would not have achieved much fame otherwise. The greatest prominence given to the title was its incorporation in the names of several companies operating Manly ferry services, particularly the Port Jackson & Manly Steamship Company.

Phillip told the British Government in a letter sent home in May 1788: 'When I first went in boats in Port Jackson the natives appeared armed near the place at which we landed and were very vociferous, but, like the others, easily persuaded to accept what was offered them. The boats, in passing near a point of land in the harbour, were seen by a number of men. They examined the boats with a curiosity that gave me a much higher opinion of them than I had formed from the behaviour of those seen in Cook's voyage. Their confidence and manly behaviour made me give the name of Manly Cove to this place.'

Phillip had an encounter of a different kind with the Aborigines in September 1790, when he went with a party in a boat to Manly Cove, intending to land there and walk overland to Broken Bay and the Hawkesbury River. Nearing the beach, they saw about 200 Aborigines cooking and eating the putrefying flesh of a dead sperm whale which had come ashore. The whale had caused some excitement a few days earlier when it entered the harbour. Parties had put out in several boats, from which they tried to harpoon the whale, and three men were drowned when their boat was upset. Governor Phillip had been talking to the Aborigines for about half an hour when one, with a spear in his hand, came forward and stopped 30 metres from where Phillip stood. The Governor held out his hand and called to the man, walking towards him at the same time, but the nearer Phillip approached, the greater became the man's terror and agitation. Phillip thought he might remove the man's fear by throwing down a dirk he wore at his side. It had the opposite effect, however, because the man fixed the spear in his throwing stick, which was like cocking a gun. Phillip, thinking it would probably be more dangerous now to retreat than to advance, called out 'Wee-ree, Wee-ree', meaning 'Bad. You are doing wrong'. Suddenly, the man stepped back and threw the spear with such force that, striking Phillip's right shoulder just above the collar bone, the point, which glanced downwards, came out at his back.

There was instant confusion on both sides. The fellow who had speared the Governor raced off into the woods. Several more spears were thrown, fortunately without hitting anyone else, and the landing party retreated to the boats. Governor Phillip scrambled to the water's edge with some difficulty because the pole of the spear, at least three metres long, was protruding in front of him, impeding his flight. Naval lieutenant Waterhouse tried in vain to break it, but they had no chance of extracting the barb until they could break off the shaft. Eventually they did break it off and assisted Phillip into the boat, where he bled considerably during the dash up the harbour in the frantically rowed craft. Medical examination back in town dispelled any grave fears. According to Captain Watkin Tench, of the New South Wales Marines: 'It was doubtful whether the subclavian artery might not be divided. On moving the spear, however, it was found that it might be safely extracted, which was accordingly performed.'

After that, the manly Aborigines of Manly Cove were left alone for another 20 years. No attempts were made to settle there until the first land grants in 1810. Two of the first landholders were Richard Cheers and Gilbert Baker. Cheers took 100 acres and Baker 30 acres. Both grants would be worth more than a small fortune today. Cheers' land covered what is now Eastern Hill and Fairy Bower and Baker's land was the heart of present-day Manly, from the harbour beach through The Corso. A mere twelve families lived in the whole of Manly.

The first ferry of any kind was provided for a time by a small sailing boat, operated by Barney Kearns, which took a few passengers between Balmoral and Balgowlah at the top of North Harbour. That was in the 1830s, when about 50 people lived between Manly and Pittwater, engaged mainly in agriculture. From Balmoral, the passengers went overland to Milsons Point, where a waterman took them across the harbour to Sydney. Nobody has kept a record of how long the service lasted. It ceased after a while, leaving the pioneer settlers the long overland trek if they wanted to go to Sydney town. Nothing else disturbed the peace until 1848, the year the little steam boat called *The Brothers* began to paddlewheel its way across The Heads, offering up to 50 passengers the first direct passage between Sydney and Manly for a fare of threepence return. *The Brothers*, 67 ft long 10 ft 9 in wide and displacing 23.4 gross tons, was built of wood in Sydney for the brothers John and Joseph Gerard, after whom it was named. The vessel was in use until 1884, when its hulk was broken up at Port Stephens. Its dimensions are very small compared with the 70.4 metres by 12.4 metres (231 ft by 41 ft) of the 1159 tonnes modern Freshwater class Manly ferries.

Other small paddlewheelers followed when it became possible that there might be money in the business. And things began to move when one of Manly's pioneers, Henry Gilbert Smith, seeing the possibilities of sun, sand and surf, invested extensively in real estate. He built the Pier Hotel and the first ferry wharf. In 1853, when he had subdivided some of his land and it was ready for sale, Smith chartered *The Brothers* from the Gerard brothers and went into the ferry business to make sure there were buyers for his land and drinkers for his beer. The *Sydney Morning Herald* of 25 March 1856, told of the crowds flocking to Manly by the steamer, *The Brothers*, three times a week. From *The Brothers*, the service grew until ferries became the main form of transport for people and cargo between Sydney and Manly. The *Phantom* arrived on the scene in 1858, and with her really began the colourful history of the ferries. *Phantom* was the first double-ender and her long white funnel tipped with a wide black band became the distinctive colours of the Manly ferries for more than 100 years until the State Government took them over in 1974 and the green hulls and white and black funnels disappeared into the white and blue uniformity of the inner harbour fleet of smaller ferries.

Phantom was the first Manly ferry to come from abroad, but not under her own power. She was built in sections on the River Clyde in Scotland, and the iron frames and other parts were exported to Melbourne as cargo in a sailing ship. Assembled at Williamstown, the

Advertising material for the Phantom, *used probably in the 1860s.*

Phantom paddled around the Melbourne waterfront for a while before Henry Smith had her steamed up to Sydney to work with *The Brothers*. She was not a comfortable ship. Her narrow beam of only 13 ft in proportion to her length of 120 ft and a very shallow draught of 3 ft 6 in did not provide the good sea boat Manly ferries had to be.

She was known as 'Puffing Billy' because she huffed and puffed, sometimes taking nearly two hours for the trip, and frequently she blew smoke rings from her funnel. Caught in a bad storm crossing The Heads one day, *Phantom* shipped a big wave which put out her fires and left her drifting. The crew raised a jury mast and sail and ran in to Quarantine Beach for shelter. Another bout of bad weather nearly finished her. This time she shipped several big rollers, taking enough water aboard to put out the fires and stop the engine. Again they rigged a jury mast to get out of trouble and battled their way to Sydney safely, though two hours late. To counter the bad roll *Phantom* developed in big swells, the crew used to hang weights on poles slung out on the windward side like outriggers.

Associated with the *Phantom* was the Hot Potato Club, headed by Mr Robert Grant, who devised the idea of roasting potatoes on the boiler grate while they were waiting for the frequently delayed departure from Woolloomooloo, where the ferries called en route in those days. They had the potatoes with hot coffee and bread and butter on their way home to Manly. Similar ideas have taken on at various times in the form of shops or coffee bars aboard the ferries. At one stage the *South Steyne* opened a breakfast bar to sell passengers breakfast and coffee on their way to work, but it did not attract enough patronage and was closed. Shops on the Freshwater class vessels, however, seem to have been very popular, selling anything from ice cream to fairy floss at the weekends and coffee and sandwiches to commuters during the week.

In 1868 Smith sold his interest in the *Phantom* for £2240 to his partners, Tom Heselton and T.J. Parker, whose name was to figure later in the coastal shipping firm of Huddart Parker. That year the Brighton & Manly Steam Ferry Company was formed and Manly began to see a rapid growth in ferry services by boats big and small. Many of these were only part-time ferries. They were essentially tugs, used to tow sailing ships in and out of the port through the week and cutting in on the growing Manly tourist trade at weekends and on public holidays.

Frequently, if a sailing ship was sighted through The Heads, the Manly 'ferry' would divert from its route, taking the load of passengers with it to race out to sea and get the tow into port before a rival tug arrived.

Paddlewheelers plying the route in those early days included *The Nora Creiner* (1854), *Warlington* (1851), *The Huntress* (1854), *Herald* (1854), *Breadalbane* (1853), *Goolwa* (1864), *Royal Alfred* (1873) and *Brightside* (1877). Birds' names seem to have been very popular. Early paddlers included *Emu I* (1855), *Black Swan* (1854) and *Pelican* (1854). Many of these tug-ferries appear to have come on the scene around 1854, trying, obviously, to cash in on the business Smith had built up with *The Brothers* and the *Phantom*. Details of these very early vessels are given in The Ships and the Men.

Not a great deal is known about many of them. The *Herald* was around for quite a while from 1854 until one day in 1884, when she was waiting near The Heads to pick up a towing job with a sailing ship which had been reported off the entrance to the port. Suddenly, there was an explosion. *Herald*'s boiler had burst, knocking a hole in the hull, and in a short while the *Herald* gave up the ghost and sank.

The most famous of the paddlewheel ferries, the *Brighton*, had an overall length of 220 ft—as long as the great *South Steyne*, which came later. *Brighton* was as long as the new class in service now—*Freshwater*, *Queenscliff* and *Narrabeen*—although she did not have their beam. They probably thought in those days that the paddlewheels protruding each side made up for the narrow beam. *Brighton* was as famous in her day as the *South Steyne* in later years. Both these grand ships, with their impressive two-funnel appearance, reigned for many years as queens of the harbour.

Another famous paddler was the *Fairlight*, which steamed out from Scotland in 1878, imported by the Port Jackson Steam Boat Company, the new name in 1878 for the re-organised Brighton & Manly Steam Ferry Company. *Fairlight* was quite a popular ferry in Sydney

until 1908. Built in 1878 by Thomas Wingate & Company, of Glasgow, at a cost to the Manly company of £7600, she was a ship of 315 tons, 171 ft long and with a beam of 22 ft. The 130-hp engines could get *Fairlight* up to 14 knots. She left Glasgow on 14 August 1878, commanded by Captain Roderick, boarded up along her topsides with heavy wooden planks to keep out the big seas she would meet on the way. *Fairlight* made the voyage without mishap via the Suez Canal, averaging 10 knots, and reached Sydney on 2 November. During her trip she battled some very heavy weather without suffering any damage and Captain Roderick was full of praise for the vessel's seaworthiness.

The Fairlight *heading for Manly in the 1890s. (John Darroch)*

Fairlight was involved in a nasty accident on the harbour two days before Christmas 1882, when she ran down a sailing boat near Middle Head, killing one of its three occupants, Arthur Ward. The little boat was crushed under the steamer's paddlewheel. Dr O'Reilly, a passenger aboard the *Fairlight*, told the City Coroner, Mr H. Shiell, at the subsequent inquest that on the day of the tragedy he saw a small sailing boat about 200 metres off the port bow of the steamer, moving in the direction of South Head. He said that the man at the ferry's wheel, about a minute later, turned the wheel rapidly to starboard for two or three revolutions, then sounded what they called in those days the 'engineer's alarm'. Dr O'Reilly told the court:

By that time the boat was out of my view in front of the steamer. After a few seconds, the bow of the steamer struck the sailing boat near its stern, turning it around. It then glided by the side of the steamer and, coming in contact with the starboard paddle, the boat was crushed and sank. The next thing I saw was two men coming to the surface, one of them supporting an object which I recognised to be a boy. A boat was lowered immediately and the two young men and the boy were taken

16

Manly in the early 1880s when it was practically 'the bush'. This was before St Patrick's College or anything else was built on what is now Fairy Bower and Eastern Hill, shown here as a rocky, scrub-covered ridge. The ferry at the wharf is the paddlewheeler Fairlight.

aboard the steamer. The two men were uninjured, but the boy had a large wound across the front of the forehead, revealing a fracture of the skull. This fracture, extending backwards, passed both ears to the upper part of the neck, laying bare the brain substance.' The right arm was also fractured.

The boy died within half an hour of being taken out of the water. One of the others in the boat with him, Richard Matchett Griffiths, told the coroner how they had left Woolloomooloo on that Saturday morning to go for a sail down the harbour and were just off Middle Head when they saw one of the Manly ferries, the *Royal Alfred*, coming up from Manly. They continued towards The Heads, keeping a watch on the *Royal Alfred*, when they saw the *Fairlight* coming down to Manly on the port tack. She was a long way off at that time and, Griffiths believed, had she kept on her course would have passed a long way clear of them. The *Fairlight* was off Georges Head when they put the sailing boat about with only a light wind blowing from the north-east. Griffiths said their jib sheet has just filled to windward when he saw the *Fairlight* about 100 metres off, steering straight for them: He said:

We couldn't get out of the way because the wind was so light. I thought the *Fairlight* would steer out of the way, but she still kept on the same course until she ran us down, hitting our boat about the middle on the starboard side. The boat was turned around like a top and was taken under the steamer's starboard wheel.

Neil Meikleson, master of the *Fairlight* said he saw a little boat standing out from Watsons Bay and the *Royal Alfred* coming up from Manly. He told the man at the wheel, as he had to go below to attend to some business, to keep well out from the *Royal Alfred* and under the stern of the little boat. After having attended to the business below, he

heard the engineer's alarm strike. He went to the bridge immediately and found the telegraph pointing to 'stop'. Then, seeing the sailing boat 10 or 15 metres ahead, he directed the engineer to go full speed astern. When the boat was about 30 metres from the paddle box he ordered the engines stopped, but the boat approached the paddle box and collided with it.

The bridge of these early ferries was amidships and it was customary to have a man on lookout at the front of the vessel. Captain Meikleson said he had a lookout there on the morning of the accident, but when he went below he did not put another man at the helm, although it was a customary practice to do so. He had not his full complement of seamen on board and had reported this to a clerk at the manager's office on the Saturday morning.

The jury deliberated for six hours before returning with the verdict:

That the boy, Arthur Henry Ward, met his death on the morning of the 23rd ultimo through a collision between the steamer *Fairlight* and a sailing boat off Middle Head and that this accident was caused by the steamer *Fairlight* not being sufficiently manned and there not being a proper lookout kept and the Port Jackson Steamship Company are responsible for it.

If the *Fairlight* had a good trip out from Scotland, the *Brighton* was not so fortunate when she left Glasgow for Sydney on 2 June 1883. This big paddlewheel ferry displaced 417 tons, was 220 ft long, of 23 ft beam and drew 10.7 ft. On her trials she had exceeded 15 knots. *Brighton* was schooner rigged for the voyage to Australia so that her sails could be used to assist when winds were favourable. Captain Roderick was again in command, but he left the ship at Malta—we don't know why—and the chief officer, James Japp, brought the *Brighton* on to Australia.

Japp probably would have left also had he known what was ahead. They ran aground three times, battled a savage storm in the Indian Ocean and finished up burning the wooden deck cladding as well as their coal to get them into Sydney. Off Socotra Island, just past the mouth of the Gulf of Aden, a monsoonal gale from the south-west roared in on them, bringing very high seas. Wallowing between the troughs and crests, *Brighton* took a battering. One big greenback carried away part of her deckhouse, tore off a lot of the protective deck planking, smashed nearly all the windows down that side and damaged deck furniture and fittings. There was no let up in the weather for the eight days it took to struggle down to Colombo, where two days were spent bunkering coal. She took on coal again at Singapore on 28 July and left the next day, running with the south-west monsoon to Sourabaya. Leaving there on 4 August, *Brighton* had to push into squally winds and huge seas again. Big rollers swept the length of her decks, flooding all the accommodation above and below decks. Some of the water even invaded the stokehold. Battling weather like this, the stocks of coal began to dwindle and soon they were in such a desperate situation that they had to cut up the deck cladding for extra fuel. Only by burning cabin doors and other parts of the ship's woodwork did they manage to reach Thursday Island on 16 August. Here they were able to obtain more coal and fresh water and set off down the inner passage of the Great Barrier Reef.

The big two-funnelled paddlewheeler Brighton *going astern to berth at Circular Quay in the 1890s.*

For some reason, they did not take aboard a Torres Strait pilot, although this service had become available the previous year. Today, nearly 40 pilots take ships through the dangerous reef passage, staying with them for the whole journey. *Brighton* had left behind the high seas which did so much damage, but in going through the reef she was to face dangers of a different kind—hidden shoals, sandbanks and coral patches—difficult to see by day, impossible to detect at night. Four days south, at 5 am on 20 August, *Brighton* was bowling along at full speed

when there was a sudden bump and a jolt and she shuddered to a stop, her paddles thrashing the water in vain. She had run aground on an uncharted sandbank, fortunately without causing any apparent damage, and when the engines were put astern the ship slid off into deep water. More coal was taken on at Townsville and the voyage proceeded until two days later she ran aground on another hidden sandbank. Again no damage was apparent and the *Brighton* worked herself off. Near Cape Bustard on 28 August, a hidden reef of rocks loomed up with the ship going full ahead, but this time they were able to stop her and avert the danger. Those rocks would not have been as kind to them as the sandbanks.

The *Brighton* reached Sydney early on Saturday morning, 1 September, having taken 89 days from Scotland. With *Brighton*, *Fairlight* and *Brightside* in service, the Port Jackson Steamship Company, as it was then, saw its trade increasing rapidly. At weekends the ferries were carrying full loads, 1200 passengers travelling at times in the *Brighton*. Cargo was another profitable business, even up to the opening of the Spit Bridge in 1924. Nearly everything went to Manly by water in vessels which were part-time tugs for ocean-going ships as well. This was still the day of the sailing ships, all of which needed tugs in and out of the harbour. The Port Jackson Steamship Company had several passenger-carrying tugs, including *Emu*, *Irresistible*, *Commodore* and *Port Jackson*. But as the sailing ships faded away and more steamers came into service, the company began to concentrate on building its passenger traffic, although at times the passengers didn't think so. There were frequent complaints that cargo was given preferential treatment.

Competition became very keen in the 1880s when the Port Jackson company decided to increase its ferry fare to one shilling and sixpence return because business was so good and the company thought it could get away with the price rise. But the customers complained bitterly and, before long, Port Jackson had opposition from a new operator, the Manly Co-operative Steam Ferry Company. Now there was a cut-throat war for the thriving ferry trade. The challenger was John Brown, who decided in 1893 to take on the all-powerful Port Jackson company by chartering some tug-ferries and cutting the fare to sixpence return. At one stage the fare was even reduced to threepence. It all resulted in building up a terrific tourist trade to Manly in those times when the cheaper fare meant a lot to many working families who could never have afforded a day at the beach on the one-and-sixpenny fare.

The ferries were crowded at weekends. Rival craft raced each other to get to the wharves first and gather in the customers. There were fights. Rival crews even took arsenals of stones aboard to throw at each other as their ferries passed. The public was happy and the Manly traffic

PS Goolwa. *(John Allcot)*

PS Mystery. *(John Allcot)*

PS Brightside. *(John Allcot)*

PS Irresistible. *(John Allcot)*

boomed, but the companies found that their bitter battle did not pay, and by 1896 nobody was making a profit. Tugboat owner John Brown had to declare a truce and the two companies amalgamated to form the Port Jackson Co-operative Steamship Company on 15 May 1896. The Port Jackson Steamship Company posted up a black-bordered notice which said:

Sacred to the Memory of THE MANLY CO-OPERATIVE STEAM FERRY COMPY. Born December 1, 1893; died May 15, 1896. After a long and painful illness. REST IN PEACE. Ashes to ashes, dust to dust; If Brown won't take you the Port Jackson must. With sympathy from the Port Jackson Steamship Company for their departed Friend.

Sacred to the Memory of
THE MANLY CO-OPERATIVE
STEAM FERRY COMPY.
Born December 1, 1893
DIED MAY 15, 1896.
After a long and painful illness.
REST IN PEACE.

Ashes to ashes, dust to dust;
If Brown won't take you, the Port Jackson must.

With sympathy of the Port Jackson Steamship Company for their departed Friend

This board was posted by the Port Jackson Steamship Company to record the take-over of the Manly Co-operative Steam Ferry Compy.

The paying public did not come out of the ferry war too badly. The return fare remained at sixpence for some time and the amalgamated company was induced to build bigger, better and more comfortable ships than those that were in service before the 1880s. The company was re-formed in 1907, becoming the Port Jackson & Manly Steamship Company, the last of six companies to operate Manly ferries from the time the service was started with *The Brothers* in 1848. The history of the various companies and their struggle for power is long and involved and would have limited interest today apart from a few highlights of events along the way. The Port Jackson & Manly Steamship Company days are remembered best as the age of the great Manly ferries, particularly up to World War II, when the company's fleet consisted of seven good vessels—*Balgowlah*, *Burra Bra*, *Baragoola*, *Bellubera*, *Barrenjoey* (later *North Head*), *Dee Why*, *Curl Curl* and *South Steyne*.

The *Brighton* was the last of the Manly ferries to be built overseas for nearly 50 years. In 1886, the Mort's Dock Company at Balmain designed and built for the Manly run the *Narrabeen*, an iron paddle steamer of 239 tons, 160 ft in length, which, although small, gave good

Narrabeen I *with a good paying load. In the early part of this century more attention was paid to safety standards and in 1908 the master of the* Brighton *was fined for overloading his ferry. (John Darroch)*

service up to 1911, when she was retired to cargo service with the *Fairlight*, which had also been pensioned off from passenger work. *Narrabeen* was followed by nine other good ships built for the Port Jackson & Manly Steamship Company at Mort's Dock. The *Manly* (1896) was the first double-ended, propeller-driven ferry. After her came *Kuring-gai* (1901), *Binngarra* (1905), *Burra Bra* (1908), *Bellubera* (1910), *Balgowlah* (1912), *Barrenjoey* (1913) and *Baragoola* (1922).

The *Manly* brought the first challenge to the reign of the paddlewheelers. She was so fast she could leave anything on the harbour well behind. In 1912, the *Manly* did the run in 22 minutes, a time that has never been beaten, although the *South Steyne* is said to have equalled it. This was a remarkable performance in those days and it is still remarkable, comparing very favourably with the 15 minutes taken by the hydrofoils at 35 mph in modern times. Actually, this ferry was *Manly II*. For the purposes of this story, however, she will be referred to merely as the *Manly*. She figures later in a very dramatic incident.

Kuring-gai, designed by naval architect Walter Reeks, introduced the basic design type of Manly ferry which was to follow through in *Binngarra*, *Burra Bra*, *Bellubera*, *Balgowlah*, *Barrenjoey* and *Baragoola*. They were good sea boats, fast, and offering more comforts than their predecessors, which had open top decks. *Kuring-gai* won instant acclaim for the quality of her passenger accommodation, the polished Australian timbers throughout, mirrors and electric lights. Her overall building and fitting out cost was only £23 789, which is about the cost of a small pleasure boat nowadays. Looking back, it is hard to imagine being able to build at 1200-passenger steel ferry for that price. *Kuring-gai* set a pattern for the shape of things to come and it saw little variation until the construction overseas of the three bigger ships *Dee Why, Curl Curl* and *South Steyne*. One major change was made in 1905, when Mort's Dock built another ferry very similar to *Kuring-gai*. The big difference was that for the first time there was a wheelhouse at each end instead of both being amidships on either side of the funnel. The new ferry was the *Binngarra*, the first of six built at Mort's Dock, all given names beginning with B.

Three of these Mort's Dock ferries, built years before those ordered from overseas, gave long years of service and two—*Baragoola* and *Barrenjoey*—outlasted the imported vessels. *Dee Why* is now growing feed for fishes as an artificial reef out from its namesake beach and *Curl Curl* is on the sea bed about 18 miles south-east of Sydney Heads. The Mort's Dock ferries gave splendid service during their long lives and clocked tremendous distances. Great advance claims were made in 1982 for the *Freshwater*, which was going to do 18 knots and cut the journey to 20 minutes, neither of which happened. Any of the Freshwater class ferries can do the trip in 25 minutes, but so did the *Balgowlah*, whose steam engines pushed her along easily at a good 16 knots when she appeared on the scene in 1912. *Balgowlah* is credited with having covered 715 000 miles in the 110 000 return trips she did in her 41 years. *Bingarra* lasted 28 years, travelling nearly 700 000 miles and carrying about 30 million passengers. *Bellubera* was there for 59 years and *Baragoola* for 60 years. The record-holder is *North Head*, built in 1913 as *Barrenjoey*, rebuilt in 1948-51 with diesel-electric power and renamed *North Head*. She was still working as a spare boat until 1986—a remarkable life span of 73 years. In 1987 she was taken to Hobart under her own power to be converted into a floating restaurant.

The scene was changing in 1985. People were coming back to the Manly ferries in great numbers. The new vessels might not have had the romance of their predecessors, but they were more comfortable and the people liked them. The third of these new vessels was delivered in 1984 and a fourth was ordered for 1988.

But we are getting ahead of the story. A lot of water has to flow under the ferries yet.

4. A Wild Night

The hardy folk who travelled to and from Manly in the early days had some rough and even frightening trips, with far more risk than in modern times because the harbour north of Bradleys Head was practically uninhabited and very few other craft were about if rescue was needed. The upper decks of early ferries were open to the weather, cold winds and wet spray, yet those who lived at Manly enjoyed the trip as much as the commuters of today, whose journey to and from work is a commuter's dream. For the holiday crowds, the trip to Manly was an exciting event. Some of these people tell about those early

days in a recorded series of interviews on tape in the Manly Public Library. Mr Albert Smith recalls:

When we first came to Manly we did it in picnic fashion. We were living at Dulwich Hill and we would catch a steam tram at Marrickville, load ourselves aboard with the old-fashioned picnic hamper and set out for a day's outing at Manly Beach. At Circular Quay we would board one of those lovely old paddle-wheel steamers. It could have been the *Fairlight*, the *Narrabeen* or the king of the fleet, the lovely old two-funnel *Brighton*. Off we would go down the harbour, and as I look back now I can see the greenery all the way. There was hardly a house in existence down the harbour before the turn of the century. It was just fantastic. I can't think of a better way to describe the glory of a trip to Manly by one of those ferries. Rolling through The Heads was an experience on its own.

How it was in the early days. Until the Spit Bridge was built, everything had to go to Manly by water.

Mr Smith remembered the *Manly*:

She was the first double-ender driven by propellers and she was very fast. The engines were too powerful for the hull and would nearly shake the ship to pieces at full speed. To correct the trouble, they put a steel brace right through the hull to hold it together.

In another interview, Mr Les Graham told of the changeable weather and its effect on the harbour.

In wild weather the ferries were, of course, an attraction for young people, who would dash down to the wharf to get a ride across The Heads on the rough seas before the service was stopped, as would happen if it became really rough.

A woman told of her days going to school:

> We had some very traumatic trips in those days. Very often the boat would be right down between the waves. You wouldn't be able to see anything but the waves on either side. Because the upper decks were not closed in, you would get the spray, but it was considered rather infra dig to go downstairs to the closed-in compartments. It was a matter of pride that you rode upstairs if you could.

Another woman recalled:

> The ferries took me to school. A tram into Manly, the ferry across to Sydney and another ferry to Kirribilli, where I attended school. The ferries were very homely places in those days. Everyone knew everyone else. As teenagers, we picked up our best boy friends on the ferry.

The ferry rides were not always that pleasant. For instance, on the night of Sunday, 30 June 1901, when 50 people had the ride of their lives which would leave them with much more vivid memories of the SS *Manly* than that Mr Smith recalled. The passengers and the *Manly* with its crew were nearly lost in a particularly wild gale which swept the east coast of New South Wales and caused considerable damage. The *Sydney Morning Herald* of Tuesday, 2 July, told in the multiple headline style of the day: 'A Disastrous Cyclone. Gales off the Coast. The *Protector* Capsizes. Loss of Six Lives. Another Steamboat Wrecked. The Captain and Three Men Perish.'

Actually, 10 men perished at sea in the cyclone—six when the tug *Protector* was rolled over and smothered by a huge wave on the bar at Ballina, and four when the steam drogher *Alexander Berry* was smashed on rocks near Shellharbour. Shipping was forced to take shelter wherever possible along the coast. The *Herald* told how the steamer *Innamincka*, a powerful ship of 2500 tons, had to seek refuge in Broken Bay, at the entrance to the Hawkesbury River, on her way from Brisbane to Sydney. The paper said:

> She was reported on Sunday evening as having passed Seal Rocks at 12.30 pm and Port Stephens at 5 pm, so that in the ordinary course she would have reached Sydney at 11 o'clock on Sunday night, or certainly by midnight. It will be seen that she was nearly five hours steaming 26 miles, a fact which illustrates forcibly the great severity of the gale. Broken Bay is but some 20 miles north of Sydney and that such a splendid vessel as the *Innamincka* had to break her passage there affords abundant evidence of the kind of weather prevailing between Sydney Heads and Barrenjoey.

*The SS M*anly, *the first double-ended Manly ferry with propellers instead of paddle wheels. (John Darroch)*

It was in such conditions that the *Manly* took on 50 passengers for the 10.15 pm trip to Sydney. She was a tough little ship, capable of carrying 820 passengers, designed by Walter Reeks, who was to be the designer of several more Manly ferries. The *Manly* was smaller than the 220 ft *Brighton* or the *Fairlight,* 171 ft. She was 147 ft long, with a beam of 15 ft 6 in. Her keel, frames, floors and beams were of hardwood, the decks were kauri pine and the hull was of oregon, copper-fastened to 2 ft above the waterline. There was comfortable accommodation for passengers in the saloons on the lower deck, including a ladies' cabin, tastefully decorated, with curtains and such modern facilities as electric light.

Captain Percy Davies, master of the *Manly*, knew they were in for a rough trip that Sunday night in 1901. The weather, bad during the day, became much worse after dark. The southerly wind, and the waves it created, did not make such an exposed place as Manly wharf a desirable haven while the crew of the *Manly* waited for sailing time. The surge was building up, causing the ferry to bump heavily against the wharf piles and strain at her groaning mooring ropes.

They cast off at 10.15 pm and headed out into the darkness of the foul night, not unduly worried. They were used to strong winds and big seas, and the ship was riding easily over the swell, which increased as they passed Smedleys Point, leaving behind the shelter of the peninsula dividing Manly Cove and Little Manly Cove. Now she was dipping constantly, cutting the rollers and hurling aside great showers of white spray. Captain Davis steered the usual course for bad southerly weather—beam-on as far as Dobroyd, then out into it as they began to take the full force of the big swell rolling in from the open sea. That night it was particularly bad, with the swell coming in through The Heads and the wind blowing more south-west across it. Davis headed his ship out until he was near Inner South Head, then turned to starboard to make a course which would take him up the harbour, passing the lightship *Bramble* on his port side. In those days the lightship was moored to mark the dangerous Sow and Pigs reef, just inside the harbour entrance. Davies had just altered course when he noticed that they were losing headway and the engineer called up the speaking tube that he was having trouble down below. Suddenly the engines were silent and there was that awful stillness when engines break down at sea. Usually, when engines stop of their own accord they are not restarted easily, and here they were, disabled in a howling gale which would push them on to the rocky base of the cliffs somewhere between Flagstaff and North Head. Davis could not see that far in the darkness, but he knew what it would be like over there with that sea crashing ashore. *Manly* was wallowing now, mostly beam-on to the treacherous seas as the wind drove her back. They let go the port anchor and paid out about 30 fathoms of cable, but the drift continued. Of course it would most of the way across. Some of the crew did a bit of fishing in their spare time. They knew the anchor would drag on that sandy bottom, perhaps until it caught up in the foul stretch of rocks and kelp, only a narrow strip, unfortunately, along the Inner North Head shoreline. Captain Davis ordered the crew to burn blue distress flares. They had two chances. The government yacht *Victoria*, acting as pilot boat for the port, was stationed in Watsons Bay, and then there was the *Brighton*, due to come down from Sydney very soon. The *Brighton* should see the flares. But could she reach them before they reached the rocks?

A sudden jerk and the ship slewed around to bring her head into the sea. The anchor had caught the edge of the reef bottom and the crew saw with some anxiety that they were only about two lengths out from the seaward side of Quarantine near what is known as Old Man's Hat. The anchor would surely hold now, but the danger was its chain. If that broke the *Manly* would be smashed to pieces in minutes. It was jerked constantly as the ship's bows rose abruptly on each mounting billow. Despite the roar of the boiling sea as it tumbled on the rocks and the possibility that at any minute the *Manly* could become part of that turmoil, there was no panic among the passengers. One man took off his shoes and rolled up his trousers, 'to get ready for swimming', as he said later, but the women stayed in the saloon and cheered themselves up by singing—except two who didn't care very much. They were violently seasick.

Across The Heads the black night was broken only by the beam of the Macquarie Lighthouse on South Head and the gleam of the Hornby Light on Inner South Head. The tops of the waves sizzled past the sides of the bucking ship and there was the occasional whack of the anchor chain as it flopped across the surface of the water after pulling the ship back into line. When the wind blew stronger and the waves gathered that extra strength they take on in their final dash shorewards, the anchor chain ground itself against the edges of the cleats which kept it in position on the port bow. To Captain Davis and his crew, this, while it continued, was the most comforting sound of all. Below, in the madly pitching and rolling engine room, desperate efforts were being made to get things going again. The condenser was the trouble. They found out later that seaweed was choking the injector, disabling the feed pump.

Occasionally the darkness was relieved by the glimmer of lights up the harbour, but they were not the ones Captain Davis wanted to see. He stood clutching the side of his crazily swaying wheelhouse, waiting for a cluster of lights to appear around Bradleys Head—the *Brighton* on her way down from the Quay. They had been in their perilous position nearly three-quarters of an hour before the lights emerged around the upper harbour headland. Davis then ordered rockets fired and the burning of flares intensified. Captain James Drewette, on the bridge of the *Brighton*, saw the rockets and flares with some sense of uneasiness. The *Manly* should have arrived in town long ago. Those distress signals could only be from her. He called down the tube for every bit of speed they could get from the engines, and with the wind and weather behind them it was not long before they were bowling across the open seaway of The Heads. Those watching from the *Manly* saw *Brighton*'s lights disappear from time to time, swallowed in the troughs of the tumbling walls of water. *Brighton* drew near in a cloud of spray, cheered by everyone on the *Manly*. Although he was greatly relieved to see the *Manly* still safe, Captain Drewette realised immediately the difficulty of trying to wrest her from such a delicate and dangerous position. There was no chance of going behind the *Manly* and coming up alongside to get a line across. How to get a tow line aboard and drag her out without both of them ending up ashore presented a problem requiring great skill and even more good fortune.

By skilful seamanship, Drewette and his crew eventually succeeded in getting a tow line aboard, and they took up the tow slowly, getting the weight off that anchor— another problem. But Davis was not going to try getting the anchor and chain in. 'Let it go,' he yelled to the deckhands up for'ard, and they did. The *Victoria* arrived just then, but seeing that the *Manly* was under tow, retreated back into the harbour. The passengers on both ships cheered, the *Brighton*'s engines throbbed and her big sidewheels churned a foamy wake out of the paddle boxes. Twice the tow line parted in the heaving swell and the crews had to get it fast again, but now there was room to manoeuvre in the ground they had put between them and the shore. Turning in, they headed for North Harbour and the quieter waters beyond Manly Point. Suddenly the

The grand old paddlewheeler Brighton *aground in Chowder Bay, near Clifton Gardens, after she had been holed in a collision with the collier* Brunner *in August 1900. They were lucky to beach her after the big hole had been torn in her side.*

Manly's engines came to life and she was able to proceed under her own steam again into the entrance to North Harbour, where Captain Davies put down his other anchor and the *Brighton* went on to Manly wharf to land her passengers. While she was away, the *Manly*'s anchor began to drag and Captain Davis sent a boat over to get help again from the *Brighton*. They were no sooner under tow again than this rope snapped. Now *Manly* drifted into water too shallow to risk stranding the bigger *Brighton* and, reluctantly, Captain Drewette had to leave his colleague to his fate on the sandy bottom between the wharf and the ladies' swimming baths on the eastern shore. The passengers were still aboard the *Manly* and the problem was how to get them ashore. It was solved by taking a line ashore in the boat that had gone to get help, and when this rope was made fast ashore the boat was hauled to and from the ship, hauling on the rope. It took the passengers, ladies first, four and five at a time through the heavy surf which pounded the harbour beach in Manly Cove. Three or four times the boat was swamped and it was nearly 3 am before all were ashore. They were dried off and accommodated for the night at the Pier Hotel. Both Captain Davis and deckhand John Conwell agreed they had never spent such a rough and unpleasant night in their lives. One of the deckhands who had been a master in his time said that in 27 years' experience he had not known such wild and unpleasant weather on Sydney Harbour.

The J. and A. Brown tug, *Port Jackson*, arrived at the scene soon after the *Manly* grounded and stood off during the remainder of the night. At daylight she got a hawser aboard and towed the *Manly* in another rough trip up the harbour to the Port Jackson company's works at Kurraba Point, Neutral Bay. Subsequent inspection revealed that the ferry was little the worse for her battering and she was soon back in normal service.

Six months later, on 7 December 1901, the *Evening News*, in a story headed 'Seamanship Rewarded' said:

An interesting ceremony was performed on Friday by the Sydney Underwriters' Association, when Captain Percy Davies, of the steamer *Manly*, and Captain James Drewette, of the *Brighton*, were presented with souvenirs in recognition of their smart seamanship on the occasion of the mishap to the *Manly* during the memorable gale of 30 June this year. The manager of the Port Jackson Steamship Company, Mr Fitzsimmons, also shared in the presentation as a result of his prompt action in having the *Manly* refloated. The skippers received silver liquor stands and Mr Fitzsimmons a silver salver. The proceedings were of an enthusiastic character and the recipients each made a suitable acknowledgement.

5. Profit and Loss

Operation of the Manly ferries has been almost like a primary industry, with good and bad seasons—some years a profit, sometimes a loss. The business was founded on the tourist trade, grew with a mixture of tourist and commuter traffic, and declined to a stage where the ferry service almost went out of existence, but in the 1980s it swung back into an ever-increasing and more viable operation than before. By 1984 the Manly ferry service, which nobody wanted 10 years previously, had become one of the New South Wales Urban Transit Authority's few profitable undertakings. The State Government took it over in 1974 from Brambles Industries Ltd, whose two-year reign left the Port Jackson & Manly Steamship Company a poor business proposition. Brambles, a big land transport company, acquired the ferry company in a $2.1 million take-over early in 1972. Why they did and what happened is a later part of the story. In 1974 the Government had to make another take-over because Brambles, having lost $48 000 on the ferries in 1973, lost interest in the deteriorating fleet of vessels remaining and if the Government had not intervened to save the service it would have ceased to exist. In the early 1980s, however, the ferries came into their own again, particularly after the introduction of the big new ships, *Queenscliff and Freshwater*, which were so comfortable and popular that they ate into the hydrofoil traffic rapidly. The ferries were profitable again—weekend and holiday gold mines.

It was not always so. The financial viability of the ferries is reflected in the annual reports and half-yearly reports, first of the Port Jackson Co-operative Steamship Company and later the Port Jackson & Manly Steamship Company. The report to the directors of the co-operative company for the half year ended 30 June 1898, congratulated the shareholders on 'the prosperity of the company'. It said:

> The result of the business for the past year, after maintaining the steamers inefficient working order and providing £4842 12s 0d for depreciation, leaves a balance of £3961 17s 1d, out of which it is proposed to pay a dividend of 10 per cent to the shareholders and five per cent to the debenture holders, absorbing £2968 8s 0d and leaving £993 9s 1d to be carried forward.

Two years later the profit had increased to £7424 15s 8d and by 1911 the holders of the 250 000 £1 shares in what was now the Port Jackson & Manly Steamship Company were to be paid a dividend of one shilling a share from the half year's profit of £8380 18s 9d. The chairman, Mr J. J. Eyre, and manager, Mr F. J. Doran, stated in their report:

> The SS *Bellubera* was placed in commission on the 9th September last and is giving every satisfaction. She has been running without any intermission since the above date and is very popular with the travelling public and the residents of Manly.

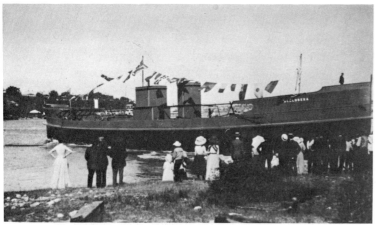

The Bellubera *being launched from Mort's Dock at Woolwich on 26 April 1910. (John Darroch)*

In the report for the half year 31 December 1911, they said:

> It was mentioned in the last report that two more steamers of the same class as the *Bellubera* had been

Bellubera, *decked out with bunting, on her trials in September 1910, when she clocked 15 knots to become the fastest ferry on the harbour at that time. (John Darroch)*

ordered. The builders, Mort's Dock and Coy. Ltd., are making good progress with the work and it is expected that the first of them will be launched early in April next.

The report for the half year ended 31 December 1912 announced:

> After undergoing successful steam trials, the new steamer *Balgowlah* was taken over from the builders and placed in commission on the 25th November last and is giving every satisfaction. The builders are making good progress with the second steamer ordered and, as stated in the last report, she will be in commission during September next.

Profit for the half year was £11781 4s 4d after paying £5044 15s 0d on account for the new ship.

By 1936, the company was making a profit for that year of £22 575 1s 3d. General manager then was Mr W. L. Dendy, a man who was to have a great influence on the company. He reported:

> Excursion traffic for another season was affected by unsatisfactory weather. It is now five years since we have had a summer season favourable to our business with continuous warm days and settled weather conditions. Statistics issued by the Divisional Meteorologist, Mr Mares, showed that the mean maximum temperature for February—75.1 degrees [Farenheit]—was the lowest for the last 77 years. The remarks made in last year's report re Manly's increasing popularity as a residential suburb still hold good and the percentage of revenue received from the sale of season tickets compared with that received from our excursion trade is a record in the history of the company.

Mr Dendy noted that the company's steamers made 32 188 trips between Sydney and Manly during the year—equal to 225 316 miles, 'thus making further history for the company as it constitutes a record'.

The annual report to 30 June 1952, however, told of decline in business, due largely to inroads being made by direct bus services to the city and greater use of private cars with the lifting of petrol rationing after the war. The service was profitable no longer, despite inauguration by the State Government of a bus-ferry diversion program to co-ordinate services to Manly. For some years after the scrapping of the Manly tramway system which had fed the ferries at Manly wharf, the Labor State Government and the bus unions had been luring patronage away from the ferries with direct bus services to the city from as far north as Narrabeen and Palm Beach. But now the competition had gone too far and the ferry company was in trouble. The Government did not want it out of business altogether. The directors' report said:

> Although every effort was made by the Government and the company to give quick and efficient service, the actual financial results have been insufficient to close the gap between revenue and expenditure. Success of the future activities of this company depends on earning considerably greater revenue and this, with other related matters, has been referred to the State Government. The Government realises the difficulties and is now examining various proposals to determine what steps might be taken to enable the company to improve the position.

Worse was to come the following year. At an extraordinary meeting held in February 1953, shareholders were informed that a budgeted loss of £40 000 was possible for the financial year, but it was hoped this would be reduced by increased fares from December 1952, and 'further economies'. The annual meeting in June was no doubt relieved to learn that the loss had been reduced to only £10 671, but the company's shareholders were also told in the director's report that 'it is a matter for regret that while the year's financial results have shown a marked improvement over the anticipations of the budget, they do not warrant payment of a dividend.'

Profitable operations returned before long, however, helped by fare increases, as well as the Sunday and holiday ocean-cruises up the coast to Broken Bay by the big new ferry *South Steyne*, and conversion of the *Bellubera* and *Baragoola* to diesel-electric operation after 1958. The profit in 1954 was £29 609.

Weather continued to play a big part in the fortunes of the ferry service. Another factor was the cheaper fares offered by government bus services, which were taking away the ferry passengers with the direct trips to the city. In addition to having to cope with higher costs of labour,

maintenance and fuel, the company battled what it described as 'exceptionally bad weather' in the summer of 1956, which was the wettest for 60 years and provided few sunny days to pack people into the ferries for a day at Manly beach. Thus, the trend in ferry patronage continued downwards, from 6 727 000 in 1955-56 to 6 036 000 in 1956-57. In 1957, tripper traffic was hit again with cold and overcast weather through January, February and March. February was the coldest for 20 years. The impact of the government bus opposition on commuter patronage was shown clearly during a strike at the Brookvale bus depot, during which the daily ferry loadings picked up by 70 per cent. Taking everything into consideration, the Port Jackson company did quite well to provide a good service all those years, build new ferries and remain in business.

The image of the Manly ferry, as it came to be known generally, evolved from the six double-ended steel vessels built in Sydney by Mort's Dock & Engineering Company between 1905 and 1922—*Binngarra* (1905), *Burra Bra* (1908), *Bellubera* (1910), *Balgowlah* (1912), *Barrenjoey* (1913) and *Baragoola* (1922). Double-ended vessels had been the most successful from the paddle-wheeler days because of the difficulty of turning around at Circular Quay in the crowded Sydney Cove, and in strong winds at Manly. Also, the requirements of speed and coping with heavy weather demanded sharp bows—sharp sterns as well if they had to go astern quickly, as happened often in heavy harbour traffic. With so much experience over more than a century as a guide, it is difficult to understand why the State Government's Urban Transit Authority ordered, in the early 1980s, three big new ships with bluff bows and sponsons which stopped short of the bows behind the anchor hawse holes. The sharp bows and wrap-around sponsons of the older ferries allowed them to cut into a big sea and throw most of it aside. In contrast, the first of the new breed, the *Freshwater*, horrified the Manly ferry faithful when she appeared in the harbour pushing ahead of her a bow wave like a barge. It was apparent at once how much green water she was going to ship over the front in heavy weather.

But back to where the story was in the earlier part of the century, from 1905-25. The six 'B class' ferries, as they might be called, were among the biggest ships built in Australia in those years. Mort's Dock executives said they were built more for prestige than profit, although they did cost slightly more than if they had been built in England or Scotland. For the Port Jackson & Manly Steamship Company, however, Mort's Dock was cheaper than steaming new ferries out from the other side of the world. The first of the new-look ferries, the *Kuring-gai*, designed by Walter Reeks, built at Mort's Dock, Balmain, in 1901 had cost £23 789. Building cost of the *Balgowlah* in 1912 was £29 000 and *Barrenjoey*, 12 years after *Kuring-gai*,

The first of the 'new look' Manly ferries, the Kuring-gai *at Circular Quay in 1904. (John Darroch)*

cost only £32 000. But the next and last, *Baragoola*, in 1922, reflected the rapid rise in wages and other charges after World War I, and the bill for her was £80 000. Australia, the lucky country, even then was pricing her industries out of business. It would be cheaper in future to have new ships built overseas. Those prices were nothing, however, compared with what lay ahead. Rebuilding and re-engining the *Barrenjoey* as *North Head* in 1951 cost £275 000. Replacing steam engines with diesel-electric in the *Baragoola* in 1960 cost £65 000. By 1983, the New South Wales Urban Transit Authority was looking at the best part of $10 million each for the three new ferries it ordered, all built in Newcastle; two at the State Dockyard and one at Carrington Slipway. Compared with the price of the *Kuring-gai* 80 years before, the cost was 210 times as much.

The *Kuring-gai* made quite an impression when she entered the Manly service. 'Pearl of the fleet', said one newspaper. 'The saloon fittings are of beautifully polished colonial woods and the ladies' boudoir is simply perfect. The electric light is installed throughout the vessel and will serve at all times as well as the beautiful but inconsistent moon.'

Mort's Dock designed the six Manly ferries which followed the *Kuring-gai*, but they all looked very much like Walter Reeks' *Kuring-gai* in their basic lines. It was a great day for Sydney when Miss Loudon, daughter of Port Jackson & Manly Steamship Company director, W. J. Loudon, smashed a bottle of wine on the bows of the *Burra Bra* at Mort's Woolwich dock at high water (10.17 am) on 17 June 1908. Thousands of spectators lined the shores and another 700 had come up river in the *Binngarra*, which the Port Jackson company had made available for invited guests to travel to the launching. *Binngarra* was decorated from stem to stern with bunting, a band was playing aboard and the guests were taking advantage of refreshments which the directors had made

available for their comfort. Reporting the event, the *Manly Argus and Northern Express* described the directors as men 'worthy to be enrolled in the niche of fame when the future history of Manly is written'. The *Argus* did not say whether its enthusiasm was entirely for the new ferry or in part for the refreshments. The paper added: 'We cannot do less than let the world know the names of the true friends of this village, who, by their enterprise, are building up the prosperity of Manly and district.' Manly was by then known somewhat affectionately as 'The Village'.

The new seaside resort was certainly becoming prosperous. Traffic to Manly was growing fast. In February 1908 the master of the *Brighton* was fined for overcrowding his ferry. Apart from the weekend and holiday trippers, many people were making their homes at Manly, some induced by the ferry company's offer of free passes for five years for those who bought land the company subdivided and auctioned, if the buyers built a house costing not less than £1000. The fare at that time was fourpence for adults and twopence for children. Manly Council tried to get the fare reduced to threepence, but there was some opposition to this on the grounds that many of the threepenny trippers would not be exactly the kind of Sydney's young people the village would want to welcome. It was, of course, a time when things were very cheap compared with modern times and ferry crews worked long hours for little pay. Firemen worked 120 hours a fortnight for £3 10s 0d (or the equivalent of $7 when this story was written). Deckhands received only £2. Overtime after 120 hours in the fortnight was paid at the rate of sevenpence an hour for firemen and fourpence an hour for deckhands.

A few months after the launching of *Burra Bra*, two almost identical accidents damaged *Kuring-gai* and *Binngarra* at Circular Quay when they overshot the wharf and crashed into the footpath. This is the perpetual nightmare of ferry skippers and it has happened at some time or other to many of them. Ferries approaching the terminal wharves at Circular Quay and Manly usually stop the propellers several hundred metres from the wharves and leave the vessel to glide in, losing way gradually. At the end of the wharf, in the steam days, they would ring down on the engine room telegraph for full astern. Nowadays, they put the engines astern direct from the bridge. The ferry at this stage still has a fair amount of drift and if there is not quick response to full astern, the ship has no brakes except the stout wall of big timber buffers and, at Circular Quay, the footpath. That is what happened at the Quay on 1 November 1905, when *Binngarra*'s engine room bells rang in vain. She tore into the footpath, scattering a scared group of spectators, tearing the steel footpath railings and dislodging big blocks of stone as she gouged a huge cavity out of the footpath and roadway. The company's cargo paddlewheeler, *Brightside*, spent half an hour trying in vain to tow *Binngarra* out, and similar efforts by Fenwick's tug, *Leveret*, failed. Another powerful tug, *Hero*, joined *Leveret*, but *Binngarra* still refused to move for another hour. The two tugs finally levered her loose by pulling from side to side.

Four days later the *Kuring-gai* did the same thing and jammed herself in the same hole. Reporting the incident, Sydney *Truth* said:

The screams of women and the hoarse cries of strong men in their agony could be heard from afar. Several lady passengers seized the occasion to faint and throw a back'un and the commotion was quite considerable for a while. The *Kuring-gai* damaged her fore rudder and had to go off under her own steam, being relieved by the *Binngarra*, which, after her smash on Wednesday, was just coming out of Mort's Dock to resume her running.

The Manly ferries have always been named after local places or have been given Aboriginal names. None of them have been called 'Sydney', as many people have imagined, seeing Sydney, the port of registration, on the stern of the ferry in which they went to Manly. Kuring-gai was the name of a tribe of Aborigines who lived north of Sydney in an area which still bears their name. Burra Bra is an Aboriginal word meaning a tongue or spit of land, thought to refer to the Spit, a well-known part of Middle Harbour. Balgowlah is a suburb, part of the Manly area. Barrenjoey is Aboriginal for little kangaroo. Bellubera is another Aboriginal name. It means pretty lady. Baragoola is a native word meaning flood tide. The *Dee Why*, *Curl Curl* and *South Steyne* ferries were given the names of those three famous Manly-Warringah beaches.

One puzzling feature is the different spellings some of the ferries' names have attracted at different times. *Burra Bra* has become *Burra-bra* or *Burrabra*, *Binngarra* became in common use *Bingarra*, although it was always *Binngarra* in the Port Jackson & Manly Steamship Company's annual reports. *Kuring-gai* became *Kuring Gai* or *Kuringai*.

Some of these old ferries, like the proverbial old soldiers, simply faded away. *Kuring-gai* finished her career at Newcastle with Newcastle Ferries Ltd, who bought her for £8000 in 1928 when the new glamour ferry, *Curl Curl*, arrived from her Scottish builders and the Port Jackson Company sold *Kuring-gai* out of service. She was used for a while ferrying dockyard workers from Walsh Island Dockyard to other parts of Newcastle Harbour and occasionally for ex-cursions from Newcastle to Port Stephens and Broughton Island. *Kuring-gai* was tied up finally at a

wharf 10 miles up the Hunter River near the road bridge at Hexham, where she eventually filled up with water, rolled over and sank into the mud. Part of her remains can still be seen in the river mud at low tide under a coal wharf.

Binngarra figured in two incidents before she was retired from her regular Manly service. One was a collision with the interstate steamer *Lady Isobel* about 5 pm on 31 January 1927, near Bradleys Head. The *Lady Isobel*, bound from Melbourne to Newcastle, was coming up the harbour to berth and the *Binngarra* was on her way from Manly to Circular Quay. Both vessels suffered only slight damage and nobody aboard was injured, but there were considerable legal repercussions. A Commonwealth Court of Marine Inquiry sat in Sydney on 24 February to investigate a charge of failure of navigation duty against the master of the *Binngarra*, Captain William Henry Mitchelmore. His defending counsel, Mr F.P. Evans, rose as the hearing was about to begin and submitted that the court had no jurisdiction to deal with any charge against Captain Mitchelmore. He contended that the court's sole function was to hold a preliminary inquiry into the cause of the accident.

As smart a ship as they had in those days. The Binngarra *(later known as* Bingarra*) leaving Manly Wharf in 1906. (John Darroch)*

After conferring with the two assessors assisting him, the chairman, Mr A. Gates, said he would proceed with the hearing. Mr Evans then commented that in these circumstances he was setting a precedent for courts of marine inquiry throughout the British Empire.

Outlining the case for the Navigation Department, Dr E. M. Brissenden KC said that at about 4.45 pm on 31 January the *Lady Isobel*, returning from Melbourne, was followed around Bradleys Head by the *Binngarra*. Ahead was Sydney Ferries Ltd *Karabella*. *Binngarra*, travelling at about 12 knots, gradually overhauled the *Lady Isobel*, which exchanged two blasts with *Karabella*.

The collision occurred shortly afterwards and, according to Dr Brissenden, it appeared to the captain of the *Lady Isobel* as if the *Binngarra* had made no attempt to avoid him. Damage to the *Lady Isobel* was £350 and to the *Binngarra*, £35. Both vessels were stopped at once, but the *Binngarra* went on again without attempting to ascertain the *Lady Isobel*'s position. Captain John Douglas Gray, master of the *Lady Isobel*, gave similar evidence and the ship's chief mate, Joseph Norris, said that in his opinion there would have been no risk of collision if the *Karabella* had not been in her wrong channel.

Captain Mitchelmore told the court that he had held a master's ticket since 1883. He said that as the *Binngarra* was swinging around Bradleys Head with the *Lady Isobel* he heard the *Lady Isobel* give two sharp whistles, which led him to believe she was altering her course. Then he saw the *Karabella*. Captain Mitchelmore said he resumed his journey after the collision because he was not aware that the *Lady Isobel* was in any difficulty. Questioned by Dr Brissenden, the Manly ferry master said he attributed the collision to the unexpected appearance of the *Kara-bella*. 'When I sounded the whistle the *Lady Isobel* was alongside me,' he said. 'I saw the *Karabella* some seconds afterwards.'

Addressing the court, Mr Evans said the accident came under the category of what could be described as 'inevitable' and Captain Mitchelmore should be exonerated. He said Captain Reid, master of the *Karabella*, was a contributing party to the collision because he admitted he was in his wrong water and for two years he had frequently broken the harbour regulations relating to this. Mr Evans submitted that Captain Gray had given misleading signals.

The court re-assembled to give its decision on 3 March, and proceeded to lay the blame for the collision on Captain Mitchelmore, who was found guilty of a breach of the navigation regulations by failing to keep out of the way of the *Lady Isobel*. Said Mr Gates:

> The court considers that the master of the *Binngarra* approached the *Lady Isobel* at too great a speed when nearing Bradleys Head, with the result that adequate control of his vessel was not maintained in the emergency that arose. The court has determined, in consideration of the long service, good record and character of the master of the *Binngarra*, not to suspend or otherwise deal with his certificate of competency. The court further considers that the action of the master of the steamship *Karabella* in keeping his vessel close to the shore on his port hand when proceeding from Athol Bight around Bradleys Head to Clifton Gardens did not contribute to the collision.

About a year later, on 29 February 1928, the *Binngarra*

caused some excitement at Circular Quay when she seemed to run amok during the peak-hour rush. In those days, before the advent of the Harbour Bridge, Circular Quay and Sydney Cove were swarming with ferries and punts of all kinds during morning and evening peak periods. Thus there was some consternation when *Binngarra* gave three sharp blasts as she was leaving the wharf to go to Manly. Why should she be giving three toots—the signal for going astern? It appeared, according to the *Sydney Morning Herald*, that there was some defect in the steering. The *Herald* reported:

> Sydney Cove at the moment was alive with steamers and the passengers hurried to the sides of the ships to ascertain the reason for the whistling. Other people lined the retaining wall at the Quay to watch the incident. At one stage it seemed that the *Binngarra* was likely to collide with one of the other vessels, but, with reversed engines, her speed was arrested and she slowly returned. She was out of her course, however, and bumped the steamer *Kurraba*, which was lying at the Cremorne wharf. Neither vessel was damaged and no one was injured.

An eyewitness was quoted saying:

> I was on the *Kaikai* when I heard the three blasts from the *Binngarra* and I hurried to the side. It appeared to me that the captain of the *Binngarra* was making a desperate effort to gain command of his ship. He was spinning his steering wheel rapidly, but this did not seem to affect the course of the steamer.

What had happened, it transpired, was that the rudder pin had dropped, fixing the stern rudder, and the ship had no steering. Manly ferries have a rudder at each end. When they are travelling, the bow rudder is fixed straight by means of a locking pin operated from the deck and the stern rudder is left free for steering. On arrival at the Quay, the locking pins had been switched over, but the one at the stern for going out had apparently fallen back into locking position.

Binngarra was retired from the Manly service in 1930, but it was to be another 16 years before she was buried at sea. In between, her engines and boilers removed, she had served at Port Stephens, north of Newcastle, as a store ship for timber waiting to be exported. During World War II the American Navy towed her to New Guinea to be used there as a store ship. Captain C. W. Henderson, a famous Manly identity who wrote many interesting articles on the ferries for the *Manly Daily*, recalled in one of the articles:

> I clearly remember it falling to my duty as the skipper of an RAN ship in Papua-New Guinea waters to tow the

Binngarra to forward area ports. It was not always easy to realise that we actually had her in tow, so smoothly did her fine lines slip through the water.

Another Manly resident actually commanded *Binngarra* as an American warship. Mr I. MacGillivray-Elder, of Daintrey Street, Fairlight, told of this unique experience in the *Manly Daily* of 7 February 1974:

Towards the end of the Second World War I was a ship's officer employed by the US Army. I had just left one ship in Oro Bay, Papua-New Guninea, and had about three months to fill in before going south on leave. So, when I was asked if I would like 'a command'—at that time I did not possess a master's ticket—I was only too willing to accept. I was immediately shipped to Dreger Harbour to take command of USS *Binngarra*. She was anchored well out of sight when I joined the launch which ferried me to my command. When she eventually came into sight I realised she was the old Manly ferry. But what a change had come over her! Seeing her riding at anchor, the stars and stripes proudly flying from her stern and listing at a most precarious angle, I began to have misgivings. Gone was all her superstructure. Two tall masts, curiously constructed of overlapping steel plates and derricks of a similar style had been installed.

The Binngarra. *(John Darroch)*

I made a circuit of the ship and noticed the bow propeller had been removed. On passing under the stern I was dismayed to find no propeller there either. Could this really be my new ship? But there above me in raised brass letters painted over in drab jungle green was quite unmistakably the name *Binngarra*. So astounded was I that I climbed aboard without uttering a word. Obviously I was the victim of a joke and I decided the best thing was to go along with it. I soon discovered that the *Binngarra*, with her engines removed, had considerable cargo capacity and was being used as a towed vessel.

The list was caused by some 40 tons of cement which had been poured over rusted plates between the frames on the starboard side to keep out the sea. When properly loaded, she assumed an even keel and rode surprisingly well.

A strange command indeed, but one with a challenge. Once loaded, we anchored in the harbour, thumbing a tow from any vessel going our way. On arrival, we would slip the tow line and drop anchor to await a tug to bring us alongside. Steering was also an experience. The *Binngarra* was built before the change-over in helm orders of 1931 and to go to starboard, the helm had to be put to port. She had no anchor windlass. To weigh anchor, the hook from the cargo winch was run forward to the point where the cable emerged from the hawsepipe and was pulled away up the mast by the petrol-driven winch. This had to be repeated several times. It was amazing how one could become fond of such an extraordinary ship. I settled into the most idyllic three months I can remember, for the *Binngarra* was a most happy ship. But it was fortunate she was never called upon to defend herself against attack for her armament consisted of four Browning machine guns of First World War vintage.

I was more than a little sad when my short command came to an end. A Danish gentleman named Kaspersen took over and, as far as I am aware, was the last of her skippers.

Where is the *Binngarra* today? My guess is she is rusting away on some beach in Papua-New Guinea. But she had the distinction of ending her days as USS *Binngarra*, at war with Japan and fulfilling a most important function—getting war supplies to forward areas. A fitting end to a fine old ship.

However, that is not how she met her end, as Captain Henderson explained in another *Manly Daily* article a few weeks later. Apparently *Binngarra* found her way back to Sydney after the war and was given an honourable burial outside the heads she had crossed so often in her nearly 80 000 trips to Manly with 30 million passengers. On 11 December 1946, her rusting remains were towed to the ships' graveyard, 18 miles south-east of The Heads, and she was sent to the bottom in 100 fathoms.

Burra Bra achieved some fame in 1928, when she was painted white, festooned with flags and, with two big white crosses amidships, was used to take crowds to Manly for part of the Eucharistic Congress being held at St Patrick's College. She also had the unique distinction of being the only Manly ferry to become an Australian warship as HMAS *Burra Bra*. Taken over for the Royal Australian Navy at Poole & Steel's Balmain yards on 13 November 1942, she was fitted out for anti-submarine training and given the pennant number 69 and bow letters BR. HMAS *Burra Bra* was commissioned as an Australian Navy ship in February 1943, after which she spent two years on anti-submarine work and was also used by the Navy and the RAAF as a target ship at Jervis Bay. *Burra Bra* was laid up in 1944, apparently unwanted by her original owners, the Port Jackson & Manly Steamship Company, to whom the Navy would have given first option. But she had been altered so much for her wartime role, as shown in the picture below, and was too old to warrant the cost of restoring as a ferry, especially now that the days of steam were nearing their end. For her wartime service, *Burra Bra* had been armed with a 12-pounder gun on the aft upper deck, a Vickers machine gun on each side of the bridge and she carried six depth charges. None of her armaments were ever used against enemy ships. She was sold at auction for £900 and passed out of Navy ownership on 24 November 1947, ending her life being broken up in Sydney in 1950.

The Burra Bra *at East Circular Quay in 1945, still in her wartime dress. (Ross Gillett)*

Other Manly ferries saw some war service in Sydney Harbour on the night of 31 May 1942, when Japanese midget submarines got past the boom net being built to prevent such an invasion and tried to sink an American heavy cruiser, the USS *Chicago*, which was in port with other ships of war. A few weeks earlier they would have had a much bigger target in the *Queen Mary*, which was in Athol Bight, near Taronga Zoo wharf, embarking troops for the Middle East. It is possible the Japanese were seeking the *Queen Mary*, which they knew was ferrying 5000 troops on each trip between Sydney and Suez. At sea she was too fast for submarines to catch, but, anchored in Sydney Harbour, she would have been a sitting shot for a submarine which could slip through the harbour defences and fire two or three torpedoes before being detected.

For most of the war years an anti-submarine net guarding the entrance to the inner harbour stretched from Georges Head, near Middle Head on the north side, to a point near the southern end of Camp Cove on the south side. In the middle it was hooked to a solid base on the Sow and Pigs reef and was guarded near each end by boom vessels which raised and lowered gates for ships to pass through into the eastern and western channels. These were former inner harbour, wooden-hull ferries of Sydney Ferries Ltd, several of which had been commandeered by the Navy for various purposes. One was the *Kuramia*. Outside the net at several places between the outer heads and the boom gate entrances were other anti-submarine defences called indicator loops which would warn of any vessel travelling between them. Manly ferries had to pass through the boom gates and keep all lights out between the boom and Manly so that the entrance to the harbour could not be seen by a lurking raider out at sea. Many couples—particularly American servicemen and local girls—had to extricate themselves quickly from compromising positions when the lights came on again.

Near the end of May 1942, the anti-submarine net was still unfinished, leaving a gap of 293 metres at the western channel end and 274 metres on the eastern side, something which must have been known to the Japanese after an aerial survey of the scene by a seaplane from one of two plane-carrying mother submarines in the early morning hours of 31 May. The Japanese pilot flew over the harbour about 4.30 am, unchallenged, and returned to his ship 20 miles out to report what he thought was a battleship and other large ships near Garden Island. Little did the Australian and American navies know that only 20 miles outside Sydney were lurking five large Japanese submarines, carrying two sea-planes and four midget submarines designed for suicide attacks on shipping in places like Sydney Harbour. They had a carefully mapped out plan for that night. The main target was the 'battleship'—actually the American heavy cruiser USS *Chicago*—and any other ships they could hit. If they escaped they were to rendezvous with the mother subs 20 miles south of The Heads.

The mother ships launched their raiders seven miles out from The Heads, taking advantage of a full moon to guide them in. How all this could have been allowed to happen is somewhat amazing, considering that the National Emergency Service had issued standby warnings two days previously, disclosing that unidentified aircraft had been reported over Sydney and Newcastle. Of course the two outer indicator loops at North Head and South Head were out of action, but both inner loops, one in 15 fathoms and the other in 7 fathoms, were operating. By the time the first midget reached the inner entrance to the main harbour the night had become overcast and the submarine ran into the net, entangling its propeller. Efforts to struggle free attracted the attention of James Cargill, a Maritime Services Board watchman, who was investigating the turbulence when the two Japanese crewmen fired a demolition charge and blew up their submarine and themselves with it. The huge explosion raised the alarm and the port was closed to outward shipping, although the Manly ferries were allowed to continue running, probably because it was thought that the more craft kept moving about, the more chance there was of keeping the submarines pinned down until daylight. About a quarter of an hour after the explosion at the boom net, gun crews on the *Chicago* saw a submarine surface 200 metres off the Garden Island ferry wharf and opened fire with everything they had, from 4-inch guns to Oerlikons. HMAS *Whyalla* also began firing, and naval auxiliary craft raced around the vicinity dropping depth charges. By this time everyone living near the harbour was out watching the fireworks, and the ferries were in the thick of it, too close to tracer bullets for the comfort of one lot of Manly passengers. The city was blacked out, but for some strange reason Garden Island was a brightly lit target. Berthed there was the Australian cruiser HMAS *Canberra*, the Dutch submarine *K9*, and the American cruiser *Perkins*. With the Dutch submarine on the eastern wall of the island was HMAS *Kuttabul*, a former Sydney Ferries ferry, used as a naval depot vessel. Down near The Heads more explosions were heard as depth charges were dropped and attempts were made to ram another midget submarine, which either escaped or was sunk and has never been found.

Also not known is why the submarine near Garden Island did not fire while the island's lights silhouetted five warships against the blacked-out city in the background. Apparently the submarine was moving in to attack about 11.25 pm when the lights on Garden Island were switched off and this is probably what saved the *Chicago*. The first torpedo it fired missed and ran aground on Garden Island without exploding. The second passed under the Dutch submarine and exploded against the sea-wall, right under the *Kuttabul*, blowing her almost to pieces and killing 19 men who were aboard. After that, the *Chicago* and the *Perkins* decided that the harbour was no place for them and made for the open sea, despite the danger that might await them out there. The *Canberra* remained at her berth and was unharmed.

The midget submarine which sunk the *Kuttabul* was never found. Many believe it was sunk by gunfire from the *Chicago* and is still somewhere on the bottom of the harbour. Two others were found and raised from the harbour bed, their pieces were combined to make a complete submarine and after a fund-raising tour on a truck, the midget was given to the Canberra war museum.

The Japanese submarine invasion of Sydney Harbour is one of the daring events of World War II, and the men who manned the submarines displayed a suicidal bravery which most of us would find hard to understand. It is generally believed that they entered the harbour by following a Manly ferry across The Heads and through the boom, confusing their own progress with that of the ferry as shown by the indicator loops. However, nobody denies that these were brave and daring men, whose initiative contrasts strongly with the apathy and unpreparedness which allowed them to penetrate the harbour and threaten many valuable ships and lives that night in May 1942. It was lucky that the *Queen Mary* was far away. Had she been in the harbour she was a dead duck. Her sinking would have been one of the achievements of the war, of immense propaganda value to the Japanese and Germans. The following year she was carrying 15 000 Americans on each trip across the Atlantic—the biggest troop carrier ever known.

PART II
THE WHITE FUNNELS

1. Havoc on the Harbour

Life was not always quiet for the *Burra Bra*, or, for that matter, any other ship on the Manly run. For days, weeks or months they would plod along with nothing happening to get them into the news and too often when they made the headlines it was bad news because of bad weather. Like that winter day of 26 June 1923, when a particularly nasty gale screamed up the coast pushing mighty seas in front of it and battering anything afloat.

The ferries and their crews were used to winter gales, which had to be really dangerous to stop them working. But this was a bad one. It belted the New South Wales' coast all day with 70-mile-an-hour winds and heavy rain, described by the *Sydney Morning Herald* as 'torrential downpours'. Said the *Herald*:

Shipping was greatly imperilled. The steamer *Belbowrie* was driven ashore north of Cronulla. Heavy seas across The Heads swept the Manly steamer *Burra Bra* and a huge wave occasioned damage to the vessel and injured four passengers. The Manly service was discontinued, but will probably be resumed this morning. On the harbour the gale played havoc with shipping. Many vessels dragged anchor. The huge crane *Titan*, with boilers for the new liner, *Fordsdale*, broke away and was driven on the rocks at Woolwich. Two steamers narrowly missed going ashore at Shark Island.

Another *Herald* story was headed in the quaint style of the day: 'Wonderful sight. Off the coast. Tremendous seas at The Heads.' The intensity of the storm, according to the *Herald*, was something novel and to be marvelled at. It said:

Along the coastline there was an unbroken ribbon of foam. Such tremendous seas as were running yesterday have rarely been witnessed. Those living at seaside resorts were treated to a wonderful sight. During the day, many people living in the vicinity walked to the Gap at Watsons Bay and there gained the most wonderful sight to be obtained along the coast. Huge waves broke over the rocks below, throwing up great showers of water to a tremendous height. The roar of the ocean could be heard half a mile away.

Even to the commuters of Manly, who were used to rough trips to town, it was obvious when they awoke that morning with rain thrashing their windows that Sydney was being hit by something more than just another winter gale. The *Burra Bra* berthed at Manly with some difficulty, pushed towards the shore by the wind and yawing sloppily in the surge around the wharf. She was to do the 8 am trip, nowadays the heaviest morning peak load, but on the morning of this gale she left with only 500 aboard. Quite a few regulars had decided, after looking towards The Heads, to take the tram to the Spit and then another tram to Cremorne, finishing the journey to the city by Cremorne ferry. These were the days before the Harbour Bridge.

The *Burra Bra* was lifting to the swell before she was halfway to Smedleys Point. Passengers could see the huge

The Bellubera *as a steamer before her conversion to diesel-electric power.*

32

rollers sweeping in through The Heads and breaking heavily on the rocks at Dobroyd and Middle Head. The entrance to Middle Harbour between Grotto Point and Balmoral was a continuous line of breaking surf, precipitated over the sandy bottom covered by less than two fathoms at low water, and the waves were higher than that. *Burra Bra* was dipping, rising, then burying her nose into the swells, spray flying over the bridge and water running all over the lower deck. She was halfway across The Heads when one mighty sea slammed into her on the port quarter, a massive wall of solid water, disintegrating with an explosive roar. The ferry shuddered and slumped under the weight of water. Dozens of windows were broken, seats, with passengers sitting on them, were wrenched from their fastenings and slid across the rolling decks, the sliding doors on the port side were stove in and shattered, leaving the sea to pour into the lower deck as the doors burst open. There were some hysterical screams, but most passengers remained calm, though many were wet and uncomfortable. Four people were injured, one badly. Several women fainted as water flooded the deck downstairs.

Burra Bra had been caught nose-down in a big trough, too close to the next roller to rise with it. The signal master at South Head estimated that at the time of the incident the gale was roaring in from the south-east with a force of 80 miles an hour. Somebody watching from the shore said the ferry disappeared from sight completely in the trough between enormous seas halfway across The Heads. Her position for a while was described later as 'distinctly dangerous', but experienced handling by the master, and *Burra Bra*'s stout construction, enabled her to weather the storm. Sloppy reporting by the Press of the day did not name the master, so that his epic goes unhonoured.

Ambulances took four passengers to Sydney Hospital when the *Burra Bra* berthed at the Quay. Three were discharged after treatment for abrasions, bruises and lacerations, but the fourth, Mr D.M. Richardson, later Sheriff of New South Wales, had a broken leg and spent three months in hospital because of complications from the accident. The *Herald,* contrary to its reputation for accuracy in those days, listed the injured treated at Sydney Hospital and discharged as: 'Jack Stewart, abrasions; James Gray, scalp wounds; Donald Richardson, bruises; Harold Muir, lacerations to hand'. Later, the paper refers to one of the injured men as Eric Stewart. Mr Stewart, whatever his first name, was sitting in the forward cabin when the ferry made her downward plunge into the trough. Suddenly the sea rose up around her and the cabin door was smashed in. A piece of heavy plate glass from the door slashed Mr Stewart under the chin, inflicting a nasty wound. The rush of water swept him off his feet as he tried to get up and swirled him outside to a position near the

for'ard gangway gates. One report said the ferry lost a lifeboat and an outside companionway to the bridge, but this was not mentioned by the company's general manager (again unnamed), who said in a statement to the Press:

> Roughly, I should estimate the damage to the *Burra Bra* at about £150. It consists of breakages to windows, seats and doors. The vessel left Manly at 8 o'clock, carrying approximately 500 passengers. Though it is licensed to carry 1100 people, the usual number on this trip is only about 650, so the rough weather had not made a great difference to the loading. Though the deluge, of course, occasioned a good deal of excitement among the passengers, there was no panic.

The Manly service was, of course, suspended after the *Burra Bra* arrived at the Quay with her story of mayhem inside The Heads and the ferry was taken off for repairs.

How lucky she was can be imagined from other news of the day. The coastal steamer *Belbowrie*, on her way up from Ulladulla, was driven ashore on the beach near Boat Harbour, north of Cronulla. The steamer *Kiama*, which left Sydney for Kiama at 12.55 am, was forced to turn back before she passed Port Hacking on her way south. It took her until 7 am to get back into Sydney. Several big ships had to heave to at sea and ride out the gale. The 13 000-ton RMS *Niagara*, well known over the years between Sydney and the United States, hove to 100 miles from Sydney and the SS *Durban*, 7000 tons, rode it out 240 miles off the coast.

Newcastle people gathered at the entrance to their harbour early in the afternoon to see what was described as a thrilling sight as Captain W.T. Hoskin, master of the coastal steamer *Boambee*, in a fine feat of seamanship, literally surfed his vessel into port over the dangerous bar which was a bad-weather hazard in those days. Watchers on shore had given the *Boambee* little chance of making it when it was obvious that she was going to try to come in through the narrow opening to the port. They feared the little ship would be smashed to pieces on the southern breakwater. It nearly happened. Just as *Boambee* was crossing the bar, she was lifted high by a mountainous roller, which swept her broadside on and carried her very close to the breakwater. The *Nobby*'s lifeboat crew raced to launch their boat. But they were not needed. Just when destruction seemed inevitable, *Boambee* plunged forward, swung round and was lifted by another roller into the fairway of the harbour entrance channel.

Even in Sydney Harbour ships were in constant danger. Shortly before 6 am, the steamers *Australmead* and *Bulga*, moored alongside each other in Rose Bay, began to drift before the gale and would have gone aground on Shark

The coastal freighter Belbowrie *breaking up on Maroubra Point after running aground on the night of 16 January 1939.*

Island but for the easterly slant of the wind. A tug had to stand by them all day. The Commonwealth steamers *Talawa*, *Dromana*, *Eromanga* and *Australcrag* dragged anchors for some distance and the Adelaide company's *Lammeroo* had to be removed from Point Piper to Waterview Bay. Tugs were racing about all day picking up big ships which could not hold bottom at anchor. The floating crane, *Titan*, lying alongside the new Commonwealth Line ship, *Fordsdale*, with six boilers ready to hoist into her, snapped her mooring lines and was blown at high speed across the Parramatta River to hit the rocks near the Woolwich ferry wharf, from where two tugs had to rescue the crane.

An intriguing part of the picture of what happened during that gale is how the coaster *Belbowrie* was driven ashore about 200 metres from the end of the beach near the Merries Reef and Boat Harbour, even now a fairly isolated spot at the end of a long beach which stretches about nine kilometres north-east from Cronulla around Bate Bay on the southern side of the Kurnell peninsula. In 1923 it would have been a thoroughly deserted area, separated from Cronulla, Kurnell or any other habitat by huge sandhills and swamps. At night, and certainly at 3.30 am when that gale was blotting out the sky, it would have been as black as the blackest ink in there because Cronulla, then only a very small village, had no street lights, although it is possible a couple of lamp lights were showing in the village and these were what the mate of the *Belbowrie* took for the lights of other ships. In any case, the *Belbowrie* was way off the course followed even today by ships coming up the coast to Sydney. They pass Bate Bay and Port Hacking well out to sea to clear Cape Banks, the northern headland of Botany Bay, and other obstacles before that, such as the Jibbon bombora near the southern headland of Port Hacking, the Osborn Shoal—visible bottom appearing suddenly in the midst of what is apparently open sea—then the Merries Reef, a veritable breakwater of rock stretching about three-quarters of a mile just under the surface south-west from Boat Harbour.

The *Belbowrie* should not have been there in the early morning hours of 26 June 1923. Pushed north-west by the south-east gale, she was more than a few miles off course. But how did she get through the Osborn Shoal and the Merries Reef? The mystery is not explained in a fairly long account of the incident in the *Sydney Morning Herald* of 27 June. First, however, consider the facts as presented by the *Herald*:

After midnight the storm gathered and a fresh wind sprang up from the south-east, freshening to gale force and lashing up big seas. The master of the *Belbowrie* had gone below and the mate was in charge. No lights were visible and the vessel appeared to be keeping to her proper course. At 3.30 am, according to a statement by the mate, he saw two vessels between him and the coast and there appeared to be no danger until the vessel took ground. The seas drove the vessel through the surf and lifted her clear of the huge breaking waves. The engines were put full astern, but without avail.

At daylight the tide had receded and she was resting less precariously on sandy bottom. *Belbowrie*'s hull was not damaged and they refloated her when the storm receded.

There seems to have been no court of marine inquiry to ask the questions the *Herald* left unanswered. Did the *Belbowrie* pass close to the Jibbon bombora and continue almost due north, just inside the Osborn Shoal and the Merries? Did she steam in a north-westerly direction, riding the roll in between the shoal and the Merries? Or, remembering that the mate, P. Cassar, had said 'The seas drove the vessel through the surf and lifted her clear of the huge breaking waves', was she lifted right over the

SS Manly II. *(John Allcot)*

SS Burra-Bra. *(John Allcot)*

The SS Barrenjoey *crossing The Heads during a 60-mph south-east gale on Easter Sunday, 16 April 1927. (Fred Elliott)*

SS Narrabeen II. *(John Allcot)*

Merries? The last theory, although the most improbable, could have happened. There is a narrow passage through the reef about one-third of its length out from Boat Harbour. Seen from either side, the break in the Merries in rough weather is an awesome sight and the wall of white water obscures the opening. Anyone who knows the passage would be wary of going through it in very calm weather in a small boat. They certainly would not want to try it at 3.30 am riding a gale in a ship the size of the *Belbowrie* —123 ft long, of 29 ft beam and drawing 8.3 ft. But at high tide, when the *Belbowrie* went into Bate Bay, there could have been enough water over parts of the reef for a huge roller to throw her across.

The *Belbowrie* seems to have been attracted to that part of the coast. She met her end not far from Bate Bay 16 years later on Maroubra Point. This time, unfortunately, she went on the rocks instead of the beach and was smashed to pieces. It happened on the night of 16 January 1939. Again the captain was down below and the mate, E. C. Ladd, was in charge. He told how they left Sydney about 8.10 pm in ballast for Shellharbour.

'The sea was rough and we were cutting through blinding rain,' he said. 'Visibility was terrible. Before we knew where we were the crash came and we were well on the rocks.' The crew scrambled ashore on lifelines. Ladd said: 'The old boat has been in a few things, but she is finished this time.' Captain P. R. Dixon was asleep when they went aground. He said: 'The first I knew was when the mate woke me up and told me we were on the rocks.'

Belbowrie broke up after daylight and was a total loss.

2. The Last of their Line

The 1920s were the era of the long white funnels with the black-banded tops which stood out so distinctly amongst the crowded traffic of Circular Quay in the years before the opening of the Harbour Bridge. They were the proud ocean-going Manly ferries, so superior to those inner harbour tubs that plied to the North Shore, Mosman and the Lane Cove River. I remember vividly seeing from my uncle's home at Watsons Bay the black and white funnels

The Bellubera. *(John Darroch)*

approaching, coming together and passing away from each other on the other side of the harbour near Clifton Gardens. My uncle, Captain Bill Roberts, was one of the pilots who brought the big ships into Sydney and saw them out again on their way overseas. One of his wife's sisters took me frequently to visit at Watsons Bay, usually in one of those inferior little harbour ferries which called at Garden Island, Nielsen Park and Parsley Bay on its way to Watsons Bay. Sometimes it was the *Greycliffe*, which on 3 November 1927, was involved in Sydney Harbour's greatest tragedy when she was cut in two by the liner *Tahiti* near Bradleys Head and nearly 40 people lost their lives. Those almost weekly trips on the Watsons Bay ferry introduced me as a very small boy to the tinkling of engine room telegraphs, the smell of hissing steam engines, the ships on the harbour and the majestic Manly ferries gliding past, smoke belching from their long funnels.

But in the early 1920s another era ended with the launching on 14 February 1922, at Mort's Dock, Balmain, of the fine new ferry *Baragoola*, making seven vessels of this type built there. Her white funnel joined those of *Kuring-gai*, *Binngarra*, *Burra Bra*, *Bellubera*, *Balgowlah* and *Barrenjoey* in the Port Jackson fleet. *Baragoola* was the last of her line. As mentioned earlier, the cost of building them here had outgrown the advantage of not having to bring them from shipbuilders on the other side of the world. These seven steamers served the company well. They were not as big as the Scottish-built *Dee Why* and *Curl Curl*, which arrived in 1928, and the magnificent *South Steyne* of 1938, nor were they as fast and commodious. But two of them, *Baragoola* and *Barrenjoey*, outlasted all the imported vessels.

The first two built after the *Kuring-gai*—*Binngarra* and *Burra Bra*—were slightly smaller and slower versions of what was to come. Respectively, of 442 and 458 tons and 190.5 and 195.3 ft in length, they each carried about 1400 passengers, but could do little better than 13 knots. *Bellubera*, *Balgowlah* and *Barrenjoey*, launched in the three years between 1910 and 1913, were around 500 tons, 210 ft long and were given more powerful engines to get their speed up to 15 knots or better for faster transport of the 1500 passengers they were designed to carry.

Balgowlah, Barrenjoey and *Baragoola* were the last of what we have described as the B class vessels, evolved from the ships designed by Walter Reeks—the *Manly* of 1896 and *Kuring-gai* of 1901. *Manly* replaced the paddle-wheels with a propeller at each end, but, being a wooden ship, had problems with engine vibration and the propeller shaft getting out of alignment.

Balgowlah was launched from Mort's Woolwich yard on 18 June 1912. *Balgowlah*, 499 tons, 210 ft, carrying 1528 passengers, was built as a sister ship to the *Bellubera*, launched two years previously. On the morning of 25 November, *Balgowlah* did her speed trials over the measured mile in the harbour and clocked 16 knots between the markers on Fort Denison and Bradleys Head, guided proudly by Captain J. Hart, no relation to the later Captain Ron Hart of the *Baragoola*. There was great excitement a few hours after the trials at an official luncheon aboard the new ship for the handing-over ceremony. Many guests attended the luncheon, arranged by Mort's Dock & Engineering Company.

Mort's manager, Mr Franki, told the gathering that the Port Jackson company had ordered the *Bellubera* and the *Balgowlah* from Mort's because they had found there was not much difference in the cost compared with British yards. But it did not leave much profit for the Sydney builders. Mr Franki added:

> We are building boats more for the sake of showing what can be done in Sydney than for what we are making out of them. I can assure you we do not make five per cent, but it is worth our while merely for the sake of prestige, for in my opinion there is none to surpass these ferry boats in any part of the world.
>
> The *Balgowlah* is as fine a boat as we could get turned out in any part of the world.

Mr J. J. Eyre, chairman of directors of the Port Jackson & Manly Steamship Company, said in response:

> With this new boat we can run 13 trips more every day than we could have 12 months ago, so we are doing our best for the people of Manly. My company regards the new boat with more than satisfaction. Every boat built by Mort's Dock seems to be better than the previous one. As far as I can gather from Mr Franki, we have been given a vessel which exceeds the requirements of the contract by something like 12 to 15 per cent.

Balgowlah was the name local Aboriginals had for the

The Balgowlah. *(John Darroch)*

area around North Harbour. It has been retained by the pleasant residential suburb around and above that part of the harbour near Manly.

It is interesting to note, more than 70 years later, that the new ferries are not much faster, if indeed they are at all. *Balgowlah* was one of the fastest of them all. She could make 16 knots with ease and frequently ran the distance in 25 minutes compared with the normal 30 to 33 minutes of later years. In her time she is credited with doing about 110 000 return trips and covering some 715 000 nautical miles.

Perhaps it could be said that the *Balgowlah*, which went into service on 28 November 1912, had a quiet life compared with some of her sisters like the *Bellubera* and *South Steyne*, which were frequently in the news. But she was in what was described as 'a peculiar incident' less than a fortnight after going on her regular run and, contrary to the usual situations in which skippers and deckhands did the rescuing, it was the engineer and his crew down below who got everyone out of trouble.

It happened near the entrance to Sydney Cove, at that time a really busy place with ferries going in and out of Circular Quay, ships being berthed or tugged out of the wharves on either side of the cove, ships moving up or down the main stream, spanned now by the Harbour Bridge, and vehicular ferries crossing between Fort Macquarie and Milsons Point. Accidents were not uncommon there, particularly around what was called P & O corner on the eastern side, where the P & O liners berthed. Most ships in those days were coal-burners and the chaos near the Quay was aggravated occasionally by colliers coming in to coal the overseas vessels.

This was the scene on the afternoon of 10 December 1912, as one of the South Coast colliers, the *Five Islands*, moved into position to coal the liner *Mantua*. The *Five Islands*, 956 tons and 215 ft long, owned by the Bellambi Coal Company, had just arrived from Bulli with a full load of coal. As she was being manoeuvred into position alongside the liner, out of the Quay came the Port Jackson company's new pride and joy, the *Balgowlah*, commanded by Captain Hart, on her way to Manly. Fortunately, Captain Hart, observing the situation, had his vessel moving at 'dead slow' and as he saw the collier let go an anchor to maintain position against the ebb tide, Hart rang his telegraph to stop engines. The *Balgowlah* then drifted slowly towards P & O corner, waiting to pick up way again when the *Five Islands* had backed clear. But that ebb tide, a fresh wind and the wash from the *Five Island*'s propeller took charge and carried the *Balgowlah* across the collier's anchor cable, which immediately proceeded to wind itself around the *Balgowlah*'s forward propeller.

Both vessels were anchored now and they drifted together alongside each other while vain rescue efforts were attempted for about an hour. Then the engineer took a hand—literally. His steam reciprocating engines had been fitted with geared equipment to enable the main engines to be turned slowly by hand for maintenance work so that the main engines and the propeller shaft could be turned slowly ahead or astern for inspection or overhaul. Had they tried to do this by driving the engines normally, it would not have been possible to move the propeller slowly enough and could have been very dangerous. Cranked by hand, the propeller turned gradually back in the opposite direction to which it had been spinning when it picked up the chain, until finally the chain dropped off and fell to the harbour bed.

While all this was going on, the *Kuring-gai* had been brought alongside and took off the Manly passengers, most of whom were more interested in getting home than watching salvage operations. *Balgowlah* went across to the company's depot at Kurraba Point, where an inspection showed no real damage and she was returned to normal service from the Quay.

Far more serious was another accident which happened almost in the same spot 15 years later, when the *Balgowlah* collided with the *Kanimbla*, one of the inner harbour ferries owned then by Sydney Ferries Ltd. Four injured people were taken from the *Kanimbla* to Sydney Hospital. Others with minor injuries declined hospital attention. The ferries met off Fort Macquarie with a resounding crash which was heard for some distance around the waterfront. *Kanimbla* was coming out of Circular Quay en route to Neutral Bay about 4 pm on Wednesday, 15 June 1927, and the *Balgowlah*, with no passengers aboard, was proceeding from its Kurraba Point depot to the Quay to go on the evening peak-hour running to Manly. The *Balgowlah* hit the *Kanimbla* on her port bow with enough force to tear a gaping hole in the wooden ferry's planking below the waterline, almost to the propeller shaft. *Balgowlah*'s sharp steel stem also cut right into the *Kanimbla* above water, tearing and splintering woodwork on both upper and lower decks. Frantic blowing of sirens after the crash brought another Sydney ferry, *Kangaroo*, to the rescue. She came alongside quickly, fearing that the *Kanimbla* was in danger of sinking, as indeed she was, beginning to settle down at the bow, but the water was confined to the first bulkhead and she remained afloat. The *Kangaroo* took the 100 Neutral Bay passengers back to Circular Quay. His passengers transferred safely, the master of the *Kanimbla* headed his stricken craft at full speed to Milsons Point to tie up at a wharf being used by Dorman Long & Company, builders of the Harbour Bridge.

Then began a dramatic salvage effort under the direction of Captain Carter, chief officer of the then Sydney

Harbour Trust fire brigade. They used the pumps of the fire float *Pluvius* and lighters which were brought in, but because the hole in the *Kanimbla* was so huge, it was impossible for the pumps to gain on the intake of water. Fearing that the bulkhead might collapse if the ferry was beached, Captain Carter sent for the floating crane *Titan* and a diver, who passed a steel hawser from the crane under the *Kanimbla*'s damaged hull. The bow was then lifted slightly above normal level while the ferry was towed slowly around Milsons Point to more shallow water, escorted on either side by the fire floats *Pluvius* and *Cecil Rhodes* with pumps working at full pressure. In the shallower water, the load was taken off the crane and the *Kanimbla*'s bow settled on the mud bottom for patching to be done before she was taken to dock for proper repairs several days later. *Balgowlah*, to the credit of her Mort's Dock builders, escaped with only minor damage to two plates above the waterline.

Passengers in the smoking saloon for'ard in the *Kanimbla* must have received an awful shock when the bow of the *Balgowlah* crashed through the wall at them, shower ing them with shattered glass, splintered wood and flying lifebelts. One was 83-year-old Robert George Enever, of Ben Boyd Road, Neutral Bay, who received a lacerated wound over the right eye and abrasions to the face and nose. Other passengers extricated him from a mangled heap of debris. But he said that had the Manly steamer cleaved its way into the smaller ferry just a fraction more he would have been crushed to pulp. He thought he owed his providential escape to the prompt action of a fellow passenger who pushed him forward as the ferries hit.

Frederick Fairbairn, 73, a retired civil engineer, also of Ben Boyd Road, who was treated for injuries at Sydney Hospital, told the *Sydney Morning Herald:*

There was a crash like thunder and I was sent sprawling to the deck. The impact was terrific. I have never heard such a crash in my life and I thought the vessel would sink straight away. Standing near amidships, I saw the Manly steamer coming towards us, just for a second perhaps, and then our ferry quivered from stem to stern and it seemed as though it was being sawn in halves.

Miss Alice Maud MacDonald, another Ben Boyd Road resident treated at Sydney Hospital, was sitting reading near the stern of the *Kanimbla*. She was thrown forward and her face hit the seat opposite. The seat on which she had been sitting was hurled on top of her.

A couple of years later, the *Balgowlah* had another collision, this time with the collier *Birchgrove Park*, but neither vessel suffered serious damage. Dented plates on the collier's port side were replaced at Mort's Dock and the *Balgowlah*'s damaged bow and sponson were repaired at her depot at Kurraba Point. The *Birchgrove Park*, a 640-ton vessel, one of the famous sixty-milers carting coal from Newcastle to Sydney over the 60 miles of sea road, met a tragic end on one of these trips in the early hours of 2 August 1956, when she capsized and sank about four miles south of Broken Bay, taking eight men to their deaths with her. Survivors said the ship, carrying 500 tons of coal, began to list badly to port after leaving Newcastle. Apparently some of the coal had shifted. They were trying to run for shelter when a big sea hit beam on. The collier just rolled over and sank, as one survivor said, like a stone.

Considering the number of collisions which occurred on the harbour, the *Balgowlah* had a fairly trouble-free life. Her first brush was in November 1913, with the inner harbour ferry *Kangaroo*, the same one that took the passengers off the damaged *Kanimbla* in the crash off Fort Macquarie 14 years later. Then, on 25 April 1921, *Balgowlah* and the Union Steamship Company's *Manuka* met in that notorious danger zone off Bradleys Heads in an accident similar to that involving the *Lady Isobel* and *Binngarra* mentioned previously. Both vessels were coming up the harbour, the *Manuka*, from Hobart, heading for her berth in Darling Harbour and the *Balgowlah* travelling from Manly to Circular Quay. *Balgowlah* fared worst. The ship escaped apparently with little damage, but *Balgowlah* had about 10 ft of her sponson torn off.

The only other newsworthy incident recorded was when she overshot the wharf at the Quay on 26 January 1939, and went aground in soft mud. No passengers were aboard at the time and the ferry suffered no damage. It happened at about 5 pm as she was coming in from Kurraba Point depot to join the peak-hour rush traffic. Some of the wooden buffer stop was broken, but the bow of the ferry was not dented, demonstrating again the sturdy Mort's Dock construction. Thousands of home-ward-bound office workers stopped to watch the efforts of the tug *Gamecock* to free the stranded ferry. For 45 minutes the *Gamecock* pulled the stern of *Balgowlah* first one way and then another, but was unable to move the bow from its muddy bed. Finally, another tug, the *Chesterford*, was brought in, and between them the two tugs eventually pulled the *Balgowlah* away from the wharf.

During the 1930s the top decks of the *Balgowlah* and *Bellubera* were glassed in and their wheelhouses extended to provide crew accommodation. In 1946 the Port Jackson company decided to convert *Balgowlah* and the *Barrenjoey* to diesel-electric propulsion because the cost of replacing them with new boats was prohibitive for what the ferries were earning. *Barrenjoey* was the first to be taken out of service for rebuilding and when she returned to duty in 1951, renamed *North Head*, with two funnels and diesel-electric engines, it was assumed that *Balgow-*

The North Head *on the afternoon of the Opera House opening waiting for Circular Quay to be opened to normal traffic.*

lah would receive a similar facelift. But the 8.05 am journey she did from Manly on 27 February 1951, was her last. The company, in grave financial circumstances after spending £261 772 on the *North Head*, could not afford the cost of reconditioning the hull of the *Balgowlah* and fitting her with new engines. She was laid up until 30 June 1953, when she was sold to Stride's shipbreaking yard at Glebe, where she was towed on 7 August. *Balgowlah* was the last coal-burning ferry in the fleet. It was unfortunate that the Port Jackson company did not reconstruct *Balgowlah* as it had done with *North Head*, which was still giving good service 33 years later, but times were hard for the ferry business.

In her 40 years with the Manly fleet, the *Balgowlah* had travelled about 17 440 miles a year up and down the harbour.

3. The Pretty Lady

Two years before the *Balgowlah* arrived on the Sydney Harbour scene, the Port Jackson & Manly Steamship Company had acquired another fine vessel, given the name *Bellubera*, said to mean in the local Aboriginal dialect, beautiful woman or pretty lady. Beautiful women have been the downfall of many throughout history and quite a bit of tragedy was to become associated with the *Bellubera*'s 63 years of service, most of it after she was taken off the run in 1935 to be the first Manly ferry converted to diesel-electric propulsion. Almost as if the pretty lady resented having her steam engines taken out and replaced by those new-fangled contraptions, she became involved in a strange series of events.

Perhaps there was an omen just after *Bellubera* was launched, while she was being fitted out alongside Mort's Dock at Woolwich. On 10 May 1910, chains holding a 40-ton boiler broke and the boiler crashed down into the hull, causing considerable damage to her frames and wiring.

Apart from sinking a tug a few years later, *Bellubera* led a reasonably quiet life until 1936, when she caught fire at the company's Kurraba Point depot while undergoing overhaul. Two men died as a result of the fire and another spent two years in hospital. Then, after she was rebuilt and returned to service, *Bellubera* was often in the news. Two captains collapsed and died at the wheel, a young man fell overboard and was drowned, she rammed and damaged a warship, she ran down a launch, whose driver went to the bottom with the wreckage, she tangled badly with an overseas freighter and she broke down several times and had to be towed to safety.

Mrs J. J. Eyre, wife of the chairman of directors of the Port Jackson & Manly Steamship Company, christened and launched *Bellubera* on 26 April 1910, at Mort's Woolwich dock, presenting the company with a fine ship, to be, when fitted out, the largest and most powerful unit of the fleet to date. *Bellubera* had been built in little more than a year from the time she was ordered, basically to the design of the two earlier B class ferries, *Binngarra* and *Burra Bra*, but retaining the distinctive lines of Walter Reeks' *Kuring-gai*. She was 210 ft long, of 32 ft beam and drew just 12 ft. Her triple expansion steam engines, also manufactured at Mort's Dock, drove single screws fore and aft. The hull was of riveted steel construction, divided into watertight compartments by five bulkheads. Two navy-type boilers, heated from six large furnaces, developed steam at a working pressure up to 180 lb per square inch, producing 1350 hp.

So, when *Bellubera* faced up for her trials on the harbour on 15 September 1910, it was no surprise that she made 15 knots. She was the fastest ferry in Sydney until the *Balgowlah* came along two years later with 16 knots. Mort's Dock chairman, Mr Kelso King, presided at the handing-over ceremony and a luncheon in the ferry's main saloon for managers, directors and officials and guests of both companies. Praising the enterprise of the Manly company in having a ship like the *Bellubera* built in Sydney, Mr Kelso King said Manly had just 'caught the bus' with the new ferry because Coogee and Bondi beaches were beginning to provide Manly with strong competition for the surfing community. *The Bellubera*, which accommodated 1529 passengers, gave the Manly ferries a fleet of seven vessels, capable of carrying 8500 people. 'The floating palace', was the description of the Manly *Argus* for the new ferry. It was said that the advent of magnificent steamers like *Bellubera* would make the paddlewheelers take a back seat and before long become nonentities on Sydney Harbour.

Bellubera's first hair-raising experience occurred on 2 April 1914, when she sliced in two a tug towing a lighter loaded with high explosives. Had *Bellubera* hit the lighter instead, her life might have been shortened considerably. Victim of the accident, however, was the tug *Kate*, sent to the bottom for the second time by a Manly ferry. Fourteen years previously, the Manly ferry *Narrabeen* collided with *Kate* and sank her between Macquarie Point and Fort Denison during a heavy fog. Now fate befell *Kate* again.

A waterlogged derelict skiff was blamed for the early morning collision off Dobroyd Point. The *Kate*, according to the *Sydney Morning Herald*, was towing in the lighter enough explosives to blow up half a township. Earlier that morning one of the Manly skippers had reported seeing a waterlogged rowboat, about 14 ft long, drifting near Dobroyd. Captain Nixon, on the bridge of the *Bellubera*, was keeping a lookout for the skiff after leaving Manly on the 7.45 am run to the city. *Kate*, belonging to the New South Wales Explosives Department, had taken a lighter to Manly and had landed six kegs of blasting powder on the cargo wharf. The tug and lighter were coming back up the harbour to Woolloomooloo Bay, the lighter still containing 20 packages of explosives, including 17 kegs of blasting powder and three cases of gelignite.

Captain Nixon saw the waterlogged skiff near Dobroyd, then, almost at the same time, noticed the tug, apparently about to cross in front of his ferry. Blasting the whistle, he rang down for full astern and starboarded the helm. But it was too late. The sharp bows of the *Bellubera* cut through the tug amidships. Ferry passengers threw lifebuoys to the four tug crewmen struggling in the water and when Captain Nixon could stop the ferry he ordered a lifeboat launched. By this time, two of the tug's crew had scrambled on to the bottom of the lighter, which had capsized. The four men were soon rescued and were taken aboard the ferry to Sydney, where the tug's master, Captain J. Collins, reported the mishap to the Super-intendent of Explosives. Returning to Dobroyd with the Harbour Trust's tug *Powerful*, the three other members of the *Kate*'s crew—engineer T. Crawley and deckhands W. Webb and H. Arnemann—righted the upturned lighter

and towed it back to the Manly cargo wharf, nowadays the Fun Pier. In those days most of Manly's requirements came via this wharf.

Bellubera did not suffer any serious damage apart from some scratched paint. She arrived at Circular Quay with pieces of the tug's wreckage hanging around her sponson. An examination dispelled fears that the for'ard propeller might have been damaged, but a piece of copper piping from the tug was found jammed between the ferry's rudder and hull. This was removed and the *Bellubera* went back to Manly, having missed only one trip.

A ferry passenger, Mr R.L. Nicholl, told the *Herald* of the accident. Mr Nicholl, travelling to business in the city by an earlier ferry than usual, was sitting almost amid-ships, facing Middle Harbour, when he heard three blasts of the *Bellubera*'s whistle—the signal for going astern—and, jumping up, he ran to the rail to see what was happening. Said Mr Nicholl:

What impressed me most was the remarkable sudden-ness with which the tug disappeared after it had been hit. It was creepy to see it duck away so quickly. I saw the tug towing a big lighter right ahead of us. Our engines stopped, but they hardly had time to be re-versed when there was a crash and I saw the stem of the *Bellubera* cutting through the tug amidships like a knife cutting through a piece of cheese. Almost immediately, the stern of the tug sank out of sight. At the same, the bow shot up in the air and, shortly afterwards, disap-peared also. When the collision occurred, two men who were sitting at the stern of the tug were thrown down on the deck and as the stern sank they both scrambled up and climbed from the sinking tug on to the bottom of the upturned lighter. I also noticed the captain climbing up the bow as that portion was sinking. I could not under-stand at the time the anxiety to be rescued of the two men on the upturned lighter. They kept shouting excit-edly for us to throw them a rope. They seemed to be perfectly safe, but when we learned that the lighter contained explosives we saw the reason for their anxiety. As far as the passengers on the *Bellubera* were concerned, there was little, if any, panic. A number of women screamed and a few girls were crying. The passengers threw over some lifebelts and lifebuoys and our boat stood by until all the men were picked up.

Nothing else of note seems to have happened to the *Bellubera* for about 20 years. She plied her way safely up and down the harbour, carrying many thousands of pas-sengers to and from work or for happy times at the beach in the weekends. It must have been the replacement of her steam engines that put the curse on her after she went to be fitted with the new diesel-electrics around September 1935.

Bellubera was only the second British vessel to be converted to diesel-electric propulsion. The first was one of the Hong Kong Star ferries, *Electric Star*. There were, of course, plenty of motor ships, driven by large diesel oil engines. Sydney Ferries Ltd had converted one or two of its old inner harbour steamers from steam to diesel. But this was something different. Diesel engines would be used to drive direct-current generators, which, in turn, would supply electric current to four electric-propulsion motors of 615 hp each. Two electric motors were to be geared by single-reduction, double-pinion helical gears with thrust blocks to each fore and aft propeller. The four diesel engines were built at Glasgow by Harland & Wolff under licence from Burmeister & Wain, of Copenhagen. They were two-stroke cycle, single-acting type engines, with five cylinders of 220 mm bore and 370 mm stroke, capable of developing up to 450 bhp at 600 rpm. Two auxiliary six-cylinder diesel engines of 85 bhp each powered the generating plant for lighting, auxiliary power for the steering and engine room pumps. Many other things were to change, too, in the process. The engine room telegraphs were to be retained, but only for emergencies. The engine speed, stopping and starting or reversing of the vessel, would in future be controlled direct from the bridge. The long white funnel was removed and replaced with two shorter, stout, medium-height funnels, giving the vessel a more streamlined appearance. But all this change removed another thing which had been a great attraction to ferry travellers—the sight, sound and smell of the steam engines. When the sleek new *Bellubera* returned to the Manly run, the open engine pit was gone, covered over by the main deck. No longer could passengers lean over the rails as the telegraph clanged and watch the engineers wind the wheels and pull the levers which made that hissing machinery throb into life, with pounding pistons pushing spinning crankshafts. The engines down below were to be heard, but not seen. They were felt, though. The *Bellubera* became notorious for the vibration, which rattled windows and doors.

The Port Jackson & Manly Steamship Company, however, was looking forward to many advantages—cleanliness, easier and better economy of operation, plus more speed. *Bellubera* had been lumbering along at about 14 knots, whereas her two new big sisters, *Dee Why* and *Curl Curl*, brought out from Scotland in 1928, were two or three knots faster. The conversion increased *Bellubera's* speed to 16 knots, the engines could be started instantly with a compressed air device as against the two hours required to raise steam and, another big advantage, the ship would have to be refuelled only every 14 days. The conversion also changed the propeller function. Previously, the steam engines had turned the fore and aft propellers simultaneously on a shaft from the engines to each end of the vessel. Most people would think this was very efficient; the for'ard propeller pulling, and the one aft pushing. But it had been found that the for'ard screw turning at the same speed as the other hindered rather than helped and so, in the new *Bellubera*, the propellers were driven by separate shafts, each geared to two electric motors. In this way, the vessel could get its full power from the thrust of the aft propeller while the for'ard screw turned at slower revolutions, reducing water resistance to a minimum.

Steam engines, boilers and pipes were taken out of *Bellubera* and the bare hull was taken to Mort's Dock, where the foundations for the four diesel engines were to be made. She then returned to the company's depot and workshops at Kurraba Point and here most of the work was done. Everything was completed and *Bellubera* returned to service on 28 June 1936, but from then on she brought a lot of trouble to everyone connected with her.

Eric Gale, 94 years old, living at Mosman in 1987, remembers much of the trouble. He was with the Port Jackson & Manly Steamship Company for 22 years, first as an engineer in the ferries and later as works' superintendent at Kurraba Point. Former traffic manager, George Marshall, paid tribute particularly to Eric Gale and another engineer named Lew Maxwell when he said:

The *Bellubera* was cheaper to operate than the steamers because the diesel-electric side of it was very successful. But the prime motors were a failure and it was only because of the tenacity of the engineers in the company that we were able to keep her going as long as we did.

Of that first trial run, Eric Gale recalled:

They were measuring out the speed from Pinchgut (Fort Denison) to Bradleys Head, but before we got to Bradleys one engine broke down. We went as far as Chowder Bay and my boss, Mr McMillan, who was the works' manager then, said 'All right. She's supposed to do 16 knots with three engines, so we'll try her on three'. We turned back, passed Bradleys Head, got to Pinchgut and then the second engine broke down. Mr McMillan said we would go back to the Kurraba yard, but as we went into Athol Bight to turn around, the third engine failed. Struggling on one engine, the *Bellubera* headed in to berth at Kurraba Point and as we put her astern to take the way off her, the fourth engine conked out. We got a rope ashore and tied her up and that was the end of the official trial. The company officials were furious and I don't know what the fellow from Harland & Wolff said.

This graphic picture of the Bellubera fire at Kurraba Point in November 1936, shows the mass of flames devouring the ferry's bridge and upper decks while five men were trapped beneath the fire in the engine room.

The engines had to be overhauled extensively before the ferry went out on the harbour again and even then, according to Eric Gale, they gave 'a terrible lot of trouble'. He said:

> They were two-stroke, started with compressed air, and they had four coiled springs on top, about a quarter of an inch thick. These springs used to break, so we had to crank the engine around with a bar to get the pistons up and screw a plate which would tip the springs so that we could take the broken ones out.

That plate was the cause of the first fatality in the sequence of unhappy events to follow. Engineer Jack Doran cut a finger on the edge of a plate and suffered blood poisoning. He was dead in a fortnight. At a subsequent inquest, the City Coroner found that 'John George Doran, 45, marine engineer, died from streptococcal septicaemia after an injury accidentally received through cutting his right forefinger at his place of employment on the ferry Bellubera.'

Frequently, between Circular Quay and Manly, they would have to stop engines to take out exhaust valves and lift the poppets. It was not unusual for the vessel to be running on only two of her four engines while Gale and Maxwell worked to get the others going again. 'Lew Maxwell was the man who kept those engines going,' said Eric Gale. 'He kept them alive for 12 years.' But Maxwell nearly lost his own life in the process, as we shall see.

4. Fire up above

Two of Maxwell's workmates died after a disastrous fire swept the Bellubera at the Kurraba Point yards about 3.30 pm on Monday 16 November 1936. Maxwell and four others, trapped in the engine room for nearly an hour, were almost suffocated by smoke and fumes. But it was not another sea story of fire down below. The fire was up above, raging through the upper decks and superstructure. It was started by sparks and molten metal from an oxyacetylene torch used by workmen repairing a steel plate on the roof of the promenade deck near the for'ard funnel. The sparks and molten metal fell on to a leather upholstered seat in the upper saloon and in less than five minutes the whole vessel was ablaze under a cloud of thick black smoke rising high into the air. The heat was so intense that the five men below in the engine room could not get out, and if they had tried to make their way up to the main deck they would certainly have been burnt to death before reaching safety.

For 50 minutes four of them lay on the floor of the engine room engulfed in acrid smoke while firemen endeavoured to reach them by wearing an asbestos suit and respirator. Fellow employees tried to cut a hole through the steel side of the ship with an oxyacetylene torch. Lew Maxwell saved his life by putting his head out a porthole and breathing air instead of smoke. Eric Gale had been down there with them, but a call from superintendent McMillan just before the fire began probably saved his life. It also saved the big steam ferry Dee Why, which was tied up nearby and, fortunately, had enough steam up for Gale and a fireman to move her away from the wharf and the fire.

42

The *Bellubera* was a burnt-out shell by the time the fire was extinguished. Damage was estimated at around £40 000. One man was dead, another died four days later and a third, in hospital for almost two years, nearly lost his life and just missed having both legs amputated. That was Andrew Rae, 29, a marine engineer. Robert Findlay, 38, a fitter, of Council Street, Waverley, died on the night of the fire. Sidney Tight, 44, a greaser, of Barton Avenue, Haberfield, was taken to Royal North Shore Hospital suffering from suffocation, burns and shock. He died on the following Friday. Sidney Cronshaw, 43, fitter, of Bank Street, North Sydney, spent some time in hospital for treatment for severe burns to his arms and legs, and shock. Frederick Thompson, 28, of Atchison Street, St Leonards, was burnt on his left arm during rescue operations. Several police, firemen and ferry depot employees received minor burns and injuries. Captain Wally Dohrn Snr was on the ferry's bridge when the fire broke out. He managed to scramble to the foredeck, from where he slid down a rope to the wharf.

Firemen had difficulty in dealing with the fire because the depot and wharves were under a high cliff at Kurraba Point. The fire engines could not get down to the wharf and without them the water pressure available was insufficient. When Chief Fire Officer Richardson and Second Officer Beare reached the wharf, the ferry was burning so fiercely that nobody could get aboard. The water supply at the wharf was not strong enough to be of any real use. Depot employees had made a gallant attempt to fight the fire with hoses, but soon had to give up and hand over to the firemen, who used a fire engine as a relay pumping station on half a kilometre of fire hose laid down to reach the wharf from hydrants in the street above.

The five men who had been working on the *Bellubera*'s diesel-electric engines were driven back as they tried to escape up the narrow companionway from the engine room, the walls and floor of which were soon unbearably hot. Lew Maxwell squeezed through a narrow opening into the adjoining auxiliary engine room, where he managed to reach a porthole and poke his head out through the side of the hull. His cries for help were heard above the roar of the flames by two fellow employees, Fred Thompson and Charles Anderson, who dashed into the workshop on the wharf, grabbed an oxy-welding plant and rowed with it in a dinghy to the side of the ferry where Maxwell was yelling from the porthole, but it soon became obvious that they would have no hope of cutting through the ship's side in time.

The *Sydney Morning Herald* report said the ferry *Curl Curl*, which was lying alongside the *Bellubera*, would also have been destroyed if water police, using a small police launch as a tug, had not towed the *Curl Curl* to safety. It was not the *Curl Curl* but the *Dee Why* and the police did not tow her out. The *Dee Why* was certainly in grave danger at No. 1 wharf, just around the corner, jutting out across the wharf where the *Bellubera* was tied up. Eric Gale was aboard *Dee Why* when the fire started. She was soon to have gone out for the peak evening traffic. Superintendent McMillan said to Gale when he came in response to McMillan's summons from the *Bellubera*'s engine room: 'Go down to the *Dee Why*. The engineer hasn't turned up. See that the fireman and greaser are there and see that we've got steam ready. The skipper is not here, either.' Gale recalls:

I went down to the stokehold. The fireman was there and I had a look at the pressure and water gauge, which is the thing you do first, but I need not have looked because you couldn't have had better greasers and firemen. They knew their job and they did it. Then I went and looked to see how the gauge was at the engine controls to see whether she had steam up and just then someone called out 'fire'. I looked at the greaser and repeated 'fire?' I ran up the stairs and saw the *Bellubera* was a mass of flames. I jumped on to the wharf, grabbed a hose and tried to do something with it to fight the fire, but it was hopeless, so I ran back aboard the *Dee Why* and told the greaser 'You man the engine-room telegraphs' and called out to those on the wharf to let go the ropes. I climbed up to the wheelhouse and took the *Dee Why* out into the stream. I stopped there because I knew the skipper would come and it was not long before Captain Wally Dohrn and the engineer came alongside in a launch. Two of the Dohrns were Manly skippers— Wally and his father, also Wally, who had just escaped the fire.

We went to Circular Quay with the *Dee Why* and then I was taken back to Kurraba Point in a launch. The fire was out then and a lot of people were about. I went down into the engine room of the *Bellubera*, which was crowded with police, and one of them said to me, 'Do you know anything about this ship?' I said, 'Yes. Why?' He said, 'A man is down there under the floor. How do you get down there?' I said, 'You can't. I don't know how anyone could get down there.' He said, 'A man is missing.' I asked, 'What man?' He said, 'A bloke named Gale.' They thought I was missing and they were looking for me. Findlay was brought up and put in the workshop, where the ambulance men worked on him and others with special inhalators, but they were not moved until some hours later. They were not rushed to hospital as soon as they were brought on to the wharf because doctors said it was better to treat them there with the apparatus the firemen were using.

Bob Findlay died that night in hospital and Sid Tight lingered on until Friday. The day of the fire was Sid's first day back at work after being off for quite a long time with pneumonia and bad lung trouble. You can imagine what happened when the smoke got him. Andy Rae had his legs badly scorched. They were burned right in to the bone. Snowy Cronshaw, too, was burned badly on the arms and legs. They were scalded with water from the fire hoses, which leaked down into the engine room, almost boiling from the raging fire above. God knows what Andy Rae went through later during 21 months in the Royal North Shore Hospital. When he was taken there the doctors thought both his legs would have to be amputated, there was so little of them left, and they thought he would die. But his courage enabled the doctors to save his legs, making seven skin grafts—three from his thighs and four from his brother. By August 1938, his legs were almost normal size again and he was taken to his home at Epping by his aged parents, who had not missed a day seeing him during the 21 months he was in hospital.

The men in the engine room were rescued after a huge quantity of water had been hosed into the ferry to make a laneway through the flames. The firemen then tried something never done previously. District Fire Officer Griffiths put on a new type of asbestos suit fitted with a respirator, climbed over the side of the ferry and strode into the fire. But he had not gone far when he was called back from what would have been certain death. Soon afterwards, when the flames were more subdued, he tried again with District Officer Currer, Sub-station Officer Condon and Senior Fireman Millege, and this time they reached the engine room, where their lamps showed four men lying unconscious on the floor plates. Said one of the rescuers:

> I still don't understand how they lived. The smoke was so thick it was impossible to see. We stumbled around in the darkness, our lamps hardly penetrating the gloom, and found two of them huddled together, one lying a few yards away and another unconscious over a dynamo. It was terrible work getting them out. Mr Griffiths stripped off his asbestos suit to move more freely. Two of the men were so heavy we had to use a rope to get them up the companionway. The only one who did not seem to be affected seriously was Maxwell, who had been getting air from outside.

Constable Baxter, of the water police, told of coming up the harbour in a police launch with Constable Anderson when they saw the smoke and noticed that the ferry was on fire. The *Herald* reported him as saying:

> We ran in close and managed to get a line to the *Curl Curl* and towed her away from the wharf. It was too

The head through the engine room porthole is that of engineer Lew Maxwell, who saved himself in this way from asphyxiation by smoke and fumes.

dangerous to take our petrol launch near the burning ferry, so I transferred to a rowing boat and paddled to the harbour side of the ferry. Maxwell had his head through a porthole. He was gasping and calling for water. I got some for him from the launch and he drank about a gallon.

Constable Baxter later fought his way into the engine room with firemen and helped to rescue the men.

General manager of the Port Jackson & Manly Steamship Company, Mr W. L. Dendy, said the *Bellubera* was insured with Lloyds and the loss would be covered, but the amount would not be known until the ship had been surveyed. At that stage there was no explanation for the sudden fire and this probably started the rumours which often spring up in such cases, including suggestions that it was 'an insurance job'. A huge array of barristers and solicitors, 13 in all, crammed the City Coroner's Court on Thursday, 10 December 1936, when the City Coroner, Mr E. T. Oram, conducted an inquiry into the cause of the *Bellubera* fire and the deaths of Findlay and Tight. Practically every company or public authority which feared it might have faced the slightest risk of blame was represented. After hearing evidence for two days, Mr Oram found that the fire was caused by molten metal and sparks falling from the sun deck, where an oxyaectylene burner was being used on a steel plate. He found that Findlay and Tight had died accidentally from the effects of inhaling carbon monoxide and smoke fumes while they were at their usual occupations in the engine room of the *Bellubera*. Mr Oram said that during the inquest he had received many letters from different people, most of which had been helpful. On the first day of hearing, however, he had been handed an anonymous letter, which, he said, appeared to have been written by somebody of unbalanced mind, making the serious allegation that the fire had been caused maliciously and the company had had something to do with it. Said Mr Oram:

There is nothing to suggest that the fire was malicious. After reconditioning, the vessel was completely satisfactory, the company's employees were satisfied and happy and there was no evidence that the company was in financial difficulties.

There was, however, a serious problem for the Port Jackson company. What would happen with the *Bellubera* obviously going to be out of action for some time? The new year of 1937 had arrived before *Bellubera* was towed to Cockatoo Island dockyard on 4 January and it was not until October that she was returned to normal service. Meanwhile, *Burra Bra* had been brought back into use temporarily to fill the gap. *Bellubera*'s engines had been overhauled while she was being rebuilt, but they still gave trouble and again it was mainly Lew Maxwell who kept them going.

The engines were replaced a few years later. *Bellubera* was taken to the State Dockyard at Newcastle in February 1954, and returned to Sydney in October that year with English Electric engines which generated the power for electric motors to drive the propellers. General manager of the Port Jackson & Manly Steamship Company, Mr W. L. Dendy, had sent Lew Maxwell to England to buy suitable machinery for re-engining the *Bellubera*, *Barrenjoey* and *Balgowlah*. They ordered 12 English Electric engines and generators, which were shipped out to Sydney and stored at the ferry company's Kurraba workshops. Four went into the *Barrenjoey* when she was converted from steam to diesel between 1948 and 1951, and three of the engines replaced the Harland & Wolff diesels in the *Bellubera*. Conversion of the *Balgowlah* never proceeded. She was taken out of service in 1951. The engines were kept until it was decided to re-engine the *Baragoola*, which became the third diesel-electric Manly ferry in service in January 1961.

Bellubera had only three of the new engines. Whereas *Barrenjoey*, renamed *North Head*, and *Baragoola* were complete conversions from steam to diesel-electric, *Bellubera* retained the electric motors and gearboxes from her original conversion. Eric Gale recalled:

There was no need to change the electric motors, generators and gearboxes, but we couldn't put four engines into her without shifting the bulkhead between the engine room and the two boiler spaces of 44 inches. I went along to a Board meeting and told the directors:

'Well, gentlemen, you haven't got the money to shift the bulkhead. Just put three engines in her and she'll go faster than she ever did, even when she was a steamer. You will have more horsepower in the three engines than she had in the steam engines or the four diesels from Harland & Wolff.' The Board agreed, and then I did get into trouble. I had all the engineers on my back. But when the *Bellubera* came out of the State Dockyard she ran very successfully on her three new engines.

Bellubera was certainly faster than she had been as a steamer, having clocked 15.5 knots on her trials with the original diesel engines; but the problems were plenty for men like Gale and Maxwell, whose job was to keep the engines going, especially when they had to stop one or more during trips between Manly and the city and do running repairs like taking off cylinder heads and replacing broken valve stems and springs or worn-out cylinder liners. Frequently, the liners were worn out within two or three weeks. The engineers down below decks had to cope with this and the company's demand for speed, requiring that over the 6.8 nautical miles between Circular Quay and Manly the time should not exceed 30 minutes between 'full ahead' from one wharf and 'stop' at the other end, which meant an average speed of around 13.6 knots. Skippers who did not run to time had to 'please explain' to the management.

That the Manly ferries run so strictly to time has always been a tribute to the men who man them, navigating them through much foul weather and the difficult conditions of Saturday afternoon sailing races and Sunday drivers of power boats who know and care nothing for the ways of the water. People who live on the harbour front can usually set their clocks by the passing of these ferries, even since the demise of the Port Jackson company and the advent of government control under the Urban Transit Authority. To keep to the timetable was no mean feat in the days when Eric Gale and Lew Maxwell were wrestling with those Burmeister & Wain diesels in the heat and noise and fumes below deck, frequently with the floor beneath them bucking around on the swell rolling in through The Heads. Maintaining an average speed of 13.6 knots needed all four of the original Burmeister & Wain engines.

Eric Gale thought he had solved the problem when they found that the engines were running at too many revolutions. With the works' superintendent, Mr McMillan, he was invited to visit in the harbour a ship from Denmark which he was told had Burmeister & Wain diesels. Eric said:

We went below with the ship's second engineer and found they were exactly the same as those in the

45

Bellubera. They had no trouble with them. So I scratched my head and thought out what was wrong with ours. The answer was twice as many revs. Their engines were doing 360 rpm whereas ours were doing 600. Our blowers were super-charging to give the 600 revs, so we set about modifying them. We got the engines all set up and Billy Scott was just about to start them when a cable arrived from England saying: 'On no account start those engines.' We were told to take the blowers off and remove the trains of gears. Harland & Wolff flew out from Belfast four more trains of gears which reduced the revs from 600 to 510.

The frequency of breakdowns was reduced, but so was the speed of the generators and they could not supply the electric motors with enough current to keep the ship running at the required speed.

Things were better with the English Electric engines installed a few years after the fire. The Harland & Wolff, Burmeister & Wain diesels were replaced at the State Dockyard, Newcastle, between February and October of 1954. Refitted again, *Bellubera* returned to the Manly service on 21 October 1954, and operated for another 19 years before she was taken out of service on 29 November 1973. *Bellubera* had seen 63 years on the harbour, regarded then as quite a long time. But records are made to be broken and *Bellubera*'s record was to be surpassed later by the *North Head*, which celebrated with a quiet grandeur its 71st birthday rolling across The Heads on the swell kicked up by the bad weather on 8 May 1984.

5. Hoodoo Ship

Life was fairly uneventful for the *Bellubera* for some time after the fire and she does not seem to have been in the news much until September 1941, when she was involved in the first of a series of strange mishaps which earned her the dubious name of 'the hoodoo ship'. If anything had to be hit on the harbour the *Bellubera* would hit it. Some even said she had the kiss of death.

A man was swept to his death during a heavy rainstorm near Circular Quay on the night of 9 September 1941, the launch he was driving dragging him down as it rolled over and disappeared beneath the *Bellubera*. The ferry, commanded by Captain W. Harris, on the 6.40 pm run from Manly to town, was rounding Bennelong Point off the present site of the Opera House at about 7.15 pm, making the turn into Circular Quay. It was raining heavily at the time. As the ferry turned around Bennelong, Captain Harris and some of the passengers who were sitting for'ard on the upper deck saw the port light of a launch appear suddenly out of the rain directly ahead of the *Bellubera*. Captain Harris sounded three blasts and rang down full astern, but the ferry was still gliding ahead when it struck the launch. He told the *Daily Telegraph*:

I didn't see the launch until it was right beneath me on the starboard side. It was raining steadily and visibility was poor. The sea was calm. I had only a fleeting glimpse of the launch before it disappeared. It was showing a dim light, but I could not make out whether

The Sydney Opera House was still under construction when this photograph of the Bellubera *was taken for publicity by the Port Jackson & Manly Steamship Company.* Bellubera *had just left Circular Quay and was heading out to run down the harbour to Manly.*

anyone was on board. It happened so quickly that I could not even distinguish the colour, type or size of the launch. I'm sure the *Bellubera* did not run it down, but struck it side on. This may have been sufficient to turn the boat over. I stopped the ferry immediately, had the lifebelts thrown overboard and searched the vicinity for 15 minutes.

But in vain. There was no sign of the launch or any occupant. Apparently the boat had gone intact, taking with it whoever was aboard. When the *Telegraph* went to press that night the water police were still trying to find out which launch had been sunk and who was in it. Just before midnight, S. G. White Pty Ltd, boilermakers, of Balmain East, reported to the police that one of their launches, the 30-ft *Sydbridge*, was missing with its driver, Sidney Rose, 54, of Gornall Avenue, Canterbury.

Mr R. T. Brown, of Redfern, a passenger on the ferry, told reporters that he had seen a man in the launch before it collided with the ferry. 'The launch seemed to roll completely over and then it was gone,' Mr Brown said. Another passenger said he rushed to the side of the ferry when he saw that a collision was inevitable. He watched the bow of the launch bobbing momentarily along the side of the *Bellubera* until it disappeared. Deckhands threw lifebelts into the water, but nobody was with them when they were picked up later.

Police and customs men in launches searched the area for some time without finding anything. There was little they could do until daylight, when a diver could be sent down. It was another two days, however, before the *Sydbridge* was found in 10 metres of water off Bennelong Point within 45 metres of where it was believed to have gone down, but there was no sign of any body. The story gained added interest when it was learned that Rose was one of the claimants for what was known as 'the Rose Millions'. Rose was a great-great-grandson of Thomas Rose, claimed to have been the first British free settler in Australia. Thomas Rose had left an estate in London consisting of very valuable property around the Tilbury Docks. This estate, in Chancery, was estimated at the time of Sidney Rose's death to be worth about £15 million.

Sidney Rose's body was found floating in the harbour nine days after the accident. A Court of Marine Inquiry was held during October and November. It was a trying time for Captain Bill Harris, who was in charge of the *Bellubera* on the night of 9 September. He had crossed Sydney Harbour 28 000 times in 11 years, he told the court, and this was his only accident. Captain Harris said he ran to the side of the bridge when the collision occurred and saw the launch swing along the port side and then founder. He cruised back and forth for a quarter of an hour, but saw no trace of anyone in the water. The court

subsequently absolved Captain Harris from any blame, finding that the launch's masthead light came on only when the motor boat, in heavy rain, was too close to avoid a collision.

Bellubera's next tragedy, four years later, involved Captain Wally Dohrn, 67, one of the best known skippers on the harbour. There were two Captain Dohrns, father and son, both named Walter. Wally Dohrn took the *Bellubera* out of Circular Quay for the 4 pm trip to Manly on 6 February 1945. As they approached The Heads and the ferry began to nod gently into the swell, Captain Dohrn collapsed into a chair in the wheelhouse. George Conwell, a deckhand who was helmsman, took the *Bellubera* on to Manly and berthed her at the wharf, where 300 passengers disembarked, unaware of what had happened. Conwell said:

There was nothing wrong with the skipper when he came aboard. He ran up the ladder to the bridge the same as usual. Just before we reached The Heads he complained of a pain in his heart and collapsed unconscious. He was dead when we called an ambulance at Manly. He must have died soon after collapsing into the chair.

Wally Dohrn had crossed those heads many thousands of times in his 33 years with the Port Jackson company and, no doubt, if he had been given his choice, this was the way he would have wanted to go.

Other strange events followed the death of Captain Dohrn. In September 1945, a young woman, feeling slightly seasick, leaned too far over the rail and fell into the water almost at the spot where Captain Dohrn died. Two soldiers who saw her fall dived in after her and held her up until the ferry returned and they were pulled aboard. The girl, wearing only blue scanties, said she had taken off her clothes so she could swim better. About 1000 people on the ferry arrived in town 15 minutes late.

Not long after that, a young fellow, jilted by his lover, jumped from the *Bellubera* and began swimming towards The Heads, shouting that he wanted to die. He ignored the lifebelts thrown to him. The ferry came back and lowered a boat, which was used to rescue him. Still protesting, the despondent lover was dragged into the boat and saved. Not so lucky was another young fellow, who, almost a year from the date of Captain Dohrn's death, fell from the top deck of the *Bellubera* and was not saved. The ferry was on the 11 pm trip to Manly on the night of 31 January 1946, and as it passed Clifton Gardens the man was seen to fall overboard. Passengers rushed to tell the captain, who stopped and searched without any success.

Perhaps the strangest story of all is told about what happened on the night of 17 August 1948. The *Bellubera* was near the part of The Heads where Captain Dohrn died when passengers heard loud moans coming from the water. Thinking somebody had fallen in, they told the captain, who put the ferry astern and searched the area with spotlights. The captain reported 'fear and agitation' among the passengers when nothing was found.

And so it continues with yet another strange story. Almost exactly a year later to the day—16 August 1949—again at night, passengers on the *Dee Why* heard shouts coming from the water. The ferry stopped and crew rescued a Navy stoker who had fallen from the *Bellubera* and had kept himself afloat in the harbour for a quarter of an hour.

In October of the following year, on the night of 18 October 1950, the *Bellubera* was involved in a nasty collision off Bradleys Head with the 7000-ton Norwegian freighter *Taurus*. Both vessels were travelling up the harbour, the *Bellubera* ahead of *Taurus*, and as *Bellubera* made her normal turn to starboard at Bradleys Head, the *Taurus*, continuing straight ahead, crashed into the ferry. *Bellubera* was damaged rather badly, but, fortunately, none of the 100 passengers aboard was injured, although the force of the impact rolled the ferry over on her side. The dramatic story, with pictures, made the headlines in the *Sydney Morning Herald*, which reported:

The *Taurus* loomed up suddenly in the dark. She sounded her siren, then her bows tore into the ferry's lower deck, smashing 15 feet of woodwork. Women screamed and there was a panic rush for lifebelts. One man was seen wearing three. The *Taurus* rolled the ferry over on its side. A flood of water poured over the lower deck, submerging it to the centre line. The 100 passengers scattered about the vessel were thrown from their seats when the crash came. Some raced for the upper deck when the ferry rolled and shipped water. One man had a remarkable escape. He was lying on a seat when the bow of the *Taurus* cut through the woodwork a few inches from him. He was showered with splinters, but was not hurt.

The *Bellubera*, which had left Manly at 10.15 pm, continued under her own power to the city, where she was taken off the run and tied up for the night, although, because the *Curl Curl* was in the spare berth on the other side of the wharf, ferries to and from Manly had to tie up alongside the *Bellubera* and had to go to and from the wharf through the disabled *Bellubera*, all of which presented a problem.

The *Taurus*, belonging to Wilhelm Wilhelmsen and Company, had left Melbourne a few days previously carrying a light cargo of timber and other goods from the United States and, under the command of a pilot, Captain J. N. Collins, was coming up the harbour to a berth at No. 4 Woolloomooloo. Neither Captain Collins nor the master of the *Taurus*, Captain T. W. Wenneberg, would tell reporters anything when the ship was berthed, but a seaman on the *Taurus* was quoted. He told of being in the bow of his ship when it collided with the *Bellubera*:

We were coming up the harbour slowly when suddenly the ferry came across our bows and we hit it almost amidships. After we hit, the ferry swung around on our starboard side. One of the crew said he saw a woman sitting on a bench on the ferry, but I didn't see anyone. We called out 'Do you want help?' and someone said 'Yes'. We went to lower a lifeboat, but by that time other boats were coming around and we continued on up the harbour. When the collision happened both boats stopped. We didn't move for about 10 minutes after the hit.

The impact bent about five feet of the *Taurus*'s bow, pushing it out of alignment, and gouged a hole about 18 inches wide on the starboard side. Some plates near the bow were buckled. The fact that both vessels were travelling in the same direction must have saved them from worse damage. It would have been very serious had they been going in opposite directions.

Mr Bill Berryman, a Manly resident who was a passenger on the *Bellubera*, said neither he nor any of the other passengers were aware of the ship or the danger until the *Taurus* appeared suddenly alongside the ferry, gave two short blasts of her siren and then came the crash. Said Mr Berryman:

She was coming at right-angles to us and hit us hard on the starboard side aft. There was a general panic, with women screaming and everyone rushing for lifebelts. We all thought the ferry was lost, seeing the *Taurus* towering high against us and water rushing in on the starboard side. Men as well as women raced for the upper deck, clinging to lifebelts. One bloke had three on. A lot of us got heavy bumps and some minor injuries.

So ended another night of excitement on the harbour and *Bellubera* plodded along peacefully for nearly 10 years before she made big news again on Saturday night, 25 June 1960, on the 10.15 pm run from town to Manly. The *Bellubera* struck an unknown object, thought later to have been a log, while crossing The Heads and drifted very close to the rocks at Dobroyd, where there is a nasty bombora, before she was finally towed to safety. Then the westerly breeze pushed her close to Smedleys Point and there was more drama before the *North Head* took off the 60 passengers and landed them at Manly more than an hour late.

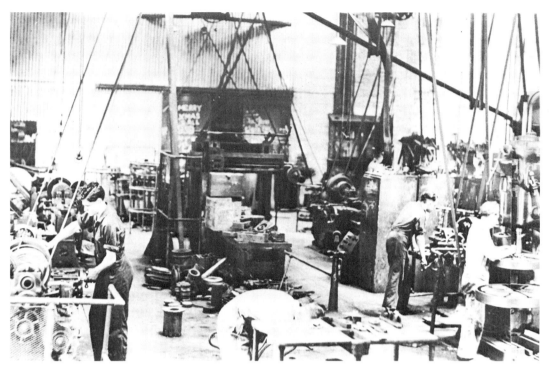

Apparently there was what passengers described as 'a tremendous jolt' and a thumping noise in the engine room when the *Bellubera* was between Middle Head and Dobroyd. The engines stopped and the ferry began to drift towards Dobroyd, lifting and rolling on the swell. Then the westerly breeze took charge and pushed the *Bellubera* slowly away from Dobroyd and across towards Smedleys Point at the end of Addison Road on the tip of Manly Cove.

Captain Albert Villiers called for help over the *Bellubera*'s radio while deckhands tried to get an anchor down and calm some of the anxious passengers. It was about 35 minutes after the engines stopped before an anchor gripped bottom and by then the *Bellubera* was little more than 45 metres from the rocks betwen Smedleys Point and Manly Point, the end of the peninsula separating Manly Cove and Little Manly. Company officials, meanwhile, had arranged for the *North Head*, on the trip following the *Bellubera*, to unload her passengers at Manly and try to tow the *Bellubera* clear. But it was not easy with a cold south-westerly blowing and the surge around the rocks making quite a joggle. Hundreds of people living in and around Addison Road were watching from their windows and high points around the water's edge. Back on Manly wharf, some one hundred young folks who had been to Manly for a Saturday night outing sat shivering, waiting to get back to town. Said 17-year-old Elizabeth Allen, of Thompson Street, Drummoyne: 'I hate to think what mum and dad are thinking. When I get to Circular Quay—and I don't know when that will be—I haven't my taxi fare home.'

Out on the water, the *North Head* crew got three ropes aboard *Bellubera* and they all snapped immediately towing began, indicating that the *Bellubera* had gone aground. It was decided then to try to take the passengers off, transferring them to the *North Head*—not an easy task with no gangways aboard and the two vessels lurching about in the swell. The 58 passengers included two babies. Some of the women had to be coaxed into jumping from one ferry to the other, especially as the gap widened sometimes to about two metres and then closed suddenly, splashing water and spray between the two hulls. Eventually they were all transferred safely and landed at Manly at 12.35 am—two hours and 20 minutes after leaving Circular Quay. *North Head* got another rope aboard and towed *Bellubera* out into deeper water, where she anchored until the tug *Waratah* picked her up at 1.30 am and towed her back to the Port Jackson depot and workshops at Kurraba Point.

Mr Edward Montanus, of Pacific Highway, Mount Colah, said:

There was a tremendous crash. Crew members told us that the propeller shaft had crumpled up. It was dangerous changing over to the second ferry. The sea was choppy and the ferries kept thrashing together. About five ropes were snapped. There were no gangways and we had to jump.

Captain Villiers said his ferry had 'hit something, which buckled the rudder and fouled the propeller'.

When the *Bellubera* was dry-docked at Cockatoo Island two days later it was found that the rudder and propeller were certainly buckled and badly bent. The propeller blades were twisted and split. Managing director of the Port Jackson & Manly Steamship Company, Brigadier C.E. Cameron, put forward the theory that a log, wrenched adrift by a tidal wave a month before, may have disabled the ferry. The tidal wave was believed to have followed an earthquake in Chile. The big Manly steam ferry, *South Steyne*, was in Cockatoo dock when the *Bellubera* accident happened and had to be taken out so that the damage to the *Bellubera* could be dealt with. 'As a consequence,' Mr Cameron stated, 'we will have to introduce a slightly restricted timetable until the *South Steyne* returns to service. This will mean a 20-minute service in peak hours and half-hourly for the rest of the day.'

The *Bellubera* made the news again twice in the following year, once when she broke down halfway across The Heads and had to be towed into Watsons Bay, much to the annoyance of one commuter, Mr D. Roberts, of Ashburner Street, Manly, who indicated in comment to the Press that he was not amused. The other occasion was the death at the wheel of another skipper, Albert Villiers, almost exactly 16 years after the death of Captain Wally Dohrn in February 1945. Captain Villiers arrived at No. 3 wharf Circular Quay on 3 February 1961, to go on duty, his first assignment being to take the *Bellubera* over to Kurraba Point for refuelling. Wharf hand Allen Conwell remembers him greeting everyone cheerily as he went through the gate and telling them he had been to his doctor that morning for a check-up. The doctor had patted him on the back and said 'You're good for another 20 years'. But it was not to be even 20 hours. Albert Villiers, commonly known as 'Digger' Villiers, died from a heart attack while trying to berth at Kurraba.

Ron Hart, a deckhand then, was aboard the *Bellubera*. He recalls:

I remember it well. It was my first wedding anniversary and it was also the day the Governor-General, Lord Dunrossil, died. I was working one of the after lines as we approached Kurraba and it was partly the fact that I couldn't lasso the dolphin at the yard which caused the trouble. We went into the yard, missed the wharf and backed out to line her up and do it again. That was where it all went wrong. The pressure was too great for Digger and he had a heart attack. Kurraba had wharves which were built originally for the paddlewheelers—a short wharf, a space and a dolphin—and to get your line ashore from the ferry you had to lasso the dolphin yourself. There was nobody to pick up the rope, as at Manly and the Quay. If you had an offshore wind and you couldn't get close enough to lasso, you would have to back out unless you were lucky, and we were not that day. There was no room to move up and have another

go coming back because the No. 4 wharf was right across the end of the berth. Harold Gibson [a captain] went in there one day in the *Dee Why*, got the wrong movement from the engineer and the *Dee Why* went right through the wharf.

The *Bellubera* did not go into Kurraba after Captain Villiers collapsed. The crew, who were nearly all up on the bridge, held her off and a message was sent to the *Baragoola* for Keith Rosser, then a deckhand with his master's ticket, to come aboard *Bellubera* and take her back to the Quay. A tug which intercepted the message met the *Baragoola* and transferred Rosser to the *Bellubera*. He took the ferry back to Circular Quay, where Captain Villiers was put ashore.

A few months later the *Bellubera* was in trouble again, having broken down and drifted near The Heads while taking a load of commuters to work in the city on the morning of 13 December 1961. The story and pictures took up most of a page in the afternoon *Sun*, which reported:

The disabled Manly ferry *Bellubera* was towed to safety this morning when only 60 yards from the rocks at Middle Head. In a two-hour harbour drama, another ferry, a tug and a pilot boat were used to save the *Bellubera* with 100 passengers aboard. In the rescue, a bollard and six feet of the *Bellubera*'s decking were torn away by a tow line as the ship drifted dangerously. Thousands of ferry passengers were stranded at Manly and Sydney as the mid-harbour rescue operation was carried out.

The drama began at about 6.20 am when *Bellubera* was crossing The Heads, five minutes out from Manly. Passengers heard a loud bang, after which the engines stopped and the ferry was left drifting. The *Dee Why*, which left Manly at 6.35 am, came alongside her crippled sister and the crew managed to get a line aboard, but a low ground swell kept the ships apart. Several more attempts were made before a heavy mooring rope was taken aboard the *Bellubera*. Then, as the *Dee Why* began to tow and the line took the strain, the double bollard to which the rope was attached pulled out of its mountings and part of the decking came away with it.

By the time the *Dee Why* was able to manoeuvre back into position to try another tow, the *Bellubera* had drifted to within 55 metres of the rocks below Middle Head. The pilot boat *Goolara* joined in the rescue attempts at this stage and, being smaller, managed to get closer and was able to tow the *Bellubera* clear of danger and took her across into Watsons Bay. There, in calmer water, the *South Steyne*, on its way to Manly, came alongside. The

Bellubera's passengers were transferred and were taken back to Manly. Some boarded a later ferry to the city, others went by road transport, having had enough of their morning afloat, and most of them arrived at work about two and a half hours late.

The *Bellubera* was to plough on for a few more years before she was pensioned off, departing, like most Manly ferries, to the sorrow of many who had become attached to them. In her last years she seemed to prefer a much quieter life, except for one last fling on the last day of February 1970, when she literally went to war with the Navy, ramming the frigate HMAS *Parramatta* and damaging the warship severely. The collision gouged a hole 6 ft by 8 ft in the side of the *Parramatta*, but the ferry escaped with minor damage to its bows and for'ard rudder.

It happened about 4.35 pm when the *Parramatta*, after refuelling at Chowder Bay, near Clifton Gardens, was being towed out backwards by a tug, right across the path, apparently, of the *Bellubera*, coming up the harbour from Manly. The master of the *Bellubera*, Captain L. Bruce, gave several siren blasts and then put his ferry full astern. But in vain. The two vessels crashed with a loud bang and an accompaniment of screams from female ferry passengers, one of whom fainted. Passengers near the front of the ferry ran back when they saw the collision was imminent and many of them grabbed lifebelts. The hole ripped through the quarter-inch steel plating of the *Parramatta* made an opening into the wardroom store. One passenger said he saw some bags and luggage drop from the hole into the water and a few beer cans landed on the bow of the ferry. An American, Mr Thomas Khan, who was migrating from the United States to Perth, said he saw the Navy ship when it was about 12 metres away and knew it would be impossible to avoid hitting it. Sailors were hurrying to lower fenders to cushion the impact. Mr Khan said: 'I was in the Navy myself and I can imagine how the sailors felt, colliding with a ferry.'

If the sailors didn't feel too happy about what had happened, the Navy top brass were even less overjoyed. Aided by the tug which had been dragging her out of Chowder Bay, HMAS *Parramatta* moved off after the collision to a Navy mooring buoy off Garden Island. As a news photographer aboard a launch tried to take a picture of the damage, sailors threw a big tarpaulin across the hole. A Navy spokesman said officers and crew would not be allowed to comment on the incident. An inquiry would be held 'as soon as possible'.

6. The Little Kangaroo

The *Bellubera* fades out of the story at this stage. Captain Harold Gibson, senior master of the Port Jackson & Manly Steamship Company, took her on her last run on 29 November 1973, and she was put into retirement, to be sold. What happened will be told later. It is linked with the decline in the service and the eventual take-over of the Manly ferries by the New South Wales Government. But we are still dealing with the good years of the Port Jackson & Manly Steamship Company and many things happened in that time. Between launching the *Bellubera* in 1910 and the *Balgowlah* in 1912 and the beginning of World War II, the company built five new ships—*Barrenjoey* (1913), *Baragoola* (1922), *Dee Why* and *Curl Curl* (1928) and *South Steyne* (1938).

Barrenjoey, Aboriginal for little kangaroo, is also the name of the landmark lighthouse at the southern entrance to the Hawkesbury River at Broken Bay. The *Barrenjoey*, built at Mort's Dock and launched on 8 May 1913, was almost an identical sister ship to the *Bellubera* and *Balgowlah*. *Baragoola* was slightly smaller. The *Barrenjoey* was re-engined with diesel-electric power and rebuilt with closed-in upper decks and two funnels between 1948 and 1951. Since then she has been known as the *North*

Two phases of the Barrenjoey. *This picture was taken in 1947 while she was still a steamer. The picture over the page was taken in 1914 — after she had been in service about a year. Note the completely open top deck.* (John Darroch)

Head, but for the purposes of the story she will be known as the *Barrenjoey* from the time of her launching until she was rebuilt. However, either as *Barrenjoey* or *North Head*, she has outlasted her three sister ships, the *Baragoola* and three ferries built overseas.

In the days when the *Barrenjoey* was built, a new Manly ferry was just as much a matter of interest as the three new types built by the State Government in 1983 and 1984. Keen subjects of discussion were her design, seating and passenger accommodation; then, most importantly, her speed and how good a sea boat she was in bad weather. *Barrenjoey* attracted plenty of attention, even though she was a look-alike of *Bellubera* and *Balgowlah*. These were big ships, among the biggest built in Australia in their day, 210 ft long, 32.2 ft beam and displacing just on 500 tons. Like her predecessors, *Barrenjoey* had an open deck and one long white funnel with a black-banded top, She could carry 1520 passengers. Two boilers provided the steam for her triple expansion steam engines to give her a guaranteed speed of 15 knots.

With the *Barrenjoey* in service, the Port Jackson & Manly Steamship Company had eight ferries which could carry 10 500 passengers, whereas 12 years previously the fleet had comprised five ships with accommodation for 4300. Those who attended the launching were told that in the previous year the ferries had operated 32 022 trips covering 209 000 miles, representing an increase of 11 648 miles on the year before. In August 1930, the open promenade deck of *Barrenjoey* was partly enclosed and the interior was fitted with reversible upholstered seating, all designed for more comfort during the winter and at night. The new *Dee Why* and *Curl Curl*, brought out from Scotland in 1928, had enclosed upper saloons and the time had arrived to make the older ships more comfortable. Goodness knows how the people of Manly had put up with those wind and rain swept open decks for so long. *Balgowlah*, *Bellubera* and *Baragoola* were altered similarly in 1931 and 1932.

In an interview with the *Manly Daily* in March 1982, Bill White, then 82, told of the exciting eight months he spent as a chocolate boy in 1915. He was one of eight boys who turned up on a Monday morning in response to an advertisement for a chocolate boy and the manager of Nestlé, a Mr Cook, was scrutinising him from head to toe outside the wharf at Circular Quay. He checked the boys' fingernails and behind their ears for lice. 'You are to sell food,' he said. 'We don't want any dirt.' Bill and six others selected were measured for summer and winter uniforms with shining brass buttons and a numbered badge. They were to be paid a weekly wage of one pound, plus a commission of twopence in the pound. The boys were inspected again next morning before they started work and were given a stern lecture on discipline. 'It was all

discipline,' Bill recalled. 'Many of the passengers were shareholders and we were terrified of being fired for skylarking.'

Naturally, the boys all wanted to work on the Manly ferries rather than the more mundane inner harbour fleet of Sydney Ferries Ltd, but they were told Manly was only for those with six months' experience. So, for six months, Bill White worked on the ferry services to Neutral Bay, Mosman, Cremorne and Lane Cove, selling from his round tray Cadbury red and blue labels, Toblerones, tins of assorted chocolates and sixpenny and threepenny blocks. After six months his big day arrived. He was to get his chance on the exciting Manly run. 'The manager took me through the turnstiles and in came the *Barrenjoey* in all her majesty,' he said. 'The captain came down, I was introduced to him and he welcomed me aboard. Four musicians played Strauss waltzes while children stood around open-mouthed and goggle-eyed.' But for Bill White the sweetest music was the hissing and humming of the steam engines driving the *Barrenjoey* and other Manly ferries on which he worked in some of the happiest days of his life.

Fog is a frequent cause of trouble on Sydney Harbour. At times it can stop nearly all ferry and hydrofoil traffic. Modern vessels with radar can cope, but before the days of radar all ships were in difficulty. The *Barrenjoey* was lost in a fog one night for two and a half hours, not in winter but in the summer month of February.

'Manly Boat. Lost in a fog,' were the headlines in the *Sydney Morning Herald* of 2 February 1914. The *Barrenjoey* left Circular Quay at 11.35 pm. It should have reached Manly around midnight, but did not berth there until after 2 am. The *Herald* told the story in the narrative style of the day, written obviously by a reporter who didn't know that you don't call craft the size of Manly ferries 'boats'. It said:

Residents of Manly were startled on Saturday night, long after the last boat had left for Sydney, to hear the

The Barrenjoey, *in 1914.*

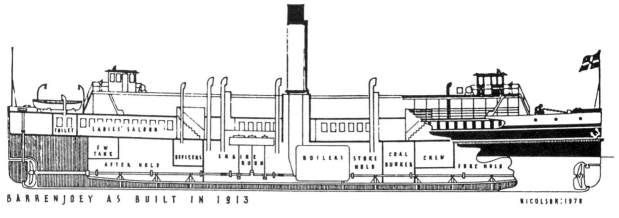

BARRENJOEY AS BUILT IN 1913   NICOLSON:1978

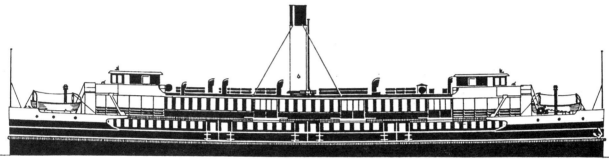

BARRENJOEY IN 1936

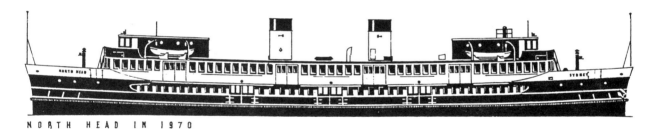

NORTH HEAD IN 1970

Three phases of the Barrenjoey: *the steamer built in 1913 with open top deck; in 1930, still a steamer, but with the top deck closed in and the wheelhouses extended for crew accommodation; as the* North Head *with two funnels, diesel electric and the wheelhouses extended still further.* (The Log)

bell which records the departure of the ferry boats on the wharf tolled loudly and continuously for over an hour. It was sounded as a guide to the last boat from Sydney, which had lost its bearings in a heavy mist and did not succeed in reaching the wharf until after 2 am.

The *Barrenjoey* left Circular Quay at 11.35 pm and soon encountered the heavy mist which had been gradually growing thicker since 6 pm. The steamer proceeded at reduced speed, as it was impossible to see even a few yards ahead and the customary lights on the shore were not visible.

The Heads were passed safely, but the steamer then lost its bearings and instead of passing the point to the left, made for Little Manly. A serious accident was only averted by the engines being rapidly reversed. After a considerable time, the skipper succeeded in backing the boat out of the cove, but it steamed in the direction of North Harbour before the whereabouts of the wharf

were discovered. Fortunately, the mist lifted somewhat about 1.30 am and the boat got alongside the wharf soon after 2 o'clock. A considerable crowd, many of whom were in night attire, had collected on the wharf on hearing the bell and the passengers were greeted with rousing cheers as they disembarked.

The *Barrenjoey* had her share of collisions. Some, only minor, involved the Sydney Ferries Ltd *Kareela* in January 1914, and the *Kiandra* on 30 December 1927. The *Kiandra* and Manly's *Dee Why* collided in more serious circumstances a few years later. The Sydney Ferries' vessels usually came off second best in these encounters. Being built of wood, their hulls were no match for the steel-plated Manly monsters. In January 1940, the *Barrenjoey* and Nielsen Park ferry *Kubu* met head on near Bradleys Head, causing severe damage to the bows of the *Kubu*. *Barrenjoey* was coming up the harbour from Manly and the *Kubu* was going from the Quay to Nielsen Park. Near Bradleys Head, two sailing boats, now more than ever a worry to ferry masters, crossed the bows of both ferries, which manoeuvred to avoid the sailing boats and found themselves heading for each other. Both masters put their ferries hard astern, which lessened the force of the impact, otherwise the *Kubu* might have been holed and sunk. Screams from the *Kubu* rose above the noise of wooden deck and railings splintering, but nobody was injured and the only damage to the *Barrenjoey* was a slight scratch on her bows.

The *Barrenjoey* ran aground on the rocks near Smedleys Point at Manly early one morning in April 1942, but accounts of the incident give no clue to why she grounded. The ferry bumped on the rocks for about an hour before the crew were able to float her off and take the passengers back to Manly, where they boarded another ferry, late for work. Apparently there was not much damage to the *Barrenjoey* and she resumed her other morning peak-hour runs.

Bad weather has to be very bad to stop the Manly ferries. In recent years they continued running during one nasty gale which closed the Port of Sydney to big overseas ships. A cyclonic storm which lashed Sydney in April 1946 damaged the *Barrenjoey* while she was crossing The Heads. In three days, the cyclone poured 25 centimetres of rain on an arc swinging 240 kilometres around Sydney, swirling the seas into fury under a 50-mile-an-hour gale. The Manly ferry service was suspended at 3 pm on Monday, 16 April after four passengers were injured when what were described as 'great waves' pounded two of the ferries. Three passengers were hurt in the *Barrenjoey* travelling to Sydney. The other was in the *Baragoola*, going to Manly. A wall of water rolling in through The Heads hit the *Barrenjoey* side on, smashing windows as it crashed over the lower deck. The blow of the wave hitting the vessel knocked dozens of passengers from their seats. Then the surge of water as it came aboard carried them along the deck to crunch into stanchions and fittings. Passengers were slithering all over the deck, their belongings swirling around in the water.

An ambulance met the *Barrenjoey* at Circular Quay and took three people to Sydney Hospital for treatment. They were: Doreen Reilly, 17, of Dee Why, strained back and shock; Muriel Edwards, of Manly, injury to ribs, and her sister, Dorothy Love, of Manly, cut over right eye and shock. Ruth Willcock, 19, of Maroubra, was cut on the face and legs by broken glass when another big wave battered the *Baragoola*. She was taken to Manly Hospital.

With heavy rain pelting down on Sydney, stopping the Manly ferry service added greatly to the many problems the weather was causing. All those ferry travellers had to be transported by road over the Spit, where they alighted from trams to get into buses for Manly and beyond. Although the buses were taking about 100 people every five minutes, there was still a queue more than 100 metres long and three deep at 7.30 pm. It was estimated that nearly 30 000 more people than usual crossed the Spit Bridge with the ferries out of action.

Many parts of Sydney were flooded and residents had to leave their homes. Huge seas burst in white foam along the coast. Spray was showered over the cliffs near the Macquarie Lighthouse, south of The Heads, which was 73 metres above the water. In Newcastle, the famous sixty-milers fleet of colliers, all loaded, remained tied up, not daring to risk the trip to Sydney. The American tanker, *Whitier Hills*, bound for Sydney, had broken down and was wallowing in heavy seas 300 miles east of Brisbane, having drifted 270 miles in the strong south-easterly wind, being blown north at four knots, although both sea anchors were out. The only available ocean-going tug on the Australian coast equipped to cope with heavy seas, the LT *454*, left Sydney to assist the tanker, but was forced back when only halfway to Newcastle. Describing the voyage as far as *Barrenjoey*, the tug's master said the seas were so rough that he was thrown from his bunk four times and the electrician injured his head against a bulkhead.

A 60-mile-an-hour gale hit Sydney again only a couple of months later, on 20 June, and in this the *Barrenjoey* was the centre of another drama inside the harbour when she broke from her moorings at the Kurraba Point depot and drifted across to Neutral Bay, blocking the Neutral Bay ferry wharf for more than three hours. Passengers for Neutral Bay had to leave their ferries at Hayes Street or Kurraba Point and walk in heavy rain to reach the Neutral Bay tram terminus. Four deckhands were on board when the *Barrenjoey* broke loose at 7 pm. They tried to get out a new rope, but could not do so before the ferry was well clear of the wharf. As the wind blew the ferry north-west across the harbour, the crew feared she would smash into several other ships, including HMAS *Adelaide*, but she missed them all and slid sideways towards Neutral Bay wharf, where, fortunately, no Neutral Bay ferry was unloading. *Barrenjoey* struck the west side of the wharf at an angle, wedging itself diagonally across the entrance. Quickly, the crew threw ashore mooring ropes, which were picked up and looped over bollards by several people who were waiting for the Neutral Bay ferry, due in a few minutes later had the wharf been clear. A tug came and dragged the *Barrenjoey* clear at 10.20 pm.

The next couple of years were uneventful for the *Barrenjoey*, which was nearing the end of her life as a one-funnel steamer. She was withdrawn from service in April 1948, and during the following three years was rebuilt mechanically and structurally to reappear as the two-funnel diesel-electric *North Head*.

7. Flood Tide

Shipbuilding was becoming expensive by the time the *Barragoola* floated off from Mort's Dock at Balmain on 14 February 1922, but the harbour traffic was growing and more ferries were needed. These were the days before the Harbour Bridge and even the Spit Bridge. Everyone and everything that crossed the harbour or its estuaries had to go by water. Between Fort Macquarie—the site now of the Sydney Opera House—and Milsons Point, the closest point of the north shore, vehicular ferries transported cars and trucks. The large Sydney Ferries' fleet carried people between Circular Quay and everywhere except beyond The Heads, which was the preserve of the Port Jackson & Manly Steamship Company.

In a letter dated 7 October 1920, the manager of the Port Jackson company, Mr F. J. Doran, wrote to the manager of Mort's Dock & Engineering Company, Balmain:

> Dear Sir, I am instructed by my Board to acknowledge your letter of the 30th ultimo offering to construct a double-ended screw steamer of the *Barrenjoey* type, length 199 ft, breadth 34 ft and depth 14 ft 4 inches, and all other particulars as per your letter. My Board will accept your offer to build the vessel for the sum of £72 000 (Seventy-two thousand pounds) under the conditions mentioned in your letter, the time to finalise the work to be 18 months from the landing of the material.

The contract drawn up subsequently stipulated that passenger accommodation on the main and upper deck should be arranged on similar lines to that of the *Barrenjoey*, modified to suit the reduced length and increased width of the new vessel, for the *Barragoola* was slightly shorter and wider than her predecessor. This was to affect her speed later as part of the fleet. She was just a bit slower than the others, even with the 15 knots she registered on her trials as against the builders' guarantee of 14 knots. They called her *Barragoola*, which is an Aborginal word meaning 'flood tide'.

On 31 August 1922, the managing director of Mort's Dock, Mr I. P. Franki, wrote a memo to directors, which said:

> Under separate cover I have pleasure in sending you photos of the new steamer *Barragoola* built by this company for the Port Jackson & Manly Steamship Company, of this port. The *Barragoola* is the 41st vessel built at the company's works and the eighth in a period of about 35 years for the Port Jackson & Manly Steamship Company. The hulls, boilers and engines of all the

Great celebrations as the Baragoola *was launched from Mort's Dock at Balmain on 14 February 1922. (John Darroch)*

vessels of the Manly service have been built at Mort's Dock and it is most gratifying to know that under applied tests of efficiency and of time, the work as turned out merits a continuance of a custom so highly valued. The *Baragoola* is a handsome addition to the Manly company's fleet, being complete with every modern shipbuilding development for that class of vessel and having increased accommodation as compared with others. At the official trials the vessel exceeded the guaranteed speed and all who were present were delighted with her performance. Business generally at the company's establishments is showing a slight revival and improvement and if we can only get a cessation of the government competition we hope to return to the position we were in before this depression.

Mr Franki's hopes were not to be realised. The cost of building ferries locally had risen too steeply and the Port Jackson company was to go overseas for its next three ships. Meanwhile, as chairman of directors, Mr H. McPherson, told official luncheon guests on board the *Baragoola* after the trials, the company had seven steamers capable of carrying to Manly on one trip a total of 10 250 passengers. Manly was benefiting considerably from the tourists the ferries were bringing across the harbour, many of whom soon became local residents. In 1926, Manly Council decided to make a take-over bid for the ferries and began negotiations with the Port Jackson's directors, but the company was not interested and declined the council's offer.

Baragoola's first taste of trouble on the harbour was a collision off Kirribilli Point with the Sydney Ferry *Kosciusko*, on Christmas Eve 1926, in which the main damage was to the *Kosciusko*, whose master was reprimanded subsequently by the Marine Court and had his certificate suspended for three months. There was far greater excitement in September the following year when the *Baragoola* ran down a lifeboat from the French steamer *Ville D'Amiens*, anchored in Athol Bight. Five people were thrown from the boat into the water and one was admitted later to Sydney Hospital suffering from shock. The ferry had left town at 4 pm on 12 September in charge of Captain J. Clarke. Just before reaching Fort Denison, passengers noticed a small boat under sail coming out of Woolloomooloo Bay. Then they heard what they described as a rending crash, accompanied by frenzied cries in a foreign tongue. The *Baragoola* had struck the small boat amidships, damaging it seriously and tossing out the occupants, Capone Antioni, Bitterlugga Antioni, Albertini Jean and two women. Two trawlers which were nearby when the accident happened picked up the French sailors and the women. Albertini Jean was nearly exhausted when pulled aboard a trawler. He was taken to Sydney Hospital suffering from severe shock. The lifeboat, one side crushed in, was towed back into Woolloomooloo Bay by one of the trawlers.

Ferries hit many things at various times in the harbour, but probably the most unusual collision was that between the *Baragoola* and a whale, an incident which was to have repercussions for several days. The whale, said to have been about 60 ft, caused great excitement when it appeared in the harbour about 3 pm on 28 August 1934, and was seen leaping and spouting near The Heads for more than an hour, followed around by several launches as it made for the open sea. But fate intervened in the shape of the 4.15 pm ferry from Manly to Sydney, the *Baragoola*, which sliced into the whale like a destroyer ramming a submarine surfacing in front of its bows. The shuddering shock of the impact stopped the ferry almost dead, and as she backed away passengers could see the whale thrashing about in water turned vivid red by its blood. The poor whale was obviously badly injured.

Mr G. H. Finnis, of Crown Road, Harbord, a passenger on the ferry, was in the smoke room when the crash came and ran out to the side of the vessel to see what had happened. Telling of the event afterwards, he said:

> The whale was submerged, with the exception of the fin, which appeared to be about six or eight feet long. After churning the water into foam for a minute or two, the whale swam away in the direction of the Quarantine Reserve and we lost sight of it.

The officer-in-charge of the quarantine station, Mr G. Ashton, saw the whale near Flagstaff Point about 3.15 pm. He and his wife watched it through field glasses, diving, then reappearing a few moments later and leaping out of the water as it headed towards Manly, spouting and pursuing an erratic course. The whale went so close to the shore at Smedleys Point that Mr Ashton thought it would

be stranded, but it swam away again after lashing the water with its huge tail. Some fishermen in a launch circled around the whale each time it surfaced, but most other small craft kept their distance. The occupants obviously did not want to be too close to that thrashing tail. Another passenger on the *Baragoola*, Mr R. S. Cristopher, of Longueville, said even a large launch could have been sunk easily if it had been too close to the wash caused by the movements of the whale.

As darkness crept in there was no sign of the wounded whale and nobody knew whether it was still in the harbour or had managed to get out to sea. South Head signal station staff had not seen it. Three days later, however, the carcass surfaced near Old Mans Hat. It was towed out to sea, but just on dusk it had drifted in again and was about a mile off the coast near Bondi. A signalman at South Head station identified the whale as the one hit by the *Baragoola*. It had a deep gash in its left side. The impact had killed the whale and it must have gone down to the bottom of the harbour near The Heads. Whales killed at Twofold Bay during the whaling days used to sink to the bottom and float up again three days later, inflated by stomach gases. This would have accounted for the reappearance of the *Baragoola* whale at Old Mans Hat three days after the collision.

The Baragoola *near Bradleys Head in 1956. She is still sporting her long white funnel. (John Darroch)*

Sydney harbour master, Captain Stringer, sent out the fire float *Pluvius* when the situation was reported to him, and the dead whale was towed about four miles clear of the coast, followed by clouds of wheeling, screaming gulls and other sea birds. When the crew of *Pluvius* cast off the tow lines they thought the carcass would drift away from the coast and they came back to port. But that whale was determined to return. Next morning, the duty officer at South Head signal station saw the unwanted guest again, floating back towards The Heads, swarms of sharks feeding on the blubber, the air above thick with gulls. At 5.30 pm the floating mass was almost two miles south-east of The Heads. At daylight the *Pluvius* was sent out to tow the rotting mess well out to sea.

It was no use. Two days later the whale was back inside the harbour, this time on the rocks near the Hornby Lighthouse at Inner South Head and there it stayed until the *Pluvius* could tow it off on the high tide. They dragged it 14 miles out, thinking that would end the problem. 'We'll get rid of it this time if we have to take it to New Zealand,' a Harbour Trust official told reporters. But that whale had no intention of going to New Zealand. The following day, 4 September, it floated ashore and stranded on Bombora Point near the entrance to Botany Bay. The commissioners of the Harbour Trust went out to consider the problem and made an on-the-spot decision that another attempt would be made next morning to tow the whale out again. The Harbour Trust tug *Hydra* hitched on to the carcass and left Botany Bay at 9 am with orders to go 20 miles out. They must have gone at least that far. It was late evening before the *Hydra* returned. But whatever happened to the whale after that nobody knows. It was never seen again, much to the relief of the crew of the *Pluvius*. From the time it was hit by the *Baragoola* it had floated around near Sydney for nine days before the Harbour Trust finally got rid of it.

In comparison with some of the other ferries, the *Baragoola* had little serious trouble. She ran through the wharf at the Quay twice and sliced into the footpath. Eric Gale recalls the first incident because it gave him his first permanent berth as engineer afloat. That was in her steamship days when Eric was working in the Kurraba Point workshops. Apparently some of these incidents when ferries overshot wharves were not altogether accidents. There were cases of friction between captains and engineers where incidents developed. Sometimes a skipper could give a wrong signal on the engine room telegraph, calling for ahead instead of astern, and if the engineer didn't know it was wrong they could be in trouble. Later, when steam went out and the engine room was controlled direct from the bridge, it was just too bad if the captain pushed the handle the wrong way.

Whatever happened in the incident Eric Gale mentions, the engineer was blamed. Said Eric:

Bob complained about the skipper quite a lot. He even went to head office and complained about him. On this occasion he said the skipper came into the wharf too fast and the triple expansion steam engines didn't respond quickly enough. They would do that—stick on the bottom and top centre if you weren't very careful. They brought Bob back into the workshop and gave me the job. I was lucky. The engines never stuck with me.

For some unknown reason, the *Baragoola* was always a popular ship with travellers, as evidenced by the emotional farewell on her retirement. Asked which ferry he thought was the best ever, Eric Gale did not nominate, as might have been expected, the *South Steyne*. He chose the *Baragoola* saying:

She was the slowest of the fleet, but she was the best sea boat. She did a good job, she had good accommodation and she never had much trouble, although her engines were tricky.

Captain Ron Hart, master of the *Baragoola* over many years, said:

The *Baragoola* became one of the most popular ferries. I don't know why, but I became quite attached to her, too. I was in a few tight squeezes with her and got out of them quickly and without any trouble. I was taking her into the Quay one day when a ship was berthing at the Overseas Terminal and, with the wash from propellers, ended up on the east side of No. 3 (Manly) wharf at an angle of 45 degrees. It was a situation where you either have to abandon the operation or try to get out stern first, which could lead to turning around off the end of the wharf with the danger of hitting it. I belted her ahead and astern a couple of times and she came in like a charm. I never had any trouble with her from that day on. Down in Manly one night in 1974 the wind pushed her around the end of the wharf, but I pulled her out, changed ends and she went in beautifully. It was often difficult berthing at Manly with strong winds. If it is coming from one side or the other you know what to do, but when it is straight behind you anything can go wrong at the last minute, as it did that night. Coming in with a straight southerly behind you, if your engines don't go astern you are in big trouble. You just keep going into the buffers. Also, with the wind straight behind, it can turn you into or out from the wharf. If it is south-west or westerly you can counteract it, but that southerly is a friend to nobody.

The *Baragoola* was so reliable. She never let me down any time in any conditions—either stopping in a hurry, avoiding a sailing boat or getting in or out of wharves. You could always rely on her. In all the years I was with her she had very few untoward incidents, none of which ever made the headlines. She went through the wharf at the Quay twice because the skipper put the handle for the engines the wrong way. That is unforgivable, I think. A skipper could forget whether he is at the bow or stern and, thinking he is putting the ship astern to stop her at the wharf, he is actually putting her ahead. Old Harold Gibson, the company's senior master, had the secret of that. He would usually walk out the wheelhouse door of the *South Steyne*, across the top of the ladder and squeeze between the handrail and telegraph. He could have walked around it, but he would say 'That's no good. That will put me on the wrong angle.' He would always walk out and squeeze between the two and grab the telegraph with his left hand. He contended that if he did this all the time he would never make a mistake. So I always walked out to the *Goola*'s telegraph and pulled it down in front of me like that. I never went around it because if you do that you can turn around and forget which way you are going.

Ron Hart was right about some of the things that happened to *Baragoola* never making the headlines. In January 1984, big headlines and lots of pictures told of near tragedy with the old Sydney Ferry *Karrabee*, which competed in the annual ferryboat race in the Festival of Sydney and was rushed to Circular Quay in a sinking condition. She was sinking fast as hundreds of passengers were unloaded on to the wharf and the last one had just landed before the old wooden tub gave up the ghost and settled on the muddy bottom, only the top of her funnel showing above the water. The incident caused a great scandal and a Court of Marine Inquiry went on for months, during which a Maritime Services Board employee agreed there could have been areas of dry rot in the vessel.

A similar thing might have happened to the *Baragoola*, probably with even worse results. Ron Hart tells the story:

Back in 1973 she came out of an overhaul and developed a leak. It was the Sunday afternoon that the Queen opened the Opera House. The *Baragoola* looked absolutely sparkling after her overhaul and we were maintaining the service because every other ferry was out on the harbour with spectators. We left Manly about 1.30 on a trip which was to take nearly two hours because the area around the Opera House was closed off. We were told to wait at Pinchgut [the common name for Fort Denison from the convict days] until we saw the release of the balloons at the Opera House to signal the end of the opening ceremony. A westerly was blowing about 30 knots and we had to drift around in it for a long time. Eventually we saw the signal and tried to go into the Quay, but there was chaos everywhere and we ended up in Woolloomooloo Bay. At one stage I had the HMAS *Lithgow* across my bow and the *Karrabee* across my stern and we were being blown sideways.

A week later, I had just signed off at Manly and told the skipper coming on, Tony Slattery, that everything was in order. There was nothing out of the ordinary to report. On the way up to town the engineer went to the

bridge and said 'We've got a serious problem. She's making water faster than we can get rid of it'. What made it even worse was that on the Friday before, I took the *Baragoola* up to Balmain yards to refuel and we did fireboat and anchor drill, in the course of which I found that the fire pump was not working, so we put the fire hose water through the bilge pump. The fire pump was an extra one which you could put on to the deck hydrants or you could pump it over the side. By running the bilge pump we got the water on to the deck, but both pumps should have been working. I told them about this in the works office and they said 'She'll be all right. We'll get it fixed'. But it was not fixed and when it was wanted on that Sunday it was not there. If both pumps had been working they could have handled the leak. They staggered into the Quay, got everybody off and rushed the *Baragoola* up to Balmain yards, where the fire brigade was waiting. With the aid of the firemen's pumps they just kept her afloat. She had sprung this leak and would have to be put into dock to weld a patch over it. That was 10 years ago and the patch is probably still there. By the time she went out of service the *Baragoola* must have had about a dozen doubling plates over other plates that were suspect. The *North Head* didn't have one.

The *Baragoola* was one of several ferries damaged when violent weather hit Sydney towards the end of June 1972. Winds gusting up to 60 miles an hour and what the newspapers always tend to describe as 'mountainous' waves wreaked havoc with ferry services on Friday, 23 June. The *Daily Telegraph* next day, under the heading 'Giant waves batter ferries', reported:

Manly ferry services, battered by 40-ft waves, were suspended last night for the first time in five years because of the treacherous conditions. Services were suspended after two ferries and a hydrofoil were damaged. Thirty feet of the *South Steyne*'s bulwark was ripped, several windows and a door on the *Bellubera* were stove in and a mooring bollard on the hydrofoil *Fairlight* was snapped. A middle-aged man on the *Baragoola* suffered head injuries when two seats were torn loose. Traffic manager of the Port Jackson & Manly Steamship Company, Mr George Marshall, crossed to Manly late in the afternoon and decided to suspend all services. Waves up to 40 ft between The Heads were playing havoc with ferries, Mr Marshall said. The *South Steyne* will be out of service until the middle of next week.

No wonder. The *Telegraph* had a picture of workmen repairing 34 ft of the *Steyne*'s bulwark, smashed when she

Riding the roll. The Baragoola *down in a trough, passing Middle Head in big seas.*

crunched into the wharf on the surge while trying to berth at Manly in the high winds and swell.

In 1946 the Port Jackson company decided to convert the *Barrenjoey* and *Balgowlah* from steam to diesel-electric propulsion rather than replace them with new ships, the cost of which would have been prohibitive in those post-war years. This was done to the *Barrenjoey* between 1948 and 1951, and when the *Balgowlah* was withdrawn from service on 27 February 1951, everyone thought she would be converted like the *Barrenjoey*, now renamed *North Head*, especially as she was the last coal-burning vessel in the fleet. But passenger traffic was declining because of bus competition and the company, in financial difficulties, having spent £261 772 on conversion of the *Barrenjoey* to *North Head*, decided that it could not afford the cost of reconditioning the *Balgowlah*'s hull and fitting the new engines, and she went to the shipbreakers. The engines were put aside for installation in the *Baragoola*, but the same financial considerations delayed the work for another five years until the end of 1958, when it was done at a cost of £65 000. When she returned to regular service at the beginning of January 1961, the *Baragoola* had a short, fat funnel instead of the traditional long, tall stack, but otherwise she looked much the same and was the only one left with the open upper decks at each end.

Her next big change came after the State Government took over the Manly ferries in December 1974, and the then Public Transport Commissioner, Mr Philip Shirley,

decided to change the colour scheme of all public transport in New South Wales to blue and cream. *Baragoola*, at Balmain for a refit, was the first to lose the bottle green and white colours which had been the Manly trademark for more than a century. The ferries have retained the blue and cream ever since.

There were many pleas to save the *Baragoola* and preserve her in some form after she was finally removed from service in January 1983. Even before that a group of Manly businessmen had applied to the Urban Transit Authority to buy the *Baragoola* and use it as a floating museum, moored at Manly. Mr John Callaghan, speaking for the group, told the *Manly Daily* in July 1980:

> We want to secure a relic of Manly's past and preserve it in working order as a floating museum, which will trace Manly's history back to when the first spear was thrown and we also plan to ask local residents to donate pictures and other historic relics. With a new hotel being built in Manly, a floating museum would be a major tourist attraction of benefit to all who live in the area.

But not everyone was enthusiastic. Even the principal of the new hotel under construction, the Manly Pacific International, Andrew Kalajzich, who was also chairman of the Manly Chamber of Commerce. 'Where are they going to moor it?' he asked. 'We don't want it becoming an eyesore.' Mr Kalajzich predicted correctly that the project would not even get off the ground.

Tall buildings of the city in the background, Baragoola *crosses Farm Cove on her way to Manly.*

Urban Transit officials must have rubbed their eyes twice in March 1983, when an offer to buy the old ferry for $100 000 was received from Fairlight businessman John Russell, who wanted to transform the *Baragoola* into a plush floating restaurant. He obviously didn't know the poor condition of the hull, but he was not concerned that his tender might have been too high. It was a matter of beating other parties who had similar plans. Mr Russell said he would have gone ahead with his idea for a floating restaurant even without the *Baragoola*, putting the restaurant on a pontoon similar to that used by Flanagans Afloat at Rose Bay. Engineers had priced a comparable pontoon at $400 000 new, or $200 000 if made from two second-hand pontoons joined together. 'A lot of people around this town thought they had it over me,' he said. 'Now they have had mud thrown in their faces.' At that stage Mr Russell was planning to spend another $650 000 to renovate the ferry, including $250 000 for a wharf to moor it at Manly.

But this was another project not destined to get off the ground. Manly Council saw no merit in having a floating restaurant that big anywhere in Manly Cove, where it could obstruct the possible rebuilding of the harbour swimming pool and be in the way of ferries and water taxi operations. By early May, however, the deal was off. The State Government ended contract arrangements because the tenderer had allegedly not paid money due on time.

Four other firms which had tendered unsuccessfully were to be offered a second chance to buy the ferry, but apparently they had lost interest and there were no takers.

At the end of 1983 the *Baragoola* was lying lonely and neglected at Cockatoo Island, her only hope of adoption being from a Melbourne group who were talking of buying her to moor in Port Phillip Bay as a tourist attraction, but that did not eventuate either. About that time a group of Sydney academics calling itself the Eureka Education Foundation bought the *Baragoola* for $12 000 and planned to turn it into Australia's first floating university. The idea was that of Mr Robert Hyde, who had lectured in education for 14 years at the Sydney College of Advanced Education. He said the university would tutor 6000 part-time students and would cater for retired and handicapped people. Lecturers had been recruited and the university would be opened for the beginning of the academic year in March 1984.

March 1984 came and went with no floating university and grave doubts by the Maritime Services Board about the proposal, which it considered 'not financially viable'. A Board official said there was a lack of comprehension by the academics in their estimates of costs for labour and maintenance. The Eureka Foundation had been paying $500 a week just to moor the ferry at Cockatoo Island after buying it. They moved later to a private wharf at Balmain, where they were paying $345 a week while volunteers tried to restore the vessel—a very costly operation requiring massive amounts of money, as voluntary groups had found out when trying to restore the fire-damaged *South Steyne* a few years earlier.

Boys watch in delight as the bow of the Baragoola *parts a roller and hurls aside green water and white spray.* (Manly Daily)

PART III
THE BIG SISTERS

1. New Twins

In the 10 years between 1928 and 1938 the Port Jackson & Manly Steamship Company had three new ships built overseas, all of which steamed out to Australia under their own power—the twin ships *Dee Why* and *Curl Curl* and, the greatest of them all, the *South Steyne*. These, being familiar to most people, were responsible for the common belief that 'all the Manly ferries sailed out from England'. They were the first to make the long ocean voyage since the paddlewheel steamers *Fairlight* in 1878 and the *Brighton* in 1883. Since then, as told already, seven vessels had been built for the company at Mort's Dock in Sydney. There was also a small wooden vessel called the *Narrabeen*, which carried cargo between Manly and Woolloomooloo until the Spit Bridge opened in December 1924. Ferry traffic was growing in those years to the extent that the Manly company had to consider acquiring bigger and faster ferries to replace some of the older and ageing smaller ones. So the general manager, Mr W. L. Dendy, went to Britain and Scotland in 1927 and on his return to Sydney by the P & O liner *Cathay*, announced that he had completed arrangements in Scotland for the building of two new steamers for the Manly service, to be named *Manly* and *Brookvale*. Mr Dendy said the new ferries, expected to be in commission by the end of the year, would replace the *Kuring-gai* and *Binngarra*. Both would be fitted for burning either oil or coal, they would be 220 ft in length, making them 20 ft longer than others in the fleet, they would be able to carry 2000 passengers and had been designed for a speed of 16.5 knots, cutting travel time to Manly from 30 to 25 minutes.

Another more detailed story appeared in the *Sydney Morning Herald* of 25 August 1927, which disclosed first of all that the new ferries would be named *Curl Curl* and *Dee Why* after two suburbs adjoining ocean beaches north of Manly. The *Herald* story continued:

Many important improvements regarding accommodation will be found in the new steamers, which are to be delivered early next year. The seating accommodation will be on altogether new lines. The three lifeboats will be placed on the bridge deck and passengers will thus be allowed to sit right out at each end of the promenade deck and have an uninterrupted view when looking for'ard. The steamers will be glassed-in on the top deck in order to give travellers protection from boisterous wind and rain. The *Curl Curl* and *Dee Why* are being constructed by Napier & Miller Ltd, whose yards are on the Clyde at Old Kilpatrick, near Glasgow. They will be 220 ft in length with a beam of 36 ft and will draw 12 ft of water when loaded. The vessels will be 20 ft longer and 2 ft wider than the *Baragoola*, which was built in 1922. Steamers now in the service have one funnel, but these new vessels will have two, oval-shaped, which should give them the appearance of ocean-going steamers. The *Curl Curl* and *Dee Why* will be engined by D. & W. Henderson Ltd, a renowned firm of Scotch engineers. The engines will be inverted direct-acting four crank triple expansion Yarrow, Schlich and Tweedy balanced type.

First to arrive in Sydney was the *Curl Curl*, on 25 October 1928, after a voyage of more than 20 weeks from Glasgow. The *Dee Why* followed on 1 November. Captain J. Abram, who had with him in *Curl Curl* a crew of 18, was enthusiastic in praising the sea-going qualities of the vessel. Several heavy spells of bad weather were encountered, but the *Curl Curl* behaved well, despite taking a battering in the Bay of Biscay where she lost part of the sponson. One broken window was the only damage to the superstructure. They called in at Algiers, Port Said, Perim, Aden, Colombo and Sourabaya. Five days were spent at Port Said and 10 days in Aden because of a broken main steam pipe. Then they had to spend two months at Aden awaiting the passing of the south-west monsoons in the Indian Ocean. Only one of the four boilers was used on the trip out, yet the *Curl Curl* averaged 10 knots. On the last stage of her run down the east coast of Australia the *Curl Curl* cut several days off her schedule and her arrival in Sydney was a surprise. For the voyage out, the *Curl Curl* had only one propeller and one rudder. Before she could go into service at Sydney another rudder and propeller had to be fitted. These were left off while travelling to Australia because, contrary to what might be thought generally, propellers at each end of a vessel, one pushing and the

The Curl Curl *decked out with bunting on her first trip to Manly in 1928.* (John Darroch)

other pulling, are not the most efficient means of propulsion. The pusher gives maximum thrust with the bow propeller turning just slowly. There had also been the risk of damage had the bow propeller hit something at sea. These four-blade propellers had a diameter of 9 ft 3 in.

Mr E. H. Mitchell, the naval architect who designed the *Dee Why* and *Curl Curl*, read a paper on the subject at a meeting of the Institution of Naval Architects, chaired by Admiral of the Fleet, Lord Wester Wemyss, in March 1928. He told of an incident in which one of the Manly ferries, not named, had the blades of one propeller stripped off entirely. But because of the heavy traffic demands at the time the company had to keep the ferry running for some days and she went one way with a bow screw pulling and the other way with the same screw pushing. It was found that she got consistently better results with the screw pulling than she did with the screw at the after end pushing.

On her service trials in Sydney on 29 November *Curl Curl* did even better than expected, covering the trip from Manly to Circular Quay in 25 minutes and, according to company officials, still had three knots in reserve. Then she gave the *Bellubera* 12 minutes start from the Quay and passed her at Middle Head. Returning to town, *Curl Curl* was speeded up to 17.5 knots, indicating that when her engines were fully run in she could reach 18 knots. This must have impressed the official party of shipping interests and other VIPs aboard. Speaking at a luncheon on board the *Curl Curl* afterwards, the Mayor of Manly, Ald. A. T. Keirle, said the building of such a steamer as the *Curl Curl* was the best answer to those pessimists who said Manly was slipping. Notwithstanding the building of Sydney Harbour Bridge, he would not be surprised if the company found it necesssary before very long to build another three steamers. Mr J. Chapman, a Port Jackson director, who presided at the luncheon, said whether the new vessels would be the nucleus of a new fleet was one of the problems the directors would have to consider. If the bridge crippled the ferry business, it would be a great pity. Mr Chapman told the gathering that excluding season ticket holders, more than 50 million people had been carried to or from Manly in the ferries in the last 10 years without loss of life. 'That is the record of the Port Jackson & Manly Steamship Company and we are proud of it,' he said.

At that time, the ferry fare to Manly was only sixpence for adults and twopence for children. In my young days it was still only sixpence—the best sixpence worth in Sydney when a big sea called for a ride across The Heads.

But the storm clouds were gathering on the economic front as Mr Chapman spoke to the guests at the *Curl Curl* luncheon. In 1914 Sydney Ferries Ltd had 42 ferries carrying about 25 million passengers a year. By 1928 their fleet had grown to 52 ferries and the gross passenger traffic to an estimated 50 million. But the arches of the great bridge were stretching over the water between Dawes Point and Milsons Point, and in December of that

The Curl Curl *lost her bearing in dense fog on 31 March 1936 and ran aground on a reef near Bradleys Head.* (John Darroch)

year estimates prepared by the ferry companies warned them that 25 million fewer passengers would cross the harbour by ferry annually when the bridge was opened for traffic in 1932. Sydney Ferries Ltd made available to the Press a survey showing the number of ferry passengers at that time compared with the probable traffic when the bridge opened. The return showed:

SYDNEY FERRIES LIMITED

Service	Passengers now carried	Estimate when bridge is completed
Milsons Point	18 291 000	Nil
Lavender Bay	4 513 000	Nil
Neutral Bay	1 254 000	834 000
Cremorne & Mosman	1 264 000	2 115 000

THE MANLY SERVICE

Manly	5 000 000	4 000 000

These figures must have caused quite a shock. Here was Sydney Ferries, a buoyant business carrying 25 322 000 passengers a year in 42 passenger-ferries and thousands of vehicles in nine vehicular punts, threatened with a complete cessation of its vehicular traffic—nobody would want to take cars over the harbour on a punt after the bridge opened—and a massive reduction from 25 322 000 passengers to only 2 949 000. Most of the passenger trade came from the North Shore railway, which transported 22 804 000 people a year into the city each day from Willoughby, Chatswood and as far north as Hornsby, dropping them on the Milsons Point side of the harbour to cross to the city by ferry. An official of Sydney Ferries commented:

> It must be realised that when the bridge is opened in three years time the ferry company will lose all this traffic. There is not the slightest doubt in the minds of those who have studied the problem that the Milsons Point and McMahons Point services cannot be continued. The comparatively small falling off in the Mosman, Cremorne and Neutral Bay services would make them unprofitable. The position is entirely new and without precedent and one cannot suggest many avenues for the employment of the company's fleet when the bridge is opened.

The end of the voyage. The Curl Curl, *her lower deck still boarded up, at Kurraba Point wharves in October 1928.* (Manly Daily)

The Port Jackson & Manly Steamship Company, however, was not nearly in such a desperate position. It could lose a million passengers who might drive over the bridge instead of going from Manly by ferry, but Mr Dendy was confident this loss of about 20 per cent of revenue would be counterbalanced by the growth in the population of Manly and district and an increase in the number of day trippers. He believed the falling off would be only temporary. Dendy was right. The Manly-Warringah area became one of the most attractive places in Sydney for living and the things that brought most people there included, in addition to the lovely northern beaches stretching from Manly to Palm Beach, the Manly ferries as a form of public transport far preferable to noisy suburban trains or uncomfortable buses. But at the time these figures of ferry doom appeared, Mr Dendy and those associated with the Manly company were comforted by the boost their tourist traffic had received from the two new sister ships. Manly traffic was increasing rather than declining and there was no immediate danger to the company's position.

The *Dee Why*'s arrival in Sydney was not nearly as auspicious as that of her sister vessel, *Curl Curl*. It was 2 am on 1 November when she arrived outside The Heads in darkness with nobody to greet her and welcome the crew except a somewhat unenthusiastic pilot, who declined to come aboard after he had been rowed across from the pilot steamer *Captain Cook*, as was the custom when that famous clipper-bowed vessel ruled the waves around everything entering or leaving the harbour. The pilot objected to going aboard over the *Dee Why*'s very wide sponson, which both *Dee Why* and *Curl Curl* had built around them as a buffer for protection against damage from wharf piles and, no doubt, collisions with other vessels. So, as happens when pilots cannot board incoming ships because of rough weather or reasons such as this, the *Dee Why* followed the *Captain Cook* through The Heads into Watsons Bay, where the ferry anchored until daylight, to the surprise of Watsons Bay and Vaucluse folk who woke to see her there. Then, as soon as medical and other formalities were completed, *Dee Why* steamed off up the harbour to the Kurraba Point depot, receiving a warm and noisy welcome from the morning traffic.

Actually, the *Dee Why* should have arrived in Sydney before the *Curl Curl*. She was the first of the two ships launched—on 23 December 1927. *Curl Curl* did not come off the slipway until 27 February 1928. It was intended originally that *Dee Why* should leave Glasgow on 16 May, but her departure was delayed until 26 May, seven days before *Curl Curl* steamed out on 2 June.

It was a most unhappy voyage, during which many things went wrong. Telling of the troubled trip when interviewed in Sydney, the master for the voyage out, Captain A.W. Brown, confessed that there had been friction between him and the officers and crew. He said one of the officers would not support him and had questioned his authority several times. But Captain Brown paid tribute to the deck crew, who had remained loyal the whole time. He said they were a fine body of men and were able, willing and experienced sailors. Nearly all the trouble had been caused by several firemen, who were always full of grievances. Captain Brown said they came to him at different times with the declaration that they were 'finished' and often they had used abusive language.

At Aden, Captain Brown said, he refused to give the men any money because they were overdrawn already. That was when the galley utensils disappeared overboard. He was unable to deal with the troublemakers and consuls in several ports would not allow him to get rid of them. Some of the firemen, on the other hand, complained that food provided for them had been bad. They said there was no bread between Port Said and Aden, where the galley utensils disappeared, and no baking could be done until they reached Sourabaya. Another complaint was that the bully beef was unwholesome and the butter was rancid.

No doubt living conditions on a voyage like this would not have been up to the standard expected of a first-class ocean liner. These vessels were designed for short-distance harbour commuter and tourist travel instead of long ocean voyages. Makeshift arrangements had been made to provide bunks, bathing and feeding facilities and the accommodation inside was dark 24 hours a day because the sides of the ship were boarded up against the possible invasion of heavy weather at sea. Nevertheless, somebody found it attractive, or was desperate enough to stow away. They found him two days out from Glasgow and at Aden he was signed on as a fireman in place of another who, it was said, could not discharge his duties.

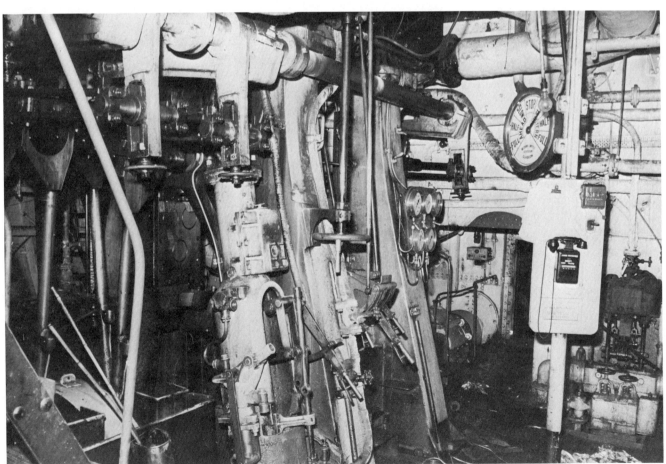

The engine room of the Dee Why.

After clearing the English coast, *Dee Why* pounded into heavy seas across the Bay of Biscay before she rounded Gibraltar into the more sheltered Mediterranean. Then, half-way to Algiers, a joint of the main steam pipe blew out and *Dee Why* drifted for more than 10 hours until an Italian tramp steamer answered her distress call and took her in tow, handing over to a tug outside Algiers harbour. *Dee Why* stayed eight days at Algiers while the steam pipe was repaired before making off again for Port Said. Here there was more trouble because the port authorities certified the ferry as being seaworthy only as far as Aden and not beyond. Both ferries were tied up in Port Said for another five weeks before they loaded bunker coal and proceeded through the Suez Canal and down the Red Sea to Aden, where they joined a whole fleet of small ships—coasters, tugs, tankers and dredgers—all waiting for the monsoon to pass in the Indian Ocean before they would be allowed to proceed to Colombo. As the time for sailing approached, the ships were put through a floating dock for their bottoms to be scrubbed off and painted with anti-fouling.

Nothing much enlivened the *Dee Why*'s subsequent passage from Colombo to Java, then through Torres Strait to Thursday Island. Inside the Great Barrier Reef at night, *Dee Why* anchored in shallow water because she had no steam winches to pull up the anchor and heavy chain. A good deal of hard labour was demanded from eight men at a time, straining and heaving on a small hand winch to drag in as much as 45 fathoms of chain and pull the anchor up to the hawse pipe. Within 70 miles of Sydney, *Dee Why* ran into strong headwinds and seas so rough she could not make progress. This situation produced another worry when the chief engineer told the captain that according to his estimates of the remaining bunker coal and the rate at which they were burning it to keep the ship's head into the sea, they would be unable to keep going long enough to reach Sydney. There was nothing they could do but run for shelter and anchor until the weather blew itself out. That is probably why the *Dee Why* turned up eventually outside Sydney Heads at 2 am on 1 November 1928.

For the Press of the day, however, the main story when *Dee Why* berthed in Sydney was the mini 'mutiny on the *Bounty*' that had plagued her most of the way out. Captain Brown spent some time with a *Sydney Morning Herald* reporter refuting the complaints about the bad food. This was rubbish, he said. The food was good and sufficient and any claims to the contrary were 'perfect nonsense'. And what about the cooking utensils being thrown overboard? Captain Brown left the reporters at that stage to go down to breakfast. But within a few minutes he was back with some more news. He had been given a drinking glass at the table for his tea. 'Now all the cups on the ship have apparently disappeared,' Captain Brown said.

The opening of the Harbour Bridge in 1932 brought the predicted disaster for Sydney Ferries Ltd. Within 12 months the Watsons Bay service was taken off—although goodness knows why the bridge should have affected that part of Sydney—and there was a general cutting back of whatever services were left. The once great fleet of inner harbour ferries and vehicular punts was struggling for its existence. But for the Manly ferries business was good. They had two things which the inner harbour fleet did not have—the ever-popular ride across The Heads and now, coming up, Sydney's biggest sharkproof swimming pool inside a promenade enclosing the whole harbour beach at West Esplanade alongside the Manly ferry wharf.

2. The *Greycliffe* Disaster

The story of the Manly ferries so far tells of a marvellous safety record which was probably unequalled in public transport. But things did happen on the harbour and tragedies did occur. The worst ever was on Thursday, 3 November 1927, when the Union Steamship Company's RMS *Tahiti* rammed and sank the Sydney Ferries' *Greycliffe* off Bradleys Head about 4.30 in the afternoon. Thirty-nine lost their lives, many of them schoolchildren, when the *Greycliffe*, sliced in two by the impact, rolled over and plunged to the bottom of the harbour in a matter of seconds.

If ever newspapers had cause to plaster their street posters with shock and horror this was it. Sydney was shocked by the horror of what had happened. The worst affected part of the community was in Vaucluse and Watsons Bay, the destination of so many men, women and children who never reached home on that fateful day. Ages of the victims ranged from six to 81. Many of them, coincidentally, were people whose livelihood was the sea and shipping—naval ratings from Garden Island Navy depot and workshops, ships' painters, a chief petty officer of HMAS *Penguin*, a senior naval medical officer, also from Garden Island, a master mariner, and lighthouse folk. These were many of the people who lived at the Vaucluse addresses most common in the casualty list— Hopetoun Avenue, The Crescent, Fitzwilliam Road. But, most tragic of all, was the listing of 'schoolboy', 'schoolgirl' from the same addresses. The *Greycliffe*, which left Circular Quay at 4.10 pm for Watsons Bay, calling at Garden Island, Nielsen Park, Parsley Bay, Central and Watsons Bay, was known as the 'school boat' and she was packed with children coming home from schools in the city and a sports meeting which the Public Schools' Amateur Athletic Association had held that day at the Sydney Cricket Ground.

The *Sydney Morning Herald* of Friday, 4 November, in the staid headline fashion of the day, spread across three of its 17-em columns, announced: 'APPALLING HARBOUR DISASTER—Ferry Boat Struck by Mail Steamer—GREYCLIFFE SMASHED AND SUNK—Killed and Missing Estimated at 37 Persons—ABOUT FIFTY PERSONS TAKEN TO HOSPITAL.' After listing the known dead, missing and injured, the *Herald*, under another single-column heading, 'THE DISASTER,' said:

> The greatest disaster that has ever occurred on Sydney Harbour took place yesterday afternoon about 4.30 o'clock, when the Union Steamship Company's RMS *Tahiti* rammed and sank the Sydney Ferry Company's *Greycliffe* off Bradleys Head. The accident was accompanied by appalling loss of life. The latest reports last evening stated that 11 bodies had been recovered, 28 persons were reported missing and over 50 had been treated at Sydney Hospital for injuries received in the collision.

Then the horrifying story unfolded from interviews with survivors, passengers aboard the *Tahiti*, people who had seen it happen and those who rescued survivors.

It was not known at the time how this terrible thing had happened. The collision occurred so suddenly that the *Tahiti*'s passengers only realised something was wrong when they heard the screams of women and children from the stricken ferry, which had been hit broadside on by the towering bows of the 7898-ton ship. *Tahiti*, a twin-screw vessel, 460 ft in length, ran a regular service between Sydney and San Francisco in those days before airlines took over the international passenger traffic. It may have been an omen that as she was casting off from No. 5 wharf at Darling Harbour at 4 pm that day a young woman fell into the water. A man jumped from the wharf and rescued her. Within half an hour the *Tahiti*'s bows cut into the wooden superstructure of the *Greycliffe*, pushing it forward temporarily, then rolling it over and ripping the little wooden vessel in two halves which slid along each side of the ship as they disappeared beneath the wreckage-strewn water. The *Herald* reported:

> In a moment all was confusion. Terrible scenes were witnessed as the ferry passengers struggled to free themselves from the wreckage, which finally sank. The engine room boiler burst when it became submerged, adding further to the terrors of the situation for the unfortunate passengers. In a moment, many were struggling in the swirling waters and many pitiful scenes were witnessed. Forgetting their danger, some of the survivors immediately went to the assistance of others

and placed them in comparative safety until assistance arrived. A fireman on the *Tahiti* dived overboard, rescued two children and assisted others.

In a remarkably short space of time, vessels of all descriptions had hurried to the scene and searched for survivors. Two Manly ferries and three others of the Sydney Ferries fleet, with small craft from all around the shores, scoured the floating wreckage to pluck many people to safety. It is feared many passengers were fatally injured when the collision occurred. The *Tahiti* swept on for some distance after cutting through the *Greycliffe* before she could be pulled up. Eventually she returned, anchored opposite Point Piper and lowered boats to help in the rescue. The steel plating of the mail steamer prevented her being damaged and all that was noticeable were two long scratches on either side of her bows where the wooden superstructure of the *Greycliffe* had scraped off the paint. She was able to continue her voyage to New Zealand last evening.

Reporters, when they arrived in boats chartered hurriedly when the news hit their offices, found a milling mass amongst the wreckage. Some boats were dashing off to Circular Quay with injured survivors. On the decks of one could be seen a group giving artificial respiration to somebody who had been pulled from the water. Just off Bradleys Head the harbour was littered with broken timber and all kinds of debris. Here was a child's gaily coloured doll, there a man's walking stick. A child's doll floating face down in the water was pathetic evidence of its owner's fate. Lifebelts which people had no time to put on hung together in broken roof racks. A felt hat drifting slowly away from the scene gradually became waterlogged and went down to join its owner. Among the wreckage, rowing boats and launches still hunted for bodies, occasionally finding a handbag or some other article which might identify a missing owner. A water police launch crew continued their search after throwing a tarpaulin over the body of a man they had hauled aboard. Nobody would have believed that so much wreckage could have come from such a small vessel as the *Greycliffe*. The roofing of the top deck had apparently been lifted off en masse, and on this a ventilator cowl rode above the water as if the ferry was there partially submerged. Passengers on passing ferries crowded to the side nearest the scene, looking at the scattered debris, including the ferry's for'ard wheelhouse, which was still floating in the vicinity. The aft wheelhouse, splintered almost beyond recognition, had drifted forlornly out into the middle of the harbour.

Aboard the *Tahiti* there was stunned horror. People, petrified, stood in silent groups. Only a few had known anything about the accident until it was all over. They had

SS Curl Curl. *(John Allcot)*

SS South Steyne. *(John Allcot)*

Baragoola *as a steamer. (John Allcot)*

MV Baragoola. *(John Allcot)*

heard a shrill blast from the *Tahiti*'s siren, followed immediately by no more than a slight bump as the big ship ploughed through the frail timber of the little ferry. Few took much notice until they heard terrified screams. Then there was a rush for the upper deck. Said one passenger:

> Looking over the side, I could see the ferry turning over slowly and then, to my horror, she split in halves. One piece swept by the side on which I was standing. It was terrible to hear the women and children screaming. I couldn't look any longer and in a minute or two the wreckage was gone.

Another *Tahiti* passenger who has been watching the ship's bow wave saw everything. He said:

> In a moment one side of the ferry had disappeared from view. The other immediately became alive with scrambling, terrified people, some clinging frantically to stanchions, railings or anything which might offer support as they clambered hopelessly upwards on the submerging wreck, terror showing vividly on their faces.

They had more hope, however, than those who had been in the saloons downstairs, struggling madly to get out of doors or break through windows. Some did escape even after the ferry went down, but many were trapped with the dead bodies of those who had been killed when the steel plates of the *Tahiti* crashed through the side of the ferry.

Passengers on the other side of the *Tahiti* told of seeing

Raising the bows of the Greycliffe *from the bottom of the harbour off Bradleys Head.*

half of the *Greycliffe* scraping along the ship's hull. This portion must have contained the boilers because after it sank people on the *Tahiti* heard a muffled explosion and saw the water boil, throwing up into the air a great cloud of steam in which hurtled flying pieces of timber. In this swirling vortex appeared suddenly the heads of men, women and children, fighting for their lives against the suction created by the sinking ferry. Some, unable to swim, clutched desperately at passing objects, several had been fortunate enough to grab lumps of floating timber, but others appeared too dazed to help themselves. It was pitiful to see tiny children struggling in the churning water. Some were brought to safety exhausted, but for many rescue was too late.

For one man on the deck of the *Tahiti* the gruesome memory remained of seeing the body of a girl sucked under the *Tahiti*'s whirling propellers. He looked to see whether she would come to the surface again, but there was no sign of her any more. Another recalled seeing a distracted woman standing on a piece of floating timber screaming as though she would never stop. Yet another shuddered as he told of watching a youth who, dragged under by the wreckage, turned staring eyes to those above on the ship before he disappeared finally after clutching vainly at a fragment of timber which could not support him.

Greycliffe passengers who escaped with their lives told graphic stories. Four schoolboys, Leslie Brook, K. Berliner, R. Fairweathers and Ken Horler, son of the Town Clerk of the then Vaucluse Municipal Council, were sitting at the stern of the *Greycliffe*, singing, shouting and 'mucking up' generally on their way home to Watsons

Bay. They heard the *Tahiti's* whistle and then saw that the ship was too close to stay where they were. No sooner had they moved than there was a crash and the ferry began to tip over. Said Leslie Brook:

> I was drawn down by the suction. The current spun me around in all directions. When I came up to the top I grabbed the biggest piece of wood I could find. I saw Doris Garrett struggling in the water and helped her to safety. Other passengers were floundering around looking for something to support them and crying for help. Launches came from all sides, but there was such confusion that nobody seemed to know what to do.

Leslie was a good swimmer and that was what saved his life. He saw another boy he knew, Ken Lankshire, who could not swim and on the night of the tragedy Leslie did not know what had become of this boy. He also saw in the water Dr C. W. Reid, chief quarantine officer for New South Wales, who lived in Watsons Bay. 'It seemed as though the boat must have been knocked into splinters,' Leslie said. 'Few pieces of the floating wood were big enough to support anyone.'

Ken Horler, also a good swimmer, said he must have been dragged down 25 feet. When he came to the top his leg was caught in a rope and he was dragged down again. This time he had considerable difficulty in reaching the surface. He had cuts and scratches all over his body. Doris Garrett said the schoolboys saved her life. They got her and Nancy Lewis on to a floating drum. She said:

> When I came up I didn't know where I was. While I was under the water I seemed to think I was asleep and when I came to I expected to find myself in bed.

Mr J. S. Bithel, a Watsons Bay resident who had boarded the *Greycliffe* from work at Garden Island, said the impact was so severe that the ferry was crushed to pieces. He was sitting on the port side when he saw the *Tahiti* coming along 'at a fair speed', which he thought was about six or seven knots. Suddenly, the *Greycliffe* seemed to cut off towards Bradleys Head. This was so unusual that he seemed to think the steering had failed. He heard the *Tahiti* give two blasts as he ran to the other side of the ferry. Then the deck heaved over and his leg was jammed under a seat, from which he extricated himself with difficulty as the water rushed in around him. Mr Bithel went straight down, almost to the bottom of the harbour it seemed to him. He said:

> I think I turned 20 Catherine-wheels. I didn't know where I was going or what was happening to me. When I came up I was dazed. I was near a buoy, but didn't

have the strength to grasp it. I got into a sort of a coma and the next thing I knew was that a lifebelt was thrown to me from a tug and I was dragged aboard. I don't think anyone in the cabins would have had any chance. The boat sank, I'm sure, in 20 seconds. It was the most nerve-racking experience I have ever been through and I've been shipwrecked two or three times.

One of the main rescue vessels was the Sydney Ferries' *Kummula*, which had left Circular Quay at 4.10 pm and had just landed its passengers at Taronga Park wharf when the accident happened in full view of these people, who were then travelling up the hill from the wharf in a tram. The *Kummula* was continuing on to Clifton Gardens and raced immediately to the rescue.

Mrs K. Carruthers, of Vaucluse, was on another ferry travelling from Watsons Bay to the city; arrived at the scene just after the collision. To her horror, she saw her son, Jim, aged 13, in the water clinging to some debris. He was picked up and admitted later to Sydney Hospital with other people who were injured.

Alfred Norman Dean, of Watsons Bay, a fireman on the *Greycliffe*, was really lucky. He would have had no hope had he been down in the stokehold, but instead he just happened to be on deck for 'a breather' and was rescued by the water police after being in the water about 15 minutes. One of the *Greycliffe's* deckhands saved a woman and her daughter. Mrs W. F. Sully, of Vaucluse, was struck by the ferry's propeller while under the water and received severe internal injuries. Her daughter, Nurse Sully, of the Royal Alexandra Hospital, was trying to keep her mother up when the deckhand swam to Mrs Sully and insisted on keeping her afloat until they were picked up.

Two sisters went to their deaths together. Mrs Williams, 53, of Vaucluse, had her widowed sister, Mrs Terry, 65, from Victoria, spending a holiday with her. A gaping wound across the head and forehead indicated that Mrs Terry had been killed instantly in the crash. Mrs Williams was suffering severely from immersion when plucked out of the harbour and died soon after being admitted to Sydney Hospital.

The Sydney Ferries' vessel *Woollahra*, which left Nielsen Park at 4.10 pm, went to the rescue and lowered two lifeboats. A man dived from its deck to save a woman who was becoming exhausted. The two boats came back to the *Woollahra* with seven survivors and two mangled bodies. While they were standing by, a shout from the *Woollahra's* passengers drew the crew's attention to the body of a woman floating just beneath the surface and being drawn slowly under the *Woollahra*. She was picked up and two passengers with a knowledge of life-saving restored her to consciousness.

Mr R. K. Angus, a visitor from New Zealand, was

returning from Taronga Park Zoo in the *Kummula*, which had just unloaded its passengers from the city at Taronga Park wharf and was heading for Clifton Gardens when the accident happened. He was watching the *Tahiti* coming down the harbour because he had friends on board going back to New Zealand. He heard the *Tahiti* give one blast and then the ferry appeared across her bows. Telling of the crash and the rolling over of the ferry, he said:

> When about halfway down the waist of the *Tahiti*, the half of the ferry visible to me exploded. The *Tahiti* passed clean through the remaining wreck, leaving only a few survivors visible clinging to the wreckage. When we arrived there lifeboats were lowered and we picked up several survivors. The suddenness of the tragedy was unbelievable and the grim experiences immediately afterwards are too terrible to tell in detail.

The first survivors and bodies of those who had not survived were landed at Man-o'-War Steps, near the eastern side of what used to be the Fort Macquarie tram depot, now the Sydney Opera House, about 5 pm, half an hour after the collision. The open space in front of the little naval office which used to be there was turned into a temporary casualty station, from where ambulances rushed water-sodden people to hospital. Bodies of those who were beyond help were lying on the footpath and ambulancemen were trying to resuscitate others showing some signs of life. They were assisted by police and some tramway men from the nearby depot. There were what the newspapers described as heart-rending scenes as wet and injured people, shivering with cold, inquired anxiously about relatives or friends who had been with them in the *Greycliffe*. One woman was crying piteously and screaming for her mother. Another, wrapped in a Navy man's overcoat, lying across the bows of a Navy launch, was dead when they took her ashore. Some survivors were almost covered with blood and most of them were suffering from exposure. A young woman, obviously in great pain, had her clothing torn to shreds, her stockings almost ripped off her legs. She was helped off the Navy launch by a bluejacket, but was unable to walk. The sailor, without any hesitation, took her in his arms and carried her to a waiting ambulance. Despite her suffering, the young lady muttered grateful thanks to the Navy man, who answered quietly: 'That's all right, Miss.'

One of those picked up by the *Kummula* told of the terribly tragic end to his holiday in Sydney. Mr John Corby, a railway fettler from Moree, had arrived the previous Tuesday with his wife and daughter for a holiday. From the Hotel Burlington in the Haymarket they had set out for a trip to Watsons Bay, but they never got there.

Trembling violently, blood streaming down his face, Mr Corby was among the first to be landed on the Mosman wharf at Circular Quay. Staggering ashore, he said in a dazed voice to the first person he saw: 'Oh God. My poor wife and child. They're gone.' Assured by people in the crowd on the wharf that many had been saved, Mr Corby told how he and his wife and six-year-old daughter had been sitting talking on the top deck of the *Greycliffe* when they heard some women scream and they looked behind them to see the big ship almost on top of the ferry. He said:

> I sprang for some lifebelts and shouted to my wife to rush down the stairs. I grabbed a lifebelt and was just making for the stairs to join them when there was a terrific crash. I was immediately thrown into the water and went down with the anguishing screams of women and children in my ears. My next recollection was coming towards the surface of the water. I thought I would never reach there, it was so long before I surfaced. There I was, clutching hold of something, looking about for my wife and daughter. Everywhere around me were struggling women and girls, some with their faces horribly mutilated. What happened after that I don't know until I came to on the ferry that rescued us.

Mr Corby was not reassured. He said his wife could not swim. Then he collapsed on the wharf and was taken to hospital.

Sydney Hopsital had been transformed into a semblance of a war-torn casualty centre. Doctors, nurses and wardsmen were rushing about, directed by the medical superintendent, Dr C. K. Winston, and assisted by some 30 doctors and medical students who had been commandeered to help in the emergency. They were hampered by a never-ending stream of anxious people pouring through the hospital gates. Distracted mothers cried for their children and ran from ward to ward seeking them. Some found their children terribly hurt, but were relieved to know that at least they were there and not at the bottom of the harbour. One of the most terribly injured was John Barrett, engineer of the *Greycliffe*. But he smoked a cigarette bravely, without a murmur. They said he had implored rescuers to leave him in the water while they saved others more badly injured. 'He waved us on with a grin on his face,' one rescuer said afterwards.

The *Tahiti* was anchored near Shark Island after the collision and when an examination showed that she was not damaged she resumed her voyage to New Zealand, clearing The Heads at 8.08 pm. The search for bodies continued in the harbour under searchlights of the fire float *Pluvius* until 8 pm, gathering up the wreckage, which was a danger to navigation. The crew of the *Pluvius* found many lifebelts in the water, indicating that the *Greycliffe*'s passengers had little or no time to put them on. They piled all available space on the *Pluvius* with broken timber, seats, lifebelts and other debris. The harbour where the ferry went down is about 24 metres deep.

The master of the *Greycliffe*, W. T. Barnes, was taken home suffering from immersion and shock, which must have been considerable. The same could no doubt be said of the master of the *Tahiti*, Captain Aldwell, and the pilot who was taking her out, Captain T. Carson. At the inquiry later it was claimed that the ship was travelling too fast. Fortunately, her engines were stopped quickly, or more would have been sucked into the churning propellers.

When the New South Wales Parliament met the next day, the Premier, Mr Bavin, moved that the House adjourn as an expression of grief at the tragedy and sympathy with the relatives of those killed. Members stood in silence, after which the House adjourned.

During the weekend, divers recovered three more bodies from the wreck, which they had found lying in the mud 24 metres below the surface. The ladies' cabin had drifted 24 metres away from the hull. It was described as smashed practically to matchwood. No bodies were in that cabin. The divers found two of the three they located buried under a mass of twisted and tangled steel in the engine room. The third, a girl, was lying on her back imbedded in the mud alongside the *Greycliffe*. On Saturday and Sunday afternoons thousands of people assembled around the Fort Macquarie waterfront waiting for any news brought ashore by the launches which went to and from the wreck. Others waited on the western side of Circular Quay, where police launches brought in the corpses for removal to the City Morgue.

Bodies were still being recovered nearly two weeks after the accident. Some floated to the surface when the wreck was moved above the mud. Some were picked up by water police. The divers had been working continuously to try to search the wreckage and get slings under the hull so that it could be raised. They told pathetic stories of what they found. Diver W. Harris found the body of a schoolgirl, Betty Sharp. He said:

Just before finishing on Friday I decided to have a look around a portion of the wreck which had not been explored. You can imagine my feelings when the figure of a little girl, standing upright and with outstretched arms loomed up in front of me. Her clothes were torn to shreds. I found that one of her feet had become jammed between some twisted steel rods. I wrote on a slate 'Have found the body of a little girl' and sent the message up to my tender on the pontoon. After a great deal of difficulty, I managed to release the girl's foot and sent her body up to the surface.

Much of the time they were working below, Harris and the other diver, Tom Carr, could see only a few centimetres in front of them and had to feel for the dead bodies. They had to use hacksaws to cut their way through parts of the wreckage, working in positions of great danger to themselves if parts of the wreck collapsed on them. They were greatly disturbed emotionally after finding the bodies of schoolchildren, some clutching school cases and other belongings.

It was 27 November, nearly a fortnight after the accident before all the missing people were accounted for. Two bodies found during the second week of searching brought the total of dead in the disaster to 37. One man, Mr Arthur Hardy, was the last on the missing list, believed to have been among the *Greycliffe*'s passengers. He called at the water police station on Saturday, 26 November, and assured the police that he was very much alive. Explaining the mystery, he said he had intended to travel in the *Greycliffe* with a friend, but when the friend did not arrive in time he decided he would not go and left the ferry just as the gangway was being taken aboard. He would go to the country instead. But in his haste to get off before it was too late, he left his attache case behind and when this was found floating near the scene of the collision the police assumed that Hardy was among the missing. He went to the country on the evening of the disaster and remained there, blissfully unaware that divers were searching for his body until he returned to Sydney more than three weeks later. By that time the main part of the wreck had been lifted and beached near Taronga Zoo and various people were telling their stories before the City Coroner and a Court of Marine Inquiry.

The City Coroner, Mr Fletcher, heard Sergeant Shakespeare, of the water police, tell of picking up 11 survivors just after the accident and being on the scene all the next day when the divers recovered 13 bodies.

But the main interest was in the Court of Marine Inquiry, which was concerned with establishing what had caused the disaster. Both produced much conflicting evidence, but the one thing on which most witnesses agreed was that *Tahiti* was going too fast for a ship of her size in the traffic lanes of the harbour. Over three days several witnesses swore that the *Tahiti* did not change her course, but the *Greycliffe* altered hers to port so as to converge with that of the *Tahiti*. Others said they saw no change by the *Greycliffe*, some said the *Tahiti* changed her course to starboard towards the ferry and still others claimed that both vessels turned to port just before the collision.

Naval Chief Petty Officer Bryant told the inquiry that when the *Tahiti* went past Garden Island at a distance he reckoned as 170 yards out, the pontoon of the ferry wharf was rocked as he had never seen it rocked before. Bryant, a crew member of the destroyer *Success*, said he was used to judging speeds from 14 knots up and in his opinion the *Tahiti* was doing about 12 knots when her wash rocked the pontoon. The Sydney Harbour Trust regulations at that time provided, for vessels other than ferry boats, a maximum speed of 6 knots between Goat Island and Fort Denison and 8 knots between Bradleys Head and the Shark Island light. But according to one witness after another, the ship was going much faster than that.

Petty Officer Halliwell, also of HMAS *Success*, said that after the *Tahiti* passed Garden Island she would have been doing about 12 knots and the wash was such that he expected the rocking pontoon to damage the wharf piles. Joseph Kirkham, Chief Yeoman of Signals at Garden Island, said that after 30 years' experience he could judge the speed of vessels and his estimate for the *Tahiti* was 12 knots. Leslie Blakeney, master of the tug *Bimbi*, also estimated the ship's speed at 12 knots. This was supported by Adrian Galjward, a cook on HMAS *Success*, who said the *Tahiti* was doing 12 to 13 knots and she was overhauling the *Greycliffe*.

Rupert Nixon, who was at the wheel of the Manly ferry *Burra Bra* on her way to Manly said that as they rounded Bennelong Point, where the Opera House is now, the *Greycliffe* had left Garden Island and the *Tahiti* was passing Fort Denison. The *Greycliffe* starboarded her helm about a point, to go to Nielsen Park, and he had to turn to starboard to let the Sydney Ferries' vessel *Woollahra*, coming from Nielsen Park, pass between the *Burra Bra* and the *Tahiti*. He said the engineer on the *Burra Bra* had told them hundreds of times that they had to do 13.5 knots for the Manly trip and they were not gaining on the *Tahiti* until he saw the *Tahiti* strike the *Greycliffe*. Albert McDonald, who was engineer on that trip of the *Burra Bra*, said that as they rounded Bennelong Point he went up on deck and saw the *Tahiti* ahead of them. He then went down and began to bring the *Burra Bra* up to her business speed of 13.5 knots. When they were abreast of Fort Denison he went up again and saw the *Tahiti* about three times her own length ahead of them. As they passed Garden Island they appeared to have gained 150 to 200 feet on the *Tahiti*. Said McDonald:

I felt justified then in bringing the *Burra Bra* up to her maximum speed of 14 to 14.5 knots. But just as I got her up, the engine room telegraph rang for full astern and then the whistle went to lower the boats. That was at 4.29 1/2 by the engine room clock.

Frederick Edgar Jones, a deckhand on the *Greycliffe*, was moving about collecting tickets when they left Garden Island at a speed, according to him, of about 10 knots. He said that after collecting the tickets he looked out a window and could see Bradleys Head on the port side. Then he turned to the stern of the ferry and, to his horror, could see halfway up the bow of the *Tahiti*. He told the inquiry:

The stern was level with the bow of the *Tahiti*. I saw the *Tahiti* coming at tremendous speed and called out to passengers to run for their lives. They all ran to the starboard side and the next thing the water came up and met us. We went down. The *Greycliffe* was pushed at a tremendous rate under the water. When I came up I could see the *Tahiti* down the stream. There was plenty of wreckage about and many people in the water, a number of whom I saved.

In reply to questions by Mr F. P. Evans (for the pilot of the *Tahiti*, Captain T. Carson), Jones said: 'I should say the *Tahiti* was doing 15 knots. The *Greycliffe* was dead ahead of her.'

William James Silva, holder of a harbour and rivers certificate for 39 years, was master of another Watsons Bay ferry, the *Woollahra*, on the afternoon of 3 November and was almost alongside the *Tahiti* and the *Greycliffe* when they collided. He had left Nielsen Park and was proceeding to Garden Island, coming back from Watsons Bay to the city. When he passed the *Greycliffe* she was on her usual course. He lost sight of her temporarily, then, after passing the bow of the *Tahiti* he could see that the two vessels were on parallel courses. Captain Silva said the *Greycliffe* was travelling at her usual speed, but the *Tahiti* was travelling at 'a great speed' and was certainly overtaking the *Greycliffe*. He was astern of the *Tahiti* when he heard two whistles and then saw the ferry run down. Edward Weatherbone, a deckhand on the *Woollahra*, said in his evidence that his attention was directed to the *Tahiti* by 'her tremendous speed'.

The master of the *Greycliffe*, Captain Barnes, gave his evidence that day. Telling of the trip from Garden Island, heading for north of the Shark Island light, he said:

I was standing on the starboard side of the wheelhouse against the telegraph when I heard two blasts. I looked over my shoulder through a window at the back of the wheelhouse. I did not see anything at all. I stepped to the port side and looked out and then I saw the bows of the *Tahiti* right on my port quarter aft, only a few feet away. Just as I moved across I felt a wave hit my stern and swing me to port. I immediately stepped back to the centre of the wheelhouse and pulled the wheel over to starboard, but it did not take effect. Then crash, bang. The *Greycliffe* went over on her starboard side with her stern down and I was thrown into the water. I came up and got on to a raft and the *Kurraba* picked me up.

71

The following day, Captain Carson, the pilot who had been taking the *Tahiti* out of the harbour, gave evidence. He said he had been employed as a pilot by the State Navigation Department since 1909, before which he had been a master at sea. He said he piloted about 250 ships a year and had never had an accident before. On the afternoon of the *Greycliffe* collision he took the *Tahiti* from her berth and after passing Çircular Quay had the engines at half speed. The first time he saw the *Greycliffe* was when the *Tahiti* was near Bennelong Point and the *Greycliffe* was leaving Garden Island wharf. The *Tahiti* was then two ships' lengths behind her. Captain Carson said:

After the *Greycliffe* got on her course she was about two points on my starboard bow, heading for Shark Island, and I steadied my ship for about the north end of Shark Island. We proceeded in those positions. After leaving Garden Island the *Tahiti* began to overtake the *Greycliffe* rather rapidly. Passing Garden Island, my ship was working up from about 6 knots to about 7 knots. Then the *Tahiti* practically ceased to overtake the *Greycliffe*, which seemed to keep stationed about four points on my bow, about a ship's length from the bridge of the *Tahiti*. When we were nearly abreast of Shark Island I noticed the *Greycliffe* alter her course very rapidly towards us, closing in very quickly. I made an exclamation to the captain of the *Tahiti*, ordered the helm hard to starboard, stopped both engines, then ordered the port engine full astern and sounded two short blasts. I thought the two ships would clear, but the *Greycliffe* seemed to cross more than ever. When the *Greycliffe* seemed to swing, I ordered both engines full speed astern, but, unfortunately, the ships collided.

Captain Carson said that just before the collision the speed of the *Tahiti* was 8 knots. When the *Greycliffe* was struck he ordered both engines stopped because he knew there were people in the water and there would be very great danger of them being injured by the moving propellers. After the *Tahiti* drifted clear of the wreckage Captain Carson had her turned around to lower lifeboats. In reply to Mr H.E. Manning (for Sydney Ferries Ltd), Captain Carson said there had been a gradual increase in the speed of the *Tahiti* from the time it passed Garden Island until it struck the *Greycliffe*.

Captain L.E. Lucas, chief examiner of masters and mates' certificates in the Navigation Department, said he had read the evidence before the inquiry and had made certain calculations. From a point marked H (which he indicated on the chart) to the divers' punt over the wreck scene was 4040 feet. If a vessel traversed that 4040 feet in 3 minutes 15 seconds, as had been given in evidence, that vessel would be travelling at 12.25 knots.

Captain Basil Meredith Aldwell, master of the *Tahiti*, showed deep emotion as he told his story when the inquiry resumed on Wednesday, 28 December. Captain Aldwell had never had an accident in 22 years as a master with sailing vessels as well as steamships. He told of leaving Darling Harbour at 4 pm and clearing Millers Point 10 minutes later, proceeding down the harbour on the usual course on about 4 knots. He said that from the end of Circular Quay the speed was increased to about 5.5 knots and when passing Garden Island he rang for full speed. He reckoned that after passing Garden Island the *Tahiti* was doing 7.5 knots. When he came to tell of the collision, Captain Aldwell was deeply affected and had to sit down for a few minutes to recover. Resuming, he said everything appeared to be all right. They were not expecting any trouble. They passed a ferry boat coming in on the port side and just as they did so the pilot looked over the bridge and made an exclamation. It was then that he saw the *Greycliffe*, which had been parallel with the *Tahiti*, change her course suddenly and pull in towards the bows of the larger ship. The pilot immediately ordered 'Hard to starboard'. Captain Aldwell ran to the engine room telegraph, sounded two blasts on the whistle to indicate that they were turning to starboard and rang down for full astern. The orders were carried out at once, but as soon as the *Greycliffe* altered her course, Captain Aldwell said, he knew there was no chance of avoiding a collision. He continued:

A few seconds more might have saved the situation. The *Tahiti* would have swung round like a saucer and the *Greycliffe* might have been able to straighten up. But there was no time. The engines of the *Tahiti* were put astern and emergency boats were lowered but not launched because of the heavy wash from the propellers. I saw 13 lifebelts thrown from the promenade deck.

To Mr Manning, Captain Aldwell said the *Tahiti* was easily manageable at 7.5 knots. 'I was horrified when the *Greycliffe* changed her course,' he said 'I knew it was going to be a sure hit.'

Mr Manning: You had Shark Island slightly on your starboard bow?—Yes.
Did you know the *Greycliffe* was a Watsons Bay ferry?—I assumed she was.
You knew she would have to turn to port at Nielsen Park?—Yes. We knew that.

Captain Aldwell said the *Tahiti* could not turn further to port. The *Greycliffe* was on the starboard side, the *Woollahra* was coming in and the *Burra Bra* was behind them. Had they gone further to port a collision would have been likely.

Mr Manning: In all the circumstances do you consider a speed of 13 knots by the *Tahiti* dangerous?—We were not travelling at that speed. She never came up to 8 knots.

Captain Aldwell said the *Greycliffe* seemed to fall to pieces when hit. 'She simply collapsed like a barrel,' he said. 'We felt no impact.' Asked what was the ship's maximum speed, Captain Aldwell said 15.5 knots, depending on conditions. 'She has covered 408 miles in 24 hours with a strong equatorial current and we are very proud of that,' he said.

Mr Manning: How long would it take you to reach full speed?—Sometimes the whole trip. On ordinary occasions we would take an hour and a half to reach full speed. She was not travelling more than 8 knots down the harbour. In fact she did not reach that speed. Unless the boilers had been heated for a number of hours it would be impossible for the *Tahiti* to reach a speed of 12 knots on the run from Millers Point to Bradleys Head. I don't know what is the greatest speed to be attained by the vessel between those points. I am unfamiliar with the currents and there is a great deal of traffic. It might be possible to get a speed of 10 knots.

The *Tahiti*'s chief engineer, Lawrence K. McMurrich, said that when the vessel left Darling Harbour one single-ended and three double-ended boilers were in use. He remembered getting several orders going down the harbour, all of which were carried out. Mr McMurrich said the engines were not properly warmed up, but in other respects they were in perfect working order. He told the court he could not estimate the speed of the *Tahiti* going down the harbour. In reply to questions by Mr Manning, Mr McMurrich said 'full speed' did not indicate the maximum speed of the vessel.

John Augustine Thompson, a British naval expert, enlivened proceedings at the inquiry somewhat when he was very critical of the evidence about how long it took to warm up the boilers and get speed out of the *Tahiti*. He said they were not entitled to be engineers on a passenger-ship like the *Tahiti*, and if it took them all day to warm up the boilers 'they should be thrown overboard'. Dr Brissenden (for the Union Steamship Company) questioned Mr Thompson on his criticism of evidence by the *Tahiti*'s engineers:

Do you know that it takes from 10 in the morning until 4 in the afternoon to warm up the *Tahiti*'s boilers?

Mr Thompson: If it takes them all day to warm up the boilers the machinery should be thrown overboard and the engineers with it.

Dr Brissenden: I will have the matter attended to directly the ship returns to Sydney.

Mr Thompson: I am averse to British engineers going into a British court where everybody will get justice and giving evidence which is not wholly true. They should have been able to correlate the speed of the vessel with the number of revolutions. They ought to be ashamed of themselves. They are not entitled to be engineers on a ship like the *Tahiti* carrying passengers.

At this stage Mr Justice Campbell had to intervene and redirect the cross-examination, which was becoming quite heated.

The Court of Marine Inquiry was crowded on Saturday morning, 7 January 1928, when Mr Justice Campbell delivered judgment. He found that the cause of the collision was the failure of the *Tahiti* to observe the regulations and keep out of the way of the *Greycliffe*. Mr Justice Campbell found also that the speed of the *Tahiti* when approaching the point of the collision was 'greatly in excess of that prescribed for outgoing deep sea vessels'. He said the necessity for observing a proper speed limit in the harbour should be the subject of inquiry by the port authorities. In his opinion, the master of the *Greycliffe* did not cause the collision and was not culpable for it. The judge said in his finding:

I am unable to accept the case put forward on behalf of the *Tahiti* and those in charge of that vessel that the *Greycliffe*, when she was about 400 ft away from the *Tahiti*'s bridge and about four points on the starboard bow suddenly swung to port with a sharp angle of turn that would head her almost north and to the west of Bradleys Head. No one was able to suggest any reason for this as a voluntary act and it is not otherwise sought to be explained or accounted for and it is flatly denied by the master of the *Greycliffe*.

The finding pointed out that the master of the *Greycliffe* was totally ignorant of any danger, but those in control of the *Tahiti*, having the *Greycliffe* in full view, should have been aware of it.

That was the crux of the whole matter. On 8 February 1928, the City Coroner made similar findings after concluding the long series of inquests, and the following day the Minister for Customs, Mr Pratten, laid the blame officially, saying that the Court of Marine Inquiry had found the *Tahiti*, being the overtaking vessel, solely to blame for the collision. He added:

The New South Wales Superintendent of Navigation, Captain J.E. Morris, has therefore suspended Pilot

Carson from duty for breach of Article 24 of the Collision Regulations and for exceeding the speed limit as laid down by Regulation 43 of the Sydney Harbour Trust Regulations.

Regulation 43 prescribed a maximum speed of 6 knots between Goat Island and Fort Denison and 8 knots from Bradleys Head to the Shark Island light. Obviously, according to the evidence, the *Tahiti* was doing much more than that. But more interesting, and more important, was the breach of Article 24, which, shorn of its legal jargon, states that every vessel overtaking any other vessel shall keep out of the way of the vessel being overtaken. The situation was similar to that of the driver of a motor vehicle running into the back of another vehicle in front of him. Almost invariably, he would be charged with negligent driving.

Mr Pratten said the New South Wales authorities would lay a charge against Pilot Carson under the Pilotage Regulations of New South Wales, and Federal authorities were giving careful consideration to the liability, if any, of the master and officers of the *Tahiti*. By then, however, a round of litigation was about to begin which would take years to wind up, starting with a writ on the Union Steamship Company, issued on behalf of Mrs Ada Lee Brown, widow of Dr Lee Brown, of Greystanes Avenue, Vaucluse, claiming £5000 damages for the loss of her husband in the *Greycliffe*. In those days, of course, £5000 was a lot of money. They pointed with awe to the man who earned £10 a week.

After the *Greycliffe*'s remains were salvaged from the harbour, the engines were taken to New Zealand, where they were used in a dairy factory until 1964. They are still in New Zealand and visitors to Auckland can see them in the Museum of Transport and Technology. Grim justice befell the villain of the piece, the *Tahiti*. In 1929 she threw one of her propellers while steaming across the Pacific. The propeller shaft, as it broke loose, tore a hole in the ship's hull and she settled down slowly and gracefully, but fortunately with no loss of life, to her own grave beneath the sea.

3. The Harbour Pool

There were many who saw the *Greycliffe* disaster as an ominous prelude, giving Sydney Ferries Ltd the kiss of death before the opening of the Harbour Bridge in 1932 inflicted the coup de grâce. In December 1927, while the coroner's inquests and the Court of Marine Inquiry were still proceeding, the annual report of the Sydney Harbour Trust, tabled in the State Parliament, showed that 8366 vessels with a total registered tonnage of 16 526 796

entered Port Jackson during the year ended the previous 30 June, representing the highest aggregate tonnage in the port's history. During that year the various ferry services had carried 47 046 000 passengers compared with 42 731 000 in the previous year, an increase of 4 315 000, but even before the bridge opened, the patronage of the inner harbour ferries operated by Sydney Ferries Ltd was dropping. The figures disclosed by that company a year after the loss of the *Greycliffe* showed that the inner harbour ferries had carried 25 322 000 passengers in the preceding year. This did not include Watsons Bay, where patronage was being lost to road travel. The service to Watsons Bay closed down completely 12 months after the bridge opened, although the bridge, surely, could not have had that much effect on water transport between the city and Watsons Bay.

Sydney Ferries struggled on until 1951, when the State Government took over the ailing business, which was on the verge of folding up, acquiring all the company's assets for £25 000 and £1 each for the 15 ferries. The Sydney Harbour Transport Board was formed then and the inner harbour ferries put under the management of the Port Jackson & Manly Steamship Company. But the story is running ahead of itself. We are still in 1928, when the big new *Dee Why* and *Curl Curl* have arrived to add their glamour and prestige to the Manly ferries. Plying the harbour with 'Manly Beach Excursions' painted on their sides in big white letters, they were part of a growing instead of a declining business at a time when the great depression was beginning to infect the nation's prosperity. Manly, of course, had something the inner harbour ferries never had—the exciting trip across The Heads. But much of the boom which came with the *Dee Why* and *Curl Curl* was due to the building of a big sharkproof pool to enclose the harbour beach on West Esplanade with a net, topped by a promenade, between the ferry wharf and what is now the Manly Marineland.

Several other places had similar swimming enclosures, but none were as big and as interesting as the one at the end of a ferry ride to Manly. It was claimed to be the biggest in Australia, if not the world. Covering more than nine acres, it was 300 yards long, with an average width of 75 yards, and its deepest parts varied between 14 and 20 feet. It had, too, shallow parts with a clean sandy bottom, which were ideal for children, and this made the ferry trip and a dip in the pool a real family attraction. As well as those who went in the water, those who merely watched from the promenade had plenty of fun. The pool contained quite a few novelties which provided all the fun of the fair. Floating logs, anchored at the end, rolled and bucked at the slightest touch. To climb on them required a great deal of skill and practice. A circular platform on metal floats tilted from side to side, according to the number of

This was a typical weekend or holiday scene at the Manly Harbour Pool in the days when the Port Jackson & Manly Steamship Company ferries transported thousands of tourists and holiday-makers to the great aquatic playground provided by the harbour pool. On busy holidays the timetable was abandoned and the ferries steamed back and forth as fast as they could load and unload. The ferry at Manly Wharf is either the Dee Why *or* Curl Curl. *Both ferries are now at the bottom of the sea and the harbour pool ended its days in 1974 wrecked by a fierce gale.*

swimmers who climbed aboard. Another floating platform had two steep slippery dips. There were nine water wheels as well as an Olympic-standard springboard. A great thrill for watchers as well as riders was the 50-ft-high slippery dip built on to the walkway across the pool. No other slippery dip was as high as this one. At night the pool was floodlit. At the western end were dressing sheds, a kiosk and tea rooms, at the other end were shops on the wharf, and across the road was The Corso with the many wonders it had to offer in food and other fare. The wharf shops included Burt's Milk Bar, one of the first of these in Australia. When it opened you could get a milk shake for fourpence and soon there were fourpenny milk bars all over Sydney. The one on Manly wharf—still under its original name of Burt's Milk Bar, but not under the original ownership—does not display the price of a milk shake now as prominently as it did when '4d' was painted on these shops in big letters. A milk shake today costs more than a dollar.

Fourpence for a milk shake, threepence for a meat pie, threepenny and penny ice creams, sixpence for a beer at the pub across the road, except, of course, on Sundays. But the pool and all its wonderful attractions for the family was free. These were the days when not everyone had a car. A day out at Manly, even in the depression, was a possibility for many families. By the mid 1930s the

harbour pool had become one of Sydney's most popular summer venues, and with it Manly and the ferries were booming. On summer Sundays the ferries ran every 20 minutes and if the crowds warranted it, extra ferries could be brought on to provide a 15-minute service. On the eastern side of the ferry wharf a marine aquarium had been built on piers. Here, the visitors to Manly could see sharks and fish swimming around. Also on that side of the ferries, the old cargo wharf had been converted into the fun pier which was still there at the time of writing.

The new twins kept out of trouble for nearly 18 months after their arrival until *Curl Curl* spoilt the record by clashing with a passenger-carrying launch, the *Nimrod*, on 28 April 1929, in what was described as a narrowly averted tragedy. The harbour was crowded late that Saturday afternoon with craft of all kinds returning from the Greater Public Schools regatta up the Parramatta River. The *Nimrod* was passing the entrance to Sydney Cove as the *Curl Curl* emerged from Circular Quay on her way to Manly. The master of the *Curl Curl* thought the crowded launch was perilously close and rang down for full astern. It was fortunate that he did so because the ferry was actually going astern when the launch collided with it, despite the efforts of its driver. The impact was not severe, but several passengers on the launch either jumped overboard or were thrown into the harbour. Passengers on the

The Curl Curl *tossing aside the spray from a south-east chop off Dobroyd soon after entering regular service in 1928. (John Darroch)*

Curl Curl threw about 20 lifebelts overboard and the people struggling in the water grabbed them until nearby launches picked them up within a few minutes.

More than a year later, while early morning fog shrouded the harbour on 30 April 1930, the *Curl Curl* and the Sydney Ferries' steamer *Kiandra* tangled in almost the same spot at the entrance to Sydney Cove in what was a most unusual accident. The steel bow of the *Curl Curl* smashed into the wooden hull of the *Kiandra*, cutting through the partition separating the fore cabin of the *Kiandra* from the outer deck. Masters of both ferries realised that if either one withdrew a gaping hole would be left in the starboard side of the *Kiandra*, the water would rush in and the *Kiandra* could sink. So, the captain of the *Curl Curl* kept the bow of his ferry stuck fast in the *Kiandra* and, locked together like this, the two cripples struggled to the P & O Wharf at Circular Quay. There was no panic among the passengers, most of whom did not know the extent of the damage because they could see only a few metres in the fog. Not long after they reached the wharf the firefloat *Pluvius* and the salvage steamer *Petrel* came alongside. A pump was put aboard the *Kiandra* from the *Petrel* and as this began to cope with the intake of water into the *Kiandra*, the *Curl Curl* returned to the Quay and landed its passengers. There, as these commuters disembarked, they saw a large hole in the *Curl Curl*'s bows ohoked with smashed timber from the *Kiandra*. Several plates in the bows were buckled, but otherwise there was surprisingly little damage.

A gang of workmen who arrived to repair the *Kiandra* found a much worse situation. The heavy sponson had been splintered badly when the stem of the *Curl Curl* ripped through it, splintering to matchwood the solid beam which ran around the ship and snapping an outer steel rim which protected the sponson. Deck planking was ripped up and unbroken seats were twisted over splintered ones. The awning which formed the top deck was crumpled and torn back and glass from the windows was splattered everywhere. Some of the 80 passengers who had left Mosman aboard the *Kiandra* at 7 am and were sitting near the point of impact must have feared the ferry was going to sink. Several made a rush and climbed up to the deck of the *Curl Curl*, reckoning that she would have a much better chance of staying afloat. The steel hulls always fared better than the wooden vessels. Damage to the *Curl Curl* amounted to only £150.

It might appear that the story of the Manly ferries is just one collision after another, but there were years between many of the incidents when they carried huge loads of passengers without any mishaps. During those periods, of course, there was no news in what happened, or rather what did not happen. Over five years in the early 1930s very little disturbed the daily routine and the *Dee Why* and *Curl Curl* churned their way up and down the harbour with their sister ships of the fleet. In November 1931, the *Dee Why* was involved in a clash with Sydney Ferries' *Kirrule* off Kirribilli Point which became the subject of a Court of Marine Inquiry. Captain Harold Liley, a rather colourful old skipper in charge of the *Dee Why* for many years, was in trouble before the inquiry, where the evidence seemed to be against him. Captain Liley, it appeared, had got on the wrong side of Fort Denison and put himself on the wrong side of the court when he hit the *Kirrule*.

Then, as now, ferries en route to Manly went down the harbour on the southern side of Fort Denison and the Bradleys Head marker light. Coming up to the city, they passed Bradleys close in and were on the northern side of Fort Denison. Captain N. Nutt, of the *Kirrule*, accused the *Dee Why* of trying to force a passage against him, with the *Dee Why* in a position where it should not normally be. He said he ported his helm and had the *Kirrule*'s engines going astern for about 10 seconds before the collision occurred. Captain Liley told the court that the *Dee Why*, after leaving Circular Quay for Manly, rounded Bennelong Point fairly wide and straightened up on Fort Denison. By that time the *Kirrule*'s stem would have been level with the *Dee Why*'s midships. Captain Liley said it was usual to go on the southern side of Fort Denison, but he decided to go on the northern side to allow the *Kirrule* plenty of room. On the southern side he would have had to cross the *Kirrule*'s bow. When he found the *Kirrule* converging on the *Dee Why* he threw his helm hard to port to lessen the impact and make it a glancing blow. He also rang down for more speed.

The court found that the master of the *Dee Why* knew he was endangering the *Kirrule* and was to blame for the collision. Captain Liley was censured and the court ordered suspension of his master's certificate for two months.

The harbour pool at Manly had its attraction for ferries as well as swimmers. In February 1932, the *Curl Curl* ploughed through the fence. She did not stop quickly enough when berthing at the wharf just before 8 am on 24 February. There was not a great deal of damage, however. The *Curl Curl* resumed running after a diver cleared a rope which had curled itself around a propeller and the hole in the pool fence was repaired in time for the weekend. Port Jackson's engineer-superintendent, Mr McMillan, denied that the mishap had been caused either by engine failure or a lack of room between the steamer's berth and the pool, as some had predicted when the pool was being built. He said the ferry's failure to stop was due solely to the inadvertent closing of the emergency throttle valve, shutting off steam from the engines when they were required to go astern to check the vessel's way. Such an accident, he emphasised, was not likely to occur again. To the critics who maintained that the pool was too close to the ferry berth, Mr McMillan pointed out that the distance between the berth and the boardwalk across the front of the pool was much greater than the corresponding distance between the berth and the footpath at Circular Quay.

It was more than four years before the *Curl Curl* made the news again. In dense fog on the morning of 31 March 1936, she lost her bearings and ran on to a reef at Bradleys Head, where she was held fast on the rocks for more than seven hours. The 50 or so passengers were taken off by a passing launch nearly an hour after the ferry grounded. This was a remarkable feature of the accident. Nobody knew the *Curl Curl* was there all that time. Although other ferries passed within 100 metres, the fog was so dense that the *Curl Curl* was hidden. No notice was taken of the continuous siren blasts because every other vessel was advertising its presence similarly in the fog. The launch which found *Curl Curl* while passing was the first to know what had happened to make this big vessel just disappear.

The *Curl Curl* had left Circular Quay for Manly at 7.10 am which explains the small number of passengers. Had she been going the other way to town she would have been carrying a fairly full load. She ran into the heavy fog blanket soon after leaving the Quay, groping her way down harbour with no modern aid like radar to alleviate the blindness of thick fog. Captain V. Nixon gauged the turn around Bradleys Head nicely, but apparently turned just too far and the vessel went aground instead of continuing on towards The Heads. There was no immediate danger and no untoward excitement among the passengers, but disablement of the *Curl Curl* in addition to the trouble caused by the fog disrupted the Manly service and thousands of people were late for work.

Three tugs, straining for 20 minutes, were needed to drag the *Curl Curl* off shortly after 2 pm and she was docked for repairs. One of the propeller blades was broken, the for'ard rudder was smashed and several hull plates were dented and damaged. As there was no spare ferry available at the time, the summer timetable was discontinued, cutting out several peak-hour trips until *Curl Curl* came back more than a week later. Modern commuters are quite used to cancelled trips because of accidents, breakdowns, frequent strikes at the Balmain works depot and regular four-hour, stop-work union meetings, but in the Port Jackson company days, keeping up the service was almost like that other long departed Post Office concern about getting the mail through. The Port Jackson & Manly Steamship Company was fastidious about its ferries running on time and if any services had to be cancelled, which rarely ever happened, it was a matter for great concern.

Fog is not usually regarded as a summertime hazard on the harbour, but it was responsible for putting the *Dee Why* aground on Christmas night, 1946, in Obelisk Bay, between Middle Head and Georges Head. Obelisk Bay gets its name from the two white obelisks, one on the point and the other behind the beach, which, lined up, were early navigation markers for ships coming in through The Heads to clear the shallow area around South Reef, where the waves break off shore from the Hornby Lighthouse on inner South Head.

The ferry left Manly at 9.45 on Christmas night with about 700 passengers, including many tired children who had been up at dawn to see what Santa had brought and then went with mums and dads to spend Christmas Day with grandparents. The weather was fine and clear, no wind stirring the smooth darkness of the water as they left Manly, homeward bound, and the usual course was set to take the ship clear of Middle Head. Halfway across The Heads a heavy fog bank loomed up unexpectedly, especially at that time of the year, and the captain pulled back on the engine room telegraph to reduce speed to 'slow ahead'. They proceeded slowly, sounding the regulation fog signals on the ship's whistle. A deckhand was put up in the bow as lookout, another watched from the port wing of the bridge, and the skipper took the starboard side, standing by the engine room telegraph. Minutes later, land appeared suddenly through the fog haze and although the captain rang down immediately for 'full astern', the *Dee Why* crashed aground on the rocks, sliding along the bottom with a shuddering shock.

Dee Why was stuck fast. Although passengers did not know it at the time, she was resting in about 45 centimetres of water on the shore while the stern floated in more than 18 metres. Noise of the crash brought sailors from the nearby Balmoral Navy depot, who took ropes ashore from the ferry and tied them to rocks. Nobody was hurt on board the *Dee Why*, but some women passengers were screaming their alarm, caused no doubt by a senseless fellow who ran around yelling 'abandon ship'. A man and four youths decided to do so, climbing ashore hand-over-hand on one of the ropes. Everyone else, however, waited calmly to be rescued as soon as they saw there was no cause for alarm, although they all wore life-jackets. A crowd gathered around the piano on the upper deck for community singing to pass the time while they waited to be taken off the stranded vessel. As the fog began to clear, many were amazed that the *Dee Why* had gone so far off course and that no apparent serious damage had been caused when she ran on the ledge at the bottom of the rocky cliff.

The Dee Why *berthing at Circular Quay in 1929. (John Darroch)*

Passengers crowded on to the open decks at the stern, cheering the water police and occupants of other small boats who came to see what was happening. Special cheers were given each time the bulbs of news cameras flashed. Rescue was to be some time away. The ferry had gone aground at 10.05 pm. Because of what had happened in the fog, the Manly service was suspended until the fog cleared, by which time it was getting rather late. Two fire-fighting tugs, *Hydra* and *Pluvius*, were sent out from the Maritime Services Board's upper harbour Goat Island depot at 11.40 pm and reached the *Dee Why* about 12.10 am, joining the naval tug *Wattle*.

Meanwhile, the *South Steyne* had arrived on the scene and was taking aboard people who were transferred by naval launches. About 40 of these people arrived at Circular Quay after 1.20 am, complaining loudly about the delay in taking them off the stranded ferry. They didn't know how lucky they were. The *South Steyne* had been tied up at the depot. A few men were rushed over there to raise steam, which took more than an hour, before the big vessel could be moved from her berth and taken to Circular Quay to ship a skeleton crew for the rescue trip. Then, when she reached the *Dee Why*, it was deemed unwise to take her in too close because of her size. The *Bellubera* arrived at 12.45 am and tied up alongside, enabling gangways to be placed between the two vessels to transfer the passengers. Although the ferry company tried to arrange special transport to get these people home when the *Bellubera* landed them at Circular Quay about 2 am, the Public Transport Department said this would be impossible. The travellers would have to get home the best way they could. Many of them rushed 12 taxis waiting outside the wharf, squabbling for possession. A group pleaded with police in a patrol wagon to take them home. Some, going to Bankstown, had to wait until 4.10 am for a train, trying to placate worn-out children, who had been up since 4 am the previous day with Santa Claus. Two Bondi trams which arrived and would normally have departed almost empty were rushed. So were the taxis which came in to take advantage of the situation.

One of the tugs put a tow line aboard the *Dee Why* at 1.45 am, but had no chance of moving her. She had been aground nearly four hours when the combined efforts of the three tugs dragged her clear and refloated her. Fortunately, the *Dee Why* was not holed, but she was towed to dry dock, where an inspection showed that the for'ard rudder had been torn off, the propeller and some of the hull plates were damaged and part of the keel was buckled. The repair bill was £6500, which was quite a lot considering that the *Dee Why* then was valued at only £37 000.

A Court of Marine Inquiry pondered several questions as to why the ferry should have stranded north of Georges Head, nearly half a mile from where she should have been on her usual course. In normal weather, Manly ferry helmsmen steered by the fixed lights marking the main harbour channel, but in fog and poor visibility they used a compass course. To see for themselves, members of the court did a night trip on the bridge of the *Dee Why* and what they found was rather interesting. It was revealed that the compass, instead of being graduated around its edge from 0 to 360 degrees, as would have been expected, had marked on it only the main points, which, the court pointed out, was totally unsuitable for precision work in narrow harbour channels.

The *Dee Why* was to run aground once more, this time

on Kirribilli Point after a collision with the tug *Himma* midway between Kirribilli Point and Fort Denison. *Dee Why*, on an early morning trip from Manly with about 225 passengers, was preparing to turn into Circular Quay when the *Himma*, owned by J. Fenwick & Company and commanded by Captain John Boothby, came down the harbour. Hearing sirens blowing, passengers looked up and seeing that a collision was inevitable, ran from the port side, where the impact would be. There was a lurch as the two vessels collided. People were thrown from their seats and the chief engineer was hurled across the engine room. Another crash followed seconds later as the ferry ground ashore on the rocks at Kirribilli, smashing the for'ard rudder and propeller. Port side plates and a large part of the sponson had been damaged in the collision. Water police came alongside and took the passengers off in their launches, helped by launches from the hire fleet of Stannard Brothers. The *Himma*, which had suffered only slight damage, joined with three other tugs to refloat the *Dee Why* soon after 8 am and tow her to Cockatoo Dock for repairs.

Captain Keith Rosser, master of the *Dee Why* for some years, was a deckhand the day the ferry was involved in the incident. He recalls:

I don't think the skipper was on the bridge of the tug just before we hit. I saw a chap running up the bridge ladder with a pipe in his mouth. In those days, when a tug came down from Balmain the skipper would often be down below. They used to wait for their ships near the dol-

phins at Kirribilli and that is where the *Himma* was going. She came down the harbour heading east and all of a sudden she turned over towards the dolphin and went straight into the port side of the *Dee Why*. Captain Liley was pulling away, but he pulled so far away that he had nowhere left to go and the *Dee Why*, going at full speed, hit the rocks with an awful crash.

When the tug first hit I came flying out of the mess room along the port side and saw the tug slew around so that its stern hit the ferry again right amidships. The impact blew out every rivet on deck level. The ladies' toilet was at the end hit in the collision and all of a sudden I became aware of screams coming from there. A woman who travelled on that trip every morning used to go into the toilet with a flask of Remy Martin brandy. It was her all right. We had to chop through the door to get her out.

The collision ripped off a lot of the *Dee Why*'s sponson. This was rebuilt beautifully at Cockatoo Dock, but it was ripped off again in the same place on the port side not long after when she hit the north-west corner of No. 3 wharf at the Quay on her last trip one night. That was put down to an over-zealous engineer. The old Chadburn telegraph was in the 'stop' position on the bridge, but after a bit of wear, the indicator in the engine room was pointing to 'dead slow' ahead. Apparently the engineer had kept it slow ahead and when the skipper realised he was approaching the wharf too fast he reversed, which was a deadly thing to do. Making a port side wharf, putting her hard astern like that, the thrust of the propellers pulled her into the wharf. The propellers had starboard thrust ahead and when the skipper put her full astern he got himself into a worse position because the port thrust on the propellers then pushed him into the wharf. It happened again to the *Dee Why* at Manly with the same master. He hit the southeast corner of the wharf with a crunch which drove the hawse pipe through the deck.

Keith Rosser had much affection for the *Dee Why*. She was a great ship when, aged 14, he started work with the Port Jackson & Manly Steamship Company in 1949 as a yard boy. Then, when he graduated to deck boy, he was assigned to the *Dee Why* with 'Scupper' Smith as master. He recalls:

I felt like running away. Some of the masters in those days were pretty tough. No matter what the weather was like it was: 'Boy, get up and clean the scuppers.' I cleaned them out with the stick from an old distress rocket. Soot from the funnels made those boats very dirty. It would blow under the life-rafts every day and when rough weather came or it rained, soot would wash into the scuppers and choke them up. Still, she was a good ship.

At the age of 23, Keith Rosser got his master's certificate—the youngest Port Jackson skipper in 100 years—and his first ship was the *Dee Why*. He spent most of his time with her until she went out of service in 1968. In recent years he switched to hydrofoils, being attached much of the time to the hydrofoil *Dee Why*. You might think Captain Rosser would have lived at Dee Why, but his home is at Belrose with his wife, Jeanette, whom he met when she travelled to work in the city on his ferry. Said Captain Rosser:

They were good times. The *Dee Why* and the other Port Jackson ferries were painted and polished, the stairway balustrades varnished and the decks scrubbed. In the engine rooms every bit of brass shined. You don't see that today.

4. Davy Jones's Locker

For more than 10 years the two big sisters were the proud leaders of Sydney Harbour's ferry world. Nothing was as big, as fast and as stately as the *Dee Why* and *Curl Curl*, although when viewed later alongside the really beautiful *South Steyne* they were almost the two ugly sisters. Their straight flush decks had none of the *Steyne*'s lovely flair, rising gracefully from amidships to each end, their stems

were too straight and their tall funnels seemed rather thin when you looked comparatively at the proportions of the beautifully designed *South Steyne*. But they were built for a purpose. At £73 000 each—just about the price of a good-sized pleasure boat today—they were 'cheapies', ordered at a time when shipbuilding costs in Australia forced the Port Jackson Company to look elsewhere than its old friends at Mort's Dock who had built every Manly ferry since the early part of the century. But they offered several new features designed to attract passengers. They were the first Manly ferries with glassed-in upper decks and reversible padded seats; they were fast and they looked impressive against the older ships which had only one long funnel.

During their years on the harbour—33 for *Curl Curl* and 40 for *Dee Why*—they gave good and reliable service, but neither lasted as long as the older ships built by Mort's in Sydney. The 1913 *Barrenjoey* remained part of the regular service as the *North Head* years after both *Dee Why* and *Curl Curl* had been laid to rest. Still, the two sister ships were not much trouble and they were good sea boats.

The Curl Curl *photographed by John Darroch, on the crest of a wave crossing The Heads.*

The *Curl Curl* was battered several times by big seas which caused damage and injured some passengers. On Tuesday night, 13 October 1942, seas crashed over her during a trip from Manly to the city, buckling the steel gangway doors and smashing windows on the port side. The water surged through the lower deck of the ferry, wrenching seats from their fittings and breaking doors on the starboard side as it tried to get out. Some passengers who had been sitting on the outer deck ran inside when they saw the big wave begin to tower over the ship's side. Before they could reach the stairs to the upper deck, a solid mass of water struck the port side of the *Curl Curl* and pushed its way through the window glass. Passengers inside on the lower deck were swept off their feet and had their clothing saturated, although nobody was injured. Fortunately, the *Curl Curl* was not carrying many people on that trip and most of those aboard were riding on the upper deck, which was showered with spray but suffered no damage.

'It was the biggest wave I have seen during my 20 years' experience,' Skipper G.R. Clark said later at the Kurraba Point works depot, where the *Curl Curl* was taken after landing its passengers at Circular Quay. The ferry service was suspended for the night after what had happened. Deck boy M. Hancock, who was on the bridge at the time, told the *Daily Telegraph*:

I was thrown against the chap at the wheel, knocking him away from it for the moment. I had to hold up the furniture for a while. I think three big waves hit us. Oil cans splashed over on the top deck and water poured into the stokehold.

Said engineer F. Young:

I thought it was a bomb exploding, glass and water showered into the engine room all over us. All the stuff was thrown out of the locker. Another member of the crew said he picked up a woman he found lying in water in the foc'sl.

A passenger, Mr J. Mandelson, of Sydenham Road, Brookvale, said:

The wave that hit us was a beauty. The ferry heeled over and spray shot over the top deck. Water swept over the lower deck, wetting passengers to the waist. It was a wonder nobody was cut by the glass flying from the broken windows. Two men and a girl sitting outside were almost swept from their seats and had to be helped inside. Most passengers were thrown off balance, but they were very good. Only one girl became slightly hysterical.

Two passengers in the *Curl Curl* were cut by flying glass in a similar incident during rough weather on 18 February 1956. Again, fortunately, she was carrying a light loading on the 9 am trip from Sydney. Crossing The Heads, the *Curl Curl* shipped a big sea which stove in eleven windows and two double sliding doors. Two passengers were cut by broken glass. The ferry company received a claim from a Mr and Mrs Wheatley for compensation for injuries and damage to clothing.

On the same day, about an hour later, the *North Head* received a battering crossing The Heads. A Mr Harris, of Ryde, was standing on a seat when the ferry rolled in a big sea and, in an effort to prevent himself from falling, he put his arm through a window. He received ambulance treatment after landing at Manly Wharf.

Manly wharf needed ambulance treatment after the *Curl Curl* crashed into it on the night of 13 February 1953. Damage to the ferry and the wharf was quite extensive, especially the part which housed the offices of the Manly and Warringah Tourist Bureau on a projection over the water. The tourist bureau offices were almost demolished. As the bows of the ferry sheared off half the building, chairs, desks, a typewriter, a records' cabinet, boxes and thousands of booklets and leaflets fell into the harbour, which was littered with floating wreckage. Woodwork was ripped off in pieces as big as four and a half metres by three metres and blocks of windows four and a half metres high were shattered. What remained of the tourist bureau was a shambles of splintered wood and overturned furniture. None of the 200 people aboard the *Curl Curl* was injured, but the bow of the *Curl Curl* was pushed in and several large holes appeared nearby. Damage to the ferry was estimated at several thousand pounds. Chairman of the tourist bureau, Manly alderman L. A. Ellison, placed damage to the bureau offices at more than £1000, not including the wrecked wharf. 'It is a wonder someone was not killed,' he commented. A Court of Marine Inquiry subsequently found that the ferry's engineer was to blame.

Two engineers died on duty when about to take the *Dee Why* out from Manly wharf on morning peak-hour runs. The first was Don Campbell, who had been an engineer in the *Dee Why* for some years. Eric Gale remembers the incident:

The boss rang me at home at Mosman one morning and said 'Jump in a car and get over to Manly as quick as you possibly can. Don Campbell has dropped dead and the *Dee Why* is held up at the wharf.' I raced over to Manly and there was the *Dee Why* still tied up, a lot of people on the wharf and no engineer. I went aboard and took the ferry up to town, where another engineer was waiting to take over. Don's death was a great shock. He had a friend who went to town on that trip every morning and they were sitting on one of the ferry seats yarning while they were waiting to leave. When it came time for departure, Don got up, went down to the engine room and stood by his engines ready to take the ship out from the wharf. The engine room telegraph clanged 'stand by' and then 'slow ahead' and just as Don reached up to turn the wheel he let out a moan and fell on the floor. His mate ran up the stairs and told the boys to keep the lines on the ship. The passengers had to go ashore and take the next boat up to town.

The other victim was Joshua Tight, brother of Sidney

Tight, who received fatal burns and injuries in the *Bellubera* fire in November 1936. By a strange coincidence, both brothers were to meet their death in the engine rooms of Manly ferries. Sid was a greaser, and Joshua an engineer who had been with the *Dee Why* for some time. Like Don Campbell, he was waiting to take the *Dee Why* out of Manly for the first trip on the morning of 9 November 1953, and he died almost 17 years to the day after his brother Sid.

Captain Keith Rosser who was a deck boy on the *Dee Why* that morning recalls:

> Joshua Tight was sitting down in the engine room having a cup of tea with the greaser. About 10 minutes before departure time he stood up and screamed out 'Get an ambulance'. Then he crashed down on his back on the engine room plates. He had hit his head as he fell. He was a very big man and you can imagine how hard it would be to get him up the iron ladder which was the only way out of the engine room. He was dead, of course, when the ambulance men came and we had to remove the steel grates of the deck-level floor around the engines so that they could pull him up on a cane stretcher.

In July 1951, two Manly ferries—*Balgowlah* and *Dee Why*—fulfilled the unusual role of helping the North Shore Gas Company to produce gas for more than 60 000 homes on Sydney's North Shore. Supply of gas to these homes became very precarious when one of the gas company's big boilers broke down and had to be taken out of the production process. With a mid-winter gas shortage imminent, somebody had the bright idea of using the boilers of a Manly ferry to keep up the steam required for the gas plant. The *Dee Why* was taken to the gas works and moored at the gas company's wharf in Oyster Bay, near Waverton, where her boilers supplied enough steam to keep the gas producing process going and maintain full gas pressure to customers. After a few days the *Dee Why* had to return to the ferry service, but the *Balgowlah* was substituted to supply steam until the gas boiler could be repaired.

At that stage, in 1951, the *Dee Why* and *Curl Curl* were doing most of the work in the Manly fleet. In the year ended 30 June 1951, the *Curl Curl* did 6810 trips and the *Dee Why* 6658, a total of 13 468 between them. Considering that the four other ships—*South Steyne* (4128), *Baragoola* (4828), *Balgowlah* (19) and *Bellubera* (5932)—made a total of 14 907 trips in the year, the tall-funnel twins did nearly as much work between them as the four others. The figures show the amazing distances covered by these ships. The *Balgowlah* did only 19 trips before she was taken out of service in February 1951, so,

disregarding this, the six other ferries covered nearly 200 000 miles in the 12 months carrying people to and from Manly—28 356 trips and 198 492 miles to be more precise. Of this, the *Dee Why* and *Curl Curl* did 94 276 miles between them.

The romantic days of the big steamers were being numbered fast, however. They were becoming costly to operate and maintain and already three of the older steamships—*Bellubera* (1910) and *Barrenjoey* (1913)—had been converted to diesel-electric propulsion.

Within 10 years, by 1960, the diesel-electric *Bellubera* and the *Barrenjoey*—converted similarly and renamed *North Head*—had displaced the *Dee Why* and *Curl Curl* as principal carriers. In that year *Bellubera* topped the list with 8392 trips and *North Head* made 7158, a total of 15 550 trips or 108 850 miles between them, while *Dee Why* (2734 trips) and *Curl Curl* (5077) covered just 54 677 miles in 7811 trips. *South Steyne* made 2683 trips on her regular run, but in that year she did 33 ocean cruises between Sydney and Broken Bay which occupied her on more than half the Sundays in the year.

An aerial photograph taken for the Port Jackson & Manly Steamship Company, shows the Bellubera, *ploughing into a south-easterly swell.*

The pattern became even more evident in the following year when *Baragoola*, added to the diesel-electric fleet, ran 7452 trips out of a total of 26 208. The three converted vessels—*Baragoola* (7452 trips), *North Head* (7093) and *Bellubera* (5849)—made 20 394 trips compared with 5814 by the *South Steyne* and *Dee Why*. *Curl Curl* was no longer in service and *Dee Why* was on borrowed time. The three diesel-electric boats were doing the work much more cheaply than the three big steamers, which were burning costly bunker fuel oil.

How that arose is rather ironic, especially when the *Dee Why* had been so helpful to the North Shore Gas Company. It was not generally known that the Manly steamers burned coal tar in their boilers for many years. At first it was cheap fuel. Before selling the coal tar to the Port Jackson & Manly Steamship Company, the Australian Gas Light Company used to have the coal tar taken out to sea and dumped, like a lot of other things disposed of by polluting the sea and littering the sea bed. The ferry

The hydrofoil Fairlight. *(John Allcot)*

Bellubera *at Circular Quay not long before being retired in 1972. (John Darroch)*

Dee Why *going astern at Circular Quay in 1958. (John Darroch)*

The Curl Curl *stripped of all her former glory, being towed on her last trip down the harbour on the morning of 13 August 1968. She was scuttled 18 miles south-east of Sydney Heads. (John Darroch)*

company found that with a simple alteration of the burners into the boilers, coal tar could be burned like kerosene in a primus stove. The gas company was glad to sell it for twopence a gallon, saving the cost and the trouble of dumping it at sea. But it was not long before others saw the potential of coal tar as boiler fuel. All the hospitals wanted it for their boilers. Soon it was dearer than twopence a gallon and became nearly as dear as bunker fuel, to which *Dee Why*, *Curl Curl* and *South Steyne* reverted.

The bunker oil cost a little more, but it was cleaner and far less trouble. Former traffic manager George Marshall recalls:

> When we burned coal tar we had to get it delivered in steam-heated punts. Then we had to hold it in steam-heated storage tanks, which meant keeping donkey-boiler operators in the yards. That might have been all right when the coal tar was available cheaply, but when it was costing as much as the bunker oil it was just not worth it. The steam ferries were costing too much to operate and so they were withdrawn from service years before the motor vessels for that reason—no other.

Curl Curl was withdrawn from service in 1960 just before the *Baragoola* returned to work with diesel-electric power instead of steam. A couple of years later she was sold to Stride's, Balmain shipbreakers, and, stripped of anything with commercial value, she rusted away as a hulk until, on 13 August 1969, she was towed out and scuttled south-east of The Heads. A few weeks previously, Keith Rosser took his beloved *Dee Why* on her last trip up the harbour and it was not long before she, too, became a hulk in Stride's wrecking yards.

As with most twins of anything, there were interesting things about these two ships. They were identical dimension hulls, with identical engines built in Glasgow by the same maker, David and William Henderson & Company Ltd, and each had four single-ended, Scotch-type boilers with coal and oil burning equipment arranged in pairs, back to back in two stoke-holds, exhausting through both funnels. They were fast ships, capable of covering the seven nautical miles of their route in 22 minutes at a speed better than 18 knots, which has not been bettered in the years since, even by the *South Steyne*, despite her claim of being the world's biggest and fastest ferry, or the three $10–million vessels of recent years, the *Freshwater*, *Queenscliff* and *Narrabeen*.

Built for a speed of 17 knots, at their trials *Dee Why* did 17.65 knots and *Curl Curl* 17.75 knots. Their high speeds eventually contributed to their demise because apart from the cost of the fuel they burned, the two stokeholds required two firemen whereas the *South Steyne* needed only one fireman for her one stokehold, where the four boilers, arranged in pairs facing each other, exhausted through one funnel. The other funnel was a dummy.

So it was that *Curl Curl* was taken out of service on 25 October 1960, and laid up at the Kurraba Point depot while the company decided what was to be done with her. The problem solved itself when *Curl Curl* began popping rivets and taking water through the empty rivet hole and in July 1963, she was sold to Stride's, where she remained until they towed her out that August day and sent her down to Davy Jones's Locker in what had been regarded as the graveyard of ships outside The Heads. *Dee Why* plodded the harbour for a few more years, mainly as a relief boat before she went to the breakers. The Warringah Mall

Merchants' Association bought her bridge and wheel-house and used it for a children's playground at the Brookvale shopping centre for some years.

The *Curl Curl* departed fairly quietly, but much more publicity surrounded *Dee Why*'s send-off when she was scuttled out from Long Reef, North of Manly, on 25 May 1976. Her burial had the added interest that she would be the beginning of the State Fisheries Department's first offshore artificial reef to attract fish and provide shelter for them on a sandy bottom not previously abundant with marine life. In later years she was joined by other hulks and today offshore fishermen who can find this reef of ships can often find plentiful fish.

In the week *Dee Why* was taken to her funeral, work-mates farewelled one of her old crew, Alf Whybrow, who retired after 51 years with the ferries. *Barrenjoey* was his favourite ship and they presented Alf with a painting of her. But he loved the *Dee Why*, too, and the day before she was towed down to The Heads for the last time Alf went around to Balmain to say goodbye. 'It's only a bit of iron now,' Alf said sadly. 'But you could write a book about it.' Sitting on the wharf alongside the once queen of the harbour, his thoughts went back to 1925, when as a 14-year-old change boy he earned approximately £1 3s 6d a week giving passengers change for tickets. Later he became a deck boy on the ferries and eventually a deck-hand. He said:

> The *Dee Why* as a coal burner was a virtual sweat box for the crew. But we had lovely times together. They were hard times, but very good. It seems to be a different kind of atmosphere today. Young fellows want only speed, speed, speed. We had plenty of time to go nowhere.

Mention of speed, of course, brought up the subject of hydrofoils, which by then were offering a 35-mph, 15-minute trip to Manly compared with the half-hour ferry ride. 'Hydrofoils?' Alf snorted. 'Don't mention them to me. Hydrofoils and I have never seen eye to eye.'

Two tugs dragged *Dee Why* out of her condemned cell in Rozelle Bay around dawn on 25 May. They cleared Glebe Island bridge and were moving down the harbour by 6 am, passing Bradleys Head for the last time just before the sunrise at 6.47 am. It was almost like a solemn funeral procession. The *Baragoola* and a hydrofoil moved closer as they passed to pay last respects. About 7.15 am at The Heads the tug *Fern Bay* took over the tow and, with *Dee Why* nodding gently behind, moved out into the golden light of a wintry morning, followed by a growing entourage of small spectator craft. A stiff south-west breeze was cutting up a fair chop on the sea when they opened *Dee Why*'s sea cocks out from Long Reef after 9.15 am and she filled with water slowly and quietly for nearly three-quarters of an hour. Then, suddenly, her bow dived, up from the water rose her stern and the *Dee Why* slid with a gurgle and a final shower of spray to her resting place at latitude 33°41'S longitude 151°20'E, about two and a half miles north-east of Long Reef. Within minutes, divers went down to check that the hulk had settled properly and reported that she was on an even keel in 45 metres of water. Two weeks later another inspection by divers found that the ferry was 51 metres down, six metres deeper than reported originally. But they warned inexperienced divers against going down to see for themselves because of the depth and the strong currents, which they said made movement dangerous.

Dee Why *slides beneath the swell two and a half miles off Long Reef on 25 May 1976* . (Manly Daily)

PART IV
THE GREATEST OF THEM ALL

1. A New Star is Born

This stage of the story brings in two characters through whom the Port Jackson & Manly Steamship Company reached its greatest fame in its brightest era—Walter Leslie Dendy, general manager from 1925 to 1944 and managing director until his death in 1948, and the greatest ferry of all, Dendy's creation, the magnificent SS *South Steyne*. W. L. Dendy was a man of great vision and foresight. Born in 1876, he had been with the Manly ferries for many years when he became general manager in 1925. There was not much he did not know about ferries even then. He had grown up with them and they were to grow up with him. Mosman resident and lifelong ferry enthusiast Brian Verey, who lived near Walter Dendy in the days of Dendy's eminence, remembers W.L.D, as he called him, as a fatherly figure and a very great friend. It is not hard to agree that Dendy built the Port Jackson & Manly Steamship Company to its peak because in those days W. L. Dendy was the Port Jackson & Manly Steam-

ship Company. His was the drive behind the building of the biggest ferries which brought not only prestige but the extra business the company wanted in the years after the opening of the Harbour Bridge had ruined the massive inner harbour operations of Sydney Ferries Ltd.

So successful were the big two-funnel ships *Dee Why* and *Curl Curl* in the early 1930s that Dendy envisaged a design even bigger. This was to be the *South Steyne*, a ship more like an ocean liner than a harbour ferry boat, hailed when she arrived in Sydney from her Scottish builders in 1938 as the biggest and fastest ferry boat in the world. Allen Conwell, an employee of the Port Jackson company in Dendy's day, worked with the ferries for more than 50 years, including service with the State Government control of the service in later years. According to him, Dendy was convinced just before World War II that the motor car was going to make huge inroads into the ferry business on Sydney Harbour and he saw the future in

The greatest of them all! The South Steyne, *flying the Port Jackson Company flag, inside the Hawkesbury River on one of her ocean cruises to Broken Bay. (Port Jackson and Manly Steamship Co Ltd)*

Pittwater and the Hawkesbury River. Encouraged, no doubt, by the business the Manly harbour pool had brought the ferries, he saw the Hawkesbury estuary with tourist attractions as the basis of another ferry service in that area. With this in mind, in 1942 he had the Port Jackson & Manly Steamship Company buy out the Palm Beach ferries and associated undertakings of the Goddard family, including, in addition to the ferry services between Palm Beach, Patonga, The Basin, Mackerel Beach and Scotland Island, the Palm Beach general store and its liquor licence.

Dendy also bought out the Hawkesbury River ferries operated by Windybanks between Brooklyn and Patonga, he acquired the ice works at Narrabeen and built another ice works at Newport on land the company had owned for many years. Goddard's store and boatshed at Palm Beach sold practically everything—bread, meat, groceries, ice, even liquor. Dendy bought another store at Newport.

In November 1943, the Sydney *Daily Mirror* published a story which told about some of Dendy's plans for turning the Broken Bay-Hawkesbury River estuary into a tourist wonderland. It said:

Extensive post-war plans to turn a portion of Palm Beach, society's summer playground, into a resort for picnickers and tourists have been laid by the Port Jackson & Manly Steamship Company. The plans envisage a transformation of the Pittwater side of 'The Beach' into a pleasure ground. Some of Sydney's most palatial homes, whose rentals in holiday periods go as high as 20 or 30 guineas a week, overlook this section. The scheme covers establishment of a ground for picnickers at Jerusalem Bay, with the sanction of Kuringgai Chase Trust, and a picnic ground and a sharkproof swimming pool at Little Mackerel Beach, opposite Palm Beach.

Specially built pleasure craft carrying 600 people and able to ferry cars would operate between Newport, Palm Beach, Brooklyn and Bobbin Head. Some time ago, the only deep water frontage at Newport, Goddard's boatshed and store at Palm Beach and 57 acres of land at Little Mackerel Beach, were purchased. The distance from Newport to Brooklyn along the Hawkesbury River via Bobbin Head is 35 miles.

Motorists would drive to Newport and then be conveyed with their cars by ferry to points along the river and Cowan Creek, skirting Lion Island and passing through Broken Bay. They would disembark at Bobbin Head or Brooklyn and then drive back to Sydney. The company intends to negotiate with the Transport Board for the provision of special buses from Wynyard to connect with steamers from Newport and other buses to go from Bobbin Head to Wynyard.

Those 'palatial homes' at Palm Beach, available for 20 to 30 guineas a week in 1943, were costing up to $1000 a week 40 years later, by which time Dendy's plan could have been making a fortune. It was not to be, though. With the end of the war and the lifting of petrol rationing, what Dendy had forecast proved to be correct. During the war, when petrol rationing kept pleasure cars off the roads, the Manly ferries were carrying passengers by the million, but with petrol available freely again the motor car was certainly making inroads into the ferry business on the harbour, as Dendy had predicted. Things began to go badly in Sydney and the Port Jackson & Manly Steamship Company had to stop spending money on plans for expansion, although perhaps Dendy was right. If the company had gone ahead with its scheme it might never have fallen on the bad times which finally brought it to its knees after more than a century of growth.

Dendy received considerable recognition here and in the United Kingdom for the part he played in planning the *South Steyne* and in building the ferry service the way he did. In an article in *The Log*, journal of the Nautical Association of Australia, in August 1983, A. M. Prescott and R. K. Willson state:

The credits given to *South Steyne* are, of course, not without justification. Her remarkably beautiful lines are a tribute to her designers, Walter Leslie Dendy, general manager of the Port Jackson company from 1925 to 1948, and John Ashcroft, chief draughtsman for the builders, Henry Robb Ltd of Leith, Scotland.

But before we build the *South Steyne* it is worth knowing a little more about the man behind all this. I never knew W.L. Dendy, but I was always aware of him through the notices on the wharves which said: 'Passengers are warned against disembarking before the steamer is properly moored and the gangways in position. W. L. Dendy, General Manager.' Those notices were there until recent years, long after the steamers had given way to motor vessels. An interesting picture of Dendy is given by Brian Verey, with whom I was associated for some time in the South Steyne Steamship Preservation Society. Here is W.L. Dendy as Brian knew him:

In 1937, as a boy of eight, I would ride my scooter along Spruson Street, Neutral Bay, with my cobber, Jim Webster, who lived opposite me. Just up the road we would pass a garage where a tall stately gentleman would often be washing his car, a handsome six-cylinder 1934 Hillman saloon. His name was Walter Leslie Dendy. One morning he called out 'Would you boys like to help me wash my car?' Our 'yes' began an association which lasted until W.L.D., as he was

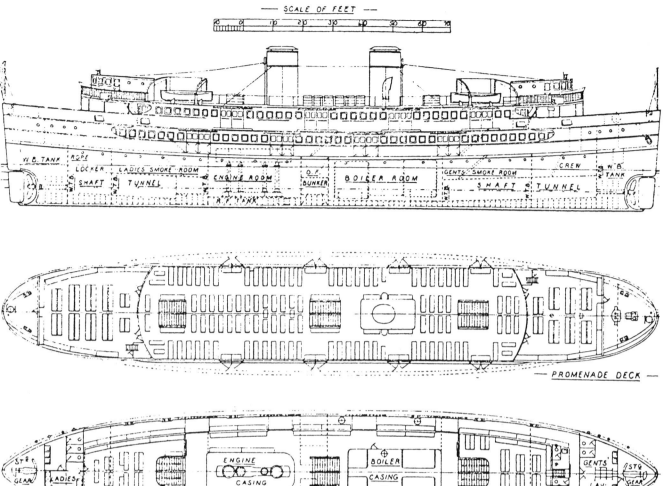

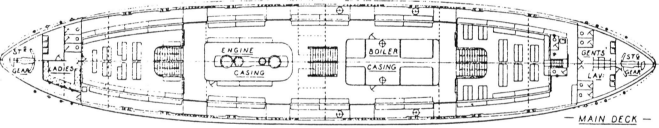

DOUBLE-ENDED PASSENGER FERRY STEAMER
"SOUTH STEYNE"

Double-ended passenger ferry steamer South Steyne.

known affectionately around the Sydney waterfront, died on 3 July 1948.

Mr Dendy was born in South Australia, the second youngest son in a family of three boys and, I think, two girls. His father was Bishop Dendy, of the Adelaide Anglican Cathedral. After young Walter had wagged school several times, the Bishop warned him that he would be sent to boarding school if he did it again, so, W.L.D., then 14, ran away from home, went to sea and served before the mast until he was 20, when he joined the Port Jackson & Manly Steamship Company in Sydney as a junior clerk.

W.L.D. was a man of commanding appearance—a big man, a tall man, a strong man—both in physique and in mind, a man of few words who demanded respect and good manners from everyone he encoun-

tered. Perfection was his goal in everything he undertook. At the time when he asked Jim Webster and me to help wash his car he was manager of the Port Jackson & Manly Steamship Company with 41 years' service in the company. He was to have another 11 years in office, the later ones as managing director.

Dendy lived in a large, single-storey residence in Spruson Street called 'Pajingo'. The house was full of relics of his past, all to do with ships. There were clocks in every room, at least four of which were ships' clocks and they would strike bells instead of chimes. Mr Dendy's time was always ship's time. To him, time was very important. He would often stand on the wharf at Circular Quay to clock a ferry coming in and if it was more than two minutes late the captain would have to explain why. When he went on holidays he would give me the keys of the house and I had to make sure those clocks were kept wound up.

Nearly every morning Jim Webster and I would arrive at 'Pajingo' at 5 bells or 6.30 am and we would whistle at the back gate until W.L.D. appeared at the door and beckoned us in. We had to shake his hand and say 'Good morning, Mr Dendy'. He had taught us early in our association to grip a man's hand firmly when shaking it, look him straight between the eyes and say 'good morning'. After this greeting he would hand us the keys of the garage and tell us what we had to do to the car. About half an hour later, having left us to ourselves, he came out to the garage and inspected our work. We knew that unless the results of the jobs undertaken were perfect we could expect a cuff over the ears and be told 'Do it again and do it properly this time'. That is how the Manly ferry company was run in those days before World War II—paintwork and varnish glistening, brass work polished and decks scrubbed. At 7 bells (7.30 am) we would leave 'Pajingo' with a handshake and 'Goodbye, Mr Dendy', after being given our wages, a piece of the beautiful fruit Dendy brought home every week from a fruiterer at Circular Quay.

Soon after we met Mr Dendy he told us he was going to the United Kingdom to call tenders for construction of a new Manly ferry which was to be called *South Steyne*. Little did we realise then what a famous ship this was to be—the last, the best and the biggest of the traditional steamers built for the famous seven-mile run to Manly. Dendy toured the length and breadth of the United Kingdom before selecting Henry Robb & Co. of Leith, Scotland, as the successful tenderer. W.L.D. spent some months supervising construction of the new ferry before returning to Sydney early in 1938 with a beautiful new Wolseley 25-hp saloon, one of only two of its type imported into Australia from England. This magnificent vehicle with black baked enamel was known by many around Sydney as Dendy's car. Jim Webster and I washed that car, BG 232, nearly every day for the next 10 years. It still looked brand new when W.L.D. died. During the school holidays I went to town sometimes in 'Annie', as the car was known, sitting there quite proudly as the policeman on point duty at the corner of Arthur Street and the Bradfield Highway at the Harbour Bridge intersection stopped the traffic from North Sydney and waved W.L.D. through, saying always 'Good morning, Mr Dendy'. W.L.D. usually acknowledged the greeting with a nonchalant wave of the hand, almost like a royal salute.

The SS *South Steyne* arrived in Sydney on 9 September 1938, after a 64-day voyage out from Scotland. It was hailed immediately by ferry lovers as the ultimate in Manly steamers and remained the flagship of the fleet for the next 36 years. Jim Webster and I were privileged to be on board her the Saturday she did her inaugural cruise on the harbour with massive greeting from everything afloat. Flags were flying, ships' whistles blowing cock-a-doodle-do. It was a grand day. Dendy was very proud of this great ship and well he should have been, although, in spite of his love for the big steamers, his favourite ferry in those days was the *Bellubera*. After the fire, *Bellubera* gave lots of trouble and was breaking down repeatedly, but Dendy and his younger brother, known as 'Punch' Dendy, who was the company's chief engineer, never gave up hope.

Arriving in Sydney Harbour on 12 September 1938, boarded up still, but with all flags flying, having made a triumphal voyage through stormy seas right across the world. (John Darroch)

I was sitting in 'Annie' one morning in 1942 at Neutral Bay Junction when a double-decker bus passed on its way to Palm Beach. Mr Dendy said 'Do you see that bus? That and many more buses on the northern peninsula will run my company out of business one day.' Thirty years later that is just what did happen when the New South Wales Government took over the service with *North Head* and *Baragoola* the only two serviceable ferries left. Today, of course, the wheel has turned again and the Manly ferry service is booming once more. When the Port Jackson company, through W.L.D., acquired Goddard's Palm Beach store, boatshed and Pittwater ferries, it proved a profitable venture at a time when revenue from the Manly ferry service was declining. There was a brass plate on the front door of the shop at Palm Beach which said 'Walter Leslie Dendy, licensed to sell fermented and spirituous liquors'. Mr Dendy was very proud of this plate. He said to me once 'I have always wanted to be a publican and now I am'.

W.L.D. owned a block of land at Salt Pan Bay on Pittwater, near Newport, which had a large boatshed and launching ramp, one bedroom and a kitchen. He had been a great sailing man. In his earlier years he was very successful in sailing races on Sydney Harbour. The walls of his home were covered with photographs and models of memories from his sailing days. Occasionally he would take us up to Newport for the weekend if we did some extra work at 'Pajingo'. Dendy always worked on Saturday mornings and he would say, 'If the lawns are cut and the edges clipped before noon when I come home we may go to Salty for the weekend.' That was our cue to work at the jobs feverishly while our mothers packed our clothes and baked rock-cakes. Dendy loved rock-cakes. After arrival at Salty on Saturday afternoon we would clean the boat— a 12-ft skiff painted Manly green outside and varnished inside. All fittings were brass and the boat was powered by a 1927 Austin Seven engine. It was a beautiful little boat, named *Sea Nymph II*. When W.L.D. had approved the cleaning it was time for dinner, so the launching was postponed until Sunday morning, when we went for a cruise around Pittwater. Then we returned to Salty to winch *Sea Nymph II* back into the shed and wash her down before going home. Of course Dendy expected a lot of work from us, but we loved every minute of these excursions and the many other trips he arranged for us on the harbour in the big Manly steamers—on the bridge with the captain, in the engine room or just as ordinary passengers. There were also the visits to Cockatoo and Mort's docks during the school holidays to inspect ferries in dry dock for maintenance, repairs and survey.

One day, many years after W.L.D. died, I was talking to the engineer on the *South Steyne* going to Broken Bay on a Sunday afternoon ocean cruise and I mentioned W.L.D. 'Dendy was the Port Jackson & Manly Steamship Company,' he remarked. 'The day Dendy died the company started to die.' Strong words, perhaps, but they indicated the remarkable type of man Dendy was and the reputation he had achieved. He was a man with a stern, tough exterior, but with a hidden heart of gold for those who responded to his challenges and worked as hard as they could. I attended his funeral service with my father at the old Garrison Church near the Harbour Bridge in Argyle Cut. The church was filled to capacity and to the mourners assembled the minister said: 'Walter Dendy loved the harbour and the ships and ferries that sailed on it. What more fitting way for this man to end his days on earth than to be in this church overlooking the harbour.'

And what a delightful picture of W.L.D. from one who enjoyed his friendship from boyhood through his youthful years. Prescott and Willson describe Dendy, a company secretary and accountant by occupation, as 'multi-

talented', a man who during his period of managership created so much of the image for which the Manly ferry is still fondly remembered. Of him, they said in their article in *The Log*:

Dendy was gifted with a sound engineering knowledge, a flair for aesthetics and publicity and was an astute businessman. During his period were introduced the famous green and white colour scheme, diesel-electric propulsion, the harbour pool and pavilion and other facitities at Manly, a flood of still remembered advertising literature and, as his pinnacle of achievement, the *South Steyne*.

The Port Jackson & Manly Steamship Board of Directors sent Dendy to Britain in December 1936, to look at developments in sea transport and to investigate ordering a new Manly ferry. He was obviously after a ship which would be an improvement on the *Dee Why* and *Curl Curl*. Manly by then had become quite a big residential area and for the first time more residents than tourists were using the ferries. This called for bigger carrying capacity and travelling times faster than the 14 knots of the older steamers. Diesel-electric propulsion had made the change with the *Bellubera* and it seems that Dendy was contemplating this form of power for the new *South Steyne*. But the *Bellubera* had brought problems with its new engines, which were so noisy that waterfront aldermen at Vaucluse complained, and which vibrated so much that passengers complained. So, while Dendy was having tank tests done at the National Physics Laboratory, Teddington, on a model of the proposed new vessel, his Board cabled him from Sydney its decision to have steam reciprocating engines driving a continuous propeller shaft, one propeller pushing and the other pulling. A new model had to be made and new tests undertaken before tenders were called from 12 shipbuilders. The quote accepted eventually from Henry Robb Ltd was £96 000, plus £5900 delivery charge, but the total cost was close to £150 000 by the time the *South Steyne* went into service in Sydney.

South Steyne was 220 ft long, 10 feet longer than the *Dee Why* and *Curl Curl*, but she was a bigger ship in many ways and this was the impressive fact about her. If the others looked like big ferries, the *South Steyne* had the looks and the atmosphere of an ocean liner. *Dee Why* and *Curl Curl* were just on 800 tons. *South Steyne* was 1203 tons. She was higher out of the water, her beam of 38 ft was wider, and her beautifully flared bows thrilled anyone who likes the nice lines of a well designed ship. She was built with much stronger frames and plating than her predecessors of 10 years before and, as an indication of her big ship size, *South Steyne* had four-bladed manganese bronze propellers of 9 ft 3 in diameter. Prescott and

Willson dealt with these matters in some detail in their article written for *The Log*, in which they stated:

As a further improvement on earlier ferry boats, *South Steyne* was built of much stronger framing and plating, with hull frames extending through to the promenade deck (not just the main deck as previously) and the promenade deckhouse was built of steel rather than wood. The number of watertight bulkheads was increased, panting stringers were fitted at each end and the frames were scarfed below the stern tubes. These improvements gave the vessel greater strength in heavy seas and in the event of grounding and enabled damage repairs to be effected more easily. To reduce the effect of pitching in rough weather in a lightly loaded condition, ballast tanks, each of about 40 tons capacity, were installed in the fore and aft peaks of the hull. Finally, this greatly improved hull design was polished into an aesthetic masterpiece. The double-ended hull was gracefully streamlined, the identical bow and stern were raked and flared, and finely curved steel plate hances and stanchions framed the open shelters on the main and promenade decks—a considerable change from the tubular stanchions and guardrails of earlier steamers. For the first time on a Manly ferry boat, the promenade deckhouse was integrated into the total design. The whole effect was completed by the symmetrical funnels, varnished wheelhouses and an unofficial company coat-of-arms on the stemheads.

One problem Dendy had to overcome while in Britain was that he had been instructed to ensure that the ship's tonnage was in excess of the 1000 tons specified in the schedule to the Sales Tax Exemptions Act, 1935. Otherwise, the import of the ship into Australia would have attracted a substantial tax. Indeed, the building of *South Steyne* overseas led to some resentful questions in Federal Parliament. By contrast, when *Dee Why* and *Curl Curl* were built, efforts were made to keep the gross tonnage as low as possible. Dendy recalled that he had been advised by the Board of Trade that if sliding doors were fitted at either end of the promenade deckhouse the whole deck would be excluded from measurement for tonnage. This had resulted in a reduction of 222.7 tons in the capacities of the 1928 vessels. As a result, after discussions with the Board of Trade, the solution adopted for *South Steyne* was to fit swing doors for the voyage out while the builders provided sliding doors and associated fittings for installation in Sydney, although for some reason this was never done. Herein lies the explanation as to why *South Steyne* (1203.37 gross tons) and the 1928 twins (799.44 gross tons) are of such differing tonnages in spite of having similar hull dimensions (217 x 38.25 x 14.9 ft for *South*

Getting ready for the 12 690-mile voyage from Scotland to Sydney. (John Darroch)

Steyne and 220 x 36.15 x 14.8 ft for *Dee Why* and *Curl Curl*), design and accommodation. If the promenade deckhouse had been measured as enclosed space in the 1928 boats, as in practical terms it should have been, these vessels would have been of 1022.14 gross tons.

There was no doubt that the *South Steyne* was going to be one of the most exciting events for Sydney in 1938. Imagine those commuters travelling to and from work each day in this magnificent ship with three decks for passenger accommodation. Below the promenade and main decks were a ladies' lounge and a smoking room for the men. The crew had good sleeping quarters, shower and toilets, and the master and engineer each had a cabin behind the wheelhouses. Satisfied that he had achieved something monumental, Dendy left for New York on 16 June 1937, aboard another great ship which had been in service not very long—the *Queen Mary*. During the trip across the Atlantic he studied her massive engines and equipment, reporting later to his Board in Sydney: 'Everything was huge and most interesting, but I did not see anything new that I could embody in our little engine and boiler room.' By ferry boat standards, *South Steyne*'s engine and boiler room were not so little. The triple-expansion steam engines, built by Harland & Wolff in Belfast, could produce 3250 hp and they were going to push *South Steyne* along at a very fast rate. Before leaving Scotland, Dendy endeavoured to arrange for the *South Steyne* to depart on her voyage home before the end of March 1938, to avoid the monsoon season in the Indian Ocean which had caused some delay in delivery of the *Dee Why* and *Curl Curl*.

The keel of the ferry was laid in Henry Robb's Leith shipyards on 14 October 1937. Five months later, on 1 April 1938, Mrs Henry Robb launched this new ship, named after the most famous of the Manly ocean beaches and promenade area—or rather, it should be said, the ship launched itself. As if impatient to get afloat, the *South Steyne* took off unaided and slid gently down the slipway. At the end of June the vessel was ready for trials in the Firth of Forth, where, on 23 June, her speed over what is known as the Burnt Island mile was recorded as 17.015 knots ahead and 17.23 knots astern. She was not ready to leave for Australia before the end of March, as Dendy had wished, but he need not have worried. The monsoons did not trouble his beloved *South Steyne*. In fact the monsoons, a few gales and other very bad weather provided her with the opportunity on the way out to show what a splendid ship she was.

2. With Flying Colours

So much publicity surrounded the delivery voyage of the *South Steyne* from Scotland to Sydney that it is no wonder nearly everyone thinks all the Manly ferries steamed out under their own power. The story was written several times for the *Manly Daily* over the years by Captain C.W.T. Henderson, a Manly man, who signed on for the trip out as navigating officer. Such a voyage would have held no terrors for Captain Henderson, who had sailed around Cape Horn on two very rugged trips in the days of sail. He spent 20 years as one of the Sydney Harbour pilots in the famous old pilot steamer *Captain Cook*, and also worked as a pilot in Bermuda, Newcastle (New South Wales) and Port Kembla. He was one of 17 top seamen who crewed the *South Steyne* out to Australia.

Master for the voyage was Captain R.M. Beedie, who returned to Britain after reaching Sydney. First officer was Captain A.E. Rowlings, of the Port Jackson & Manly Steamship Company. Both he and Captain Henderson were navigating officers and there were also chief, second and third engineers. All these had a single cabin, and in the crew's quarters below the main deck were six seamen,

three firemen, a cook and a steward. Writing of it later in the *Manly Daily*, Captain Henderson recalled:

When first I saw the *South Steyne*, she lay alongside an old stone wharf in an old-world dock in the old-world harbour of Leith, Scotland. Freshly painted and varnished in her gay bright green and gleaming white, she presented an incongruous picture among the ships with which she shared the sheltered waters of Leith docks. Fitting out for her voyage to Australia, she reminded me a little bit of Circular Quay removed to Scotland— my first glimpse of home for nearly 10 years. Looking over the ship, every detail of her construction met with my approval. Faithfully built in the best tradition of British shipyard skill, she had first taken salt water the previous April in the harbourage of this ancient port, acquired by Edinburgh from Mary Queen of Scots and Lord Darnley in 1565.

The ship was unlike anything else that sailed the high seas. Stem and stern were exactly alike and a propeller revealed itself at either end. The whole of her superstructure was boarded up to protect the window glass. She had two funnels, but the after funnel was a dummy one containing water tanks and our bosun used it as his sleeping quarters. Old Captain Beedie, a shipmaster of the old school, lectured us not to be too soft with the seamen and to see that they received not more than the Board of Trade allowance of rations, which included one tin of milk every three weeks.

South Steyne weighed anchor in Leith Roads at 5 am on 7 July 1938, and headed out on the first leg of the voyage, to Algiers. In the Bay of Biscay thick fog reduced our speed, allowing no rest for the watch below with the ear-shattering whistle sounding day and night. After weathering the bad weather in the Channel and Biscay, the ferry passed Gibraltar and, entering the Mediterranean, caused a flutter among French and Italian naval ships on patrol there. She became an object of suspicion for the commander of a French

After some years of thought and planning, the dream becomes a reality. The South Steyne *being launched at Leith in Scotland, on 1 April 1938. (John Darroch)*

cruiser, who looked her over and shadowed her for some time before steaming off the other way. Then an Italian submarine displayed similar curiosity before escorting us to a specially patrolled lane. Nine days out from Leith, a French pilot boarded and took us into picturesque Algiers harbour for fresh provisions and bunker oil.

One day in Algiers and we were off east to Port Said and the Suez Canal, where again there was consternation over this strange ship. After much animated discussion among the port authorities as to whether she should be allowed to proceed, especially without steam winches or windlasses on deck, we were eventually allowed in as 'a vessel without priority', which meant that we had to pull over to allow any other ship to pass during the passage of the canal. Soon after, our Italian pilot ordered us to make fast alongside the bank to allow a clear passage for a deeply laden British tanker, but we were so close to the bank that the huge wash from the tanker put us aground and there she remained, despite all efforts with hand winches and heavy mooring lines. It took a mighty effort by a French tug to refloat us. Then followed a heated argument, not uncommon in such circumstances, in French, Italian, Greek, and English as a stop gap, during which the tow line was let go from the tug and became wound with a dozen good hard turns around the *South Steyne*'s bow propeller, completely immobilising the ship. Divers were sent for to cut the line away. A British pilot boarded us and we were given full precedence over all other traffic. The canal authorities had 'had' the *South Steyne* and they wanted her out of the canal before anything else happened.

In the Red Sea, steaming towards Aden, we were compelled to heaveto in an exceptionally severe sandstorm. The relevant part of the log book reads: 'Saturday, 3 July. Gale force winds, rough sea, heavy rain squalls with lightning, shipping heavy spray over all.' With the sandstorm and rain, every inch of the ship became plastered thickly with heavy yellow mud.

While they were hove to in this gale they sighted a Greek tramp steamer, also hove to, but they didn't know until a few months later what effect the sight of the *South Steyne* had on somebody aboard the Greek ship. Mr I. J. Horn, a young man from Sydney, who was radio operator on that Greek ship, the wheat carrier, *Pindos*, looked through his porthole and saw a sight so strange he thought his last day had come. Lying almost alongside his ship was a Manly ferry. Back in Sydney a few months later he told how he read on the bow of the ferry which loomed up out of the Red Sea fog: 'South Steyne, Sydney'. 'I could hardly believe my eyes,' he said. Mr Horn returned to Sydney as

wireless operator on the maiden voyage of the *Matthew Flinders* and the morning they berthed at Circular Quay the *South Steyne*, then in regular service, glided in to the Manly ferry wharf nearby. 'She looked much more respectable than when I last saw her rolling around in that Red Sea gale,' he remarked.

After that gale and sandstorm the *South Steyne*, continued on her way to Aden in temperatures of 31°C on deck and 49°C in the engine room. Captain Henderson's story continued:

To cope with this heat, the second engineer had stored up some cool beer for relaxation when off duty. Before we reached Aden a report came up to the bridge that the steward was missing, probably overboard. 'Hard-a-starboard,' ordered the Old Man and extra lookouts were stationed as the ship turned back on her course. But the steward was not found in the sea. He was hiding beneath a canvas cover aft, consuming some of the engineer's cold beer and he was in such a fighting mood that the cook had to lay him out with a meat chopper.

At Aden the crew of the *South Steyne* learned that the monsoon season had begun and the weather in the Indian Ocean was so bad that two Dutch tugs, which had left two weeks previously for the East Indies, had been forced to turn around and come back. Captain Beedie decided, however, that monsoon or no monsoon the *South Steyne* would steam on and so, ready for the fray, she left Aden for Colombo. Out in the Arabian Sea, *South Steyne* ran into the full force of the southwest monsoon with its warm, rain-bearing winds of the northern summer and the accompanying huge swell. Life was not very comfortable aboard with the sticky heat and with the ship rolling and tossing. Overcome by the heat one night, a fireman went berserk and invaded the captain's cabin, demanding that the ship be turned around and taken back to Aden. He was taken back to the stokehold.

In Sydney later the story was told of a three-hour struggle to save drums of fuel oil which broke loose in the monsoon off Cape Guardafui, north-east Africa. Members of the crew described how the huge drums were flung about the enclosed deck like big tins of jam and several men had narrow escapes from serious injury before they were secured. 'We got the full force of the blow at night,' said the cook, James Mckay. 'The first warning was a loud crashing sound on the saloon deck. The drums were being whirled about by the heavy rolling and pitching as the lashings carried away.' The second engineer, E. Slater, gave the alarm and all hands turned out to try to re-lash the drums. With the vessel rolling and pitching alarmingly, it was a very dangerous job. A leg or any other part of the

Riding in on a south-east swell, the South Steyne *steams towards Manly past Smedleys Point. Spring Cove is on the right.* (Manly Daily)

body in the way of these rumbling monsters risked being smashed to pieces. The danger increased when one large drum began to leak oil after a heavy pounding as it crashed against other drums from one side of the ship to the other. Because of the oil spilling from it, keeping a foothold on the crazily tilting deck was harder than ever. The oil drums were not the only hazard in that wild night. A stack of 30 bags of coal, carried as emergency fuel, collapsed in the galley, nearly crushing the cook, Mckay, who just managed to jump clear as the bags came down. Captain Beedie decided it was time to change course until the weather moderated next day.

No doubt everyone, including Captain Beedie, was glad to see Colombo, where they filled the bunkers with fuel oil and the water tanks with fresh water. Across the Indian Ocean towards the East Indies, the weather improved and they made good time. Captain Henderson said:

On this passage, a welcome change from our normally unpalatable messroom fare was a meal of flying fish, caught on board. One night, 85 flying fish, attracted by a deck light, flew out of the water and landed on the outer deck, where they were promptly scooped up and taken to the cook's pan. It was no use trying to keep them in that hot climate. There was no such thing aboard in those days as refrigeration. At daylight on 22 August we picked up a Dutch pilot off Sourabaya and steamed 24 miles up the river to the port, where gangs of Malay coolies in their sampans were hired to clean and paint the ship in readiness for an impressive arrival in Sydney, still 3000 miles away. They swarmed all over the *South Steyne* and soon had her clean and bright.

August 31 gave us our first glimpse of Australia as we signalled our name and were answered by Thursday Island. Then south-east trade winds became strong enough to reduce our headway to seven and a half knots. Through the Great Barrier Reef, passing many small islands, reefs, cays and beacons, the *South Steyne* ploughed on her way as the strong south-easterly continued throughout, rough seas spraying heavily over all. Weather moderated as we made our way through the Whitsunday Passage. We passed the AUSN coastal passenger ship *Orungal*, whose passengers lined the rail and cheered us.

But their worries were not over. Off Cape Moreton, passing outside Brisbane, with less than 800 miles to go, they ran head on into gale force winds and high seas again, providing another test of the ferry's seaworthy qualities, to which she responded splendidly, and on Friday, 9 September 1938, the *South Steyne* entered Sydney Heads triumphantly, with all flags flying, to a grand welcome from other craft in the harbour.

There was no prouder man in Sydney than Walter Dendy and he was determined that the city would share his pride. The *South Steyne* remained at the Port Jackson company's workshops from 10 September to 18 October while workmen prepared her for harbour trials, removing all the boards covering the windows, repainting the hull and repairing any damage caused during her turbulent 64 days at sea. On 21 October, at her official trials in the harbour, she covered the measured mile between Fort Denison and Bradleys Head at an average speed of 17.1 knots—nearly 20 miles an hour. On board during the trials was Henry Robb, who had travelled out from Scotland to be present at the trials. At a luncheon aboard later in the day, Henry Robb, as managing director of the ship's builders, replied to the toast of 'Success to the ship'. Other speakers included the chairman of directors of the Port Jackson company, Sir Archibald Howie; the deputy mayor of Manly, Alderman Hanson-Norman, and the deputy president of Warringah Shire Council, Councillor T.A. Nicholas. Said Mr Robb:

I find myself today in the extraordinary position of having to reply for a second time to the same toast. After the *South Steyne* had been launched at Leith there was a little ceremony in my company's board room following the tradition that has been observed in British shipbuilding for centuries. The invited guests drink a toast of success to the ship and her owners and the builder is subsequently called upon to speak, usually in reply to a toast to their success, proposed by the owner if he is sufficiently pleased with the vessel he has just seen in the water.

Let me say at once that I am proud and pleased to have been able to join you today. My firm was honoured at being asked to construct for you what we believe to be the fastest and most modern ferry steamer in the Empire. As she took the water after the launching and naming ceremony, which my wife had the honour of performing at the invitation of your Board, we saw that she was a bonny ship. Her trials some weeks later proved all theories and calculations correct. Now she has had a further severe test of journeying halfway round the world and I was gratified to learn that the long voyage, for which she was never designed, was accomplished without the slightest incident or delay. Indeed she made the voyage so well that I began to have serious doubts whether I would arrive in time to participate in this interesting occasion.

I would like you to look on this ship—and I am sure many of you do so—as something even more than an interesting new vessel, the best of her type and constructed to the highest standards of British shipbuilding and engineering. As I prefer to see it, we sent you a piece of the mother country embodying a wealth of history and tradition which I need not describe in detail. The men who built this ship did not do so by mere accident. For more than 600 years their forebears have built ships on the shores of the Firth of Forth. I should like to remind my English friends that so seriously did they at one time regard the menace of Leith shipbuilders that in the 13th and 15th centuries they burned their yards to the ground. Since those days the axe may have become transformed into an electric welding machine and the hammer into a pneumatic riveter, but while the tools have changed, the shipbuilder has been able to preserve in a greater degree than in most other industries the skill and craftsmanship of his ancestors.

Behind this ship is the accumulated knowledge and experience of many centuries—surely one of the chief reasons why the best type of British ship is still unrivalled in any country in the world.

Mr Robb paid a tribute to Mr Dendy's 'outstanding knowledge of ship designing and construction', which, he said, was quite unique in a general manager, so much so that it had given him great pleasure in being one of the proposers for Mr Dendy's membership of the Institution of Naval Architects. Mr Robb continued:

Although we eventually secured the order, by the time the contract was signed that pleasure was somewhat subdued as we realised that if Mr Dendy was not born in Scotland he had certainly imbibed the Scottish, or shall I say that particular Aberdeen gift of getting the best of a bargain, so, with all modesty, I can tell you that this ship represents very fine value for the money your company paid for her. I wish to thank you most cordially on behalf of my firm for the warm reception you have given to this toast and to express the wish that the *South Steyne* will give you many years of faithful and profitable service running on your beautiful harbour to such a lovely place as Manly.

The Port Jackson & Manly Steamship Company showed off its new ship proudly in two special cruises from Circular Quay on Sunday, 23 October and next day, a wet and windy Monday, she began her regular run on the 8.10 am trip from Manly, the first of thousands she was to make in 36 years as one of Sydney Harbour's main attractions.

3. Harbour Lights

One problem that had not been foreseen when the *South Steyne* settled into regular work on the harbour was the big wash her size and speed caused. It was all very well for ship lovers to revel in the sight of the beautiful bow wave curling away from her stem and the wash rolling up astern, but for people too close in small craft the sight was often quite terrifying. It soon caused trouble. In January 1939, sailors were working on a punt alongside the cruiser HMAS *Sydney*, which was attached to a Navy mooring buoy near Garden Island. They paused in the job they were doing, painting the hull near the waterline, to admire the proud new *South Steyne* steaming past. Then they resumed work again, brushes spreading light grey paint over the warship's steel plates. Suddenly, almost like a surprise enemy attack, the wash from the *Steyne* hit, overturning the punt and throwing the sailors, paint, brushes and all, into the water alongside the *Sydney*. Able

Seaman E. Wainwright was squeezed between the punt and the ship's hull, suffering bruised thighs, arms and legs. His companion, Ordinary Seaman H. O'Sullivan escaped with a ducking. Both men climbed out of the water on to the capsized punt and were hauled aboard the *Sydney*, but all their paint and gear was lost on the bottom of the harbour.

The steam ferry engine rooms were always an attraction for boys, young and old. Here, below decks in the South Steyne, *Chief Engineer George Todd explains how it all works.*

Two Italian fishermen had a narrow escape when the *South Steyne* ran them down in their launch near Taylor Bay a few weeks later. Yachtsmen rescued Steve Defina, 36, carrier, of Darling Street, Balmain, and his nephew, Frank Matarazzo, aged 10. Telling of the incident, Defina said:

The launch was out of control through carburettor trouble. I saw the ferry coming fast and was cleaning the carburettor furiously when the boy screamed 'It's on top of us'. Then we went down and the launch rolled over and over.

The launch, damaged only slightly, was beached at Taylor Bay. Captain A. McIntosh, master of the ferry at the time, said he was trying to avoid a yacht and the launch was in the fairway.

The next incident, later that year, could have had much more serious consequences. Hundreds of children at a picnic in the Manly harbour pool were in the path of the *South Steyne* when she overshot the wharf and crashed through the promenade, tearing and splintering a gap of about two metres. The children, attending a railway locomotive workers' picnic, had been standing on the promenade watching the ferry coming in to berth, waiting for the ever-fascinating spectacle of the propellers going astern and churning up that spreading circle of white water. When it became apparent that the ferry was not going to stop in time, the inspector in charge of the pool, Mr U. Gorman, ran along the promenade, shouting to the children to run from where they were standing. The children, terrified as they saw the danger, ran away and escaped being hurled into the water or crushed in the wreckage of the promenade. Two people who watched, fearing tragedy, suffered from severe shock and received ambulance treatment.

In grave danger, too, was a ferry company diver, Samuel Taylor, who was examining under water some of the wharf piles near where the wharf joined the pool enclosure. Those were the days of helmets and air hoses for divers. Taylor saw the keel of the ferry sliding towards him and felt the turbulence from the whirling propeller. The swirl of the rushing water being pushed ahead of the approaching ferry sent Taylor off balance and flattened him against the pool's steel net. He feared that his airline would be severed, but it was not. The ferry backed out of the wreckage it had caused and Taylor was walking under the wharf towards the shore when his assistant took him unharmed aboard their work punt.

The *South Steyne*, on her first trip since being repainted and cleaned in preparation for the busy summer season, was not damaged, apart from having some paint scraped off. She resumed her normal running after diver Taylor went below again and found that none of the hull plates had been damaged.

Three years passed in which nothing untoward happened to the *South Steyne*. She was clearly the favourite of both commuters and tourists. People would ring the ferry office to ask what time she would leave Manly or the Quay so they could ride in her. Some commuters had their regular seats and would glare ferociously at anyone who usurped their place. The *Steyne* took her share of rough weather and handled it as well if not better than the others. She was usually the last ferry to be taken off in very bad weather. On 19 March 1942, a huge wave crashed into the *Steyne* as she was crossing The Heads about 4.45 pm. Several windows were smashed, some seats were torn from their fastenings and passengers were showered with broken window glass, but nobody was injured.

A 15 metre whale provided a diversion at Manly wharf in October 1943, surfacing near the wharf about noon. It remained in the vicinity of the wharf for several minutes, but was frightened apparently by the *South Steyne* coming in to berth and dived. The whale was not seen again. A wharf hand commented: 'The whale was a disappointment. It lay in the water like an oversized log and didn't spout.'

There was much more excitement at the wharf on Saturday evening, 31 October, when more than 500 people were involved either actively or vocally in a series of fierce brawls which followed police intervention in an incident on the *South Steyne*. Police reinforcements and Army provosts were called in to help arrest 15 men, who were charged with 35 offences. The *South Steyne* was waiting at Manly wharf to make the 6.45 pm trip to Sydney when three sailors climbed up to the wheelhouse and told the captain they were going to see to the sailing of the ship. They took charge of the wheelhouse and navigating bridge, defying the captain and crew, and police had to be called in by blowing the ship's whistle. The wharf was crowded with servicemen and civilians returning to the city from Manly when sergeants Grimes, McClelland and Miller went aboard the ferry and dragged the struggling sailors from the wheelhouse. The police

This photograph, taken in Cockatoo Dock, Sydney, shows the massive size of the South Steyne *and the ship's graceful lines.*

were subjected to a barrage of abusive language as they took their captives on to the wharf, and that was where the real trouble began.

Scuffles began after somebody in the crew punched one of the policemen. Dozens joined in then and the police had to draw batons to defend themselves. The police were outnumbered heavily, surrounded by an abusive, screeching mob of people, who, by some strange reasoning, were attacking those who had been trying to defend them from the irresponsible behaviour of larrikins. These were the days of the six o'clock swill in the pubs and many of the *South Steyne*'s passengers had no doubt imbibed up to the final bell. But only a few of the 1000 or so people on the wharf gave the police any help. Men prevented the police from using their batons by pinning their arms to their sides. Sergeant Grimes had a finger nearly bitten off, Constable Turbett was punched behind the ear and knocked unconscious and three men threw Constable North to the ground and jumped on him.

The wharf was described as 'a confused battleground', in which the weapons were fists, boots and batons. The tide turned in favour of the police because of two things— departure of the ferry about 10 minutes after the brawl started, taking with it most of the crowd, and arrival of police reinforcements from North Sydney and Narrabeen, plus Army provosts from Sydney. Those who were prepared to miss the ferry to see out the brawl surged off the wharf to follow the police and prisoners to the police station, a few hundred metres away in Belgrave Street, still sniping with stray punches, and another large-scale brawl developed outside the police station when a new attempt was made to rescue those arrested. The disturbance took nearly an hour to subdue.

Most of the 15 arrested appeared in Manly Court a few days later and were fined on charges ranging from riotous behaviour, to assaulting police, resisting arrest, malicious damage to a police vehicle, inciting to resist arrest and indecent language. Sergeant Grimes told the court that when he and other police boarded the ferry, one of the soldiers called to his mates: 'Come on, boys. We'll chuck the police car in the harbour and take the boat out The Heads.' Sergeant Grimes continued:

> The crowd seemed hostile and a number of civilians and other servicemen joined in the fight or incited the soldiers to resist arrest. Only three of about 1000 supposedly intelligent and civilised people who were there assisted the police.

The sergeant told how a sailor pulled the windscreen off the PD car and another man tugged at its radio aerial. Both seized a mud-guard, screaming 'We'll tip the bloody thing over'.

Mr Leiberman, a solicitor appearing for the three soldiers, asked for leniency. He said the men were aggrieved because they had been put on wharf work after having served in Greece, Crete, Libya and New Guinea. The magistrate, Mr Harris SM, was not very impressed, commenting:

There is little doubt that a disastrous situation would have arisen if the three soldiers had taken control of the ferry. A first-class panic would have ensued. These men threatened a public utility and a section of the public upheld their attempt. Such conduct merits the deepest disgust of all decent folk. But for the soldiers' overseas service, I would certainly have sent them to jail.

Instead, the various offenders were fined.

When the *South Steyne* was in trouble it was usually at Manly wharf. Coming in to berth at 9.35 am on 11 May 1944, she overshot the berthing space and crashed through a baffle board to crush some of the wharf buildings, wrecking the tourist bureau and part of the men's toilets. The sponson of the ferry became jammed under the wharf, causing the vessel to list dangerously until she was pulled clear. Miss Dora Martin, of Alexander Street, Manly, was typing in the bureau office seconds before the ferry tore into its wall and had just risen from her chair when a wooden beam weighing about 150 kilograms crashed across her chair and the roof began to fall down around her. Miss Martin escaped with slight bruises and shock. An American soldier took one startled leap from his seat in a toilet as the wall burst asunder. One leg of his trousers was torn off and he was lucky to escape being buried under the debris. The soldier was treated at Manly Hospital. An attendant, Ralph Langton, of Golf Parade, Manly, cut about the face and hands, said:

I heard a rending crash. One wall flew at me in a shower of glass, marble and doors. How I escaped death is a miracle. I have a lump on my head as big as an egg.

The few passengers aboard the *South Steyne* were badly shaken, but only one required hospital treatment.

In the early 1950s the *South Steyne* added to her fame by starting her famous ocean cruises up the coast past the northern beaches to Broken Bay and into the Hawkesbury River estuary. George Marshall and I both remember it well. I was deputy chief of staff of the Sydney *Daily Telegraph* when, in October 1953, a fellow came into the office one morning and said he wanted to give us a story about the *South Steyne* going on ocean cruises up to the Hawkesbury. The Sydney to Newcastle passenger ships, *Hunter* and *Gwydir*, used to do this on public holidays and

Captain Harold Gibson, famous ferry skipper and commodore of the Port Jackson & Manly Steamship Company, ringing down for 'Full Ahead' as his favourite ship, the South Steyne, *leaves Manly Wharf.*

it had been a popular trip, but since that passenger service ceased there had been nothing to replace the Hawkesbury excursion. As far as I was concerned it was worth a small story in the *Telegraph* and when the first cruise left the harbour on 1 November with nearly 800 passengers at 15 shillings a head I went along to write a piece for the paper. It was the ferry's first ocean voyage since coming out from Scotland 14 years previously and for most of the passengers it was their first trip outside The Heads. Fortunately, the sea was fairly calm, despite a strong north-east breeze, and only about 15 were seasick. The others enjoyed the novelty of looking in on the northern beaches from the sea and watching several whales and porpoises. The ocean cruises were established and became very popular in the years they operated. The Port Jackson & Manly Steamship Company took over the venture itself and extended the idea to following the Hobart yacht race down the coast as far as Port Hacking.

It had not been easy to get it all going. George Marshall recalls:

It wasn't our thought, but we jumped at it. Brigadier Claude Cameron, who was managing director, went with me to see the harbour master, a jovial old Scotsman, Captain Murchison, who was inclined to help us whenever he could. 'Why not?' he responded to the idea and called in the Maritime Services Board surveyors. 'The Port Jackson company wants to do this and I want to help them,' he said. 'Get to it and see that it works.'

But Captain Murchison's surveyors did not share his enthusiasm. In fact they didn't like the idea very much at all. They applied all the rules of bureaucracy. 'Wait a minute,' they said. 'You've got to do your sums. You've got to cut wash ports in the bulwarks, you've got to keep your doors open in case you ship a sea, you've got to put extra men on to launch the lifeboats, you've got to put an extra man on in case the skipper drops dead, an extra engineer in case he drops dead and, oh yes, you can't carry the *South Steyne*'s normal load of 1781 passengers. You can carry only 1000.' The figure chosen did not relate to lifesaving gear or anything, but it didn't matter because 1000 people at sea is enough anyhow. We were allowed to operate only 26 miles to sea—26 miles up or down the coast, or we could have gone 26 miles straight out. They did help us with one thing and that was the requirement for a mate. Since we had a percentage of foreign-going men, we were allowed to have as mate an ordinary harbour skipper on condition that he had served two years at sea and had first been an AB. We had several of these, but a special Act of Parliament had to be passed to put everything in order.

It was not long before we had trouble with the charter operator. If there was a cyclone on the Queensland coast on the Saturday and he was chartering the boat on the Sunday he would rush in and say he wanted to cancel the trip because there was a cyclone 600 miles away. This happened two or three times, so we decided to operate the cruises ourselves instead of chartering the ship. We used to operate about 35 cruises a year on Sundays, public holidays and during school holidays on Wednesdays. It was a successful summer operation, but if you ran into winter you did not get sufficient loading. It was a cheap trip. It cost $2.50 when it ended in 1973. On today's costs it would probably be a $10 fare.

The cruises ended in 1973 because the Maritime Services Board's demand for a large amount of work to be done to the hull was not met and her sea-going certificate was cancelled.

On one cruise, in January 1965, the *South Steyne* went to the rescue of a yacht in difficulties with four people aboard off Long Reef, Collaroy. The yacht, which had left Kirribilli in Sydney Harbour at 9 am for Pittwater, several hours ahead of the *South Steyne*'s departure, got into difficulties off Avalon when the cringle, a loop on the rope edging of the mainsail near the top of the mast, burst. The yacht had turned around to come back to the harbour and was making slow progress down the coast off Long Reef with a strong north-east wind and heavy rain behind it when the *South Steyne*, returning from its cruise to Broken Bay, caught up with the yacht about 5 pm in answer to distress flares signalling that the boat was in trouble. Hundreds of people watched from the shore as the

ferry diverted about half a mile from her course and hove to near the yacht. Many of those watching thought the ferry was in trouble and rang police and newspapers to give the alarm. The police launch *Colin J. Delaney* was going out to investigate when the *South Steyne* approached The Heads with the disabled yacht in tow.

The cruises were cancelled, of course, if the weather was very bad. Seasick passengers were not happy ones. Sometimes they left in reasonable weather which went bad before the return home. One such cruise was on New Year's Day, 1970, when the *South Steyne* ran into heavy southerly weather coming back from Broken Bay. Off Mona Vale they shipped a couple of big curlers, which came aboard. Two families were injured. Victor Garchevich, of Lyons Road, Drummoyne, was sitting with his family inside on the lower deck when the first wave struck. He said it left him, his wife, Mary, and their children gasping for air, half drowned. Others injured were a couple from Victoria and their teenage son. Two nursing sisters on board gave them all first aid and when the *South Steyne* returned to Circular Quay they were taken to Sydney Hospital, where doctors put seven stitches in Mr Garchevich's cuts and two stitches in cuts sustained by his daughter, Irma, 15. Mrs Garchevich was treated for a cut ankle and a bruised shoulder and their four-year-old son, Louis, was treated for shock. The Victorian family also had stitches put in cuts.

It was certainly a rough day. Earlier in the afternoon, a jet-powered lifeboat rescued 16 lifesavers from treacherous seas at a surf carnival at South Curl Curl. Before rough conditions forced abandonment of the carnival, three surf boats were damaged. Two were smashed when they were pounded on rocks at the end of the beach and nearly all their equipment was lost in the surf. Several seats in Maroubra club's surf boat were broken when a three metre wave caught the boat broadside on during a heat of the senior surf boat race. Six beaches north of Sydney had to be closed because of heavy rain and rough seas. Mona Vale was closed at 11 am after four people were carried out by rips within half an hour, and at Long Reef 11 rescues had to be made before it was decided to close the beach at 2 pm. Apparently there was a pretty good sea running when the *South Steyne* left Circular Quay at 1.30 pm for her 60-mile ocean cruise, although it was not too bad for her to handle.

Friday March 13, 1964, was an unlucky day for the *South Steyne*. About 3.58 pm, when the *Steyne* was off Bennelong Point on her way from Circular Quay to Manly, she collided with the Blue Funnel line freighter *Jason* and discovered that her 1203 tons was no match for the *Jason's* 10,160. The upper port section of the *South Steyne's* bow was smashed in, woodwork was torn apart and railing on the top deck was twisted and cracked. The only damage to the *Jason* was a large area of paint scraped off its hull. None of the ferry's 100 passengers was injured, although many were hurled from their seats by the impact. Both vessels were steaming about 10 knots when they met, the *Jason* on her way out to The Heads. Merchant Navy officer O.E. Provis, going home to Collaroy aboard the ferry, told of looking up from a paper he was reading and seeing the black hull of a ship very close on the port side. He said:

At first I didn't worry because I thought we would swing away, but the ferry and the freighter came closer. All I could see from the window was a huge black wall coming closer and closer. Then we hit with a terrific bump and many passengers were hurled from their seats. A few women screamed, but nobody panicked or became hysterical.

South Steyne had two clashes with the Royal Australian Navy. The first, in May 1954, involved a 34-ft launch from the frigate *Barcoo* between Garden Island naval headquarters and Bradleys Head. The master of the *South Steyne*, proceeding down the harbour to Manly about 3.30 pm, blew a long blast when he saw a naval launch coming around the eastern side of Garden Island. Then he saw that the launch would go fairly close to the ferry and had the ferry's engines stopped. When the launch was a few metres away, it swung around suddenly and crashed into the ferry about seven metres from the bow on the starboard side. Three men from the launch were pulled aboard the ferry and two others dived into the water when they saw that a collision was imminent. The launch, its engine still running, became jammed under the ferry's sponson for a few seconds, then rocked free and careered off down the harbour with nobody aboard. The officer in charge of the launch said the steering had jammed and he had been unable to control the launch. Other Navy launches rescued the two men who had dived into the water and pursued and caught the runaway boat, which they towed back to Garden Island. On the return trip from Manly, the *South Steyne* stopped at Garden Island and put off the three men who had been taken aboard after the collision. The Navy, always the 'silent service', lived up to its reputation. Questioned by the Press, the duty staff officer at Garden Island said: 'I have learned that a launch from *Barcoo* has collided with the ferry *South Steyne*. I have nothing more to say.'

The *South Steyne*'s other naval target was the aircraft carrier, HMAS *Melbourne*, moored to a buoy about 200 metres off Garden Island. The *Steyne* had left Circular Quay at 2.30 pm on Wednesday, 30 September 1970, and was giving her 100 passengers a pleasant trip down the

harbour when two yachts, obviously skippered by those innocent folk who believe in the divine right of sail and think everything driven by power has to give way to them, loomed up in the ferry's path. Trying to avoid them, the ferry crashed into the stern of the *Melbourne*. The *South Steyne* looked like the cow with the crumpled horn when the two vessels separated, the bulwark around her bows having been pushed back at an angle of about 45 degrees.

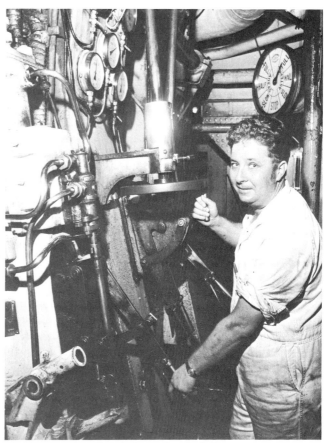

Don Pirie, standing beside the engines built by Harland and Wolff in Belfast, puts the South Steyne *full astern as she comes in to berth.*

Another typical statement from the Navy said: 'The *Melbourne* was secured to and standing at No. 2 Navy bouy in Sydney Harbour when struck in the stern by the Manly ferry *South Steyne*. Melbourne suffered minor structural damage, but there were no casualties.' The *South Steyne* returned to Circular Quay and was taken out of service after unloading her passengers. The *Melbourne* was an unlucky ship. During exercises off Jervis Bay on the night of February 10, 1964, the destroyer Voyager cut across her bows and was torn in two, sending 83 men to their death. In a similar tragic incident in exercises with the US fleet near Hawaii in June 1969 she sliced into the USS Frank E. Evans and another 74 men died.

It may seem to the casual observer that ferries like the *South Steyne* and the *Bellubera* were accident-prone ships, but, as remarked previously, accidents always made the news whereas years of quiet and uneventful running attracted no attention. Actually, the safety record of the Manly ferries is remarkable, especially when the size and speed of vessels like the *South Steyne* is considered in relation to the crowded and congested sphere of operations at weekends and holidays, when the harbour is taken over by swarms of Sunday drivers in anything that floats. At weekends in recent years the harbour has become a bedlam of sailing boats, many of them racing on the most unpredictable courses and too many smug in their belief that if they just keep going those big ships and ferries will get out of their way. They have no idea how hard it is to stop a vessel even the size of a Manly ferry travelling at speeds of around 15 knots. In latter years, ferry masters have had to contend with growing numbers of sailboard riders falling over in front of them until the harbour authorities were forced to ban sailboards from the shipping and ferry lanes. That there have not been more serious accidents is a tribute to the skill and patience of the men who man the ferries.

The Port Jackson & Manly Steamship Company set a very high standard of safety. A harbour and river ticket required to command a Manly ferry is very low in the order of priority compared with a sea-going master's certificate, but before they get their harbour and river certificate the Manly ferry skippers have had long and valuable experience as deck boys and deckhands, taking the wheel under the captain's supervision between Bennelong Point and the beginning of the run in to Manly wharf. By the time they become a certificated master they are already very adept at handling the ferries. The Port Jackson company maintained from 40 to 50 per cent of higher ticketed men who did not necessarily serve their time with the company, but they brought to the lower ticketed men the benefit of their experience at sea.

George Marshall agrees that the higher ticketed men from big ships were not always a success because some of them had never actually handled a ship in their lives, having stood by and given orders for others to do the handling. He recalls a P & O man who was in the *South Steyne* for some time, but never acquired the knack of guiding it in and out of wharves like his colleagues with only harbour and river tickets. He said:

> The same thing applied to the engineers. The requirement for a steam vessel was a 2nd class, foreign-going steam ticket and those in the motor vessels had to have a 2nd class motor ticket. For many years we had the dual ticket and 1st class steam and 1st class motor.

Towards the end of her career the *South Steyne* was used fairly frequently for charter work. When the World Law Society convention was in Sydney, the *South Steyne* was

Captain Wally Dohrn at sea with SS South Steyne *on one of the ocean cruises to Broken Bay and the Hawkesbury River.*

used two nights in succession to give 1000 people each time a night out on the harbour. That, according to George Marshall, was the biggest charter ever held on the harbour. Other large charters at different times were for the World Hereford Society, the World Shorthorn Society and the Aberdeen Society.

One charter the company could well have done without caused a riot of senseless destruction and had to be cut short. This happened on the night of 5 May 1964, when the vessel was chartered for a cruise by 1200 Sydney University students on the eve of their annual Commemoration Day. The Commemoration Day committee assured veteran skipper Harold Gibson, commodore of the Port Jackson line, that the students would behave themselves, but the undertaking didn't even last until the ferry had cleared the wharf. Between Circular Quay and Bennelong Point the students began climbing around the sides of the vessel, throwing crackers, firing rockets and dumping parts of the ship's equipment overboard. The 1200 students, half of them girls, had carried cases of liquor and kegs of beer aboard before the cruise left the wharf. Near Bennelong Point, Captain Gibson stopped the ferry and remonstrated with those in charge. He continued the cruise after another assurance that the students would behave themselves.

Not so. The vessel was hardly under way again before youths sprawled across seats with bottles of beer and glasses, throwing beer around, smashing bottles and glasses and destroying seats in mindless vandalism. A green skyrocket was fired from an empty beer bottle directly across the bridge of a passing Manly ferry. The rioters threw overboard about two dozen lifebelts and set off a high pressure fire extinguisher in the roof of the top deck, flooding that deck and cabins below. Fire sprinklers sprayed water for more than 10 minutes before Captain Gibson realised what was happening. Deckhands tried in vain to shut it off, and seats and everything else were saturated. At 10.15 pm Captain Gibson decided he had had more than enough of the drunken hoodlums who were threatening the safety of his ship, especially with the fire extinguisher system out of action, so he headed back to town and radioed for police to await the ferry's arrival.

Two captains always went on the South Steyne'*s ocean cruises. On this trip, Wally Dohrn (left) was with Captain Alfred Rowlings and helmsman Arthur Clarke.*

Thirty plainclothes and uniformed police and six ambulances were there when the *South Steyne* tied up and as the students began to stream ashore six young men were arrested. Ten more were treated aboard the ferry by ambulance men for cuts from broken glass and two were taken to Sydney Hospital. Several hundred students stood outside the wharf, jeering, booing and throwing crackers at the police who were trying to get those arrested into paddy wagons. The cruise cost the students 15 shillings a head. The proceeds, believe it or not, were to be in aid of Sydney University's charity appeal for the South African Committee for Higher Education.

Harold Gibson was fuming. It was bad enough having his beloved ship damaged by rough seas. Watching it being torn apart by 'higher education' yahoos was more than he could stand. The *Steyne* did get damaged in rough weather a few years later. Terrible weather pelted Sydney

on 23 June 1972. The *Sydney Morning Herald* reported the following day:

Heavy seas, whipped by winds reaching 70 mph, damaged two Manly ferries before services were suspended last night. The *South Steyne* had about six metres of her bulwarks badly damaged at Manly wharf. The *Bellubera*, brought in to replace the *South Steyne*, had windows and cabin doors stove in by the fierce wind and seas. A spokesman for the Port Jackson & Manly Steamship Company said the *South Steyne* would be off the run until next week.

The wind built up 12 metre waves across The Heads, tore many small boats from their moorings in the harbour and unroofed houses all over Sydney. More than five centimetres of rain caused other havoc. The *Daily Telegraph* reported:

Manly ferry services, battered by 12 metre waves, were suspended last night for the first time in five years because of the treacherous conditions. Services were suspended after two ferries and a hydrofoil were damaged. Nine metres of the *South Steyne*'s bulwark was ripped, several windows and a door on the *Bellubera* were stove in and a mooring bollard on the hydrofoil *Fairlight* was snapped. A middle-aged man on the *Baragoola* suffered head injuries when two seats were torn loose. Port Jackson traffic manager George Marshall crossed to Manly late in the afternoon and decided to suspend all services. Waves up to 12 metres between The Heads were playing havoc with the ferries, Mr Marshall said. The *South Steyne* will be out of service until the middle of next week.

I assume that in 1972 the *Daily Telegraph* still followed the practice, as when I was chief of staff in previous years, of cutting and pasting all *Telegraph* and *Herald* stories on comparison sheets. Any discrepancies were marked and reporters or sub-editors had to 'please explain'. No doubt the *Daily Telegraph* reporter had to explain why his story said nine metres and the *Herald* accounted for only six metres of the bulwark being damaged.

On 7 February 1974, cyclone Pam ravaged the New South Wales north coast and its backwash battered Sydney. Again, it was much like 1972, when the *South Steyne* and *Bellubera* were damaged and the ferry service had to be suspended. I travelled to Manly on the *Steyne*'s last trip before the service was stopped. It was a great ride. Turning around the Murchison light at Bradleys Head you could see the big white roll on Flagstaff, the inner point of North Head, promising a really good rock on the way across. Passing Clifton Gardens, just before Middle Head, the engine room telegraph clanged loudly several times, obviously to warn those down below that we were approaching the rough stuff and to keep out of the way of all that whirling mass of crankshafts. The *Steyne* rode those huge waves like the true champion she was, heading out between The Heads until she was turned to ride the big rollers in like a giant surf boat. Near Flagstaff the turbulence was churning up the sand from the bottom, colouring the boiling sea yellow, and the surge around Manly Wharf presented some problem to those who had to berth the ferries, especially one the size of the *Steyne*. Three ropes were snapped by the rise and fall of the surge before the big vessel was secured, and then getting ashore on the bucking gangways was almost a rodeo act. One woman standing near me during the long wait to disembark was terrified. She was not comforted when I said to her: 'It will be better still on the way back to town, going into it.' 'Not for me,' she replied. 'All I want to do is to get off this thing.' It wasn't for me, either. I was chairman of directors of the *Manly Daily* at that time and had told the editorial staff on arrival there of the great ride over on the big seas and how I was looking forward to the return trip. Not long afterwards, Noel MacDonald, then editor of the paper, came and told me:

> Sorry to disappoint you, but you won't be going back on the *South Steyne*. You came over on her last trip. They've stopped the ferries because of the heavy surge at the wharf here.

He drove me to Mosman on his way home and I had a placid ride to the Quay on the Mosman ferry, thinking of what I had missed across The Heads.

The big seas produced by cyclone Pam were the last the *South Steyne* had to weather. She was being used less and less now in a badly run-down service, taken over in 1972 by Brambles Industries Ltd, who were more interested in assets of the Port Jackson & Manly Steamship Company other than the ferries and least of all the last remaining steamship, which *South Steyne* had been since retirement of *Dee Why* in 1968. In 1974 the *South Steyne* was on borrowed time. Her days were numbered. But that is another part of the story.

4. *North Head*

One more ship was to play an important part in the story of the Port Jackson & Manly Steamship Company, but it was not a big new vessel like the *South Steyne*. It was the *Barrenjoey*, rebuilt and converted from steam to diesel-electric power and renamed *North Head*. In 1986, while this was being written, the *North Head* was still part of the Manly ferry fleet, by far the longest serving ship (73 years) and the only traditional Manly ferry left in service. There had been talk several times of phasing her out, but in January 1985, she had just been given an extensive overhaul and looked like being around for some time to come as a spare boat to fill in for the three new vessels— *Freshwater*, *Queenscliff* and *Narrabeen*—when they were due for overhaul or out of service at any time because of mishap. Before the advent of the new vessels, the *North Head* had been top boat since the departure of the *South Steyne*.

Her conversion was one of necessity rather than desire on the part of her owners. In 1946 the company realised

North Head *was the pride of the fleet between 25 August 1974, when fire ruined the* South Steyne *at the Balmain depot, and December 1982, when the new-look* Freshwater *came into service.* North Head *is seen here leaving Manly one afternoon in November 1982.*

that it had several ageing vessels, but business was not good enough to afford replacing them with new ships like the *South Steyne*. The best they could do, the Board decided, was to convert the *Barrenjoey* and *Balgowlah* from steam to diesel-electric propulsion as the cost of building new vessels was becoming prohibitive. The hulls were quite sound and diesel-electric power would be faster and, more importantly, give cheaper operating costs. The *Barrenjoey* did her last trip as a steamer on 12 April 1948, after which she was put in for a survey and failed to get a certificate for her boilers. That solved the problem. She was to be converted to a motor vessel. Most of the work was done by her original builders, Mort's Dock & Engineering Company, who altered and strengthened the frames of the hull, replated the hull and put in engine beds for the new machinery. Because of the post-war shortages of labour and materials, the work went slowly while the costs rose quickly. The *North Head*'s steam engines were replaced with four 7-cylinder, British Thompson-Houston diesel generators supplying current to four 500-hp electric motors, arranged in pairs at each end of the ship to drive short propeller shafts through 5:1 reduction gears. This enabled the pushing propeller to have 90 per cent of the power, leaving only 10 per cent for the pulling propeller for'ard and reducing the impedance caused as a steamer with long continuous shafts turning both propellers at the same revolutions. The steam steering gear was taken out, too, and electric-hydraulic equipment installed.

The redesigned ferry was going to look quite different. Two short funnels were much smarter than the one big long funnel of the SS *Barrenjoey*, and her straight stems were to take a lesson from the *South Steyne* and be transformed with the bulwarks at each end by flaring to produce a slightly raked 'clipper' appearance. The wooden superstructure of the upper deck was rebuilt in steel, closed in to the bridge fronts where formerly it had been open, and the boats were removed up top to the bridge deck. Two more access gates were provided for loading and unloading, making a total of 14, gates equal in width altogether to a 112-ft pathway. The theory, never achieved, was that 1500 passengers walking at two miles an hour could be disembarked in 20 seconds if gangways were used at every gate. All this was with the object of getting there more quickly, and loading and unloading more quickly.

Smith's *Weekly* noted in December 1949, the modernisation of the *Barrenjoey* at a cost of about £250 000, commenting:

> This is eight and a half times what it cost to build her in 1913, but at that she will still be a bargain, because on today's cost of ship-building it would take about

£400 000 to replace her with a new vessel. *Barrenjoey* cost about £30 000 originally. To have her built in 1928-29 would have cost nearly £70 000, and in 1938, £144 000. A shipwright's estimate to *Smith*'s this week was that modernisation and conversion of the *Barrenjoey* would cost now about £250 000. General manager of the Port Jackson & Manly Steamship Company, Mr Cameron, said it would be impossible to say exactly what the cost would be until the *Barrenjoey* was finally ready for service again. 'But we know it will be an awful lot, he added.'

Actually, the final figure was £261 772. Mr Cameron told the *Manly-Warringah News* in July the following year that the company hoped to speed up the service with the refitted vessel later in the year. He said the ferry would embody all the latest in nautical design and would resemble the *South Steyne* in appearance. In August, Mr Cameron announced after the annual meeting of the company that the *Barrenjoey*, when completed, would be the equivalent of an entirely new vessel and because of this it had been decided to rename her *North Head*. The new name did not find immediate favour with the public. Nor were they all enthusiastic about the new look. Some passengers said they liked the *Barrenjoey*'s name and her old-fashioned construction.

Mr W.J. Marsden, 60, of Pittwater Road, Manly, who had travelled on the Manly ferries for 28 years, told the *Daily Telegraph* he was sorry the company was renaming the *Barrenjoey*. 'I think *Barrenjoey* is a grand name that has some historical meaning,' he said. 'Dance floors and green and cream upholstery will spoil the old-fashioned effect of *Barrenjoey*.' Mr William Cotter, 61, of Lismore Avenue, Dee Why, said he had travelled on the Manly ferries for 50 years. His opinion: '*Barrenjoey* was a good enough name for the old ship, so I don't see why it's not good enough for her when she's rebuilt.' Mr H.T. Kay, 63, of North Steyne, Manly, said that if the company wanted to change the name of *Barrenjoey* they should have chosen North Steyne, to complement *South Steyne*.

The *North Head* did harbour trials on 5 May 1951, and two days later was commissioned by the then Minister for Transport, Mr W.F. Sheahan, at a ceremony on board to show off the virtually new ferry. The brass commemorative plate unveiled by Mr Sheahan can still be seen on the aft dummy funnel casing on the main deck. After spending so much money the owners expected the *North Head* to enter service and begin earning revenue soon after the commissioning ceremony, but the Maritime Services Board had other ideas and it was some months before the vessel could be put to work to recoup some of the money spent on its conversion. The Maritime Services Board demanded stability tests and a reassessment of tonnage figures before giving the ferry a certificate. Building up the bows with extra steelwork, and moving crew accommodation, lifeboats and rafts to the top decks had affected the craft's stability. The life-rafts were moved from the sun deck to the fore and aft ends of the promenade deck, but then it was found that they would be too heavy to be lifted over the bulwarks in an emergency. Many have often wondered why the *North Head* had hinged sections of the bulwark like a gate at each end fore and aft. They were cut into the bulwarks so that they could be opened and the wooden life-rafts could be pushed overboard quickly if they were needed.

Ships that pass in the day. Aerial photo of Bellubera *(nearest camera) and* North Head *crossing The Heads, rolling beam on to the swell.*

All this took a long time. It was three and a half years from 12 April 1948, when the *Barrenjoey* was taken out of service to be rebuilt, until 29 September 1951—six months after her commissioning ceremony—before the *North Head* resumed duty as a regular Manly ferry. *North Head*, former traffic manager George Marshall recalls, came back to the harbour with a grand fanfare of publicity, and she attracted a great deal of attention with her sleek lines and two funnels, looking like a sister to the *South Steyne*. George said:

We were in trouble and the new vessel promised to give things a lift. We were losing passengers and had been promised State Government assistance. The Government was setting up a Ministry of Transport and Highways under a commissioner, Mr Reg Winsor, and had promised to divert back to the Manly ferries all the traffic which had been taken away after the end of petrol rationing by the direct bus services between the

northern beaches and the city. That could have been the salvation of the Port Jackson & Manly Steamship Company, but it was a failure because the commission, a non-revenue earning body, was subject to every political objection by people who wanted to use the buses instead of having to change to the ferries at Manly, especially as the original bus routes which had fed the ferries wound snake-like all over the place to pick up passengers. The idea lasted about 12 months and then fizzled out. All this time the ferry company was losing more and more passengers and then, when the scheme folded up, it was open go for the direct city buses, which crept closer and closer to Manly wharf.

The *North Head*, having been out of service for three and a half years, was nearly out of action again only a few months after her return. What happened and how she was saved is quite an extraordinary story. Again Eric Gale happened to be in the right place at the right time and it was through his initiative and quick action in a situation similar to that in which he drove the *Dee Why* out of the *Bellubera* fire at the Kurraba Point depot in 1936 that the *North Head* was saved from serious damage. It happened while the ferry was being docked in Chapman's floating dock at Balmain on 14 January 1952. Eric tells the story:

Young Wally Dohrn was the skipper that day. He took the *North Head* across to the dock and delivered her in, then went back to town. I went over to the dock to inspect the hull when it came out of the water. When I arrived there I saw the *North Head* in the dock and she was up at an angle and there were no shores from the sides of the dock to hold her upright. 'What's the matter here?' I asked. They said they couldn't raise the dock. I said, 'Well lower it.' But they said they couldn't lower it either. They had started to pump out the dock, but the inshore tank was the only one pumped and that was not fully emptied.

Lew Maxwell was there as engineer. I went down and said to him: 'Lew. Start one engine. We've got to drive her off. We can't leave her here like this. She'll capsize when the tide goes down.' I went on to the bridge and tried to take her off, but she wouldn't move. We started a second engine and that didn't move her. Neither would three. I told Lew to give her all four engines and then I felt her move. 'You beauty,' I yelled. One line was still on the dock as she moved and I called out to the dock men not to let it go, but they threw it off as soon as she floated, so I took her out into the stream and held her there until Wally Dohrn came back in response to an urgent phone call from the dock and we took *North Head* back to Kurraba Point and tied her up. I telephoned Cockatoo Dock then and arranged for the

North Head to go in there next day. I was just a bit worried about what we might find. We had pulled at least six chocks out of Chapman's dock as we dragged the *North Head* off. But there was no damage to the ferry's hull. It was a risk doing what I did, but had the vessel fallen over she could have been badly damaged.

So, Eric Gale saved two of the Manly ferries. He didn't get much thanks for saving the *Dee Why*. Said Eric:

I got into trouble that time because I wasn't a skipper and didn't have a ticket. The shipwright surveyor went stone mad and said I had no right to move her. What should I have done? Left her there to burn? The varnish was scorched all around the wheelhouse. Another five minutes and she would have been ablaze.

But the Port Jackson & Manly Steamship Company appreciated what he did with the *North Head* and sent him a letter dated 22 January 1952, which said:

Dear Mr Gale. The situation associated with the attempted docking of the *North Head* in Chapman's floating dock on 14 January was reported to the Board last Friday. Your initiative in moving the vessel from the dock to avoid possible damage was commended and, as directed, I wish to convey to you the Board's appreciation of your timely action. Brigadier Claude Cameron, Managing Director.

A few years later, on a Saturday night, 28 May 1955, the *North Head* was aground again, this time on a reef about 200 metres off Bradleys Head. Thick fog had smothered the harbour when the *North Head*, carrying about 200 passengers, left Manly at 10.15 pm and because of the poor visibility, Captain Bill Benecke kept his vessel at a very slow speed. About half an hour later, the ferry ran on to an area of rock and sand covered by thick kelp 200 metres north of the fog siren on the point of Bradleys Head. Slithering over this mixture, the ferry ground to a halt within 75 metres of the shore, where, held by the bows, she rocked gently on whatever movement there was in the calm water. Two deckhands dived overboard and swam ashore to telephone the water police, who arrived fairly quickly in the police launch *Nemesis*. The passengers took the accident very calmly. Most of them resigned themselves cheerfully to a long wait, stretching out on the seats to make themselves as comfortable as possible. Others stood against the rails shouting to people on the shore. The fog siren, it turned out, had not been switched on, as should have happened when the fog descended. Two and a half hours later, at 1.30 am, the two-deck cruise launch *Radar*, known then as *La Radar*, came alongside

and began transferring passengers, who arrived at Circular Quay just before 1.45 am. The fog had closed down all harbour transport about the time the *North Head* left Manly. People rushed taxis at the Quay when they found the fog had stopped ferry services.

A subsequent Court of Marine Inquiry found that failure to switch on the Bradleys Head fog signal was the primary cause of the *North Head* going aground. The court found that the fog signal was not switched on, as it should have been, when the fog came down on the harbour, because a telephone line between Bennelong Point and Bradleys Head was out of order. No action was taken on the certificate of Captain Beneke.

In 1964 the Port Jackson company was asked to take the *South Steyne* down to Melbourne for that city's Moomba Festival. George Marshall went down to investigate the practicability of the idea of sending a ferry to Melbourne for a month. At the time, five ferries were being used on the Manly service, but one was a spare boat, used only when one of the other four was on refit, so that for about three months of the year there was a spare vessel. It was decided to send the *North Head* for a month. The venture was very successful both that year and the following year, when the *North Head* went down in March for the Moomba Festival and was away for six weeks. George Marshall recalls:

It was the right time of the year in March with the Moomba Festival and it was very successful. But the following year the management became dreamy and decided to take the little hydrofoil *Manly* down for 10 weeks in January. This was a fiasco because neither the management nor I knew Melbourne. Sydney, from Christmas to Easter, is full of visitors with people from the country and other States. During that time of the year we had been used to carrying big loads of trippers in the Manly ferries. But Melbourne we found to be completely different because at Christmas time, and through January, Melbourne is cleared out of holiday-makers. They all go down to the bottom end of Port Phillip Bay or up to Lakes Entrance and in January we found you could hardly put a passenger in the boat. These people come back to Melbourne in February and the first two weeks are taken up with getting the kids back to school or doing their shopping and they're all broke after their holidays. You can't take a bob [shilling] in February and the whole idea of the Moomba is to get the economy moving again from about the 10th of March.

So, through being greedy we came unstuck. There was one other thing, too, with which we had not reckoned. That was the southerlies in Port Phillip Bay. We took the hydrofoil first to St Kilda, where it was smashed up the first day, being on the weather side of the bay. We took it to Port Melbourne and that was almost as bad. Then we had 41 consecutive days of southerly weather, which made it impossible to operate on that side of the bay after 11 am. The southerly there is like the nor'easter in Sydney. In Melbourne the wind comes up regularly every day, even more than in Sydney at that time of the year. You get up in the morning and the bay is like glass—not a ripple on it— but by 11 o'clock you can have waves four metres high and it is impossible to operate a small hydrofoil. The whole venture that year was a failure—a complete disaster.

In Sydney, the *North Head* became more and more the work horse of the fleet after the departure of the *Curl Curl* and *Dee Why* and, in 1973, the *Bellubera*. Only three ferries remained in service then—*North Head*, *South Steyne* and *Baragoola*—and passenger business was declining.

The *North Head* caught fire while travelling from Manly to Sydney on 6 August 1976, and more than 100 passengers had to be transferred to the *Baragoola*, which was brought alongside near Bradleys Head, that fateful part of the harbour where nearly everything seems to happen. The fire, which started in the control switch-board, was put out by crew members with the ship's own fire-fighting equipment. Water police, Maritime Services Board boats and a Navy torpedo recovery boat came out to help, but the passengers were in no danger and they were evacuated without fuss to the *Baragoola* when it tied

up alongside. A tug towed the *North Head* back to its Balmain depot, where the burnt wiring was replaced and the ferry returned to work the following day.

An electrical fault caused *North Head*'s next mishap three years later in January 1979, when she overshot the berth at Circular Quay on her last trip just before midnight, glanced off the buffer and crashed into the footpath. None of the 300 passengers aboard was injured and apparent damage to the ferry was slight. A large slab of concrete was gouged out of the footpath, and at the Balmain depot a diver removed a lump of concrete from the propeller at the city end—usually the aft end. *North Head* was back on the run the following afternoon, much to the relief of the commuters, who found conditions at Manly chaotic that morning with only the *Baragoola* and *Lady Wakehurst* available and the service cut by a third. By this stage the Manly ferry traffic was beginning to pick up again and in peak hours the *Lady Wakehurst* and *Lady Northcott* were too small. They did a valuable relief job for several years, but they were not Manly ferries and were being asked to do work for which they were never designed.

On 31 July 1979, the *North Head* did not arrive at Manly with her usual promptness to pick up the biggest morning peak-hour load at 8 am. She had lost one of her rudders near Bradleys Head on the way down from town. After turning around the Bradleys Head marker buoy, the deckhand who was steering reported to Captain Dave Stimson that the vessel was not steering as she should. They stopped the ship and did some tests with the steering in the presence of the engineer, who had been called up to the bridge. Said Dave Stimson:

Manly on the starboard quarter. In the wheelhouse of North Head *approaching the end of a run from the city. Captain Noel Heath will soon stop engines to glide in to the wharf and will take the wheel from helmsman Tony Geronicolas.*

This picture of the North Head, *partly hidden behind a big roller, appeared in the* Manly Daily *on Friday, 11 December 1970.*

Then we went down and, looking over the side, could see nothing wrong with the rudder, but when we set off again it was obvious that something was wrong. We lost steering way altogether. The engineer and I decided that we would lock the rudder by dropping the pin into it, turn the vessel around and proceed to Manly using the other rudder. It was 8.20 when we reached Manly and the wharf was crowded. When we berthed, the engineer, George McAskill, jumped ashore to make an inspection from the wharf. Standing immediately below where I was on the bridge, he looked up at me and said 'It's gone'. I couldn't believe what I was hearing so I went on to the wharf to see for myself and, sure enough, there was no rudder at the for'ard end. It had been sheared off at the palm. We had to back out with the 8 am and 8.15 am crowds aboard, turn around clear of the wharf and get back to the city as fast as we could.

The Public Transport Commission called in the Navy to search for the lost rudder, but it was a hopeless task in the deep water with soft muddy bottom near where the *Greycliffe* had gone down years before. The mishap meant that the *North Head* could be used only sparingly for the main peak-hour trips while a new rudder was made and fitted at Cockatoo Dock. For several weeks the Manly service was carried on by only two ferries—the *Baragoola* and the little *Lady Wakehurst*. Commented the *Manly Daily:* 'The *North Head* accident again highlighted the narrow margin left on the Manly run when a ferry is put out of action.' At this time the other small relief vessel, *Lady Northcott*, was not available because she was out of service undergoing her annual refit.

Four years later, when the *Queenscliff*, second of the new-look, $9.5 million Manly ferries was commissioned, there was talk that the *North Head* had reached the end of her long life. A third new ferry was to be built. But several things decided that *North Head* could not be put aside and would have to be given another refit so that she could be used as a relief boat, perhaps until a fourth new Manly ferry was built. The Urban Transit Authority, as the Public Transport Commission had been renamed, was in grave trouble because it did not have enough ferries for the inner harbour services to spare the *Lady Wakehurst* or the *Lady*

Northcott for Manly. Things became really serious in January 1984, when the *Karrabee*, one of the ancient wooden ferries used on inner harbour routes, sank at the wharf at Circular Quay after taking part in the Festival of Sydney's annual ferry race, fortunately after her passengers had been put ashore. Findings of a subsequent inquiry on the condition of the old *Karrabee* no doubt helped the Urban Transit Authority decide that the days of wooden ferries were over. The last of the survivors from the old Sydney Ferries days—the *Karrabee, Kameruka, Karingal* and *Lady Edeline*—were 'put to grass' at Balmain. This left the Urban Transit Authority terribly short of inner harbour ferries pending delivery of the new catamaran-type craft which would replace them. The only one of the original Sydney Ferries fleet left in service then was the steel-hulled *Kanangra*. Although around the same vintage as the *North Head*—built in 1912—she was still a very good ship, capable of carrying more than 900 passengers. With the *Lady Wakehurst* and the *Lady Northcott*, the *Kanangra* was the backbone of the Mosman service, the most heavily patronised after Manly.

That was until the night of 5 November 1984, when the *Kanangra* and the *North Head* came to blows off Bennelong Point in front of the Opera House. The *Kanangra* left Circular Quay at 7 pm with about 200 passengers for Mosman during very heavy rain which had been pelting down on Sydney for most of the day. The *Kanangra* came out of Sydney Cove just as the *North Head*, returning almost empty from one of the last peak-hour runs to Manly, was turning into the cove. But, according to petrified passengers on the front of the *Kanangra*, the *North Head* turned too soon and if the *Kanangra* had not been in its way would have crashed into the front of the Opera House. The *Kanangra* was knocked about quite badly in the impact, which sent screaming passengers rushing back towards the stern. Many grabbed lifebelts and put them on, fearing that they might have to swim to the Opera House steps. Nobody had to swim, but the *North Head*'s stern ripped into the *Kanangra*'s wooden superstructure, making quite a mess.

There was not much apparent damage to the *North Head*. She was back on the Manly run the following day. But a couple of weeks later she broke down near Manly wharf and had to be towed back to Balmain. Later, in Cockatoo Island dry dock, shipwrights found that she had broken a propeller shaft, damaged, no doubt, in the collision with the *Kanangra*. Reporting this, the *Manly Daily* predicted that the *North Head* may have made her last voyage. Not so. Passenger traffic to Manly was growing so much then that three big ferries were needed to handle the crowds and the Urban Transit Authority patched up the *North Head* to keep her going as a spare boat for a few more years.

PART V
DECLINE AND FALL

1. Standing Room Only

In the 10 years between 1973, when the *Bellubera* was withdrawn from service, and the advent of the new large Freshwater class ferries at the end of 1982, the story of the Manly ferries is something like the decline and fall of the Roman Empire. The demise of the *Bellubera* began the disintegration of the once proud fleet. Commercial interests which took over the Port Jackson & Manly Steamship Company became disillusioned with their venture and dumped the ageing vessels and the responsibility for maintaining an essential public transport service into the lap of the State Government. The Government can claim some credit for having accepted a seemingly hopeless task and in the space of 10 years succeeding in restoring the Manly ferry service to something similar to its former efficiency.

Things were going badly for the Port Jackson company as far back as 1964, when the shares fell as low as two shillings and fourpence. But trouble had appeared even before then. In July 1947, the sixpenny fare for adults and the penny fare for children were increased by a penny and season tickets went up proportionately. To avoid altering turnstiles, tokens were sold. The Manly company's chairman, Mr H.N. Pope, told his annual meeting in August 1947 that fares would have to go higher still because an enormous increase in the company's expenditure was likely next year. The fleet had carried 923 438 fewer passengers than in the previous year—a drop of nearly a million. With basic wage increases, introduction of the 40-hour working week and weekend penalty rates, expenditure for the next year should increase enormously.

Next year, 1948, passenger traffic dropped another 537 830, making the total loss in two years close to one and a half million. Mr Pope told the annual meeting that year that the traffic had been affected by wet weekends, transport stoppages and gas and electricity restrictions. A new fare rise was inevitable and in December the Prices Commission approved another twopence for the adult fare, taking it up to ninepence. Letters of protest appeared in the Press. In May 1950 came the third increase, taking the fare to a shilling for adults and threepence for children. The company issued a statement pointing out the continuous and heavy increases in operating costs since the war. Fuel and maintenance costs had risen by 115 per cent.

In the boom days of the Manly ferries people sat on the stairs when there were no seats in peak hours. The man on the right looks like former NSW Premier J. T. Lang, but he would hardly have been a Manly commuter.

Some travellers tried their own solution to the fare rises. Poker machine tokens began finding their way into the turnstiles instead of shillings. One Manly resident pleaded guilty in court to a charge of having evaded payment of his fare on the ferry and was fined five pounds. Traffic manager George Marshall told the court that since the fare had been increased from ninepence to a shilling, cash was being used in the turnstiles, but as it was found that many brass discs were being put into the turnstiles instead of money, a close watch had been kept the previous night and the defendant was seen to drop a brass disc into the slot. The man, a fitter by occupation, told police that a fellow employee made the discs for him.

The ferry company was concerned about the public unrest and tried in other ways to keep the travelling public happy. In July 1950, passengers were handed papers

108

asking them to vote on whether they wanted to hear commercial radio programs during peak-hour travel. They were asked to give their usual travelling time, their opinion on the proposed broadcasts and their objections, if any. The idea was voted out by a narrow margin when 51 per cent decided that they preferred to keep the peace and did not want radio programs broadcast on their ferries. Of the 51 per cent who voted against radio, 59 per cent said they preferred 'peace and quiet', 13 per cent disliked radio 'in every form', 10 per cent disliked radio 'in most forms', five per cent thought fares would be increased again to pay for the broadcasts, 11 per cent said the broadcasts would put the musicians who played on the ferries then out of work. Another two per cent just said flatly that they would transfer to bus travel if radios were installed.

The travellers expressed their opinions in English, French, German and shorthand. One woman, who preferred to be nameless, said her husband was a radio announcer and she heard enough of him. Another, male, asked for a liquor bar to be installed instead of the radio. Then there was the night traveller who said the radio broadcasts would interfere with his love-making. Most of the 49 per cent who voted in favour of the radio were teenagers or schoolchildren.

In 1964 control of the Port Jackson & Manly Steamship Company changed hands and also changed direction. A group of four businessmen bought the controlling interest in the company and overnight the old board of directors was gone. In their place were Roscoe W.G. Hoyle (solicitor), R.E. Martin (solicitor), Neil Barrell (accountant), Bjarne Halvorsen, of the famous boatbuilding family, and as managing director, J.C. Needham, who had some experience in ferries with small inner harbour services. A few years previously he had taken over Hegartys' ferries, which replaced the bigger Sydney Ferries fleet on the short runs to Kirribilli and Lavender Bay.

At this point the old traditions of the Port Jackson & Manly Steamship Company began to fade. Neither this group nor the transport operators, Brambles Industries Ltd, which took the company over in February 1972 were interested in the ferries as such. Their interests were purely business and both saw profits not in the ferries but in other activities of the Port Jackson company. At that time there was talk of extensive oil exploration off the coast of New South Wales and servicing this looked like a very promising investment. Another object of the Needham group was the introduction of hydrofoils to Manly and other harbour services. They saw hydrofoils, their speed halving travelling time to Manly, as the answer to the slower and ageing ferries, whose replacement costs would be prohibitive. But they could not operate hydrofoils unless they had an operating service in existence, hence another reason for acquisition of the Manly ferries.

The new management had contacts with an oil search company in America which was anxious to get Australian representation providing oil rig supply services and building the necessary vessels. They had built an oil rig servicing vessel which was then chartered to Esso oil exploration, operating as Tidewater Port Jackson Marine Pty Ltd, an associated company of Port Jackson. Next they introduced the hydrofoils. First of these, the 30-knot, 72-passenger *Manly*, went into service on 7 January 1965. It looked as if hydrofoils were the answer. Three larger ones were ordered subsequently from Italy—the *Fairlight*, which began service in November 1966, *Dee Why* (1970) and *Curl Curl* (1973). Although the ferries were no gold mine for their new owners, things began to look up for the company generally and some money was spent on improvements to the *South Steyne*, including a bar and a food café. The idea was to have breakfast going to work and afternoon tea on the way home. George Marshall recalls:

It lasted a week. Nobody wanted it. I think we sold two cups of coffee the first morning. The bar on the ocean cruises was not much more of a success because it was used mainly by those who couldn't get into a pub or a club on Sundays and they just sat in there drinking and didn't enjoy the scenery, especially if the trip up or down the coast made them seasick.

The Port Jackson company extended its activities in 1951, when Sydney Ferries reached the end of the road and the New South Wales Government had to take over those inner harbour services, paying £25 000 for the Balmain depot and workshops and £1 each for the 15 ferries remaining from the 52 used on the inner harbour routes before the Harbour Bridge opened 19 years previously.

The Government formed the Sydney Harbour Transport Board of three members, comprising the Commissioner for Government Transport as chairman, the Under Secretary of the Treasury and the president of the Maritime Services Board. This was to deal with policy aspects only, not to operate the ferries the Government had been forced to acquire. The Sydney Harbour Ferries Act, introduced to deal with the situation, provided for an agency agreement whereby an agent company was appointed to operate the former Sydney Ferries fleet as Sydney Harbour Ferries Pty Ltd, the directors of which were the directors of the Port Jackson & Manly Steamship Company. What all this meant was that the State Government appointed the Port Jackson company to manage and operate the inner harbour ferries for the Government at a fee of £3000 a year. Later, the Port Jackson company had representation on that board.

Before this new control, the Port Jackson company had

hopes of improving its situation by developing some of its real estate, principally the Kurraba Point waterfront land and another waterfront property at Manly with an old residence on it called 'Moncrieff'. This was near what was known as the coal wharf, alongside the old Manly harbour swimming baths. The company used to ship coal and bricks to that wharf at Manly in the days when nearly all the cargo to Manly went by water. A lighter loaded with bricks sank somewhere between the wharf and Smedleys Point and as far as anyone knows is still there. The then general manager, Brigadier Cameron, had ideas of a big residential development at Kurraba Point which would return a good profit to the ferry company. This land was zoned light industrial, for use as a ferry depot and work-shops and it had to be re-zoned residential. Cameron had been looking around for some time for an alternative site for the workshops for both the inner harbour and Manly ferries, but eventually the search was given up without finding a suitable place and the entire ferry maintenance was moved to the Sydney Ferries workshops at Balmain.

If Brigadier Cameron thought he was going to rejuve-nate his company's fortunes by residential development he was in for a big disappointment. North Sydney Council did not re-zone the point for residential development and it was resumed for a park. At Manly, the State Govern-ment took the company's land there at its price for Housing Commission flats. This was a political move to dilute the non-Labor vote in Manly rather than any desire to give Housing Commission tenants a choice waterfront residence. Certainly it provided housing for a lot of people, although, environmentally, a waterfront park like that at Kurraba Point would have looked more attractive than the austere Housing Commission flats at Manly which some ferry travellers have named San Quentin and Alcatraz.

Meanwhile, from all its activities, the company was not doing too badly and its 1971 annual report and balance sheet no doubt attracted another take-over, this time from the big transport group, Brambles Industries Ltd. For the year ended 30 June 1971, the Port Jackson & Manly Steamship Company and its subsidiaries showed a profit of $111 526 after providing $104 600 for taxation. Unap-propriated profits brought forward from the previous year totalled $94 065, which, after adjustment for a transfer of $6390 from the asset realisation reserve and allowing for tax overprovided, added $100 545, making a total avail-able of $212 073. The directors' report included these interesting extracts:

> With three hydrofoils operating to Manly, it has been possible to provide a greatly improved service fre-quency, which your directors have reason to believe is appreciated by the travelling public.

The activity of the hydraulic division of the subsidi-ary company, Palm Beach Marine Service Pty Ltd, has continued to increase and during the year specially designed and manufactured sets of steering gear were supplied to all States of the Commonwealth and ex-ported to Singapore, Noumea, Papua-New Guinea, Fiji and the British Solomon Islands.

Operations of the fleet of large conventional vessels continued in a satisfactory manner, but of course, as a whole, these vessels are nearing the end of their service. Hydrofoil traffic has been most satisfactory and a new large craft of 140-passenger capacity, to be named *Barrenjoey*, is now on order for delivery to Sydney in September 1972.

The associate company, Tidewater Port Jackson Marine Pty Ltd, has continued to trade in a satisfactory manner and at present has an additional vessel of 4000-hp building in South Australia.

On 12 November 1971, the Port Jackson & Manly Steam-ship Company received from Brambles a take-over offer worth $1 572 000. Brambles general manager, Mr W. J. Holcroft, said he saw 'excellent growth prospects' for the ferry services on the harbour. He said:

> We believe the services are under-utilised and we would hope to expand them. We do not plan to interfere in the way the services are run. We would prefer to see ourselves in the role of benevolent bankers.

Mr Holcroft made it clear, however, that a large part of his company's interest in the deal centred on Tidewater Port Jackson Marine Pty Ltd, owned 50 per cent by Port Jackson and 50 per cent by a company in New Orleans, USA, at that time operating six oil rig supply vessels and building another. Said Mr Holcroft:

> We believe there is going to be a tremendous develop-ment of industries based on offshore oil, particularly if the Government adopts a more realistic policy on oil exploration subsidy.

Brambles was a highly diversified company with assets of $60 million spread over 14 transport and distribution undertakings. In March the previous year it had bought Fenwick Holdings Ltd and added two line boats and five new tugs to Fenwick's fleet of nine tugs, at a cost of more than $2 million. Brambles' 1970 profit was $4 287 500. The Port Jackson company rejected the initial take-over offer, but accepted a later offer of $2 112 000.

It soon became evident that Brambles had only a minor interest in the ferries and before long would endeavour to offload them on to the State Government. As a member of the New South Wales Parliament then and chairman of the

Government Transport Committee, I warned the then Minister for Transport, Milton Morris, that this would happen. I told him that I was appalled at the condition of ferries which the Port Jackson & Manly Steamship Company had always kept spotless, predicting that as the ships deteriorated further they would be dumped into our lap to patch up and keep going. The Government should not wait until then, I suggested. It should prepare for the inevitability of having to build at least two new ferries for the Manly service. The Government Transport Committee made a similar recommendation to the minister some time later in a report after an inquiry into Sydney Harbour ferry services. It also recommended that the *Lady Wakehurst*, being built then for the Mosman and Cremorne route, and the *Lady Northcott*, which was to follow, should be modified with higher bows and extra gangway access so that they could be used as relief vessels on the Manly run. It was very fortunate that this was done, as events turned out, because these two small ferries, although never intended to be Manly ferries, did much better than expected and filled in for several years while the new Freshwater class vessels were being built.

A week after Brambles took over they sold the hydrofoils to Waltons Finance and leased them back on a monthly rental, a move known to very few until the Government had to take over the ferries in 1974. Not that the State Government could complain very much about that. Brambles may have done it for tax purposes. The Government sold the State's trains and buses to stave off financial troubles. Most people are unaware that the New South Wales Government does not own trains and buses it operates under the Urban Transit Authority and the State Rail Authority. The Auditor-General's report, tabled in Parliament at the end of September 1982, disclosed that the State Rail Authority had been directed to sell rolling stock for $221 million, then lease it back. The Government gained $220 million to cut down its soaring deficit, which, otherwise, would have topped $290 million, but paid back $21 million in leasing charges. A year later, leasing charges for the railway had risen to a massive $69 600 000 in a total SRA loss for the year of $783 600 000. They could not very well have sold the ferries. They were not worth much at that stage.

The Manly ferry fleet when Brambles took over consisted of four vessels—the *South Steyne*, *North Head*, *Bellubera* and *Baragoola*. It was soon to be reduced, despite the pre-takeover speech by Brambles general manager predicting big expansion for the ferry services. The hard facts of the situation were that whereas the old Port Jackson & Manly Steamship Company of the W.L. Dendy era had real pride in its ferries and the service it gave the travelling public, the company, under Brambles, was a hard business concern and had little sentiment for

ageing ferries, on which it proposed to waste as little money as possible and would try to unload them on to the State Government as soon as it could.

In May 1973, new fare increases were announced, putting daily fares up by 10 per cent and weekly tickets by 33.3 per cent. Monthly, quarterly and half-yearly season tickets were to be discontinued on the grounds of increased costs and insufficient demand.

A few months later the *Herald* carried a story which said the four Manly ferries were likely to be replaced in the next few years by new conventional vessels. It said: 'The ferries' operator, the Port Jackson & Manly Steamship Company, believes the present fleet is obsolete and is concerned at the high cost of maintaining it.' The company hoped to receive government help to replace the vessels, each of which was expected to cost about $1 million to build in Australia. General manager, Tom Gibson, hoped to discuss this with the New South Wales Minister for Transport, Mr Milton Morris. Nothing, of course, came of that. The Government, its head in the sand, would resist, until the last minute, the problem it had to face ultimately.

On 14 December 1973, Mr Gibson disclosed to the Press that the 63-year-old *Bellubera* had been withdrawn from service because of increasing operating and maintenance costs and reduced off-peak patronage. The ferry services were then cut back from nine trips to five on week-days between 9 am and 4 pm. 'The people of Manly are served too well,' said somebody described as 'a spokesman for the company'. Mr Gibson said that with the withdrawal of the *Bellubera*, the *South Steyne* ocean cruises would be suspended indefinitely. He was still saying the old ferries would be replaced with new vessels. But worse was to come. In January 1974, the company threatened to withdraw the *Baragoola* as well as the *Bellubera*. Saturday services by ferry were to end in February, when only hydrofoils would be used. Naturally there was a public outcry. Apart from losing the ferry services, there was a big difference in fares. A single ferry ride then cost 45c for adults and 20c for children, but on Saturdays it was going to cost 75c by hydrofoil, with no half fares at all.

When it was confirmed early in the new year that the *Baragoola* was going to be taken off on 7 February, there was public anger and three trade unions affected by the cuts—the Firemen and Deckhands Union, the Merchant Service Guild and the Institute of Marine and Power Engineers—demanded that the State Government accept responsibility for the Manly ferries, as it had done when Sydney Ferries collapsed in 1951. A Save the Manly Ferries campaign was started immediately, taken up with double enthusiasm by some Manly Labor Party identities, who saw it as a good political opportunity to blame the

State Liberal-Country Party Government rather than the Brambles management of the Port Jackson company. The campaign did not lack support, irrespective of the political implications. More than 3000 pamphlets were distributed on Manly wharf and, at a noisy public meeting in Manly, scores of local residents, members of the Labor and Australia parties, involved trade unions, pensioners and representatives of resident action groups pledged their support for the Save the Manly Ferries Committee. At the meeting, Brambles Industries was accused of allowing the ferries to run down because it was more interested in the company's other assets, a claim which Brambles did not deny. Brambles' chairman, Mr R.A. Dickson, said his company would consider a Government take-over bid. Angry Manly-Warringah residents had put 6000 signatures on two petitions which were presented to Mr Milton Morris and they were planning a mass demonstration to demand that the Government take over the ferry service.

Chairman of the campaign was a Manly solicitor, Mr Marc Gumbert, who was active in the Labor Party. He was quoted in the *Sydney Morning Herald:*

There have been moves and statements by Brambles showing that they intend to terminate the service. The

---

THURSDAY, SEPTEMBER 12, 1974.

▌ *Your report . . . claiming overcrowding on ferries heavily relied on a photograph of about 10 people standing and another of a few people sitting on the the stairs.* ▌ — Mr. Milton Morris Minister for Transport in yesterday's Manly Daily

OUR EVIDENCE!

In a strongly worded letter to the Manly Daily yesterday Mr. Milton Morris, Minister for Transport, attempted to refute all the evidence pointing to overcrowding and inadequacy of the Manly ferry service.

Mr. Morris belittled all the reporting and photographic work that the Manly Daily has published recently.

He suggested that isolated incidents were photographed to make a point.

Today we publish further photographs from the series taken last week to reinforce our submission that the Manly ferry peak hour services are overcrowded.

These photographs tell their own story.

We reiterate that the peak-hour services are overcrowded and probably dangerously so.

The people on the north side of Sydney Harbour have every right to expect reasonable public transport.

The complaints of travellers are too numerous to dismiss with an impatient sweep of the hand as Mr. Morris tried to do yesterday in his letter — which was published IN FULL with all its biting comments on the Manly Daily's campaign.

Mr. Morris has promised to take "a special look" at the 5.15 p.m. from Circular Quay.

We hope this means that Mr. Morris will take the trip himself.

The 7.40 a.m. to Sydney, Sept. 3

The 5.15 p.m. to Manly, Sept. 3

The 7.40 a.m. to Sydney, Sept. 3

THIS picture of passengers sitting on the stairs of the 7.40 a.m. ferry to Sydney was published last week and referred to in Mr. Morris's letter to The Manly Daily. On the left are other pictures taken on the same day but not published previously. They show the general overcrowding on peak-hour services.

A feature in the Manly Daily *highlighted the problem of overcrowding on the ferries.*

Minister for Transport has made no statement and the people of Manly are becoming increasingly perturbed. If the ferries stop, at least five or six thousand more people will be thrown on the roads every morning and we cannot expect the Harbour Bridge to get any wider.

Mr Gumbert said it was surprising that the ferries had all become too old at the same time. 'After all,' he added, 'the Manly ferry is to Sydney what the Eiffel Tower is to Paris.'

Brambles announced within a couple of weeks that the *Baragoola* would not be withdrawn. The day before, Mr Gumbert, with the Mayor of Manly, Alderman W.A. Manning, had given Mr Morris a petition containing 25 300 signatures of people who wanted an assurance that the Manly ferry service would continue. Another petition, signed by 300 people in an independent campaign, went to the Premier, Sir Robert Askin; the Leader of the Opposition, Mr Wran; the Federal Minister for Transport, Mr C. Jones and the State Minister for Planning and Environment, Sir John Fuller. A few weeks later, on 26 February 1974, Sir Robert Askin announced that the Government had reached an agreement with the owners of the Port Jackson & Manly Steamship Company that the Government would wholly subsidise the service before taking it over finally later in the year. The Government would meet all direct and indirect costs from 1 March up to 30 November. Until then, the company would continue to manage and operate the ferries without charge. The Government had the option of paying $25 000 each for the three remaining ferries and would take over the company's lease of the four hydrofoils. The Government had no other option. Said the Premier:

> The arrangements mean that the management expertise of the company will be available to the Government while a technical and economic evaluation is being made of the most effective manner of maintaining this essential transport service. The remaining conventional ferries cannot be kept in operation indefinitely and the Government has asked a special committee to investigate urgently the construction of alternative vessels.

Next shock for the public was to learn a few weeks later that the *South Steyne* would be withdrawn from Sunday service to Manly as well as ocean cruises, leaving only the *North Head* and *Baragoola* to do all the Sunday traffic in 22 ferry trips instead of the usual 30. In August, Mr Morris broke the news that the Government did not intend to buy all three ferries. He said it would buy only two and would refit them at a cost of up to $400 000. Defending the decision to buy only two of the vessels, Mr Morris said a

survey had shown that two ferries and the hydrofoils could accommodate passengers using the service, which, he said, Government intervention had saved. Brambles were reported as having said they would stop the ferry service to Manly by November. The Government had not decided which of the ferries it would buy. The options would expire on 28 August (*South Steyne*), 3 October (*Baragoola*) and 18 November (*North Head*). Each vessel would be docked for inspection between 26 August and 20 September.

Mr Morris had accused Brambles earlier in the year of trying to dump a worn-out fleet and unprofitable service on the Government. He said they had expected to get $6 million for the three ferries, which was 'just not on'. A special pamphlet was printed and distributed to Manly ferry patrons as 'A message from the Hon. Milton Morris MLA, Minister for Transport'. In this he said the two main factors in the Government's decision to purchase and refit two of the three large ferries were:

> The fact that any two of these ferries could comfortably handle peak passenger loadings with room to spare. An origin and destination survey has shown that any two of the ferries, working two trips in the morning peak and three in the evening peak, would accommodate commuters now using the ferries with hundreds of vacant places remaining.
>
> The age and poor condition of the ferries and the prohibitive cost of bringing all of them up to a satisfactory standard. One ferry is thought to be uneconomic to repair.

Mr Morris said the two ferries selected would be taken out of service and refitted one at a time, which would leave only one Manly ferry operating from mid-September until early December. During this period, the new inner harbour ferry *Lady Wakehurst*, to be ready soon, would be diverted to the Manly run. He concluded:

> The Government will be spending a great deal of the taxpayers' money to avert the threatened shutdown of the service. In return, it asks you to make a slight adjustment to your travelling times and to bear with the difficulties while the ferries are being overhauled.

Mr Morris, like most ministers, was quoting what he had been advised by his departmental officers rather than expressing what he knew himself. The *Manly Daily* of Saturday, 7 September, came out with a front page story headed 'The 700 commuters they didn't count.' This said official figures on passenger counts aboard Manly ferries were widely out because season ticket holders had been forgotten. The story said:

> The reason is that the Transport Department uses turnstile figures for its daily count of passengers, but season ticket holders use separate gates (where they are not counted). The Minister for Transport, Mr Morris, has consistently used the turnstile figures to show that the ferries are not overcrowded, but actual experience shows that the ferries are packed at peak hours, with many standing passengers and others blocking gangways.

The *Manly Daily* followed this up with front pages showing the crowds streaming through the ticket gates at Circular Quay and scenes aboard the peak-hour ferries with people sitting on the stairs and standing everywhere. By this time, however, the situation had gone too far to remedy in a hurry and nothing was going to be done in the immediate future.

2. Save the *Steyne*

On 25 August 1974, the *South Steyne* caught fire mysteriously at the Balmain depot, just three days before the Government had to make up its mind whether it would buy this vessel. It was not generally known at the time, but the Port Jackson & Manly Steamship Company knew, and probably the Government representatives concerned with doing the deal knew, that the *South Steyne* needed work costing around $100 000 if she was to retain her certificate for the Manly service alone. Much more was involved if she was to resume the ocean cruises to Broken Bay. But it seemed almost unreal that a ship like this could be sold for $25 000, which was all the Government intended to pay if she was chosen as one of the two ferries to be bought. This was not as much as the price of a nine metre pleasure cruiser in those days.

Heading into another big roller over near Dobroyd.

The *South Steyne* was taken off the Manly service after her last run on Friday night, 23 August, and was tied up at Balmain, where her boilers were blown down and she was left to await her fate five days later, when the option was to expire. About 5 pm on Sunday a fire broke out in a fan room above the boilers and burned for more than an hour before fire brigades were called. Then it was another three-quarters of an hour before the air supply down the funnel was cut off and the firemen could get to the seat of the trouble. They had feared that if they opened the boiler room doors, the flames, fed by air coming down the funnel, could have raced away out of control. They were also afraid that 9000 litres of diesel fuel stored below the boiler room could catch alight.

The firemen, from Balmain, Pyrmont, Leichhardt and headquarters, took more than three hours to bring the fire under control. Just when they thought it had been contained, it broke out once more and spread quickly among the life-jackets on the upper deck, smothering Mort's Bay around the depot with choking black smoke. There was extensive damage to seats and fittings on the upper deck, which looked a real mess with everything blackened by the fire and smoke and drowned by water from the fire hoses. The piano, though charred, was still playable. Damage was assessed at $130 000. What a despairing outlook.

The day the option expired, 28 August, the Minister for Transport announced that the Government would not buy the *South Steyne*. Mr Morris said Government officials had reported that refitting the ferry would cost about $1 million. He said a two-ferry service would continue with the *Baragoola* and *North Head*, which could both be refitted, and the new inner harbour ferry, *Lady Wakehurst*, would be brought on the Manly run while the others were being overhauled.

News of the fire dismayed everyone who had hoped that the ferries chosen would be the *South Steyne* and *North Head*. Arson Squad detectives began investigations into the fire, but if they found anything, nothing was heard of it and no proper inquiry was ever held. Many refused to believe that this great ferry could not be salvaged after a fire nowhere near as bad as that which ravaged the *Bellubera* in 1936. The damage seemed to be much less extensive. Surely the *South Steyne* could be repaired and returned to service. But there was no official enthusiasm—just an ominous silence. Two days after the fire the new two-ferry timetable went into operation and with it came the chaos that everyone except the bureaucracy knew would be inevitable. With only two ferries operating a 45-minute service, hundreds were left stranded in peak hours. Members of the Save the Ferries Committee were at Manly wharf from 6.30 am displaying posters and collecting money for the campaign. There were still two

South Steyne *en route to Manly. (John Darroch)*

MANLY

Australia's Premier Seaside Resort

Seven miles from Sydney and a thousand miles from care

TRAVEL BY STEAMER FROM CIRCULAR QUAY AND ENJOY THE GLORIOUS HARBOUR SCENERY

THE PORT JACKSON & MANLY STEAMSHIP COMPANY LIMITED
NO. 2 JETTY, CIRCULAR QUAY, SYDNEY, N.S.W.

A familiar sight in Sydney's trams, these advertising signs proclaimed the Port Jackson & Manly Steamship Company's slogan 'Seven miles from Sydney and a thousand miles from care'.

days before the option on the *South Steyne* expired. Meanwhile, the Public Transport Commission pushed the crowds on to *Baragoola*, whose survey certificate was due to expire in October—only two months away—and *North Head*, whose certificate would lapse a month later. What would happen if one of these vessels caught fire or had an accident nobody cared to think.

The *South Steyne* was not left alone and forgotten, however. In September, Mr Bob Pritchard, described as a promoter, disclosed that he had ideas, with a Sydney company, Entertainment Headquarters, of turning the ferry into a floating casino after spending $250 000 on a refit. 'She would be taken outside the three-mile limit and operated as a gambling ship,' he said. 'We would have a full liquor licence, plus entertainment.' The idea was to turn the lower deck into a bar-restaurant and have all the gambling equipment upstairs—roulette wheels, black-jack and poker machines. This idea did not last long. The State Government was not keen on having his casino floating around, even outside the three-mile limit. It had other plans for casinos.

By October 1974 the two-ferry service was reduced to one real Manly ferry when the *Baragoola* had to undergo a much needed refit to retain her survey certificate, leaving the *North Head* to carry on the service with the inner harbour ferry *Lady Wakehurst* trying valiantly to carry the crowds and keep up the timetable. The Government Members Transport Committee, of which I was chairman, went up to Balmain to inspect the fire-damaged *South Steyne*, having to grapple with considerable departmental reluctance to let us aboard. We held a meeting of the committee subsequently at Parliament House, during which we heard evidence from quite a few departmental heads, most of whom tried to dissuade us from any ideas

of salvaging the *South Steyne*, mainly on the grounds of the cost of restoration and the operating costs of the vessel if she was restored. Other members of the committee with me were Messrs Gordon Jackett, member for Burwood; Alan Viney (Wakehurst), David Arblaster (Mosman), Peter Coleman (Fuller), Keith Doyle (Vaucluse) and Lerryn Mutton (Yaralla).

The committee voted five to two in support of trying to salvage the *South Steyne*. We were convinced that the cost of restoring the vessel was nothing compared with the cost of replacing her, which would have to be done if anything happened to either of the two much older ferries the Government had retained. We were convinced also that running the Manly service with only two ferries was sheer madness and told the minister (Milton Morris) so in a detailed report. In the first week in January 1975 I received a letter from the minister, addressed to me as chairman of the Government Transport Committee, which said:

Dear Mr Mead. You will recall submitting to me a short time ago a majority report of your committee which recommended among other things that the former Manly ferry *South Steyne* be acquired and restored by the Government for further service. Subsequently, your committee's recommendation was incorporated in a minute I submitted to Cabinet. A copy of the committee's full report accompanied my minute. I should now like you to know that after consideration of all factors, Cabinet concluded that it could not proceed along the lines recommended by your committee.

That should have been the end of the matter but the *South Steyne* had become the symbol of a cause which had to be pursued. To those of us who followed the cause there seemed to be no reason why this small amount of fire damage could not be repaired and a beautiful ship returned to the harbour she had graced for so long. The only reason generally accepted was that as a steam ship she was a nuisance to the bureaucracy, who did not want her back at any price. But under the surface there were several reasons which throw some light on the Government's refusal to salvage the vessel and a strange reluctance to give some of those reasons. This silence was, in effect, to make a martyr of the *South Steyne* and produce masses of newspaper and other media comment and speculation about her over many years. A great many people gave their time and money to try to bring this much loved ferry back to life.

Part of the background centred around discussions in the party meetings at Parliament House, where, for some time, I had been accusing the Government of being 'conned' by the militant Teachers' Federation into pouring nearly half of the entire Budget into the bottomless well of education, while the badly run-down public transport system was being neglected. I had spoken in the House, too, about the state of transport, particularly the Manly ferries. In the party room I warned that the excessive demands for education would continue until little more could be done, then the Opposition would concentrate its attack on the dilapidated trains and ferries. This is exactly what did happen, culminating in public transport being the winning issue for the Labor Party in the 1976 New South Wales State election. It was assisted by the upheavals which followed the retirement of Sir Robert Askin as Premier in 1974 and the power struggle for the Premiership which followed between Tom Lewis and Eric, later Sir Eric, Willis. Lewis had been cultivating votes behind the scenes for a long time and when the leadership ballot was taken his win upset the Willis followers, who had been sure that Eric, Sir Robert's loyal deputy leader of the Liberal Party since the victorious 1965 election, would be the new Premier. Between then and May 1976, when Sir Eric Willis, who had won back the Premiership but lost the State election, there were to be three new Ministers for Transport, two of them country members and all three having little knowledge of ferries. There was no ministerial enthusiasm for doing anything about the *South Steyne* or, for that matter, the struggling Manly ferry service.

Of course we did not know at that time why there had been a similar lack of interest in the *South Steyne* by the Brambles management of the Port Jackson & Manly Steamship Company. It went back to one day when the *Steyne* went into Manly with a heavy sou'easter behind her. The deckhands took the strain on the starboard bollards with the for'ard and aft lines and the usual groaning of the ropes was interrupted by a loud crash as the bulwark pulled out and lay down almost flat at deck level. She was taken off for repairs and it was found that beneath the concrete gutter everything was rotten and rusted. The bulwark—about a third of the starboard side—was welded back into position at deck level and the ferry was kept going, but what had happened was the revelation of years of neglect. At another stage the rudders had to be repaired. They were hollow and had filled with water through holes eaten into the metal by corrosion.

While the *Baragoola* was having its refit after the *South Steyne* fire, the new inner harbour ferry, *Lady Wakehurst*, was assisting the *North Head* in the two-ferry Manly service. If people hoped the Government would see reason and keep her on the service to make a three-ship timetable when the *Baragoola* and *North Head* had been refitted, their hopes were soon to fade. Within a few months she was down in Hobart, out on loan to the Tasmanian Government with several of the very old inner harbour ferries helping to overcome the crisis caused by the collapse of the big concrete bridge over the Derwent River in a terrible tragedy when a ship hit one of the piers and sent cars and people hurtling to destruction in the water below.

The first effort to save the *South Steyne* came on 16 April 1975, when a syndicate of three bought the unwanted and abandoned ferry, reputedly for $15 000, and called for help to repair the vessel and get her working again. Spokesman for the syndicate was Mr John Bryant, a director of the ship, launch and yacht brokers, Tasman Charters. Other members of the syndicate were Mr Frank Markert, a tug-boat owner, and Mr Mike Lee, a marine engineer. Mr Bryant, holder of a master's certificate and a third-class motor engineer's ticket, told how, as a schoolboy, he had been on one of the *Steyne*'s first trips to Manly and told his father he would like to be captain of the *South Steyne* one day. 'Over the years I have not given that statement much thought,' he said. 'But now it looks as though this might be the fulfilment of a childhood dream after all.'

The dream did not come true. Six months later, on 17 October, contracts were exchanged between the syndicate and a group called the South Steyne Steamship Preservation Society for the society to take over the salvation of the ship. A deposit of $2000 was paid on a total price of $40 000 and full-page advertisements appeared in newspapers seeking donations and members, especially those prepared to work on the restoration project. People responded to the appeal, but not enough money was forthcoming. Just before Christmas, the *South Steyne* was towed around to Circular Quay and tied up for the weekend at the wharf where many thousands of people passed on Saturdays and Sundays on their way to the Opera House. It was hoped they would contribute generously to the $200 000 needed to recondition the ferry's massive steam engines and remove the barnacles and corrosion from the hull. During the weekend the *Steyne* was at the Quay, the Manly Fun Pier gave its Saturday takings to the restoration appeal and members of the society sold 'Save Our *Steyne*' T-shirts and balloons. President of the society then, Mr Michael Muter, said the society already had 1800 members and $18 000 dollars.

The Budget session of Parliament which ended before Christmas had discussed the Sydney Harbour Transport Bill, which contained the machinery legislation to authorise the Public Transport Commission to take over the Sydney Harbour and Manly ferry services from 1 December. In a front page story on 15 November 1974, the *Manly Daily*, with a seven-column heading 'South Steyne Saved', 'Cabinet also looks at 3 new ferries', said:

The *South Steyne* may return to the Manly ferry service early next year. State Parliament was told yesterday that Cabinet is considering a recommendation that the fire-damaged ferry be restored and brought back into use. The Government is also considering a recommendation from its Transport Committee that three new ferries be built especially for the Manly run.

Chairman of the Government Transport Committee, Mr T.F. Mead (Lib., Hurstville) said yesterday that a few years ago the Government did not foresee the necessity of taking over the Manly ferries, but, unfortunately, their demise had made it necessary.

Mr Mead said in Parliament on Wednesday night that the Manly ferry service should be operated with three instead of two ferries. The Transport Committee has recommended this and the building of three new Manly ferries to carry at least 1000 people and do a round trip in one hour.

Mr Mead said that the new ferries would take three years to build and in the meantime the *South Steyne* should be restored and used as the third vessel.

This, of course, was the report which Milton Morris submitted to Cabinet and was rejected. He advised Manly Council of the decision in a letter written on his last day as Minister for Transport. The council reacted strongly and decided that the Mayor, Alderman Bill Manning, should continue negotiations with the new minister, Wal Fife. Alderman Joan Thorburn attacked the Government's decision to send the *Lady Wakehurst* to Hobart at a time when harbour transport was so short in Sydney, describing it as 'unbelievable'. Other moves followed, including asking the Federal Government to intervene. I spoke again in Parliament, urging the Government to make a loan of $80 000 available to the Preservation Society so that work could be done to get the ship

mobile and enable it to earn some money to pay for restoration work.

Wal Fife attended a meeting of the Transport Committee in April 1975, which dealt with several matters, including an inquiry which the committee was undertaking into the operation of private bus services, and an invitation which the minister and I accepted to attend a meeting convened by Mosman Council to consider the unsatisfactory state of Mosman ferry and feeder bus services. The minutes of that meeting include:

Discussion then centred on a 'three-ferry' service to Manly. The minister would not commit himself to such a service, but rather a two-ferry service with one in reserve. Two suitable ferries were to be ordered for the Manly run and the whole question to be reviewed in the light of their operation. The minister stated that a hydrofoil had already been purchased from Hong Kong and should be put into operation in June.

At 12.30 pm the committee was joined by Mr Shirley, Chief Commissioner of the Public Transport Commission, and Mr Trott, Under Secretary of the Ministry of Transport, together with Messrs Gibson and Blake.

Mr Mead raised certain matters on behalf of Mr Arblaster (member for Mosman, who was absent) relating to hydrofoil maintenance and the lack of service to Musgrave Street wharf on Sundays. Discussion ranged from these points to the question of feeder bus services to ferries. Mr Shirley made the point that the quality of the ferry service had been improved in recent years with the introduction of four new ferries of the 'Lady' class and the quantity was sufficient to meet demand.

The meeting closed at 1.15 pm with an obvious united front departmentally and ministerially against restoration of the *South Steyne* and a three-ferry Manly service. The Mr Gibson who attended the committee meeting was Tom Gibson, general manager of the Public Transport Commission's ferries division. The committee at another stage heard evidence from various departmental officers, including Mr John Wallace, then chief engineer of the Maritime Services Board. Departmental evidence after the fire claimed that it would cost $350 000 to repair the fire damage and a total of $550 000 to put the *South Steyne* back into service for three years. Something like $3 million was mentioned if the ship was to be kept going for another 10 years. It was also maintained that, in any case, the *Steyne* was too costly to operate because of the high-priced imported bunker fuel oil used in her boilers.

Later in 1975 the Transport Committee heard some more very interesting evidence from a qualified marine surveyor, after which I telephoned Mr Fife, then wrote to him stating:

Dear Mr Fife. Following my telephone conversation with you on Friday night last, 19 September, I submit for your information a matter which members of the Metropolitan Transport Committee believe should be conveyed to Cabinet urgently. This information strengthens the opinion I conveyed to your predecessor and the former Premier more than 12 months ago that the Government could have been seriously misled in the advice it was given about acquisition of the Manly ferry *South Steyne*.

You may recall that at the request of the then minister (Morris) and with the support of Sir Robert Askin, the Transport Committee conducted an urgent inquiry into this matter and submitted a report for Cabinet, a copy of which is enclosed. I enclose now a copy of a survey report signed by Captain J.W. Burch, of Innes and Burch, marine surveyors and loss assessors, dated 9 September 1975, only a fortnight ago, stating that fire damage to the *South Steyne* could be restored for only $25 000. Estimated cost of returning the vessel to condition to get a Maritime Services Board certificate as a passenger ferry is given at $45 000 and another $20 000 is the estimated cost of docking and maintenance, making a total of $90 000. Captain Burch estimates the present value of *South Steyne* at $125 000.

Now according to Mr Keith Doyle MLA, who was a member of this committee last year and has wide professional experience of insurance, this survey report comes from a most reputable firm of marine surveyors. I am not attempting to say who is right and who is wrong, but I believe, and the other members of the Transport Committee agree, that the wide discrepancy in these assessments should be the subject of an immediate inquiry.

We were also told last year that the ship did not have to use bunker fuel (one of the reasons for the high running costs). She could be adapted to burn local diesel oil, as the Railways Department had done previously with some of the 59 class Baldwin steam locomotives.

I also enclose a copy of a letter from Manly Council to Mr M. Muter, president of an organisation known as the South Steyne Steamship Preservation Society, which has been formed to conduct a public appeal to acquire and restore this ferry. The letter and the survey report came into my possession on Friday, when they were referred to me as Chairman of Directors of the *Manly Daily* newspaper.

Manly Council has agreed to support the society's public appeal and will allow the Council Chambers to be used for collecting donations to the fund. The *Manly Daily* has been approached to sponsor and help promote the appeal. I have delayed a decision until Friday next, 26 September, when it will be submitted to the Board of Directors of the newspaper. I feel that the public appeal will succeed, especially if it is assisted by the *Manly Daily* and Manly Council and I suggest that the Government be seen to support instead of obstruct the return of the *South Steyne*.

The purpose of this report is to inform you and the Government that the enclosed documents could be used in a way not to our liking by our political opponents. There are still gross discrepancies between the figures given to the Government recently and those quoted now by Captain Burch. I understand, for instance, that the Government figure was $12 000 to replace glass windows. A quote used in the latest assessment was given by the O'Brien Glass Company, one of the biggest glass firms in Sydney, to replace the windows for only $5000—more than 12 months after the Government quote and despite price rises that must have occurred in that time. The appeal is timed to be launched on Saturday, 4 October, less than a fortnight away. It is therefore imperative that the Government acts quickly.

South Steyne *going astern to pull her up as she comes in to berth at Manly.*

That letter probably did more harm than good. To suggest that the Government might have been misled in the advice it had received was only going to make those who had given the advice close ranks and stick to their story, if it was wrong. Whether they were right or wrong I don't know. We had conflicting stories, different sets of figures and quotes for restoration of the fire damage and it looked at the time that even if the *South Steyne* could be repaired economically and restored to efficient working order, the departmental bureaucracy did not want her back at any price and was determined to keep her off the harbour.

Anyhow, nothing happened except that the society took over the project from John Bryant and his partners and launched the campaign to raise funds and get working bees busy cleaning up the mess aboard the *South Steyne*, which was still there 12 months after the fire.

Legal helpers drew up a constitution for the South Steyne Preservation Society and I supported an application to speed up registration of the society under the Charitable Collections Act. The society, of which Michael Muter was then president, agreed to purchase the vessel for $40 000, but as it did not have this much money an agreement was made, secured by mortgage, for an initial payment of $10 000 and the balance in instalments of $10 000, payable in April 1976, October 1976, and April 1977, with interest on the outstanding amount of 12 per cent reducible. Nearly $20 000 was also involved in the initial advertising campaign to raise funds, using full-page advertisements in the *Sydney Morning Herald*, which, unfortunately, did not raise anything like the money needed to get the project off the slipway.

Early work was concentrated on the fan engine room. The decking above was removed and the fans taken out, stripped and overhauled. Then sandblasting equipment was brought in to clean up the charred woodwork, painting of the hull outside began and the wrecked seats were taken from the promenade deck to be stored away for possible rehabilitation later. But it was not to be. Brian Verey had the seats stored in a shed on the edge of the Georges River at Liverpool. One Saturday afternoon in the very hot and dry Christmas holiday period a raging grass fire swept up the river bank, destroying what had been left of the seats after the original fire.

I joined the society in 1976 and took part in the weekend work parties, scrubbing, sanding, painting. The society then had about 2000 members contributing a total of $20 000 a year. Between trying to pay off the mortgage, plus interest, keeping the vessel insured and trying to meet the ever increasing cost of the work in progress, the money did not go far. At the beginning of that year $37 616.96 had been spent on various things, including: newspaper advertising, printing and stationery $12 487; towards purchase of vessel $12 087.50; equipment, repairs $3243.25; contract labour $2100; equipment hire $827.06; registration and legal fees $493.49. Income of $37 050 included: membership fees and donations $22 125.32; day's takings from Manly Fun Pier $422.21; Manly Music Loft donation $565; Don Burrows concert $1967; sale of T-shirts, raffle tickets, balloons $575.75; *Manly Daily* donation $5000. Everything cost money— $200 for 90 litres of red lead primer, $300 for bolts, nuts, studs, jointing and steam packing for boilers, $900 for bunker oil.

If we were worried at the cost of the ordinary work we were doing, we were appalled in March 1976, when the Maritime Services Board served on the society a long list of survey requirements considered necessary after a preliminary survey at Balmain in January. These included repairing and caulking main deck wood sheathing, renewing any timber on the upper deck which had been badly charred in the fire or reduced by wear to a thickness of less than five centimetres, anchors and cables to be taken out from lockers for inspection and joining shackles to be broken, lifeboats to be presented for survey, buoyancy tanks to be removed for inspection. These were normal things which should have been done while the vessel was in service, but obviously had not been done for some time. Now, the struggling group of volunteers had to try to finance the complete overhaul of the ship to rectify the results of considerable neglect while the ferry had been capable of earning some income.

In September 1973 the Maritime Services Board had written to the Port Jackson & Manly Steamship Company after a survey, submitting an extensive list of major repair work and advising that the vessel could be considered suitable only for harbour and river service until this work was carried out. Sandblasting and hammer testing had revealed holes in port and starboard strakes B,C,D and E in the way of the boiler room and engine room. These had been covered by welding doubling plates over them and the Maritime Services Board required that they be repaired permanently in 'the approved manner'. The port and starboard E strake plating was to be renewed in the way of the oil fuel bunkers and all suspect and defective rivets which had been seal welded were required to be renewed at the next docking of the vessel. It was suggested that in order to avoid future extensive repairs, doubling plates might be welded along A strakes, an approximate length of five metres from stem and the stern, port and starboard sides. The Board's letter added: 'Patches of wastage are evident over much of the areas mentioned and if permitted to deteriorate further will eventually warrant complicated repairs.'

No wonder Brambles wanted to be rid of the Manly ferries. No wonder the Government did not share the public enthusiasm for the *South Steyne*. Nobody wanted to foot the bill. This magnificent and beautiful ship had been driven into the ground, if such an expression could be applied to a ship. But now, if she was to be mobile again, somebody had to pay out huge amounts to put the house in order. There was nobody left for more buck passing except the enthusiastic amateur members of the South Steyne Steamship Preservation Society, who did not have the kind of money needed for the pages of expensive work the Maritime Services Board required to be done if the *Steyne* was ever to steam again. Just a few extracts from the list received in March 1976:

*It will be necessary for the vessel to be dry docked for renewal of platings as determined by ultrasonic testing, renewal of doubled plates and welded rivets and repairs as found necessary when dry docked.

*Forward and aft propeller shafts to be removed, propellers to be removed and shafts crack tested.

*Forward rudder stock to be removed.

*Engine and boiler room bilges are to be cleaned and all floor plates lifted for inspection of the inner hull.

*The main engine is to be opened up as follows: all cylinder covers to be lifted and junk rings and piston rings removed. All valve chest covers to be lifted and valves removed. The weight shaft bearing caps are to be lifted. The top and bottom ends are to be opened up. The reversing gear is to be opened up. All auxiliary engines are to be opened up. Steering engines are to be opened up.

In other words, the whole ship must virtually be taken to pieces for Maritime Services Board inspection. What a prospect! The main engine was pulled down by a volunteer work gang headed by Wesley Mallet, a former engineer in the *South Steyne*, who was living then at Jannali. They spent weeks on this work. When it was done finally and the engine lay in pieces, the Maritime Services Board people looked at the mess and said: 'That's all right. You can put it all together again now.' Not for Wes Mallet and his team. They had had enough. There was nothing wrong with those fine engines. But there would be eventually if the parts were not put together again. Taking the engine apart was one thing, but reassembling it with the fine tolerances required was another. We had been treated very generously by Jubilee Engineering, a waterfront ship-repair firm at Birchgrove, who offered to do the job for $1500. But we owed Jubilee enough and did not want to add another bill for which we did not have the money. So the engine remained in pieces while the society, Micawber-like, waited for something to turn up.

3. A Lost Cause

It was obvious now that the State Government would do nothing to save the *South Steyne*. The only hope was to find one or more sponsors in the business or commercial sector who could provide the money necessary to get the vessel mobile so that she could earn something to balance the outflow of money. In March 1976 I presented a submission prepared by the South Steyne Steamship Preservation Society president, Michael Muter, asking the Government to carry out the remaining repairs and lend the society $70 000 to meet the overhead expenses

Hardly recognisable, the South Steyne *in April 1987 in the process of restoration at the Ballina Slipways and Engineering Company in Ballina. (Bill and Gay Storer, Rileys Hill, NSW)*

and the cost of establishing an administrative structure. In return, the society would offer the ship for use in peak hours, in return for which the Government would have the fare revenue as reimbursement for the cost of the repairs and repayment of the loan. Manly Council also continued its representations for a third ferry, preferably the *South Steyne*.

Nothing came of this proposition, but it was beginning to dawn on those responsible that something would have to be done. On 23 March yet another new Minister for Transport, Tim Bruxner, Country Party member for Tenterfield, announced that two new ferries would be built for the Manly service. But he could not say when tenders would be called. Mr Bruxner said a report was expected within the next few weeks suggesting possible designs for a suitable type of craft, including a twin-hull design. Manly Council wrote to Mr Bruxner welcoming this news, but pointing out that it was all going to take some time and asking why, in the meanwhile, the *South Steyne* could not be brought back into service. Manly Town Clerk, Cec Menzies, sent me a copy of the letter and a Press statement which the Mayor, Bill Murray, had issued. Bruxner replied, informing the council that the proposal to use the *South Steyne* during peak hours was impracticable. He indicated that current thought was towards vessels 'more compact and more operationally flexible'. Referring to suggestions that the ferry terminal at Manly might be given some attention, Mr Bruxner told the council:

Due to financial strictures, the Public Transport Commission has no plans for any alterations to the terminal at present. The best I can do at this stage is to state that the subject of improvements will be kept in mind should funds for projects of this nature become available.

Believe it or not, that letter was written on the eve of a State election. A few weeks later we were out of government, having been literally kicked to death on public transport. We had built new inner harbour ferries and rust-bucket suburban train carriages were being replaced rapidly with new double-deck cars. But it was too late. The damage had been done.

It was not long before the new Premier, Neville Wran, was paying special attention to the Manly electorate and funds were found for doing up the ferry wharf and planning a new bus terminal and interchange at the wharf. When another State election came up in 1978, Manly and the adjoining electorate of Wakehurst were lost to Labor candidates.

But the new Government in 1976 was not going to save the *Steyne*, as some had hoped. Peter Cox, the new Minister for Transport, had come to Parliament from the Department of Motor Transport and had some experience of transport matters. In answer to questions in Parliament in August by the Liberal member for Manly, Douglas Darby, Mr Cox said he had received a report from the South Steyne Steamship Preservation Society proposing that the Government spend $330 000 to restore the ferry and return it to the Manly service, but the costs had not been fully investigated by his Department. 'Personally,' Mr Cox said, 'I think the cost of restoring the *South Steyne* will be much more than the estimate put forward.' Hinting that there was hope the Manly service would be improved, Mr Cox said his Department had just completed a report on ferry services generally, which contained a proposal he thought would be much better in the long term than bringing back the *South Steyne*. A few weeks later it was revealed that the Public Transport Commission had recommended that no new ferries be more than 18 metres (60 ft) in length because these could be crewed by two operators. *North Head* (210 ft) and *Baragoola* (199 ft) had minimum requirements of seven crew.

These ideas, fortunately, were not proceeded with, but it was obvious that new ferries had to be built, as promised by the previous Government. At that time the State Dockyard at Newcastle was facing impending doom, with 1100 employees to be dismissed. In an editorial, which I wrote, the *Manly Daily* suggested that the State Dockyard crisis could be helped immensely by taking the *South Steyne* there for restoration work, which, the Preservation Society had been assured, could be done for $300 000. The editorial also suggested that the Government could assist the dockyard by pushing on with the much discussed plans proposed originally by my transport committee, of building three new Manly ferries. The gravity of the situation had been emphasised recently by an electrical fire aboard the *North Head* as she travelled up the harbour. Had this been more serious and she had been taken out of service at a time of prolonged heavy weather, the *Baragoola* would have been left to carry on alone. The editorial concluded:

To keep the *South Steyne* idle while this most unsatisfactory condition continues is tragic and it will continue while the people of this area do nothing to let the Government know of their concern. Write this weekend to the Minister for Transport and tell him you believe the proposals of the South Steyne Steamship Preservation Society are worth supporting.

We had seen Peter Cox in October 1976, in a deputation I arranged, and asked him about a submission we had given him containing detailed estimates of cost by Cockatoo Dock and Jubilee Engineering Pty Ltd for the complete restoration and all survey work required by the Maritime Services Board. According to these estimates, the *South Steyne* could have been made as good as new, with a sea-going certificate, for $239 600. Cockatoo Dock estimated $135 100 for docking, replacing hull plates, sandblasting and repainting and doing all the work required by the Maritime Services Board for sea-going survey. Jubilee Engineering quoted $104 500 for complete restoration and repainting of the hull and contents, plus all engineering work. Cockatoo Dock would even have taken out the propeller shafts and rudders for inspection and any necessary work. Cox expressed interest in the submission, which, he said, was being given earnest consideration by the Public Transport Commission and the Maritime Services Board. The deputation invited him to inspect the *South Steyne* on her next visit to Circular Quay for a fund-raising day.

Soon after, we received notification from the Maritime Services Board that intake pipes around the boilers would have to be disconnected for an inspection by Maritime Services Board officials. The inspection was duly made by the officials, who subsequently reported to us that three of the ship's four boilers had thermal cracks around the intake pipe area of shell-casing and the boilers would have to be replaced—an enormous and costly undertaking which would involve dismantling a large part of the vessel's superstructure to get the boilers out. It seemed that everything possible was being done to prevent us from getting on with the main work of restoration by demanding impossible and expensive work. There was no hope of the Preservation Society finding the amount of money required to meet these demands. In February things were given a lift when the National Trust listed the *South Steyne* under a preservation classification. But, unfortunately, this did not provide any money.

The society, although somewhat demoralised by the Maritime Services Board condemnation of the boilers, sought a second opinion from outside experts, who advised that the boilers could be saved and suggested two methods by which this could be achieved. We were in the process of discussing this with the Maritime Services Board and had advised Mr Cox accordingly when, on 13 April 1977, he released news that the Public Transport Commission was planning to spend up to $19 million on new ferries and hydrofoils for Manly. He said the commission was considering three combinations:

*A $2 million 140-passenger hydrofoil, an $8.5 million 1100-passenger monohull ferry and an $8.5 million 500-passenger Boeing Jet-Foil. Total $19 million.
*One hydrofoil and two monohull ferries. Total $19 million.
*One hydrofoil, one monohull ferry and the *South Steyne* refitted at a cost of about $1 million. Total $11.5 million.

The outlook was hopeless. Most of us knew that Sydney would never see the Jet-Foil as well as the *South Steyne*. It was just a political ploy to fend off those who wanted the *South Steyne* back. There was only one hope. There would have to be a public campaign and the possible support of big business sponsors. The project was soon to be dumped into my lap. At a meeting on board the *South Steyne* at Balmain on 15 March 1977, Michael Muter resigned as president and Steven Milgate resigned as secretary. I was elected president and David Bennetts became secretary. Brian Verey, with an accountancy background, remained as treasurer. We were certainly

trying to flog a fairly dead horse and the position looked worse the more we went into it. There was a frightening burden of debts, going back to the beginning before any of us were associated with the venture. Nevertheless, we undertook the responsibility we felt the society had to these creditors and the people who had subscribed to the ideal of saving this fine ship.

They were a dedicated team of workers and they gave most of their leisure time willingly to whatever they felt they could do best. Garry Downes was a Phillip Street barrister. His knowledge was very handy in many problems. The late Ken Rowley, who was secretary in the early stages, was an enthusiastic leader of weekend working bees while his wife, Merle, provided refreshments for the workers from the ship's canteen or bar on the promenade deck. Ione Paul, who worked in the advertising business, turned up at weekends ready to wield a paint brush or sand down old varnish. Warwick McDonald spent most of his time down in the engine room overhauling the auxiliary engines or attending to mechanical matters. John Darroch, many of whose pictures appear in this book, was always active doing something. Others who were there regularly included John Stirling, Terry Cook, John Hopper and Bruce Miller. Bob Kentwell had been active before my time, but left after a dispute over the spending of $15 000 he wanted to put into the funds to be used for repair of the boilers, while Ken Rowley maintained that the money should go towards paying off the debt owed to John Bryant and the other vendors, neither of which happened. Kentwell was soon to reappear in the saga, but I had never met him.

Tragedy strikes. Promenade deck of the South Steyne *after fire raged through the ship at the Balmain ferry depot on the night of 25 August 1974. The fire was the excuse for the NSW government to abandon the* South Steyne *and take over the two ageing ferries,* North Head *and* Baragoola.

By the end of 1976, from membership renewal funds and the balance of the *Manly Daily* sponsorship, the society workers had been able to reinstall the fan engines and do some boiler repairs, clean the engine and turn it over by hand. The volunteers had substantially completed painting the exterior of the hull and superstructure, they had sandblasted completely the upper deckhead to remove blistered and charred paint and had applied two coats of paint in preparation for enamelling. The work continued until about halfway through 1977, helped by extra funds from raffling a colour television set donated by Sydney Wide Discounts and selling *South Steyne* T-shirts, tie bars, brooches and colour slides.

Suddenly, about April 1977, the horizon looked brighter. Two possibilities had presented themselves which could have made all the difference. In the search for sponsors I had spoken to David Evans, group national advertising and public relations manager for EMI (Australia) Ltd, the big recording group, who wanted to discuss a plan for using the *South Steyne* in advertising promotion. The other possibility arose from a talk I had with Leo Port, then Lord Mayor of Sydney. He agreed that the *South Steyne* was a symbol not only for Manly but for the whole of Sydney and we should launch a public appeal for funds through the City Council as well as Manly Council. He offered to call a public meeting for this purpose in the Sydney Town Hall, but before he could do this fate intervened. I was at a meeting in Sydney one evening shortly after the talks with Leo when somebody came up and said: 'That was bad luck about Leo Port, wasn't it?' 'What?' I asked. 'Didn't you know?' I was told. 'He dropped dead tonight.' I almost did the same. Apart from the end of the proposed City of Sydney appeal, the death of Leo Port was the loss of a good friend who had done an immense amount for Sydney. He was a man whom I admired very much.

During May I watched with apprehension in the finance pages the varying fortunes of EMI, which was going through a period of trouble. I had written to David Evans on 9 May suggesting, following our preliminary talks, a conference to devise a basis for concrete proposals between EMI and the South Steyne Steamship Preservation Society, hoping this would produce a satisfactory proposition which could be put to the State Government. Without disclosing who was involved, I had already given to Tom Gibson an outline of a plan, seeking his response to the possibility of the ship being made available, without cost, as a commuter carrier on the Manly run. What was in it for EMI? The ship would be carrying, up and down the harbour, illuminated advertising signs which EMI could change for its various purposes and there would also be on board a plaque in recognition of the help given by EMI and other sponsors.

The South Steyne *lay idle at Ballina for most of 1986 while Michael Wansey tried to find the money needed to finish the restoration.*

It was possible that the *Manly Daily* would add to its earlier contribution. Since I had spoken to David Evans, the *Manly Daily* had published the results of a public opinion poll on the three proposals the Minister for Transport said he had under consideration and the results were very interesting. They showed that 66.87 per cent voted for the return of the *South Steyne*, with one new hydrofoil and one new ferry. Support for the Government's favoured proposal—one hydrofoil, one new ferry and a superjet hydrofoil—was only 21.69 per cent. Only 11.44 per cent wanted the other proposal for one hydrofoil and two new ferries. The letters and coupons sent in by the voters were made available to Mr Cox, who told the *Manly Daily*: 'I can give an assurance that the views as expressed in the *Manly Daily*'s poll will be taken fully into account. It will not be a case of deaf ears.'

It was proposed that the EMI venture would be controlled by a trust or company, to be formed with a Board or committee, on which would be represented EMI, the South Steyne Steamship Preservation Society, the *Manly Daily* and the State Government. That was the hopeful idea at the beginning of May. But the news in the finance pages became worse and worse and it was no surprise when a letter dated 3 June arrived in which David Evans said:

My apologies for the delay in replying to your correspondence, but as I have mentioned to you, the company is going through a reasonably tough period. I have spoken with EMI's managing director regarding this matter, but he would like at this point in time to allow the company a bit of breathing space before we venture into the proposal, as discussed. I think you must agree that after having explained to you the problems we are suffering, it would be in the best interests for the company to allow a reasonable length of time to pass before we undertake this venture with yourselves and the State Government. I sincerely hope you keep me in touch with your negotiations with the State Government and wish you every success with Mr Cox.

EMI was a solid company and its difficulties were only temporary, but this on top of Leo Port's death came as a terrible misfortune. With the EMI venture and a public appeal backed by the Sydney City Council and the Lord Mayor, there could have been a good chance of getting the *South Steyne* back in business and earning something towards its keep. At that stage the society still owed $30 000 on the vessel itself and trade creditors totalled nearly $15 000, many of them a legacy from the early days of the society. We published a bulletin for society members in which I said:

We are endeavouring to pay these [creditors] as equitably as possible, although it is very difficult at this time of the year with new subscriptions not due for another couple of months and the vessel still not capable of earning any real revenue. Even posting this bulletin costs around $370, making it almost prohibitive in the present situation unless it results in sufficient donations or membership renewals to cover the cost. In the nine months between July 1976 and the end of March this year, income amounted to only $23 100, of which $5000 came from the *Manly Daily*, the society's only major supporter financially. This is not very much towards a project of these dimensions, especially when it began this financial year carrying a substantial financial backlog from the previous year. Members might be interested to know where the money goes. If you take postage alone, that item has cost $1104 in total administrative charges of $1560. We have paid out $3523 in interest on the vessel, $760 for insurance, $779 for fuel, $468 in Maritime Services Board and associated charges. These items are classified as expenditure in furtherance of our objects. On restoration work itself we have spent in the nine months $14 265. This is where the money really goes. However, voluntary work by members and other generous helpers has saved many thousands of dollars.

The society was still awaiting a reply to my letter to the Minister for Transport, dated 18 April, in which I had asked him to meet us again and took the opportunity of conveying to him that there were alternatives to the boiler problem other than scrapping the ship's boilers and replacing them. We had found that the boilers had been poorly maintained when the ship was last in service and we had done a tremendous amount of work on them. Some of the boiler tubes were so bad that it was no wonder fuel consumption was excessive. Cox had said replacement of the boilers would cost $1 million. One of the main arguments for scrapping the *South Steyne* had been the high cost of operating her with bunker fuel oil as a steam ship, including the long time it took to get steam up before going into service and several other related difficulties. I told Peter Cox we had been advised that if the boilers had to be replaced, another type known as water-tube boilers could make the ship very economical to operate because this type of boiler required only half an hour from cold to steaming and could be switched off like diesel engines when not required. Moreover, one water-tube boiler could replace two of the existing Scotch boilers.

At the end of April I sent John Bryant a cheque for $1500 in part payment of the principal owing for the society's purchase of the vessel and, in the weeks following, Brian Verey and I had talks with him about arranging future payments. For some time the main payments to his syndicate had been by way of interest at the rate of 12 per cent. Beyond April we had to pay 14 per cent, a fairly high rate in those days. Until then it had seemed unlikely that anyone would want to buy the nest of trouble we had on our hands, but now it appeared that a buyer could be hovering around. But who? Who would want it? Towards the end of June we received a demand for payment in full, failing which the vessel would be sold. Strenuous efforts were made, without success, to find somebody who would pay off the mortgage and issue another for $30 000.

In the midst of all this, Mark Dalton, who had been living as ship keeper aboard the *South Steyne* at Balmain, rang me on the night of 10 July and told me that the ship had sprung a leak and was taking a lot of water. He said the water police were there, but their pump was not sufficient and they had called for a fire float to assist. The fire float *Pluvius* and a police launch were both pumping when I arrived at the Balmain wharf where we kept the vessel. When they got the water level in the bilges down we could see what had happened. This was a Sunday night. There had been a working party aboard during the day and they had removed a piece of equipment which water-cooled the oil in the tail-shaft bearing for the bow propeller. Sea water was fed into this through a ducting pipe and after circulating, the water went out again and was discharged overboard. As a temporary measure, a wooden plug had been pushed into the inlet pipe, but apparently the water pressure had forced the plug out.

The mortgagees had advised us that Mr Kentwell wished to purchase the *South Steyne* and unless we could pay the $30 000 still owing by 13 July the vessel would be sold. Of course we could not find $30 000 so quickly and the ship was duly sold. That day I sent out with the notice of the society's second annual meeting, to be held on 26 July, a note which said:

In the process of restoration, the South Steyne *showing the state of steelwork on the upper deck.*

Dear member. The annual meeting on 26 July, notice of which is enclosed, will consider a motion to wind up the affairs of the society. This action, regrettably, has to be taken because of the sudden foreclosure of the mortgage and sale of the SS *South Steyne* to Mr R. Kentwell. Towards the end of June the mortgagees advised that Mr Kentwell wanted to purchase the vessel and unless we could pay the $30 000 still owing they would have to sell. We made efforts to raise the money, but could not do so at short notice. Solicitors for the mortgagees advised subsequently by letter that *South Steyne* would be sold unless the balance of the mortgage was paid. The due date was today, 13 July.

This is a sad end to the long months of hard work put into the restoration of the *South Steyne* by many people who gave up their weekends to work aboard and by committee members who attended meetings almost weekly. At this stage little more can be said other than to thank all those who tried so hard to bring about fulfilment of a most difficult and ambitious project. [Signed] T. F. Mead, President.

P.S. Souvenirs remain available for those who wish to retain a memento of this magnificent ship.

The souvenirs included T-shirts at $5, large coloured prints of the *Steyne* for $2, wall plaques of the ship, ready to hang for $28.95, badges $3, cuff links $8, tie bars and brooches $4, colour slides $3 a set of five. Some 1200 members of the National Trust were to visit the ship at Balmain on Saturday, 30 July; a full-page article I had written appeared with pictures in the *Women's Weekly* on 20 July; the society had been invited to take part in the Model Railway Exhibition in Sydney Town Hall at the beginning of October and a *South Steyne* members' day had been arranged for Sunday, 21 August at the Tramway

Museum, Loftus. Trains, trams or ferries, all those working on restoring them helped each other. After our annual meeting we were to show the film *A Steam Train Passes*, based on that grand locomotive, 3801. These messages went out only by the dedicated efforts of volunteers who typed approximately 2000 envelopes and folded and assembled 8000 sheets of paper.

To a somewhat stunned annual meeting at Manly on the night of 26 July I presented the president's annual report, which said:

Loss of the *South Steyne* does not necessarily mean the end of this society, which was established for the restoration of Sydney's most famous ferry. The committee feels that the society should not be wound up and later in the meeting you will be asked to consider a motion to this effect. We feel that the society should continue to try to honour its commitments and perhaps in some way to assist the eventual restoration of the vessel.

The sudden sale of the vessel on 13 July was somewhat of a surprise to the committee, members of which feel that if she had to be sold to satisfy the mortgagees' demands, a more realistic figure should have been obtained than the $24 000 we understand was the amount paid by only one bidder in a direct sale. Taking into account the work done by the society, quite exclusive of labour, most of which was voluntary, she should have been worth about $70 000. The ship is shown in our accounts at cost plus restoration work done to 30 June at a value of $69 470 compared with $55 314 at the end of the previous year. Yet she was sold within hours of foreclosure for $24 000.

It could be said that the society set itself an impossible task when it made the original agreement with the vendors back in April 1975. The vendors had purchased the *South Steyne* in fire-damaged condition for a figure we understand was $15 000. Our original president, Michael Muter, and others, agreed to buy *South Steyne* from them for $40 000, making a first payment of $2000 deposit. Subsequently they paid another $3000 and $2456 in sundry charges in the form of refunds to the vendors of harbour dues and berthing charges ($2087), legal costs incurred by the vendors ($269) and purchase of the name ($100). Another payment of $5000 in June last year reduced the capital owing to $30 000, which was to have been paid by April this year. As at 30 June last year the vendors were owed $30 000, plus $2800 accrued interest. In the year ended 30 June last we have paid $4200 in interest and $2550 off the principal, leaving the principal amount owing at 30 June last $27 450, with accrued interest $2790 making a total of $30 240.

Altogether, the society paid the mortgagees a total of $19 206, including $4200 in interest. With the $24 000 received for the sale, the vendors, apart from the $2456 refunded to them for sundry charges, received a total of $40 750 out of the venture. The society has in hand at this stage $325 and has accumulated debts of $19 600. Some were incurred in the first year of operation, before I was a member of the committee. In that year the gross amount received was $32 012, but advertising costs took up $19 732, leaving a net gain of $12 280. In the year up to 30 June last, advertising costs totalled only $267, leaving a net gain of $19 767 from $20 034 received. Members' subscriptions in the first year totalled $18 320 and last year they were $12 355. The society was faced constantly with the problem of trying to pay off the vendors and ignore the work to be done or trying to do work to get the ship mobile enough to earn some revenue. A total of $267 014 was spent on restoration work and another $15 465 on items associated with this work, such as fuel, Maritime Services Board charges, interest payments and insurance. In the last year insurance virtually doubled, accounting for about $2000.

Inquiries so far indicate that the new owners are very vague about what will happen to the vessel. We can only hope something eventuates which will lead to her restoration. I am not aware of having met either party involved and do not intend to indulge in any recriminations. I wish only to say that the story might have ended differently if everyone had worked together.

The starboard side of South Steyne's *top deck, showing props put in to bolster work which had been commenced. At the time of writing work was to be restarted within a few days on the final stages of the restoration.*

Something did happen which led to the *South Steyne*'s restoration, but some time later. Those who attended the annual meeting at Manly on 26 July 1977 decided that the society should continue with the aim of recovering the vessel and paying its creditors. One of the committee members was barrister Garry Downes, and on his advice a statement of claim was issued out of the Equity Division of the New South Wales Supreme Court. Garry also obtained a written opinion from another eminent barrister, who believed the society had a very good chance of succeeding in such action. His best advice, however, was that in one sense no legal action would do the society any good if it could not raise the money to buy the ship outright, and that was what we decided finally. The task of raising a large amount for legal costs on top of the original commitments to pay off the mortgage, pay credi-

tors and pay for what remained to be done to the vessel was the deciding factor.

The society tried to carry on for another three years, but it was difficult to maintain real interest without the ferry as the objective, the main purpose being to pay off past debts which several of us had not even incurred in the first place. As the society was registered as a charity, we kept in touch with the New South Wales Department of Services and lodged returns each year. Financial members received a copy of the annual report and accounts, but from more than 1800 in 1976 membership had dropped to 90 in the last year. The society was wound up on 30 June 1980, with a deficiency of $14 096 in working capital and final payments to creditors were made on the basis of pro rata balance of funds to those creditors who continued to send bills during the last year of operation. Some others, very generously, had written off the debts.

PART VI
A NEW ERA

1. Fashions Change

At this stage the Manly ferry service had reached the lowest level since the early days before the big paddle-wheelers. With only *Baragoola* and *North Head* available, everyone had their fingers crossed that neither became involved in an accident which could put it out of action for some time, leaving only one ship to carry on and creating a ludicrous but tragic situation. In May 1977 it nearly happened to the *Baragoola*, approaching Garden Island on her way to Manly with a big load of holidaying school children, parents and other passengers. Out from Garden Island came the destroyer HMAS *Vampire*, manoeuvring into the harbour to turn and head off towards The Heads. The *Baragoola*'s siren blasted and she hove to with the *Vampire* at right angles across her bows. The warship turned slowly and made off towards The Heads and the *Baragoola* proceeded slowly until the *Vampire* was clear. She arrived at Manly 10 minutes late, but, as the old saying goes, better late than never, or, in this case, off the run for extensive repairs.

A couple of months later, in July, *Baragoola* had to go off for one of the delayed annual refits, which were not annual any more because of the two-boat service which the Government had been assured was adequate. The new inner harbour ferry *Lady Northcott* was brought on as relief boat, but four days later overshot the wharf at Circular Quay and crashed into the footpath. She was withdrawn for repairs, leaving the *North Head* to carry on alone. Towards the end of the year, in November, the *Northcott*'s sister ship, *Lady Wakehurst*, returned from Hobart, where she had been used for 18 months as a Derwent harbour ferry after the collapse of the Tasman Bridge. The Minister for Transport, Mr Cox, released the news at the end of November that *Lady Wakehurst* would join the Manly service on a three-month trial from 9 January and passenger response would be monitored to see whether she should continue. The *Wakehurst* was being overhauled after her Tasmanian service, two gangway gates were being made, the upper deck was being reinforced and crew accommodation modified.

Of course it was a success. After only one month passenger figures were well up, but nobody would say anything officially until the expiration of the trial period. The *Lady Wakehurst* was not withdrawn at the end of the three months. She remained there, helping to provide a three-ferry, half-hourly service and the people were using it. Mr Cox told Manly Council in November that the trial would almost certainly become permanent. Figures had shown that ferry patronage had risen considerably and was increasing at a far greater rate than that for the hydrofoils, contrary to some official predictions. Ferry patronage over 140 days between February and June was 1 366 000—an increase of 250 000 compared with the

The new era of fast water transport. The hydrofoil carries 240 passengers the 7 miles between Sydney and Manly in 12 minutes and is capable of speeds of more than 40 miles an hour. (Robert Needham)

Not a good day for the Queenscliff *when big seas rolled up in November 1984, providing thrills for some and discomfort for other Manly ferry passengers. (Robert Needham)*

passenger total of 1 116 000 in the same period of the previous year. Hydrofoils during this time carried 750 000 people compared with 702 000 the previous year. These figures represented increases of 22.4 per cent for ferries and 6.8 per cent for hydrofoils. More than 12 months before the Liberal-Country Party Government went out of office, the Minister for Transport, Mr Fife, said Manly would get two new ferries within the next three years. That was on 11 February 1975, during the naming ceremony for the *Lady Northcott*. He said they would be 'new concept' ferries. The Government was not interested in restoring the *South Steyne*. A year later, Peter Cox, as the new Labor Government's Transport Minister, told the Press that tenders would be called for a Manly 'super ferry', probably before the end of 1976 if hull tests were successful. He said the ferry would carry 1200 passengers at speeds of up to 18 knots and would cut seven minutes off the 35-minute, Manly-Circular Quay trip. The new ferry was to be built in Newcastle at the State Dockyard. Neither the Government nor the dockyard would comment on the tests ordered more than a year before by Mr Fife or say why they had taken so long, although it was fairly clear that the tests were the same ones for the same purpose. But more than two years later no tenders had been called for one, let alone two new vessels.

In June 1978 the *Lady Wakehurst* took a battering in rough seas at The Heads and had to be taken off for a few hours for repairs. A big wave forced open a pair of lower deck gangway doors, straining the doors in the process so that they could not be closed. These little ferries were never built for such rough usage, but if the Transport Committee's advice to modify them so that they could be used had not been heeded they would never had been available and the Manly service would have been in a

sorry state until arrival of the new ships. The *Manly Daily* of 16 December 1978 published an editorial headed 'Foiled again', which said:

A question in State Parliament this week spotlighted again the extraordinary Government complacency that has been going on for years over the plight of the Manly ferry service.

The Minister for Transport, Mr Cox, disclosed in reply to a question by Mr David Arblaster (Lib., Mosman) that tenders had not been called yet for construction of a new Manly ferry—six months after Mr Cox was supposed to have done so.

And even if he does call tenders within the next fortnight, as promised now, it could be at least three years before the new vessel is in service.

Meanwhile, the Public Transport Commission will be keeping its fingers crossed very hard, hoping that nothing serious happens to the rest of the fleet, particularly the two older vessels, *North Head* and *Baragoola*.

The previous government did announce in 1975 that it would build two new ferries and went out of office having done no more than talk about it.

Then, by the time the present government had to say something on the subject the two ferries had dwindled to one, to be built at the astronomical cost of $8.5 million.

When the *North Head* lost a rudder near Bradleys Head in August 1979, the problem was highlighted again. Until a new rudder was made, *North Head* made only two trips a day in peak hours in a brave effort to help shift the commuter traffic, back once more to a two-boat service with the *Baragoola* and the *Lady Wakehurst*.

The keel of the first new ferry, the *Freshwater*, was not

laid until 19 December 1980. During the ceremony, Mr Cox said he expected to see the ferry in service by October, but it was two years before she was commissioned. Meanwhile, a second ferry of the same type, the *Queenscliff*, was also being built at the State Dockyard. The *Freshwater* was launched on 27 March 1982. A great fanfare heralded the new 'super ferries', whose unique features would include a computer control system to give the skipper, it was said, complete control of the vessel.

The Freshwater class ferries, as these new ships were to be known, were completely different to the Manly ferries that had gone before them. Each was to cost more than $8.5 million. They were designed to carry 1100 passengers at a maximum speed of 18 knots on two engines or 15 knots on only one engine. They were the most powerful of the type ever built, being powered by two Daihatsu eight cylinder diesels, each developing 2940 bhp. The propellers, with controllable pitch, can be used separately or together for ahead or astern and a transverse thrust facility enables them to push the vessel sideways into the wharf. The eight-cylinder Rolls-Royce diesel engines drive alternators for generating the ship's electricity requirements and radar. The new vessels were fitted with retractable gangways like drawbridges, for which the wharves at Manly and Circular Quay had to be equipped with two level ramps capable of being raised or lowered according to the state of the tide. Their overall length of 70.4 metres (230.97 feet) was 10 feet longer than the *South Steyne* and their beam of 12.5 metres (41.01 feet) compared with the *South Steyne*'s 38 feet, although one of the reasons given for scrapping the *South Steyne* eight years before was that she was too big. An interesting point was that whereas the *South Steyne* had been known to carry as many as 1751 passengers, these slightly bigger ships were designed to accommodate only 1100. A large amount of space was provided for crew quarters and amenities.

For some strange reason, they were built with bluff bows and with the lower deck open at each end, which makes them very wet boats in rough weather. Instead of parting a sea and throwing it to each side as the older boats did, these hit the water with a big expanse of hull and throw it over the open deck and the top of the wheelhouse. Nevertheless, they offer passengers far more comforts than the old ships and have proved very popular, boosting the passenger traffic to new records and proving what everyone had been trying to tell the government for years—that people would use the ferries if a good service was provided for them.

Captain David Stimson accepted the *Freshwater* on behalf of the Urban Transit Authority at the official ceremony at Manly wharf on Saturday afternoon, 18 December 1982. After the ceremony and the celebra-

tions Dave Stimson steered his new ship proudly up the harbour to begin four hours of free travel on the ferries for the public to try the new vessel or ride on the *North Head* or *Baragoola* to see the *Freshwater* as it passed. On the Monday morning the commuters were full of praise for the new ferry.

Earlier in 1982 the *Lady Wakehurst* was involved in a tragic accident near Fort Denison on 11 April, colliding with a yacht in which John Leslie Ferguson, 27, of Sans Souci, was killed. This was what many ferry skippers and ships' pilots had feared for a long time because of the growing congestion of the harbour at weekends with sailing boats and sailing races, and worse still, the 'Sunday drivers' of the water. Many of these people have no knowledge of the rules of the road afloat and are also oblivious to the danger of crossing close in front of fast-moving ferries or the even faster hydrofoils. With power boats it is possible to get some idea of where they are going, but the ferry skipper's weekend nightmare is a mass of sailing craft twisting and turning in any direction at any minute, many in the mistaken belief that sail has absolute right of way over power. That is not so. The Manly ferries have an orange-red, diamond-shaped sign hanging from each mast, signifying that they have right of way, although if a collision is likely the ferry skipper has a responsibility to avoid it.

Ferguson was chopped to pieces by the *Wakehurst*'s propeller when the collision with the yacht *Soho* threw him into the water. Captain Bernadus Geradus Geveling, 65, of Guildford, master of the *Lady Wakehurst* at the time of the accident, was subsequently committed for trial on a charge of manslaughter after an inquest into Ferguson's death. A passenger on the ferry told the City Coroner, Mr Norman Walsh SM, that he saw flesh and blood in the water as the *Lady Wakehurst* went astern near a fleet of becalmed yachts. The witness, Geoffrey St George, of Maroubra, said that between Bradleys Head and Fort Denison he heard a long blast on the ferry's siren. Looking out, he saw some becalmed yachts in front of the ferry and then heard the siren again. He waited for the ferry to alter course or the yachts to get out of the way, but they were becalmed 'as if held in irons'. Mr St George said he heard another blast of the siren and saw the top of a mast appear in front of the ferry. Running to the other side of the ferry, he saw a yacht pass down the side with nobody on board and then, as the ferry reversed, he saw some flesh and blood in the water. Ferguson's body was not recovered for four days and had to be identified from dental charts.

A District Court jury acquitted Captain Geveling on 7 October 1983. Geveling was not steering the ferry at the time of the accident. According to normal practice with Manly ferries, a deckhand was at the wheel and the captain was in the wheelhouse. Mr Ken Horler, counsel for

Captain Geveling, told the jury that the actions of the racing yacht were primarily responsible for the accident. He said the regulations governing ferries and the directions given to ferrymasters were not clear and had led Captain Geveling to believe he had right of way. He said it did not matter that the captain's belief might be mistaken when assessing whether he was guilty of the very high degree of negligence necessary to convict him of manslaughter. Mr Horler said the instructions given to yachtsmen on the day of the accident were also unclear. Similar situations between ferries and yachts arose frequently on the harbour at weekends.

Interviewed by the *Sydney Morning Herald* after his acquittal, Captain Geveling predicted that there would be more fatalities on the harbour unless something was done about the weekend and holiday congestion and lack of adequate policing by the Maritime Services Board. He described conditions as 'nightmarish', made worse by the fact that there was no compulsory licensing for those in pleasure craft travelling at less than 10 knots while those who did hold licences were not required to pass any practical test. He said:

A lot of people in pleasure craft on the harbour behave in a completely stupid fashion. For instance, if you give them a blast to attract their attention, they poke their fingers rudely at you or hold up a can of beer.

Captain Geveling's local knowledge ticket, a compulsory requirement for ferrymasters, was suspended after the accident and he was given other duties. Nearly 12 months later, on 4 April 1984, a Court of Marine Inquiry found Captain Geveling guilty of a serious breach of duty and ordered that his certificate of competency be cancelled. Judge Sinclair, who presided over the inquiry, said the collision had been caused by the entry of the ferry at full speed into a group of racing yachts with a deckhand at the wheel. The judge said the collision occurred because the master was not keeping a proper lookout and had left the conduct of the ferry to a deckhand whose training and experience rendered him incapable of navigating the ferry safely through or around the fleet of yachts. Judge Sinclair recommended that ferrymasters should be reminded that displaying an orange diamond shape did not give the ferry absolute right of way. But despite the warning and the lesson that should have been learnt from this tragic accident, the situation became even worse, weekends becoming a bedlam of sailing boats and power craft.

If the *Freshwater* provided new comforts for her passengers, she was a constant trouble to the Urban Transit Authority. The ship's highly sophisticated mechanical equipment took temperamental turns and did strange things. After little more than a month in service, in January 1983, passengers had to wait in the drifting ferry near Middle Head while the engineers repaired failed generator circuit breakers. Next month she was held up again off Bradleys Head because of a fuel supply problem. A few weeks later the circuit breakers failed again and the *Freshwater* had to be towed back to Circular Quay from Mrs Macquarie's Chair. The circuit breakers played up for the third time early in March, stopping the ferry off Bradleys Head. But worse was to come. The *Freshwater* was one of the first ferries in the world to use a computer for the various mechanical propeller and rudder adjustments, a tiny control lever replacing all the old functions of engine room telegraph and doing many other sophisticated things not possible before. A Honeywell TDC 2000 computer had been installed on the advice of the Dutch technicians who designed the ferry's propulsion system and they had programmed it. Whatever happened, when the *Freshwater* came into Manly just after 9 am on Thursday, 10 March 1983, she refused to tie up at the wharf, snapping the rope and careering ahead again to run through the swimming enclosure net and ground herself hard and fast on the harbour beach, where she remained stubbornly until after 3 pm, when, with the tide rising again, tugs finally managed to get her off. Divers inspecting the hull at Circular Quay found no damage.

Why the *Freshwater* ran aground was a mystery. Technicians could find no malfunction in any equipment, although the skipper, Captain Merv Kramer, blamed the computer system. Parts of the computer were replaced and the original parts sent back to Holland for testing. *Freshwater* was back at work the day after the incident. An official of the Urban Transit Authority told the *Manly Daily*:

The UTA is satisfied everything has been done to ensure the *Freshwater* is in safe operating condition and passengers can travel on the ferry again with confidence. We have not discovered any electrical, mechanical or computer faults and have no indication what went wrong.

It was only a few days before trouble struck again. The *Freshwater* broke down for the sixth time since it was commissioned four months previously. Four trips were cancelled on 14 March after a fault was found in the warning system and a replacement circuit board was rushed from Newcastle. Engineers worked throughout the night to fit and test the board, which had been taken from the *Queenscliff*, still under construction at Newcastle. The component was one of nine microprocessor circuit boards which make up the ferry's monitoring system. That happened on 14 March. Two days later the *Freshwater* broke down again, spending more than an hour tied up

Riding the waves. Freshwater *drops back in a cloud of spray, her for' ard rudder and propeller right out of the water with a large length of keel. The white water in the background has been left behind by one of the hydrofoils. (Robert Needham)*

The seas were rolling in through The Heads when Freshwater *deckhand Robert Needham took this dramatic picture of the* North Head, *one rudder and propeller out of the water.*

at Manly after transferring her passengers to the *Lady Northcott*, which, like other ferries, had to tie up alongside. This time the cause of the trouble was a faulty governor on one of the diesel engines. The governor was repaired later in the day. An official of the Urban Transit Authority said:

> The problem was nothing to do with the computer system. This is a new vessel with systems which are nothing like those on the old ferries. It's likely to take a while for everything to settle down and work without mishaps.

He was right. Although everyone maintained that the mishaps were nothing to do with the computer system, the State Government had experts flown out from LIPS, of Druen, Holland, to make a thorough investigation into possible causes of the *Freshwater*'s continuing breakdowns. Until the investigation was complete, the skippers, who are members of the Merchant Services Guild, decided that they would man the trouble-plagued ferry only for morning and evening peak-hour runs. A member of the State Parliament, Mr Terry Metherell, Liberal member for Wakehurst, an electorate adjoining Manly, tried to raise the *Freshwater* issue in the House as 'a matter of public importance'. But the Labor Government, which had proclaimed its part in building the *Freshwater*, didn't let things like this get out of hand. The Leader of the House, Mr Frank Walker, opposed the motion, claiming that it was 'not of sufficient public importance' to debate and he was seconded by the Minister for Transport, Mr Cox, after which the Speaker, Mr Kelly, ruled it out of order. It all depends which side of the House you are on whether a matter is of 'public importance' or Government embarrassment.

According to a story in the *Manly Daily*, it was both. The Urban Transit Authority knew now what had caused the ferry to run aground at Manly, but was not saying anything. The problem had been traced to part of the Dutch-designed electronic control system and it had been repaired, but the superintendent engineer at the Urban Transit Authority ferry division, Mr Bill Heading, declined to elaborate. He said full details of the incident and its cause would have to come from the Maritime Services Board preliminary inquiry. The Maritime Services Board said results of that inquiry should be available within three weeks.

Despite the apparent tantrums of the *Freshwater,* it was obvious that the new ferries were going to be popular with the public and in April 1983 the Government announced that a third vessel of the same type would be built at Newcastle by Carrington Slipways, which had built the *Lady Wakehurst* and *Lady Northcott*. This time the con-

tract was for $8.9 million. Said the Premier, Mr Wran:

> It is a further step in our multi-million dollar program to overhaul and update Sydney Harbour public transport services. The success of this is reflected in the big and increasing patronage of the ferry services. Since 1976 no fewer than 5.1 million extra journeys have been recorded on all public ferry and hydrofoil services—an increase of nearly 55 per cent.

Mr Wran said the new contract provided for completion of the ferry within 14 months. The new vessel would give Sydney a world-class ferry service between Manly and Circular Quay. The fleet would have the best equipment in the world for operation and passenger comfort. Mr Wran also said operational faults found during the initial service of the *Freshwater* would need to be remedied permanently, not only in that vessel but also in the two other ferries then on order.

Students at Narrabeen Primary School gave the new ferry its name, asking in a petition with 400 signatures that it be called *Narrabeen* and the Minister for Transport had agreed. The new vessel would be the third Manly ferry bearing the name *Narrabeen*. The first was a paddlewheeler, built in 1886, disposed of in 1917. The second was a small steamer built in 1921 for the Manly cargo

The first Narrabeen *was built at Mort's Dock, Balmain, in 1886. She remained in the Manly service until 1911 carrying passengers and continued as a cargo carrier until 1917. (John Darroch)*

Narrabeen II *was a smart little cargo steamer, built by David Drake, of Balmain, with engines installed by Mort's Dock. (John Darroch)*

service. In 1928 the Spit Bridge had cut down the Manly cargo available by water and the *Narrabeen* was sold to the Westernport Steamship Company in Victoria. Renamed *Merilyn*, she was in use as a cargo ship between Cowes and Phillip Island and Melbourne and Tasmania until 1958, when she was lost in Bass Strait.

When the new *Narrabeen* came into service in August 1984, the Urban Transit Authority at last had the opportunity to provide a Manly service which would attract real patronage with three standardised ships offering a half-hour timetable during the day and comfortable travelling conditions. But the troubles were to continue for some time yet with the *Narrabeen*. On 12 September the ferry went out of control at Manly wharf and crashed at full speed on to the beach, tearing through a new shark net being put down for a swimming area. It was the second time in 18 months that one of the new 'super ferries' had crashed ashore on the beach. The new shark netting had been erected only the day before at a cost of $8000 to Manly Council. Two of the three men inspecting the net had narrow escapes from death or serious injury as the *Narrabeen* thundered towards them, blasting its siren. Graeme Birks, manager of the company installing the net, was checking the work from a dinghy out from the beach. Another of his men, Mark Tebbutt, of Cronulla, a diver, was standing waist-deep in water waiting to make a final dive to tighten up the net. Martin Smith, 16, of Randwick, told the *Manly Daily*:

We just couldn't believe it was happening. One minute the ferry was heading for the wharf. Next minute it was heading straight for the net and our boss in the dinghy. He just had to row for it. If Mark Tebbutt had been out there diving when the ferry crashed into the net he wouldn't have had a chance.

The *Narrabeen* had left Circular Quay at 3 pm with about 150 passengers, who would normally have disembarked at Manly about 3.30 pm. None was injured, but some complained that they were not told anything about what was happening. One woman said:

We did not know what was going on. We were coming into the wharf and then suddenly we were on the beach. Then, when we got clear of the beach we went back out into the middle of the harbour.

The ferry reversed itself off the beach and went up the harbour as far as Dobroyd, dragging 180 metres of floats and shark netting strung out behind from where it had caught around the rudder. The passengers were still aboard and it was 4.15 pm before they were disembarked.

The *Narrabeen* continued to have trouble berthing at Manly. Twice in a few days the master had to drop both anchors as an emergency, once when the ferry went out of control and headed for the fun pier and again when it lost power, veered to port and became stranded in the middle of Manly Cove. The *Narrabeen* was taken off for more tests and investigation of 'intermittent fluctuations in the voltage system'. Gradually the technicians from the Dutch company which installed the control systems sorted out the problems and the three new ferries settled down to normal working. Their only incident to make the headlines for a long time was when a man tried to hijack the *Freshwater* on Saturday night, 30 March 1985, and was arrested after shots were fired. The man allegedly went up to the bridge at Circular Quay and, pointing what appeared to be a gun at the captain, Dave Stimson, threatened to kill him unless he took the ferry out through The Heads. He said he wanted to jump off out there and commit suicide because he had 'busted up' with his girlfriend. Captain Stimson convinced the hijacker that he had to radio any proposed change of course and in doing so he alerted the water police to intercept the ferry. Water police sergeant Terry Fitzgerald climbed aboard the *Freshwater* from the police launch *Nemesis* on the way down the harbour and tackled the hijacker in the darkness of the boat deck behind the wheelhouse.

Telling about it afterwards, Sergeant Fitzgerald said:

I knew he was hiding somewhere in darkness on the roof of the top deck, but I didn't know exactly where until I edged out of the wheelhouse and saw him standing at the far end. As we began approaching each other he raised what looked like the barrel of a great shotgun. There was nowhere to hide, so I fired a shot into the air and ordered him to give himself up. He didn't seem to take any notice and kept coming towards me. I then fired another shot into the air and then a third, by which time we were pretty close to each other. We had reached what seemed to be a kill or be killed situation. I don't think I will ever forget the cold fear I felt when he swung what I thought was a shotgun and levelled the barrel at my chest. I thought to myself 'this is it' and steeled myself to shoot him. Then everything happened very fast. Instead of pulling the trigger I charged straight into him and managed to bring him down. I remember thanking God that he hadn't blasted me first. It was not until I had the handcuffs on him that I discovered all he had wrapped up in paper was an empty wine bottle. I've been in the police force for 20 years, 16 of them in the water police, but that night time ordeal on the roof of the Manly ferry is the most terrifying experience I've had.

Sergeant Fitzgerald praised the captain and crew of the *Freshwater* for their coolness. He said:

The hydrofoil Sydney *crosses the harbour at sunset. (Robert Needham)*

If the captain hadn't been quick-thinking enough to fool the hijacker into believing he had to radio a change of course, nobody would have known anything was wrong until very much later.

Trevor John Brady, 40, unemployed, of no fixed address, appeared in court subsequently charged with threatening to destroy a vessel.

2. The Hydrofoils

Sydney saw a new mode of water transport in January 1965, when the Port Jackson & Manly Steamship Company introduced Australia's first hydrofoil. The company imported from the Hitachi shipbuilding yard at Kanagawa a small 72-passenger hydrofoil at a cost of £140 000. She was given the name *Manly*. This was a great novelty and many people just went for the ride to see what it was like. For the commuter in a hurry the hydrofoil offered the advantage of quick travel, covering the journey in 15 minutes against the ferry's 35 minutes. The *Manly* was certified to operate between Sydney and Port Stephens to the north and Jervis Bay to the south, but never took on a regular service to these places. In February 1967, she was taken to Melbourne for tours on Port Phillip Bay, but the venture was not a great success. For normal use in Sydney the *Manly* was not really big enough, and because of this and various mechanical troubles she had a fairly short life.

In November 1966, she was given a big sister when the 140-passenger hydrofoil *Fairlight* arrived from Italy. *Fairlight* was the first of a fleet of five similar craft which formed the basis of the hydrofoil service between 1966, when the *Fairlight* arrived, and September 1984, when the 235-passenger *Manly* made her maiden journey. All these were built by the Rodriguez shipyard in Messina, Italy, at costs ranging from $500 000 for the *Fairlight* and the next to join the ranks, the *Dee Why*, to more than $5 million for

the *Manly*, which, when it was in service, cut the running time from 15 to 12 minutes.

Little mention has been made of the hydrofoils previously, this being essentially the story of the Manly ferries, but nowadays the hydrofoils do play an important part in the overall service. They are more like an aircraft than a boat or a ship, riding on their foils by using the water like an aircraft uses the air. Initially they were profitable and they were popular largely because of the run-down ferry service, but they have been plagued by mechanical and industrial troubles and their fortunes have declined since the three new ferries have offered more comfort for lower fares.

By the end of June 1984, the number of passengers using Manly ferries had risen to 7.97 million for the year, a big difference to the doldrums of 1976, when only 2.32 million users rode the ferries. But the hydrofoils, which had attracted 2.1 million customers in 1980 suffered a decline in patronage in 1984 to 1.58 million. The Urban Transit Authority attributed the decrease to the higher cost of travel—$2 by hydrofoil against $1.10 by ferry. Manly ferry passenger figures reached a record high in January 1985. The difference in fare levels might have had something to do with it, but most people did not agree it was the sole reason. They liked the new ferries and unless they were in a hurry, the ferries would do them.

The *Dee Why* joined the hydrofoil fleet in 1970 and the *Curl Curl* followed in 1973, enabling the Port Jackson & Manly Steamship Company to relegate the *Manly* to being a spare boat and use mainly a fleet of three similar craft in the *Fairlight, Dee Why* and *Curl Curl*. Brambles sold the hydrofoils when they took over the Port Jackson company and leased them back from FNCB-Waltons Finance Ltd. The State Government had to buy out the leases when it took over from Brambles in 1974. Before the Government take-over, a departmental officers' committee in a report to the Cabinet sub-committee on ferries, submitted as one matter requiring a Cabinet decision:

The old and the new. The old ferry North Head *and the hydrofoil* Dee Why *crossing The Heads on their way to Manly.* (Manly Daily)

Options on Manly hydrofoils: The agreement presently existing between the Government, the Port Jackson & Manly Steamship Company Ltd and its parent company, Brambles Industries Ltd, requires the Government to decide on options either to accept assignment of the former company's hydrofoil leases or to purchase the hydrofoils outright at a figure nominated by the owner under the company's buy-out arrangements with the owner of the craft, FNCB-Waltons Finance Ltd.

The officers committee is agreed that the hydrofoils are an essential and established part of the Manly service. Following an investigation into the technical aspects of the hydrofoils, the Maritime Services Board has concluded that the hulls, foils and machinery of the craft are in good condition and there are no technical grounds to prevent their acquisition. The expected life span of each craft is 15 years.

The committee is of the view that to exercise the second of the two options leaves no room for the Government to negotiate a more favourable purchase price, whereas in the present financial climate the Government would be in a strong bargaining position in any such negotiations. In all the circumstances, the committee recommends that Cabinet be asked to approve that the option providing for assignment of the company's leases of the four hydrofoils be exercised and that thereafter negotiations be opened with the owner of the craft for their purchase.

If the departmental officers' report was correct, most of the hydrofoils went far beyond their expected life spans. On that basis, the *Fairlight*, built in 1966, should have finished in 1981; the *Long Reef*, built 1969, should have ended its service in 1984; the *Dee Why* and *Palm Beach*, both built in 1970, should have finished in 1985 and the *Curl Curl*, of 1973 vintage, should be around until 1988. Not all of them were acquired as new craft. The *Long*

Reef, bought in Italy in 1978 for more than $1 million, arrived in Sydney as a ship's deck cargo in April of that year, but did not begin service until well into September. In the six months it was out of action it was found that the foils were suspect, necessitating considerable work on them, and the motors had to be overhauled. This became difficult when parts could not be obtained and eventually motors were taken from the *Curl Curl* and *Fairlight* to get the *Long Reef* going.

Similar troubles have beset the other hydrofoils and this, combined with industrial turmoil and strikes at the Balmain works depot, has given the hydrofoils some heavy weather to combat. How many breakdowns the hydrofoils suffer is never really known outside the ferry offices in town, and there is also a lack of publicity to explain why hydrofoils and ferries are tied up at Balmain for weeks when union strikes and go-slows dictate what does or does not go in or out of the depot. The painters and dockers control the depot. No matter how far behind the work schedule might be on ferries or hydrofoils, no outside contractors may come in to take some of it over and none of the vessels can be sent elsewhere for the work to be done. In May 1985, the big new hydrofoil, *Manly*, had been tied up at Balmain for just on two months

The hydrofoil Manly III *carries 240 passengers between Sydney and Manly in 12 minutes.* (Robert Needham)

because of a strike by the union and then go-slow tactics after they returned to work. Meanwhile, the other 140-passenger hydrofoils like the *Curl Curl*, known as the PT50s, were being flogged in a desperate effort to maintain a service to the public, carrying reduced loadings because of their inability to get up on the foils with a full load. During that period the *Curl Curl*'s load was reduced to 120, at times to 100 and even to 90, which meant 50 people had to be left behind in peak hours.

One morning in May 1979, the hydrofoil fleet was reduced to one boat. Two had broken down and the two standby boats were imprisoned at the Balmain depot by a union overtime ban. A couple of weeks earlier another hydrofoil broke down and was out of action for more than an hour. It could not be replaced because—believe it or not—the union would not allow another hydrofoil to be taken out of the depot, where union action had impounded it. In February 1985 the *Manly Daily* reported that two separate disputes between the Urban Transit Authority and the Painters and Dockers Union had put ferry and hydrofoil services on the brink of chaos. The paper said the hydrofoil *Fairlight* had been lying idle at Balmain for 10 months because of another dispute. Demarcation disputes have caused absurd situations. The day the new hydrofoil, *Manly*, was to go into service in September 1984, the maiden voyage was delayed for hours after members of the Painters and Dockers Union walked out of the Balmain depot. Apparently the water supply had been turned off while certain construction work was done at the dockyard. The unionists were angry because they claimed this rendered the dockyard unsafe in case of fire and had left them with inadequate washing and toilet facilities.

The absurdity of some of these disputes is demonstrated in this case. When the dockers walked off the job that morning because they could not wash their hands, the hydrofoil *Manly* could have been taken out of the depot and put into service, but while vessels are in the dock only members of the Painters and Dockers Union must tie them up or cast off the ropes—jobs done normally by deckhands outside the dock. That day—and no doubt many other days—nobody dared touch the ropes to lift them off the wharf bollards until after 4 pm, when the painters and dockers would have knocked off for the day if they hadn't been out on strike. In October 1982, rain and strikes held up work on the Manly wharf bus-ferry interchange for months. At one stage the union ordered men employed on the project to stop work for two days until portable toilets were installed on the site, despite the fact that the gent's toilet on the wharf was only a few metres away.

Industrial stoppages disrupt the ferry and hydrofoil services frequently when the Merchant Service Guild, which includes the ferry and hydrofoil skippers, holds stop-work meetings to discuss union affairs. Despite the

The hydrofoil Sydney *makes heavy going crossing the harbour in choppy seas. (Robert Needham)*

fact that they are manning an essential public utility, the men stop the service, usually for four and a half hours between 10 am and 2.30 pm, causing untold inconvenience to thousands of people. These tactics were taken further on 14 May 1985, when a stop-work to discuss one captain's pay grievances was pushed into the morning peak hours, leaving many commuters stranded after 8.05 am. Previously, the service was not closed down until after most people had been taken to their work in the city. This time the last ferry left Manly at 8 am, leaving quite a few behind, and the last hydrofoil departed at 8.05 am, leaving even more behind. The ghosts of the old Port Jackson & Manly Steamship skippers must have stirred that morning. Gone were their traditions of service to the public.

There are some differences between the hydrofoils and the ferries. Despite their speed, the hydrofoils do not figure in as many accidents as the ferries. Even at high speed they are very manoeuvrable and can usually avert trouble more easily than the slower moving but less nimble ferries.

The hydrofoil *Curl Curl* killed a man in an unusual accident on 2 October 1981. Timothy Charles Grahame Wearne, 23, of Cremorne, was with his two brothers and other men aboard a hired pleasure cruiser in the harbour for a 'bucks' party on the eve of his wedding to Sally Howes, 23, described as a Sydney heiress. One wonders why anyone would want to dive into the harbour near Fort Denison for a swim at about 5 pm. In the early days the fear of sharks deterred unfortunate convicts from trying to escape from Fort Denison by swimming ashore. But Timothy Wearne was killed by a hydrofoil instead of sharks and died in the whirling propellers of the *Curl Curl*. Wearne's brothers and friends aboard the cruiser shouted a warning to him as they saw the hydrofoil approaching. He saw it himself then and dived, but apparently came up too soon, right in front of the speeding hydrofoil.

Wearne's distressed friends and relatives tried in vain to recover his body before going for help. The skipper of the *Curl Curl* was Captain Bernadus Geveling, who, less than one year later, had the misfortune to be in charge of the *Lady Wakehurst* when its propellers cut a man to pieces, as mentioned in the previous chapter. He was unaware that his hydrofoil had struck a man and knew nothing about it until police questioned him. No blame was attached to him for the tragic accident. Police said Wearne's death was one of the most horrible ever to take place in the harbour.

One other accident of note involving a hydrofoil was on 2 February 1984, when the hydrofoil *Fairlight* and an eight metre fibreglass sloop collided near Fort Denison during a heat of the world 18-footer sailing championships. Three people who had been watching the sailing race from the sloop were flung into the harbour when the yacht sank after striking the underside of the hydrofoil's port bow. They were the skipper, John Stewart-Duff, of Vaucluse, Joseph Ferguson, of Bronte, and Georgina Martin, of North Bondi. They were pulled aboard a rescue boat which was following the races and were taken to the Royal Prince Edward Yacht Club at Point Piper. Police said the hydrofoil skipper, William Grasby, had to alter course when yachts were in his way. Just before the collision he told his engineer to shut down the engine, but the collision could not be avoided. An official of the Urban Transit Authority said the increasing number of pleasure boats on the harbour was causing great problems for ferries and hydrofoils. Sailboard riders were causing the biggest problem because riders were taking risks crossing in front of ferries and hydrofoils.

Urgent talks between representatives of the Merchant Service Guild, the Urban Transit Authority, Maritime Services Board and the boating industry were held after this accident to see what could be done to lessen the risk of more serious incidents involving weekend sailors, particularly in sailing boats and on sailboards. The result was that sailboards were banned from the shipping and ferry lanes, to the great relief of ferry and hydrofoil skippers and pilots getting big ships in and out of the port. The real fear of skippers was that one of the sailboarders' frequent collapses into the water would be done right under the propellers of their vessel.

The arrival of the big new *Manly* in September 1984 was an event of considerable interest. If riding in her predecessors had been like flying in a DC3 aircraft, travel in the *Manly* was like being in a Jumbo 747. Looking out of the lower front windows of this hydrofoil gives an impression similar to rushing down an airport runway for take-off. The *Manly* knocked three minutes off the journey, covering the seven miles in 12 minutes, carrying up to 240 passengers. But in the first 12 months the *Manly*

was in service she spent more time at the Balmain depot than travelling the harbour. Two days after her maiden voyage in September 1984, a fire in the turbochargers broke out when she berthed at Circular Quay after the 9.25 am trip from Manly. She was out of service for more than a week awaiting a replacement part to be flown in from abroad. Between March and May of 1985 the *Manly* spent more than two months tied up at Balmain, allegedly because of various reasons—the strike by the painters and dockers, warranty work waiting to be done and lack of spare parts. In May of that year the *Manly* was awaiting a new propeller. One had been damaged and there were no spares in Australia.

Maintenance of the hydrofoils was quite a big and frequently expensive affair. George Marshall tells about some of the problems they had to face, particularly in the early stages:

> They were constructed with the propeller for'ard of the aft foil. This meant that if the after foil was going to hit something the propeller hit it first. We kept on doing in propellers for three years before the situation was changed. It was a major operation to put the foils in front of the propeller, but the percentage of propeller damage was cut down. I think we did 60 propellers, costing $700 each, before things were put right.

The cost of building hydrofoils has gone up considerably. The *Palm Beach*, a PT50, was bought second-hand in Hong Kong, where she had been used on the service between Hong Kong and Macau. Her purchase price was $700 000, $200 000 more than the new price of the *Fairlight, Dee Why* and *Curl Curl*. Eleven years later, the much bigger and faster 235-passenger hydrofoil *Manly II*, imported from Italy, cost $8 million. A year later again, her sister ship, *Sydney*, cost about $8.75 million. The hydrofoils are costly to operate. Apart from day-to-day breakdowns and repairs, major mechanical overhauls should be done on hydrofoils after 4000 hours of engine operation. This involves taking the engines out and stripping them down. The vessels should be docked every 12 weeks to maintain hull and foil cleanliness, which is most important to their performance and economy of operation and it presents a big worry when strikes at the Balmain depot impede docking and hull cleaning.

Maintenance on the hydrofoils is almost prohibitive, according to George Marshall—admittedly an old ferry man rather than a hydrofoil enthusiast—who says:

> The cost of operating hydrofoils far exceeds the cost of operating a conventional ferry carrying about 1200 passengers. It requires an entirely separate operation— a separate berth, separate ticket selling and separate

wharf staff. The wharf hands who take in a ferry cannot berth a hydrofoil. More than once a crankshaft has been broken and to replace it means a lot of work and a lot of money. You have to take off the deckhouse, pull up the floor, take out the engine, rebuild it and then replace it. The V12-cylinder Mercedes 1500-hp engines weigh about four tonnes, so it is no small job and it is very costly.

Keith Rosser, after years with the ferries, spent many more years with the hydrofoils from their early days on the harbour and enjoyed the life. Max Barton was with the inner harbour ferries before going on to hydrofoils. He is happy in the service and regards hydrofoils as an essential part of metropolitan transport. Says Max:

> Apart from their speed, the hydrofoils attract many people because they give a comfortable ride across The Heads in rough weather, which suits those who might be prone to seasickness. They don't roll as much as a conventional vessel and they don't pitch as much because the foils slice through the waves and the hull is above the waves. Hydrofoils offer the comfort of individual seats with armrests. Also, hydrofoils have a far better safety record, despite their speed.

Another hydrofoil enthusiast is Captain Bill Thomas, who has spent 16 of his 19 years with the Manly service in hydrofoils. A native of Liverpool, England, he spent some years at sea before coming to Australia and has a foreign-going master's certificate. Between 1962 and 1964 he was with the *South Steyne* and took her several times on ocean cruises to Broken Bay. Bill Thomas went back to England in 1964 but missed Sydney harbour, returned to it in 1970 and has been a hydrofoil captain ever since.

Not a great deal happens around the hydros, as some call them, but Bill Thomas tells of an incident one day when he was off Middle Head in the *Curl Curl* going to Sydney between 7 and 8 am and the *Long Reef* was coming in the opposite direction towards Manly. As the two vessels approached at full speed near Middle Head a passenger in the *Long Reef* opened the back gate and stepped off into the water. Bill Thomas said:

> You can imagine our horror. He must have dropped down between the foils and the back one passed over his head without hitting him. We stopped, turned around and raced back to where he was floundering in the water and, to our amazement, was singing. A policeman was on board with us. We got down and hauled the fellow out of the water, which was not easy because he was at least 200 centimetres tall and rather big. The man was obviously high on drugs. Asked

where he was going, he replied 'to Nirvana', which indicated to us that he was going to Manly to get 'a fix'. Three times during the rest of the trip to Sydney we had to restrain him from going out the door again.

Bill Thomas took the hydrofoil *Fairlight* to Newcastle in 1970, covering the 60 sea miles in two hours. In 1984 he brought the *Manly II* to Sydney from Newcastle in 1 hour 45 minutes, averaging 35 knots. He says her sister ship, the *Sydney*, built to do 38 knots, can reach 41 knots. Thomas, Max Barton and another skipper, Dick Kirkwood, describe the big new hydrofoils as 'fine boats'. Gyroscopes and computers control flaps on the after foils which keep the craft in level flight, even in heavy seas. 'This is the only hydrofoil service in Australia and we should be very proud of it,' says Bill Thomas.

Working the hydrofoils is a team effort. The captain steers and gives directions to the engineer, who controls from the wheelhouse the two powerful engines down below. The engineer is a key man berthing at wharves and leaving them, controlling the vessel through its two propellers. Tony Grasso has been with the hydrofoils as an engineer since 1974 after spending four years at sea in BHP ships as a marine engineer. He likes the life on the hydrofoils. He said:

> It is an interesting life. Things on the harbour are changing all the time. In summer every trip is different. It is never monotonous. The scene can change so quickly, too, with the weather. On the hydrofoils the engineer has more of the action than he would get in the ferries. You are up on the bridge instead of being down in the bowels of the ship shut off from everything.

But it is not always so. The engineers get quite a bit of dirty work when things go wrong. The very first trip Tony did in the *Palm Beach* was not all smooth sailing. He said:

> We wondered why we couldn't get her up on the foils. When we berthed at Manly I went down below and found that the engine room was flooded. A hose bringing sea water in for cooling the engines had come off and was pouring the water into the engine room instead of through the engines. I've been down there in underpants cleaning out the water intakes when they have become clogged with rubbish.

Tony Grasso thinks big hydrofoils like the *Manly* and *Sydney* would be very suitable for long trips, like Sydney to Newcastle. He said:

> We brought the *Sydney* down from Newcastle in 1 hour 35 minutes. This is faster than the XPT train, which

takes two and a quarter hours. These boats are good at sea, too. We brought the *Manly* down into strong southerly weather and she rode it beautifully.

They are not cheap to run, however. Two V16 engines burn up 60 litres of lubricating oil a day. They are designed to use this much oil in their lubricating systems.

These craft are so fast that few speedboats can outpace them. The *Manly* and the *Sydney* can cover the seven-mile trip in 10 minutes if necessary. It has been suggested, facetiously, that they would be good for towing water skiers. That was tried with one of the PT50 hydrofoils some years back when they were being serviced at Berrys Bay. One of the workmen thought he would like to see how it went. Waterside residents, to their amazement, saw a skier being towed along behind a hydrofoil and some rang the Port Jackson & Manly Steamship Company to query what was going on. The experiment was never repeated.

The Manly hydrofoil Fairlight *riding at speed on its foils.* (Manly Daily)

PART VII
ILL WINDS

1. The Big Blow

Weather is an important factor in the operation of the Manly ferry service. It decides whether passengers will have a comfortable ride or a rough time. Some will shun the trip in rough weather, despite assurances that a Manly ferry has never sunk and not one passenger life has been lost in more than 130 years, except where the passenger had jumped overboard or was crushed leaping from a vessel before it was moored. Others, of course, enjoy a ride in rough weather more than anything, finding exhilaration in the motion of the ship and the sight of the big seas it has to challenge. To many people who live inland, mention of the Manly ferry brings images of stormy seas and wildly bucking ferries. But it is rarely like that. For weeks on end the crossing can be quite flat. The wild weather gets the headlines because it makes news and calm seas do not.

When a westerly blows up at night and keeps on blowing, daylight is not going to bring any change for the better. On the morning of 3 June 1941 the westerly which had been blowing throughout the night turned and came in hard from the south-west. The big sea the westerly had been pushing back all night then began to roll in along the coast, crashing against the cliffs and sending cascades of spray into the air. The Sydney *Sun* reported that 'terrific seas through The Heads and difficult mooring conditions at Manly wharf' disorganised the early morning ferry service for the first time in three years. Because of the big surge at Manly, three extra mooring lines had to be used on some ferries to hold them against the wharf. The *South Steyne* was unable to berth for the main commuter trip at 8.10 am. After standing off for about 10 minutes, the *Steyne* had to go back to town with the passengers it had aboard. Said the *Sun*:

The manager of the Port Jackson & Manly Steamship Company said that every steamer carried away most of the six-inch hawsers and passengers had to be loaded with great care. Only one gangplank could be used on each boat and passengers had to watch their chance to hurry on and off as the boats were swung about by the rough seas. There were no casualties, although several people had lucky escapes when one ferry snapped all her ropes. This vessel made the trip to Sydney with only 50 people aboard. Buses were run at 10-minute inter-

vals from Manly to Wynyard in the city and were well patronised.

Captain G.R. Clark, of the *Curl Curl*, said he had not seen such conditions at Manly for more than 20 years. A wharfinger at Manly said fresh supplies of hawsers had to be obtained from Sydney as every mooring hawser at Manly had been snapped and three men were kept busy all day splicing the broken ropes.

Big seas on 14 October 1942 caused suspension of the ferry service and thousands of people could not get to their work in the city. Buses and trams were packed to capacity on all the morning runs from Manly through Balgowlah and Seaforth. At 10 am hundreds of people were still waiting for transport to the city. Nearly 2000 people were waiting for trams at the Spit. Referring to many complaints about this, Mr Dendy said: 'You can't expect trams to carry the same loads as our ferries.'

It was another three years before a similar situation occurred again. On 12 June 1945, a very strong gale stopped the ferries. Lashed by the gale, huge seas rolled in through The Heads and bombarded the ferries before they were taken off after battling it out until 11.30 am. Seas broke over the *Dee Why* on her 7.25 am trip from Manly, damaging the iron gangway doors on the lower deck. The

A wild day on the water. Another angle to the rough day on the harbour on Wednesday, 7 November 1984, when the biggest sea for a long time battered anything afloat. This picture, taken by Manly Daily *photographer Ros Cannon, won the award by the Australian Suburban Newspapers Association for the best news picture of 1984.*

Curl Curl was partially swamped by a big comber while crossing The Heads from Manly at about 11.20 am. As the terrific force of water surged over the main deck, it stove in a steel gangway door, broke a sliding door to pieces and smashed five windows. Four passengers were cut by flying glass. Twelve men who had been sitting on the outer deck were swept from their seats into 45 centimetres of swirling water, which hurled them along the deck while they grabbed frantically at the legs of seats to prevent being swept overboard.

About 200 people were aboard the *Curl Curl*, which had left Manly a quarter of an hour late and took 55 minutes to reach Sydney instead of the usual 35 minutes. Several waves which struck the *Curl Curl* were described as being nine metres high. The men who had been swirled around the outer deck disembarked at Circular Quay soaked to the skin and displaying bruised and cut legs and arms. An ambulance, summoned by radio as the ferry came up the harbour, was waiting, but only one passenger needed hospital treatment. Douglas Donaldson, 35, of Anzac Parade, Collaroy, had three stitches inserted in a gash in his forearm and received treatment for other cuts in his arm and fingers.

On 16 April 1946, the Manly service was suspended after three ferries were damaged and three women passengers had to be taken to hospital. A 19-year-old girl was taken to Manly hospital when the *Baragoola* berthed at Manly with five windows shattered. Ruth Willock, of Hannan Street, Maroubra, suffered severe cuts to her legs and face when she was showered with broken glass from the *Baragoola*'s windows. The *Bellubera* took a pounding during one morning trip and turned back to the city instead of proceeding to Manly. The worst victim, though, was the *Barrenjoey*, which, according to the *Sun*, was hit by 'a wall of water'. The sea poured like a torrent across the lower deck, lifting passengers from their seats and flinging them to the deck, bruised and dazed, showered with broken glass. Mr E.A. Shaw, of Sydney Road, Manly, said:

People were washed from side to side of the ferry after the wave, which seemed to be as high as the top deck, hit us side on.

At Circular Quay three women were transferred from the *Barrenjoey* to an ambulance, which took them to Sydney Hospital. Doreen Reilly, of Parr Parade, Dee Why, was X-rayed because she was in great pain from a strained back and possible internal injuries. Mrs Muriel Edwards, of Darley Road, Manly, had injured her ribs and her sister, Miss Dorothy Love, also of Darley Road, had a deep cut over her right eye which had to be stitched. At the hospital, Miss Love told a *Sun* reporter:

My sister and I were sitting in the ladies' saloon with our backs towards the open sea. The ferry was tossing badly. Then came a horrible sickening impact which seemed to stop the ferry. I was flung from the seat and cracked my head against a steel stanchion.

Doreen Reilly's uncle, Clive Reilly, said:

We were between The Heads when the big wave struck. It shattered two windows and, with irresistible force, a wall of water swept us from our seats. Doreen seemed to be badly hurt and my first thought was for her. Passengers' belongings were floating around the deck.

Reaction from the wave made the ferry roll heavily and water poured in from the other side. Said Mr D. Grosvenor, of Craig Avenue, Manly:

Some of us saw the huge wave coming. Some soldiers yelled out 'Here she comes'. Then the sea hit us. There was a roar as the green wall of water hit the *Barrenjoey*. Doors flew open everywhere. Women were screaming. Water swirled around the deck. Passengers were rolling in it, wet to the skin. Even those on the side opposite to the impact were thrown off their feet.

Keith Rosser remembers one day in 1965 as his worst weather ever. He recalls:

I have been in some seas in the *Dee Why* so big that the funnel stays were carried away but that gale was the worst. I was skippering the *Bellubera* at the time. At Circular Quay I went down on deck and found the engine room door open. In fact it was lashed back. I said to the engineer 'What is the meaning of this?' He said to me: 'I hope you know I am a family man and if this ship is going to go down I want to get out first.' I said to him: 'You can't have all this noise coming out of the engine room to the passengers. Close it.' On the way back to Manly, halfway across The Heads we shipped a greenie, and what a mess. Water poured down into the engine room and we lost two engines. We struggled on into Manly with only one engine and there we stayed until we could get another one going. The seas were so big that at Manly they were coming right up through the wharf, breaking every mooring line. We had to get out of Manly. We came out with the two engines at a slower speed than normal and she rode the seas beautifully. They were so high I could see into the parade ground at Middle Head from some of the rollers.

The *Bellubera* was generally recognised as a good boat in big swells, which she rode superbly.

Those seas that day nearly put the Matson liner *Mariposa* aground on Dobroyd. Coming into the harbour in that gale, she missed the turn into the main western channel off Middle Head. When she was put astern to line her up again, the wind and the sea took charge, driving the vessel backwards towards the dangerous Dobroyd bombora. During this time, the ship rolled and tossed so much that crockery was smashed, fittings were broken and many passengers were injured. Interviewed after the ship was berthed safely, the master said:

I don't know how many times I have been across the Tasman, where you can get some really rough weather, but the biggest seas I have seen were here in Sydney harbour today.

The harbour is also subject to another kind of dangerous weather in the form of storms or strong southerly blows which can cause havoc among small sailing boats whose owners don't take them home before the wind arrives. People who know the ways of the weather—and everyone who uses small craft should—can see this type of weather coming some time before its impact reaches them. A black sky down south is enough warning for the experienced fisherman or yachtsman. But so many people stay out in boats until the black sky is right above them and then battle home through clouds of spray and driving rain.

Two people were drowned when one of these storms— a very violent one—swept across the harbour on 27 December 1955. Captain Wally Dohrn, bringing the *Baragoola* up from Manly, was steering by compass in a very heavy rain squall near Fort Denison about 2.07 pm when by a lucky chance he noticed a woman struggling in the water. She was taken aboard the *Baragoola*, was given first aid and Sydney was notified by radio to have an ambulance at the wharf. The woman was Mrs Margaret Marion Holland, wife of Dr Victor Holland, of Waruda Street, Kirribilli. One of the inner harbour ferries on its way to Taronga Park picked up Dr Holland, who was taken by ambulance from Taronga Zoo wharf to the Royal North Shore Hospital.

According to newspaper reports, Dr and Mrs Holland were sailing in a 25-foot cutter with two other people, Mrs Eve Anderson, of Mann Avenue, Neutral Bay, and Russell John Bownas, 31, a city markets agent, of Albyn Road, Strathfield, when the storm swept across the harbour about 2 pm. Water police received dozens of urgent calls for help as more than a hundred small craft were suddenly in danger. The *Avona*, the boat owned by Dr Holland, was heading north under sail off Fort Denison when it was flattened by a squall and capsized. It sank within a few minutes, leaving Dr and Mrs Holland and the other two struggling in the choppy water. Dr Holland

Above and following page: After the storm. Wreckage from the Manly Harbour Pool boardwalk strewn over the harbour beach on West Esplanade after the 1974 gale. (Manly Daily)

supported Mrs Anderson in the water for some time, but efforts to save her were in vain. Mr Bownas lost his life also.

Some of the worst weather ever struck Sydney on Saturday night, 25 May 1974, when a destructive gale caused immense damage around the metropolitan waterways. Daylight on Sunday revealed a picture of havoc at Manly, where the wharf was damaged so badly that ferry services had to be cancelled temporarily. All around Sydney boats were driven ashore and smashed to pieces and sea walls and waterfront buildings were battered.

Manly's harbour front, in the direct path of the furious gale, was covered with wreckage from near and far. Perhaps the greatest tragedy, however, was the almost complete destruction of the famous harbour pool boardwalk, most of which dangled precariously on its piers, torn and twisted into an amazing snakelike pattern of S-bends. Huge masses of timber and debris from the boardwalk littered the harbour beach on West Esplanade. Damage throughout Manly-Warringah was estimated at more than $1.5 million. The bad weather continued into the week,

Wreckage from the Manly Harbour Pool boardwalk after the 1974 gale.

causing cancellation of the ferry and hydrofoil services.

That was the end of the harbour pool. The idea of rebuilding it was revived in 1984, when Manly Council included the possibility in a comprehensive study of Manly Cove. But the estimated replacement cost of $1.6 million, plus $80 000 a year for maintaining it, frightened away the good intentions. The West Esplanade beach won a consolation prize of a temporary shark net suspended from floats and most of the beach was left for windsurfing and small sailing boat activities. The shark net was moved further west after first the *Freshwater* and then the *Narrabeen* crashed through it while berthing at the wharf.

Nothing like that gale has happened since. There have been some bouts of rough weather, when television cameramen and newspaper photographers terrify people living in the outer western suburbs with pictures of the Manly ferries standing on end and being smothered in white spray, but most days there is no more than a gentle rock as the ferries glide across that mile of open sea.

Some pictures in this book of the *Freshwater*, *Queenscliff* and *Narrabeen* were taken during a couple of days of storm and tempest in November 1984. It provided a good test for the new vessels, which had not faced anything really rough previously. They were very wet outside, but remained dry inside. Their expansive bows thump into the seas and throw the spray higher than the wheelhouses, they roll heavily beam on and they do catch the wind berthing at Manly in southerlies, but they have many good points. Passengers like them because they are comfortable, clean and warm in winter, not having the draughty doors and windows of the old vessels.

2. Strange Happenings

People choose many strange and bizarre ways in which to commit suicide. In Sydney the traditional methods have included—apart from guns or poison—The Gap, the Harbour Bridge, jumping in front of trains or, last but not least, jumping overboard from Manly ferries. Sometimes those who favoured the ferries succeeded. Sometimes they did not because others dived in and rescued them. It never occurred to these people, apparently, that those who went to their rescue could lose their own lives. It is a proud record that the Manly ferries, in more than 130 years, have not lost the life of a passenger through any fault of the company. There is a trail of tragedy, however, from people who jumped overboard or were involved in accidents involving the ferries and small craft on the harbour.

Many people have gone to their deaths in Sydney Harbour. It is often not known whether they fell from a ferry by design or accident. One thousand passengers on the *Dee Why* in December 1939 saw a dramatic but vain effort to save a woman who fell overboard when the ferry was crossing The Heads. The victim was Mrs Grace Coghan, 28, of Ross Street, Forest Lodge, who, apparently, went for a return trip to Manly with a friend. They did not leave the vessel at Manly and when it was directly opposite Middle Head on the return trip, rolling in a slight swell, Mrs Coghan, who had been sitting on a rail on the top deck, fell overboard.

Captain J. G. Jewell put the *Dee Why* astern immediately he heard the passengers crying 'Woman overboard' and deckhands lowered a lifeboat with the assistance of naval cadets. They found Mrs Coghan floating face down and had her back on board the ferry in little more than five minutes. An ambulance officer who was on the ferry began artificial respiration as Captain Jewell turned the *Dee Why* about and raced back to Manly wharf, hoping to get her to medical attention in time to save her life. In those days the ferries did not have radio. They used to give four blasts of their whistles as they came down the harbour when they had trouble aboard and this alerted police and ambulance men. An ambulance met the ferry at the wharf and rushed the woman to Manly Hospital, but she was beyond help. Mrs Coghan left behind a husband and four children.

Two men jumped into the harbour from the *Curl Curl* in a courageous but vain effort to save a woman who jumped to her death just before midnight on 12 February 1945. Her body was identified later as that of Mrs Dulcie Weinberg, 45, of Collins Street, Belmore, mother of two children.

Donald Taylor, of Griffiths Street, Balgowlah, a passenger, said later that he saw the woman walk to the rails on the top deck. She looked at him for a few seconds, smiled, waved and then leapt to her death. A man jumped in after her and struggled with her in the water. He tried without success to reach a lifebuoy which was thrown from the ferry. An Army sergeant dived in and helped the other man get the woman to the buoy just as a tug stopped and pulled the three aboard, then transferred them to the waiting ferry. Two elderly men on the *Curl Curl* took up a collection for the soldier and the civilian rescuers. Every passenger contributed and the men received several pounds. When the ferry berthed at Manly the two men, still wearing their wet clothes, walked away from the wharf. The woman's body was taken ashore.

The City Coroner, Mr E. T. Oram, ruled out suicide in the strange circumstances surrounding the death on 14 May 1935 of Sir Thomas Henley, a well-known figure in public life for more than 30 years after he won the State seat of Burwood in 1904. He represented Burwood in ten successive State Parliaments, was Minister for Public Works and Minister for Railways in Sir George Fuller's Government of 1922, and he gave many years service to local government. He was an alderman of Drummoyne Council for 36 years from 1898 to 1934, being mayor for six terms, was also an alderman of the Sydney City Council, and from 1902 to 1933 was vice-president of the Metropolitan Water Board. He was knighted in 1920 for his many public services.

On 14 May 1935, Sir Thomas had his chauffeur, Percival Woodberry, drive him to Circular Quay to catch the 11.30 am ferry to Manly. Woodberry was instructed to wait there until the same ferry came back to town as Sir Thomas was going for the return trip. This would indicate that Sir Thomas had every intention of coming back. It was not the attitude of one who was going to take his own life. He walked aboard the *Barrenjoey* and 10 minutes after it had left Circular Quay, nearing Bradleys Head, he was seen to fall from the stern of the ferry. A woman passenger who saw Sir Thomas fall gave the alarm, but the ferry was travelling at full speed and it was some time before Captain George Clark could turn her around and go back. When the *Barrenjoey* was about 45 metres from where the man's body was floating face down in the water, Trevor Bennett, 23, of Norton Street, Manly, dived overboard and held up the body until a boat, lowered from the *Barrenjoey*, picked them up. Bennett said:

I think he was dead when they lifted him into the boat. His face and neck were swollen and he did not have the appearance of a drowned man. Floating near him was a small bottle or phial.

The Dee Why *in a rolling swell. (John Darroch)*

Bennett and others aboard the ferry worked hard with resuscitation on the unconscious man stretched out on the deck while the *Barrenjoey* raced down the harbour to Manly, Captain Clark sounding the emergency siren to alert police and ambulance. But Sir Thomas was dead and was taken to Manly Hospital.

Dr Guy Menzies told the inquest on 5 June that Sir Thomas Henley had been a patient of his for more than 20 years. From his observations over the past six months, Sir Thomas had been suffering from a form of cerebral neuralgia and cerebral giddiness. Dr Menzies said that for three months before Sir Thomas Henley's death he had seen him every few days and his giddiness seemed to be most distressing and intense. He was also suffering from chronic nephritis, with an increase of blood pressure which made him liable at any time to a sudden cerebral haemorrhage. From that condition it was reasonable to assume that Sir Thomas Henley might at any time have a fainting attack.

Mrs May McCarthy, of Bexley, told the coroner she was sitting on the top deck of the *Barrenjoey* with another woman and a party of children. As the ferry went down the harbour she noticed an elderly man standing nearby. She said:

He appeared as if he was cold. Opposite Bradleys Head he raised the dividing rail between the boat deck and the passenger deck and walked between the lifeboats to the flagpole. He stood there with one hand on the flagpole and the other on the support of the flagpole. Then he dropped his walking stick and held the flagpole with both hands. Shortly afterwards I saw him let go and fall forward into the water.

The coroner said he had no doubt that Sir Thomas Henley fell from the ferry accidentally and this was supported by the evidence of Mrs McCarthy, the only witness to what had happened. But it still leaves unanswered why he opened the railing and walked out to the very end of a deck which was forbidden to passengers, standing there until he fell overboard. As the coroner said, it was a tragic end to the life of a man who had given a great deal of service to the State.

Many similar tragedies attracted less attention. On 13 November 1953, on the 11 pm trip from Sydney of the *Baragoola*, a woman jumped overboard as the ferry was crossing The Heads. Captain Harold Liley's accident report stated: 'After a difficult search in the dark she was taken aboard and was placed in an ambulance at Manly. She died later in Manly Hospital.'

Captain Fred Pocock reported that when in the vicinity of Middle Head after leaving Manly at 3.15 pm on 2 December 1954, a man fell overboard. The man, a young Chinese seaman was rescued by lowering a boat and was given first aid by two police officers who were aboard the ferry, but he did not respond and was found to be dead when taken to Sydney Hospital.

Captain Ron Hart tells of a man who jumped overboard from the *Baragoola* one day as the ferry was rounding the Bradleys Head marker buoy:

We went back and picked him up and I had the crew bring him up to the wheelhouse. His answer, when I asked why he had done it, was that it was a nice day for a swim. I said to him, 'You must be off your head. Do you normally go swimming like that when you see water?' The police took him from us at Manly and the sergeant rang me at home later to say the fellow had been released the previous day from the psychiatric hospital at Morisset, so I wasn't far wrong. Six months later the same man was walking over the Harbour Bridge when he decided to jump in for a swim and this

time he did not survive. I remembered him because on the ferry I asked him his name and was told Sydney Gregory. I accused him of pulling my leg. 'Oh no,' he said. 'That's my name.'

A passenger leaving the *Bellubera* at Manly at 11.25 on the night of 20 August 1955, said to the deckhand standing near the gangway: 'Why didn't you pick up that bloke who fell overboard?' 'What bloke? Where?' the deckhand asked. Informed that a man had fallen into the water as the *Bellubera* crossed The Heads, the deckhand told the skipper, Norman Smith. 'Righto,' said Smith. 'Get her under way again. It's a small chance, but we'll go back and look for him.' Near where the man was reported to have jumped they heard somebody calling from the darkness. A boat was lowered and the lucky fellow was found swimming, but tiring rapidly from exhaustion. Back at Sydney he was handed over to the police.

The *Bellubera* seems to have been favoured by many as a jumping-off platform. On 14 October 1960, a man jumped from *Bellubera* between Georges Head and Middle Head during the 10.50 pm trip to Manly. Captain Frank Farrugia returned his ship to the area and searched without success for about 30 minutes before going on to Manly and notifying the police. While the police were coming down the harbour, the collier *Mortlake Bank* found the missing man and transferred him to the police launch. He had swum to the channel junction buoy near Middle Head and was hanging on to it, calling out for help.

A passenger in the *North Head*, which left Manly at 1.45 pm on 7 March 1962, jumped overboard off Clifton Gardens. Other passengers saw him leave his seat on the upper deck carrying what appeared to be a weight and a rope tied around his leg. He put one leg over the side of the ferry and rolled off. A red cardigan he had been carrying over his arm was left floating on the surface, but the man had disappeared. Five days later his body came up in the net of some Italian prawn fishermen who were working near Chowder Bay, giving them a nasty shock.

Some people have had very fortunate rescues. A water police constable dived into the harbour on the night of 27 February 1958 to rescue a woman who had been missing in the water for three-quarters of an hour. He dived and found her by what could only have been a thousand-to-one chance and she lived by a million-to-one chance. The ferry was the *Bellubera* again. Just after it had passed Fort Denison on the 7.30 pm trip from Sydney, Mr E. Moran, of Alison Road, Randwick, reported that a woman had fallen overboard. Mr Tony Martin, of Alexandria Street, Collaroy, also saw her walk to the rail of the ferry and fall over the side. 'It happened so quickly that we couldn't do anything,' he said. 'I ran with others and called over the din of the engines that a woman had gone overboard.' They thought the woman, fair haired, wearing a floral frock, was about 35 years old. Captain Lawrence Bruce stopped the *Bellubera* and put her astern, but was prevented from steering back along his wake because a ship was following them. When they could find no trace of the woman in the choppy wind-swept stretch of the harbour between Fort Denison and Bradleys Head, Captain Bruce radioed for assistance from the water police, who arrived and took over the search. The *Bellubera* continued on to Manly, where belongings the woman had left aboard were handed over to Manly police.

Constables Joseph Bourke and Gordon Fuller in the police launch *Adastrea* were almost about to give up hope after searching for another 30 minutes on top of the 15 minutes since the woman had gone into the harbour. Suddenly, on the choppy surface of the water, Constable Bourke saw part of an arm, but it sank almost immediately and he could see nothing more. The constable dived in, swam to where he thought he had seen the arm, and then he dived again. Miraculously, he found the woman in the darkness below, brought her to the surface and swam back with her to the *Adastrea* and Constable Fuller, who dragged her aboard. They thought she was dead and beyond any help, but Constable Bourke tried resuscitation on the floor of the launch while Constable Fuller raced the boat back to the water police boatshed at Circular Quay West, having arranged by radio for an ambulance to be waiting. The woman was showing faint signs of life as they carried her ashore to the ambulance to be taken to Sydney Hospital, where she recovered eventually. Constable Bourke, who had dived in fully clothed except for his coat, lost his watch, money and other possessions in the water.

On 11 September 1950 a 46-year-old man who had jumped from the *Dee Why*, fully dressed except for his coat and overcoat, was dragged from the harbour by the crew of a naval launch. He was swimming on his back in choppy water near Fort Denison, about 350 metres from the *Dee Why*, when the launch crew saw him and took him aboard. They wrapped him in dry coats and took him to the water police at Circular Quay. Police said the man told them he had jumped from the ferry because he was tired of living and wanted to end it all. His coat and overcoat were found folded up near the stern rail of the *Dee Why*. An ambulance took him from water police headquarters to Sydney Hospital, where he was given treatment for shock and immersion. Police charged the man later with having attempted to commit suicide and took him to the Reception House, which was normal practice then.

Three youths risked their lives on the night of 11 February 1940, when they dived from the *Curl Curl* near the Sow and Pigs to rescue a young soldier who had fallen overboard. Private Bill Murphy had lost his Digger's hat

and went around the ferry looking for it. 'I've got to get it back,' he called out as he put one leg over the rail of the upper deck to climb below and look for the missing hat. Just then the ferry rolled in the swell and Private Murphy went over the side, yelling 'hoi'. He continued to call out 'hoi' as passengers threw lifebelts into the darkness. Wallis Dean, a brass boy on the *Curl Curl*, dived in with two passengers, W. J. Donohue of Lidcombe, and D. R. Gale. Between them they brought Private Murphy back to the ferry. After he had been hauled on board with a rope he was taken down to the engine room and wrapped in four blankets while his uniform was dried—something that could always be done in those days of steam engines. Back in town, he was cared for at Phillip Street police station until the Provosts called and took him away.

The Curl Curl *crossing the harbour in a heavy swell.(John Darroch)*

A Navy man fell from the *Bellubera* on its way to Sydney on the night of 16 August 1948, and was lucky enough to be picked up 10 minutes later by the *Dee Why*, going in the opposite direction. James Fraser, 24, a stoker on HMAS *Shropshire*, fell in near Taylors Bay. One of the *Bellubera*'s deckhands told police that just before the ferry passed Georges Head he saw Fraser sitting asleep on a seat in the bow, but Fraser was not there when they arrived at Circular Quay. There would have been few people going back to town at that hour—nearly 11 pm— and a deckhand could have noticed the disappearance of a lone man. While Phillip Street police were being notified about the missing man he was yelling to attract help from the fast-approaching *Dee Why* and one of its passengers saw him. An ambulance met the ferry at Manly wharf, about 11.40 pm, and took Fraser to Manly Hospital, where he was treated for exposure and later allowed to return to his ship.

Two young Manly lifesavers dived fully clothed from the *Curl Curl* near Garden Island on the night of 22 September 1947 to save a man who told police later that he could not remember his name. The lifesavers were William Starr, 19, of Addison Road, Manly, and Kenneth

Bailey, 24, of Collingwood Street, Manly. Abraham Keefe, a fireman on the *Curl Curl*, also dived in and swam to the man's assistance. The master of the *Curl Curl*, Captain Harold Liley, dropped a flare to help the rescuers get the man into a boat lowered from the ferry. Three other Manly lifesavers, Ron Hanson, Morris Sproule and Harry Bucholtz applied artificial respiration until the rescued man regained consciousness. After the ferry berthed at Manly, police took him to Manly Hospital and later to the Reception House.

Another man who fell overboard from the *Balgowlah* owed his life to two young men who dived to his rescue off Georges Head. George Hunter, of Tebbutt Street, Leichhardt, fell overboard as the *Balgowlah* passed Georges Head. Bruce Morrison, 22, of Johnson Street, Harbord, and Jack Frederick Rogers, 23, a merchant seaman from South Africa, dived from the ferry, swam to where the man was floundering and supported him in the water for more than 20 minutes before they could be picked up. Rogers, on a month's leave from his ship, was staying at Coogee and decided to go for a short sea trip to Manly. He had no idea when he set out that it was going to give him a swim as well.

The rescued man collapsed when he was brought back on board the ferry. Private Frank Reedy, and another soldier who did not give his name, worked on the man with artificial respiration until the ferry tied up at Circular Quay, then handed him over to ambulance men, who said later that the man would have died but for the treatment he received from the two young men.

On Tuesday night, 1 July 1947, a middle-aged man struggled from the grasp of another passenger who tried to save him and jumped to his death in the harbour as the *Barrenjoey* was passing Middle Head. The *Barrenjoey* had left Manly for Circular Quay at 5.15 pm. Gordon Potter, of Ann Street, Enfield, sitting outside on the starboard side of the lower deck, saw a man climb on to the bulwark as they neared Middle Head. Potter told police:

> I sensed that he was going to jump over, so I ran to him and grabbed a sleeve of his coat. He struggled to break free of me and I shouted to a deckhand to come and help me, but before the deckhand could get to us the man wrenched himself free from my grasp and jumped overboard. The deckhand notified the captain, who reversed the ferry and steered a zig-zag course a couple of times, but all we could see was the man's blue coat floating on the surface of the water.

A three-year-old girl was saved from the propeller blades of the *North Head* at Circular Quay one afternoon by a young man who dived nine metres from the upper deck to drag her free. The girl's mother, 21, was charged later with having attempted to murder her child. It happened about 1 pm on 11 October 1975. The ferry was gliding in to the wharf when the child was seen to fall into the water. Almost immediately, a young man named Trevor Rockliff dived fully clothed from the top deck, caught the child and swam with her away from the swirl of the stern propeller, which was churning the water to slow the ferry into its berth. Normal practice is for the ferries to go ahead to Manly and astern back to the city. People on the wharf took the child and wrapped her in a blanket until police arrived and drove the little girl to Sydney Hospital for treatment. Fortunately, she was not seriously hurt and seemed to be little the worse for her experience. Later, she was taken to a children's home and her mother was taken into custody and charged. The following day the mother appeared in Central Police Court, charged with trying to drown her daughter. Police said that after dropping the child into the water, the woman calmly walked away to join her husband, who was under the influence of drugs. The same day in the same court, the husband was charged before the Chief Stipendiary Magistrate, Mr Murray Farquhar, and fined for possessing Indian hemp.

3. Odd Happenings

Allen Arthur Conwell belonged to the third generation of a family which gave a total of 146 years' service to the Manly ferries. He started with the Port Jackson & Manly Steamship Company on 10 October 1934, and finished with the Urban Transit Authority on 23 August 1984, just six weeks short of 50 years. He couldn't quite make the record 52 years his grandfather, John Conwell, spent working with the ferries, but he stayed for more than the 44 years his father, George Conwell, was an employee.

Allen Conwell shared none of the glamour associated with being a skipper. He worked for some time as a deckhand. The last 23 years of his working life he was a wharfinger, mainly at Circular Quay. But what an interesting side of life he saw in those years in which he watched the boom, the decline and finally the rebirth of the ferries. Up to the day he retired there had always been a Conwell employed by the Manly ferry service. He had worked under four general managers—Dendy, Cameron and Needham (Port Jackson) and Tom Gibson (Urban Transit Authority). Allen Conwell began on a wage of $2.75 for a 44-hour week and worked for seven months before he had a single day off. The only penalty rate in those days was time and a half for Sunday work. He told the many people who attended his retirement dinner:

> In the early days of my employment the ferry company was like a family affair, headed by Walter Dendy, who

rose from the ranks to become the managing director. We had seven steamers operating before World War II—*Burra Bra, Bellubera, Balgowlah, Barrenjoey, Baragoola, Dee Why, Curl Curl* and *South Steyne*. In 1934 the *Burra Bra* was the only boat operating with a completely open top deck, which was beaut in summer but a perisher in the middle of winter. On most public holidays in summer we ran a 10-minute service with six steamers. The *Dee Why* one day in the 1930s in perfect weather with all boilers flat out did the trip from Manly to Sydney in 19 minutes. The most people carried in one day I can recall were 70 000. Today [1984], a third of that number would be classed as a big day. In 1930 we carried 5 060 000 passengers and this increased gradually to 14 million in 1946, when the decline began. By 1951 the total had dropped to 8 million and by 1976 it was down to 2 320 000. Since then it has gradually improved and in 1982 we carried 7 700 000 passengers.

Of some interest is the fact that my father and I both started work with the Manly ferries on eight-hour days and we both had the sad experience of a workmate dying in our arms. My father was the helmsman who took the *Bellubera* into Manly after Captain Wally Dohrn collapsed and died while they were crossing The Heads. My workmate, Tom Hancock, fell and hit his head on an iron railing on No. 3 wharf at the Quay and died there.

The Conwell family's association with Sydney Harbour began in the early days of the colony. Allen's great grandparents were living on Fort Denison, still known as 'Pinchgut' because of the starvation rations for convicts, when his grandfather was born on 29 May 1860. He never bothered to find out whether his great grandparents were convicts, but he was always happy to know that the Conwells had been associated with the harbour all their lives. Allen worked in nearly every position in the ferry service, from change boy to acting traffic manager—in the change box giving turnstile tokens and change, at the Kurraba Point works, on the ferries as a deckhand, on the wharves and in the office.

After the opening of the Spit Bridge the cargo service by water began to lose business and in 1928 the *Narrabeen*, which the Port Jackson company had built as a freighter, was taken out of service. For a while, Allen Conwell recalls, the ferries would take anything Manly residents wanted. Sometimes the passengers were riding with horses, mail bags, newspapers—even coffins. Crew conditions in those days were, according to Allen, non-existent. Deckhands coaled the boats, pulled bags of ashes up from stokeholds and carried them ashore at Manly. After coaling a boat they had a bucket of hot water for washing, followed by a cold shower, winter and summer. At the Kurraba maintenance depot the toilets were at ground level with a bar on each wall to hang on to. This was, Allen Conwell says, to stop workmen going into the toilets and sitting down to have a smoke.

Thinking of the modern accommodation and facilities on the Freshwater class ships, where crew have messrooms, hot and cold showers, and cooking facilities, Allen Conwell told of his crewing days:

On the last trip at night the deckhands would pull two seats together, dump an old mattress on them and bed down for the rest of the night. They had a foc'sle where they could eat and sleep, but as it was in the bowels of the ship few took advantage of it. On one boat a deckhand did sleep in the foc'sle, but nobody else would go in there because this fellow had a small revolver and during the night he would lie on his bed and take pot shots at the rats when they appeared.

Far more people went into the water from the wharves than ever fell from ferries. During the peak years of the Manly ferries an average of two passengers a week fell or jumped into the water at Manly or Circular Quay wharves. Before the Freshwater class vessels with their drawbridge type gangways and high bulwarks made jumping ashore extremely difficult, large numbers of commuters used to climb up on the bulwarks of ferries as they approached the wharf and jump ashore before the gangways were put aboard. They ran a grave risk of falling between the ferry and the wharf and two men lost their lives when they were crushed. A 15-year-old youth, William Regan, of Harbord Street, Harbord, slipped as he jumped from the *Burra Bra* at Circular Quay on 1 October 1937 and was caught between the ferry's sponson and the wharf. He was released and lifted on to the wharf to be taken by ambulance to Sydney Hospital with back injuries and a probable fracture of the pelvis. The youth remained in a critical condition until late the following night, when he died in the hospital.

As the *Curl Curl* moved into Manly wharf on the night of 4 April 1944, horrified passengers waiting on the wharf to board the ferry for its return to the city saw a man jump to his death. Slipping as he leapt from the bulwark, he fell between the side of the ferry and the wharf and his head was crushed, killing him instantly. He was identified in the early hours of the morning as Jeffrey Matthew Kernot, 48, of Old Pittwater Road, Brookvale.

Another man, Desmond Ballard, 21, of Wentworth Street, Manly, had a very lucky escape in a similar situation a couple of years later. He slipped as he jumped while the ferry was coming alongside the wharf, but fell into the water only a second or two before the ferry's

Ferry jumpers leaping ashore from the Baragoola.

sponson hit the wharf piles and he escaped being crushed to death. He was dragged to safety by fellow passengers and ferry men.

Allen Conwell remembers a blind man who used to jump off the ferries with those who could see what they were doing. Perhaps he put to good use a very acute sense of hearing which most blind people acquire and which earned him a living as a piano tuner. Said Allen Conwell:

He would go all over Sydney without a white stick. He was marvellous to watch. He would just walk with the crowd and he would jump off the ferry with them. He would get up on the rail and when the others jumped off he would jump off. This man was a regular traveller. He could tell you which boat he was on after taking a few steps on board. Apparently he knew by the tilt of the deck. One day he did misjudge his leap to the wharf and went into the water, where he floundered about before they got a rope to him and pulled him up to the wharf. The blind man could swim, but he said the most frightening thing he discovered when he realised his predicament was that he did not know which way he had to swim. In the water he had no sense of direction. Some other blind traveller lost a glass eye which was one of the unusual items to find its way into our lost property office. Whoever lost the glass eye, we never knew. It was never claimed.

Well-dressed businessmen often gave ferry and wharf crews a surprise when they were fished out after an unsuccessful morning leap to the wharf at Circular Quay.

In winter, according to Allen Conwell, when the wet and shivering passenger was taken down to the ferry's engine room to be dried out, it was often found that he was wearing pyjamas underneath his business suit. Apparently, having slept in, he dressed in a great hurry to catch the ferry to work.

An elderly man walked on to the wharf at Circular Quay one night after the last ferry to Manly had departed. He wandered around the wharf all night, waiting for the first boat in the morning. When the wharf opened for business he paid his fare, came back through the turnstile and sat himself down on the edge of the wharf for a moment before sliding off into the water. Somebody called out 'man overboard' and again one of the wharf hands had to dive to the rescue. They took the fellow down to the engine room of a ferry—steam engines then—and dried his clothes and him out in about 10 minutes.

Allen Conwell remembers a very large woman who jumped off the wharf at the Quay one day to commit suicide:

But instead of sinking she just floated and we pulled her out again. She was screaming out to be saved. Most of them want to die when they jump in, but they want to live the moment they hit the water. Just after I joined the company—it was on a hot summer day—a chap walking along the promenade wearing a suit, hat and tie, took off the hat, then his tie, coat and shoes, climbed over the railings and jumped into the water. After swimming around for a while in front of a curious crowd which had gathered, he got ashore again, put on his tie, coat and hat, and with water still streaming from him, put on his shoes and disappeared into the crowd. To this day I still wonder whether he did it for a bet or whether he was a nut.

Then there was a dog who used to ride the ferries. Wharf hands and ferry crews knew him as Captain Seaweed. They say he seemed to know just where a ferry was going because he never stayed aboard one which was going to Kurraba Point for refuelling and would be laid up there for two hours or more. If the ferry was not going to Manly he would trot off again and wait for the next trip. Apparently Captain Seaweed had more sense than people who would hide in a ferry at Circular Quay to get a free ride back to Manly. Normally, they would have to go out through the turnstiles and pay another fare to come back. But in the steamship days those hiding aboard to return to Manly could find themselves marooned at the Kurraba Point depot for at least two hours while the vessel was coaled and cleaned.

I had lunch at North Sydney one day late in 1984 with Allen Conwell and two of his former colleagues on the wharf who had retired also—George McNamara and Frank Conroy. Frank had retired medically unfit in 1973 after 33 years on the gates at No. 3 wharf, Circular Quay. He had seen the fares rise from sixpence for adults and a penny for children in 1940 to $1.10 in 1984. The fare had been twopence for children in 1925, but when the automatic turnstiles were introduced they would not work on twopence, so the fare was reduced to a penny—the sort of thing that never happens nowadays. Frank Conroy recalled the tricks and ploys of fare evaders. They would jump over the stiles or crawl under them and would try putting washers and all kinds of things into the slots instead of the proper tokens.

George McNamara retired in 1974 after 49 years' service, mainly on the wharf at Circular Quay and the Kurraba Point depot. He started as a change boy in 1925 and worked on the manual turnstiles until 1932, after the Harbour Bridge was opened. Then the company introduced electric turnstiles and kept only a few of the turnstile staff. George went to Kurraba Point doing casual work until 1940, when he returned to Circular Quay as a gate hand, inspecting the tickets of those who went through the gates instead of the turnstiles. He came back to the wharf in 1946 after service in the Army during the war and spent 18 years at the Quay and Manly until he retired in 1974.

The accident report sheets of the Port Jackson company contain many stories which although cryptic in their content, reveal quite a few dramas that never made the headlines in the news of the day. To quote a few:

19 August 1957: K. Campbell, wharfinger at Manly, reported that a woman had jumped off the south-western corner of the wharf at 8 pm directly in the path of an incoming ferry. A lifebuoy was thrown to her and the wharfinger signalled to the master by blinking the berthing lights. The master put the ship astern and made the east side of the wharf, then lowered the work boat and took the woman aboard. Later she was handed over to Manly police.

6 May 1950: Two men involved in fight on the *Dee Why* at approximately 7.35 pm when berthing at Manly. One was battered and the other fell into the water at the wharf. Both were removed by police and ambulance. Both intoxicated.

13 May 1951: Captain Smith reported that a man was seen by a passenger getting over the rail and standing on the ship's sponson. Deckhand F. Bond pulled him back on deck and on arrival at Manly he was handed over to the police. He appeared to be under the influence.

29 May 1951: Captain Mann reported that after leaving Manly on the 12.15 pm trip a deckhand reported that a passenger had advised him he had left his 11-month-old baby on the wharf. He returned immediately to Manly wharf, where the baby was found. The trip was delayed approximately five minutes.

4 September 1950: Mr R. Basham, wharfinger at Manly, reported that a lady had been bitten by a dog on the 5.25 pm trip from Sydney.

11 September 1950: Captain N. Smith reported that on the 11 am trip to Manly a passenger told him a man had jumped overboard near Garden Island. He reversed and steamed back, but could find no trace of the man. A coat and hat with a sum of money was found on the ferry. This was handed over to police at Manly.

13 January 1951: H. Dawkins reported that as the *Bellubera* was leaving Sydney on the 11 pm trip, a sailor who had tried to jump on to the vessel fell into the water. He complained of injury and the police and ambulance were called. Later, this man, together with a soldier, was arrested for causing a disturbance. The *Bellubera* was 20 minutes late through this incident.

19 January 1951: Mr J. A. Lehaffey, of Adelaide, while watching the fireworks display from the deck of a ferry, was struck on the right ear and shoulder by a signal rocket weighing one pound. Suffered from shock and burns. Ed Lumley & Sons advised us to inform Mr Lehaffey that we decline liability.

16 June 1951: Captain Dohrn reported that on the 6.30 pm trip to Manly a fight broke out between several men. A deckhand and Captain Dohrn spoke to those concerned. Later a further fight developed and some windows were broken. Police were notified at Manly and they arrested four men, who were charged later with damage to the vessel. One was fined £12 8s 0d, one £10 8s 0d, and the others pleaded not guilty. The company was compensated for broken windows.

23 May 1957: Captain Smith reported that on the first trip, 5.55 am from Manly, a man did not get off at Sydney. Believing the man to be asleep, the deckhands went to wake him and discovered that the man was dead. The master informed the police and the body was taken off on arrival at Manly.

These are only a mere fraction of the incidents reported by the masters of ferries and wharf staff, most of which never found their way into the newspapers. Captain Bruce had another scare, this time with the *Baragoola*, while lying overnight at Manly on 7 October 1962. Between 1 am and 1.25 am it was discovered that the ship, which had been lying on the east side of the wharf, was adrift. A party of young hooligans had lifted all the mooring ropes from the bollards on the wharf, leaving the ferry adrift. Manly police arrested three youths later. They were found guilty and fined.

Boats sometimes run out of petrol, but it is an unusual event for one the size of Manly ferries. It happened to the *Baragoola* on 8 March 1956, when Captain Harold Gibson was in command. He reported that on arrival at Manly at 11.25 pm his ship was out of fuel. Two tugs were ordered to tow the *Baragoola* back to Kurraba for fuel and she resumed service at 5.55 am.

Irresponsible behaviour has on occasions endangered ferries. Captain Harold Liley was involved in two incidents, both in the *Curl Curl*. A stiff southerly was blowing down the harbour on Sunday, 6 October 1942, when a young sailor decided to climb the flagpole at the bow of the vessel. In Central Court the following day he was fined £5 with £2 12s 6d costs 'for having wilfully impeded the master of the *Curl Curl*, Harold Liley, of Aero Street, Brighton-le-Sands, in the discharge of his duty'. Captain Liley said he saw the RAN sailor climb over the rails in the front of the ferry, open a few bottles of beer, then climb the flagstaff. Captain Liley told the court:

I called to him to come down, but he took no notice, so I sent a man to get him down. The fellow came up to the bridge and said he would not get off until I told him whether the ship could do 20 knots. He took a swing at me and pushed me by the shoulder. The man at the wheel had to come to help me, leaving nobody at the wheel when we were approaching a part of the harbour where we were under naval instructions. I had received a signal to look out for a capsized launch with a man hanging to it, so I was a bit upset with having to cope with the sailor too.

Mr Doolan SM bound the sailor over to be of good behaviour for 12 months.

A few years later, on Saturday night, 3 June 1944, a young airman went on to the bridge of the *Curl Curl* when it was berthing at Circular Quay at 10.15 pm and confronted Harold Liley who told Central Court on the Monday:

I told him, 'Go below like a good fellow. Don't cause trouble'. But he refused and as I was manoeuvring the ferry to the wharf he hit me in the left eye, saying 'Take that'.

The airman was find £7 for having gone on to the bridge and assaulted Captain Liley.

'You might have caused a serious loss of life,' Mr Thornton SM told a seaman in Central Court on 24 July 1948. The behaviour of the 21-year-old seaman and two mates had stopped a Manly ferry on the harbour the previous night. The seaman was fined £20 for impeding the navigation of the ferry *Dee Why* by sending a signal from the bridge to the engine room. His two companions, aged 23 and 18, were fined £5 for offensive behaviour. Detective Donoghue said the three men boarded the *Dee Why* at Manly at 9.45 pm, threw a rope overboard and left it trailing from the stern, abused passengers and the crew and used indecent language. Near Bradleys Head, the seaman climbed to the bridge and rang the ship's telegraph to the engine room to signal astern, stopping the vessel. The seaman was still abusing crew members when he was arrested at Circular Quay. One of the others dived into the harbour and swam to a disused wharf. All three told the court they were under the influence of liquor. 'This conduct has to stop,' the magistrate told them. 'You might have caused serious loss of life, a collision or anything by your act.' Police said about 300 passengers were aboard the ferry.

Life was like that on the harbour in those war years. People then were inclined to take a more lenient view of a few escapades by soldiers or sailors on leave. But their leniency gave out when such antics threatened to endanger ships and passengers.

PART VIII
THE WHEEL TURNS

1. New Hope for the *Steyne*

One day in 1979 Newcastle businessman Michael Wansey flew down to Sydney in a helicopter belonging to his family company, Tanate Pty Ltd, and landed on the heliport at Pyrmont, on the western side of Darling Harbour. Commitments for Tanate, a holding company for the family business interests, often took him to Sydney and he was usually in a hurry. But this day, whether he was in a hurry or not, he had to wait at the heliport for others to arrive and as he looked across Darling Harbour to the wharves on the city side near Pyrmont Bridge he saw something familiar—the SS *South Steyne*. The green hull and two white funnels with black tops were just as Wansey remembered when he lived at Fairy Bower in Manly in 1962 when he was working as a circulation representative for the *Sydney Morning Herald* and travelled to and from the city in the *South Steyne*, the *Dee Why*, *Curl Curl* and other Manly ferries. He had been born into the newspaper world, with parents who controlled the *Newcastle Morning Herald,* sold subsequently to John Fairfax & Sons Ltd, proprietors of the *Sydney Morning Herald*. Michael Wansey knew the old ferry well. He went to town on the 8 am and came home on the 5.15 pm. He had always loved the Manly ferries, but never dreamed

that one day he might have a controlling share in one of them, as was about to happen.

With time to fill in, Michael Wansey walked across the bridge to wharf 35b and strolled aboard the *South Steyne*, where he found 'a bunch of guys with blueprints', who said they had been given working access to prepare plans for the redevelopment of Darling Harbour. When he inquired about the ship, they gave him the telephone number of the owner, Bob Kentwell, who had been trying to continue restoration work, helped by members of a club he had formed, though lacking the essential requirement of money. Kentwell and his club had managed to get from the Maritime Services Board a suitable berth in Darling Harbour, but they were finding the same problems, principally financial, as those which had plagued their predecessors in earlier attempts to restore the vessel.

So it was that Michael Wansey brought to the *South Steyne* money as well as enthusiam and became with Kentwell part-owner of the ship that refused to die. It attracted him as it had done hundreds of others who wanted to see it restored and returned to Sydney Harbour. Wansey recalls:

The South Steyne *being towed into dock at Ballina. (*Northern Star)

One day we made the decision to bring the *South Steyne* to Newcastle. We wanted to get a feasibility study done and have her rebuilt in Manila. She was towed to Newcastle and spent the best part of a year there while a considerable amount of work was carried out, including replacement of the main generator. Then we put her into the State Dockyard because the sacrificial anodes had gone and spent another $40 000 on slipping and repair work. At that time the State Dockyard gave us a quote of $700 000 to put her back into shape—the hull, engine and boilers. But Ballina Slipways came in about $100 000 better, so it was decided to take the job there.

The sacrificial anodes were the zinc blocks affixed to the hull below the waterline to counter the electrolysis which is such a problem in salt water. The electrolysis attacks the anodes and gradually eats them away. Without them, expensive damage would be done to hull plates, rudders and propellers. It is a wonder this didn't happen to the *South Steyne*, which had been about eight years in the water before she was docked at Newcastle, covered below the waterline with a heavy growth of weeds, barnacles, shells and slime.

Ballina Slipways won the contract for further work on the *South Steyne* and, six months after being docked at Newcastle, she left under tow for Ballina. Michael Wansey takes up the story again:

One day in November 1983, the *Levanter*, a tug owned by Pacific Tugs, of Brisbane, arrived in Newcastle to take the *Steyne* to Ballina. On the Sunday night after it had departed in fine weather, I received a phone call from Pacific and they said 'We are going to lose her. Both pumps have gone, including the electric submersible, and we are taking water at the rate of a foot every half an hour.' She was then 12 1/2 miles south of Coffs Harbour. I instructed them to save the ship in any way possible. To make things worse, one of the bollards being used for the tow had apparently come loose. I contacted the water police and asked whether they could get somebody aboard. They couldn't do very much when they got there because the diesel pump was sucking air, but they managed to get the ship into Coffs Harbour and out of trouble. Later we found that a piece of metal had jammed the impeller of the electric submersible pump and had popped the circuit breaker. We found, too, subsequently, that the cold water outlet had been left open and every time the ship rolled it let water into the bilge, something which would not have been noticeable inside a harbour. There was a hole about the size of a broom handle in the elbow. A member of the crew fixed it. Ballina Slipways sent a rescue team down to effect repairs, but we had trouble getting the ship out of Coffs Harbour. The harbourmaster would not allow us to pump the bilges. We had to hire a petrol tanker to come alongside and pump out into the tanker.

The *Northern Star*, Lismore, reported the *South Steyne*'s arrival in Ballina:

Her distinctive lines drew sighs of nostalgia from the crowds as she crossed the bar at the entrance to the Richmond River. Hundreds of people were along vantage points of the northern breakwater wall.

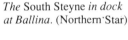

The South Steyne *in dock at Ballina.* (Northern Star)

That was on 8 November 1983. Between then and the end of 1985 an immense amount of work was done, including the removal of the whole teak decking from the main deck, cutting out the steel deck below it and replacing it with a new steel deck, to be covered with new teak timber. But before the hull plates could be renewed the ship had to be put into dock and in this another major job was involved. Thousands of tonnes of rock were blasted out of a dry dock to lengthen it to accommodate the *South Steyne*, the biggest ship ever to fit into the dock, up the Richmond River, near Broadwater.

Ballina Slipways could not take a ship as big as the *South Steyne*. The New South Wales Department of Public Works had a dry dock, cut into the bank of the Richmond River, known as Rileys Hill Dock. It had been built in 1899 and lengthened in the 1930s. In the past the dock had been used for maintenance work on river dredges and vehicular ferries and in the days of the Port Jackson & Manly Steamship Company there appears to have been a plan to take all the Manly ferries up the coast and dock them at Ballina. On 16 March 1984, the *South Steyne* was eased into the enlarged Rileys Hill dry dock, and when she was in position the dock gates closed behind her with only a metre to spare. By May 1984 quite a lot had been done. Hull plates had been renewed, which was the main purpose of dry docking, and Bob Kentwell's optimism had risen again, inducing him to tell the *Manly Daily* that the *Steyne* would steam again on 25 August, exactly 10 years after the fire which forced it out of service. He said the ship would be ready for sea trials by the end of the year. But the *South Steyne* was still in Ballina at the end of November and Bob Kentwell said he did not know how long it would take to finish the work. Already the project had cost more than $1 million. 'We really hope to sail her through Sydney Heads by Christmas 1985,' Kentwell told the *Sydney Morning Herald*.

2. Pattern for the Future

The second big 235-passenger hydrofoil, *Sydney*, was to have been commissioned on Sunday, 21 July 1985, by the New South Wales Premier, Mr Wran, in a ceremony worthy of the occasion. But there was no ceremony and the new hydrofoil went into service without being baptised, as it were. Believe it or not, the unions had decreed that there would be no commissioning ceremony because of a dispute over rostering and proposals by the Urban Transit Authority to reduce hydrofoil services. The dispute was nothing unusual. In recent years, Manly ferry and hydrofoil passengers had become quite used to having the service disrupted for most of the day while members of the various trade unions involved—the Merchant

Tina McAllister, Manly's first female deckhand, learning the ropes on her first day aboard the hydrofoil Sydney. (Manly Daily)

Service Guild, the Australian Institute of Marine and Power Engineers and Firemen and Deckhands Association—held stop-work meetings and stopped ferries and hydrofoils between 10 am and 2.30 pm. Gone was the idea of attending union meetings outside normal working hours or keeping services going while meetings were held.

The *Sydney*'s sister ship, the *Manly*, had spent most of its time out of service before the *Sydney* arrived—quite a lot of it because of industrial disruption at the Balmain depot by the Ships Painters and Dockers Union. During that time, the hydrofoil crews battled on to keep running the three older PT hydrofoils—*Curl Curl*, *Long Reef* and *Palm Beach*. Even if the *Manly* had been available, nobody would have dared take it out of the depot because although deckhands cast ropes on and off in normal service at Manly and Circular Quay wharves, only painters and dockers can do so at Balmain and if they are on strike nobody else must touch the ropes. When the hydrofoils in service became sluggish because of marine growth on their hulls or foils a diver could go underneath and scrub off some growth. But only if a member of the Painters and Dockers Union was present and if they were on strike, no diver must touch the work.

Cancelling the commissioning of the *Sydney* was the last straw, even for the Labor Government of New South Wales, which was not renowned for union bashing. So, the Minister for Transport, Mr Barrie Unsworth, indicated that he and the Government were fed up and he warned the ferry unions that the Government would consider cutting back under-patronised services if the industrial disruption continued. 'It has reached the stage where some Urban Transit Authority vessels have been out of service for longer periods than they have been in operation over the last year,' he told the media. Mr Unsworth said he would be writing to each ferry and hydrofoil employee to remind them that the harbour public transport services were more heavily subsidised by the Government than any other form of transport. Many harbour services were seriously under-patronised and ran merely for the benefit of employees, he said.

The Shadow Minister for Transport, Dr Terry Metherell, told the *Manly Daily* that commuters had had 'a gut full' of industrial disruption to the ferry and hydrofoil services, although he was quite critical of proposals to reduce the hydrofoil service. He said the Premier should sack these fellows if they didn't want to work. A few days before the *Sydney* was to have been commissioned by the Premier, the unions stopped the ferries and hydrofoils between 9.15 am and the mid-afternoon to hold a stop-work meeting and there was no commissioning ceremony. The following week, Mr Unsworth did send to all employees a letter in which he emphasised the heavy Governnment subsidisation of ferry services—in 1984-85 it was $12.1 million against a total operational expenditure of $22.8 million, not counting interest paid on borrowings. The letter said:

Despite all the efforts by the Government in providing these benefits, it has received negligible support from employees or their unions. The attitudes displayed in continually disrupting services and maintenance and repair programs, frequently over quite trivial matters, is to be deplored. It is up to all employees to recognise that they are in a service industry providing vital services to the community and this should be interrupted by industrial action only in the most extraordinary circumstances and then only when all other reasonable alternatives have been exhausted.

I am appalled at the recent industrial action by members of the Merchant Service Guild and the Australian Institute of Marine and Power Engineers which forced the abandonment of the commissioning ceremony of the hydrofoil *Sydney*. The petty-minded action in aborting the commissioning of the *Sydney* and the numerous threats and actions on previous occasions have caused loss of credibility for the unions involved. Such actions are contrary to proper trade union principles. I want to make it quite clear that neither I nor the Government will continue to provide capital funds and heavy operating subsidies to maintain the present level of ferry services when employees and their unions constantly abuse their rights and powers, resulting in disruption to services and inconvenience to the travelling public. What the Government expects is a far more rational approach to industrial relations practices and unless this is forthcoming I will be forced to review the current level of support provided by the Government.

Most people who use public transport have become

used to strikes and stoppages and accept the situation with surprising resignation, although many can never understand why employees will take action which causes huge losses to the means of their own livelihood.

The Manly ferries have come back from the real doldrums of 1975 when only two ferries were left out of a former fleet of seven vessels and passenger patronage was at rock bottom. At their peak, when seven ships were operating, they were carrying 14 million passengers a year. In 1976, the two ferries available carried 2 320 000 people, but by 1985 Manly ferry patronage was back to nearly 8 million and the total number of passengers for Manly ferries, hydrofoils and inner harbour ferries was 17 037 000. It is interesting to see the steady climb up again. In 1977-78 ferry passengers increased to 3 037 000 and hydrofoils carried 1 985 000, making a total of 5 022 000. In 1978-79 ferry loadings rose to 4 222 000 and hydrofoils 2 169 000, total 6 391 000. By 1983-84 these figures had changed to: ferries 8 017 000, hydrofoils 1 583 000, total 9 600 000. The big gain was for the ferries, and hydrofoils were slipping. The policy of building the new ferries had paid off. In the six weeks of the Christmas and January 1985-86 school holidays the Manly ferries carried 532 118 passengers and the hydrofoils took another 168 118, making a total of 700 810. The Urban Transit Authority's ferry division expected to end the year at June 1986 with a total ferry traffic for the harbour of around 18 million passengers.

A key figure behind this was the general manager of the Urban Transit Authority ferries division, Captain Tom Gibson, known generally as Mr Gibson, although he is a sea-going certificated master. Tom Gibson had never been in the public picture like the legendary W.L. Dendy. A quiet man, he worked behind the scenes, running what had become a very big business with the ferries coming back into their own again. He said:

I came into this at the bottom of the barrel. Now we are looking at patronage of around 18 million a year— more than the ferries ever carried. These increases have become apparent only in the last few years up to 1985 when these new vessels began to come into service. The Manly service showed that people were looking for a reasonable level of comfort and our hydrofoils topped the lot in relative figures for the number of vessels operated. But since the Freshwater class ferries came into service we have seen a very marked movement of passengers away from the hydrofoils because the ferries offer comfortable travel at a cheaper rate.

The *North Head* did her last run across the harbour on 12 December 1985, the date on which her survey certificate expired. She was tied up at Cockatoo Island while the

Maritime Services Board and marine surveyors prepared a report on the condition of the vessel and what it would cost to do her up for another year or two while the fourth new ferry was being built. The Board of the Urban Transit Authority decided at a meeting on 4 March 1986, that the work required would be too costly for the life expectancy it would achieve and the ferry would be advertised for sale by public tender. So ended after 73 years the long life of this grand old lady, leaving a record not likely to be overtaken. Whether they liked it or not, commuters and tourists would have to put up with the smaller and slower Ladies *Wakehurst* or *Northcott* while the fourth new ferry was being built because the Urban Transit Authority had also decided that it would not lease the *South Steyne* as a spare boat—something Michael Wansey had hoped would solve his problem of finding the money to complete the restoration of the *South Steyne*. She was lying at Ballina, nothing done for months while Wansey tried to find another $1 million to follow the $2 million he had spent on her already. Her future was very uncertain.

The scene is changing. With the *North Head* has gone the last of the traditional Manly ferries and some other traditions are going too. In 1985 the first woman crew member invaded that male holy of holies when Tina McAllister became a deckhand and joined the men throwing ropes to the wharfhands and learning how to crisscross them over the bollards. She volunteered to exchange the ticket office on No. 3 wharf at Circular Quay for the decks of the ferries and hydrofoils. Some of the old skippers of the Port Jackson & Manly Steamship Company might have stirred in their graves, but the new breed welcomed Tina. With the men she pulled her weight, even wore the official sweater of the Firemen and Deckhands Union. She lived at Manly, too. To her, Manly is, as the old Port Jackson company slogan proclaimed for so many years: 'Seven miles from Sydney and a thousand miles from care'.

3. A New Era

Towards the end of 1986 the scene on the harbour was changing rapidly. All the old Manly ferries were gone from active service, although two were still in the harbour—the *Baragoola* in Rozelle Bay and the *North Head* at Cockatoo Island. The *South Steyne* remained tied up at Ballina awaiting the long-promised finance for her resurrection. Their places had been taken by the *Freshwater*, *Queenscliff* and *Narrabeen*, which, between them, were carrying huge passenger loadings and restoring the Manly ferry service to something like its old supremacy. Ferry travel was on the way back. Many commuters were sick of the bumper to bumper peak-hour road traffic between Manly and the city and the new and comfortable ferries attracted swarms of weekend tourists and day trippers. By the end of June the harbour's total ferry services had carried more than the 18 million forecast by Tom Gibson before he retired during the year. He was replaced temporarily by Len Michaels and then Owen Eckford, a young 35-year-old naval architect recruited from the Maritime Services Board, where he had been manager of the commercial vessels branch and had a good deal to do with the survey of ferries.

Owen Eckford came to his new job as general manager of the ferry services with more than enough enthusiasm to pick up the born again water transport system and ensure that it lived through to a healthy adult life. Up to 20 September 1986, ferry traffic was up 13.5 per cent compared with 6.5 per cent in the same period of the previous year, predicting overall passenger loading of more than 19 million for the full year. Manly ferries alone would carry 9.5 million of that total, 1.5 million up on 1984-85. Len Michaels had an engineering background, which he took to the Balmain workshops and applied to rejuvenating the refitting and servicing of the fleet. The new management was determined that its ships were going to be kept in good condition.

This would be helped considerably by one of Owen Eckford's first big projects. He had arrived in time to take part in the planning of a fourth new Manly ferry, tenders for the building of which were called in November 1986. It would be a sister ship to the *Freshwater*, *Queenscliff* and *Narrabeen*, but with some modifications, making it suitable for ocean cruises similar to those operated in previous years by the *South Steyne*. Parts of the promenade or upper deck would have open space instead of the deck being totally enclosed, there would be a liquor bar and a galley below for preparing and serving food. The new ferry, to cost $12 million, would carry 1100 passengers, and, barring emergencies, would provide a year-round service by the big Freshwater class vessels with three in use at all times. The *Lady Wakehurst* had been filling in bravely since the retirement of the *North Head*, but with the traffic growing the way it was, bigger and faster ships were needed.

In reply to criticism of the delay in building a fourth ferry and ordering a new hydrofoil, published in the *Manly Daily* in October 1985, the then Minister for Transport, Mr Barrie Unsworth, revealed that the State Government had spent more than $40 million in the last three years on vessels for the Manly service. He had tried in vain to get funds for the new vessels allocated in the Government's capital works program for the 1985-86 financial year and promised he would be 'pushing' to get the money next year. 'Meantime,' Mr Unsworth said, 'passengers will continue to benefit from what I believe is one of the best ferry operations in the world.'

Rejection of the new ferry did two things. It spun out a bit longer the life of the ageing *North Head* and renewed efforts to have the *South Steyne* restored to active use. She was offered to the Urban Transit Authority for $3.5 million, or even on a lease basis, meaning that she could have been back in service in a matter of months for less than half of the cost of a new ferry. But the offer was turned down.

The *North Head* ran to Manly for the last time on 12 December 1985, and was taken out of service for a refit and renewal of its survey certificate, but the Maritime Services Board would not renew the certificate, leaving the Urban Transit Authority to ponder whether the cost of restoring seaworthiness would be too high. The authority would have liked to have seen the grand old ship receive at least a temporary certificate to allow it to be decommissioned with a ceremony befitting its years of service. By February the fate of the *North Head* remained undecided, awaiting a report on restoration costs. The report eventually recommended against restoration and the old lady was put up for sale. Leighton Developments, a property group, offered $100 000 for the *North Head*, proposing to put her on dry land as part of a big hotel, shopping and residential development in the heart of Manly, if Manly Council approved the development plans. As often happens nowadays, however, a front was set up in Manly to oppose the Leighton development, which was finally rejected by Manly Council, and the sale of the ferry fell through. The Urban Transit Authority then took an offer of $20 000 from another tenderer, a Tasmanian company, North Head Pty Ltd, which planned to take the ferry to Hobart and set her up in the Derwent River as a floating restaurant. Again fate intervened in the form of the Minister for Transport, Mr Ron Mulock, who vetoed the sale on the grounds that $20 000 was too little after $100 000 had been bid. It was really a case of $100 000 being too much, considering the condition of the vessel, but Mr Mulock obviously knew little of practicalities and was considering the political aspects. He did not want to be accused of being party to selling off a public asset for $20 000 after somebody had offered $100 000. So, in September, the *North Head* was put up again for sale by tender and this time the Tasmanian bid of $20 000 was the highest and again the departmental officers recommended to Mr Mulock that it be accepted.

Mr Mulock was undoubedly acting with the best of intentions, but his intervention caused months of delay and goodness knows how much expense to the Hobart buyers. In addition, the transaction became the subject of political concern in Tasmania.

The story is quite interesting. Newspaper advertisements on 15 March 1986, offering the *North Head* for sale by tenders closing on 3 April, attracted the attention of a Hobart group, North Head Pty Ltd, which had been interested in acquiring the vessel for a floating restaurant in the Derwent in Hobart since her retirement from service in December. These people had been looking for a suitable vessel since a similar venture went up in smoke four years previously. The MV *Kosciusko*, one of the old wooden Sydney ferries sent to Hobart as part of a ferry fleet for use while the Derwent bridge was being rebuilt, had been raised from the bed of New Town Bay, where she had been abandoned after the bridge opening, and was being cleaned in preparation for refitting as a restaurant. In August 1982 a fire broke out during repairs to the malthoid on the roof and razed the ferry to the deck, wiping out the floating restaurant until another suitable vessel could be found.

An estimate of delivery costs indicated that it would cost more than twice as much to get the *North Head* to Hobart as it would to buy her. Total estimated cost of $47 769.40, including $13 200 for fuel, $2100 for a master, engineer and assistant engineer and $2900 for insurance. There was to be a crew of up to 12 under the command of Roger Hickman, Chief Officer of the Australian National Line ship *River Torrens*, who held a master's foreign-going certificate.

Farewell gathering aboard the North Head *at Balmain the night before she left Sydney to become a Hobart restaurant. From left: Manly ferry skipper Ron Hart; managing director of the North Head Pty Ltd, the new Hobart owners, Mr Jim Hickman; general manager of the Urban Transit Authority of NSW, Mr Kel Edgar; UTA secretary, Mr Laurie Parker; and UTA ferries engineering manager, Mr Len Michaels.*

After Mr Mulock's intervention stopped the sale, Mr Hickman had hand delivered to the Minister's office on 6 August a letter asking to be able to discuss the sale of the *North Head* with the Minister or his representative before any decision to call new tenders. He pointed out that his group had made a valid tender and had agreed to the rigorous requirements of the Urban Transit Authority and the Maritime Services Board that the vessel had to leave the Port of Sydney within two weeks of the tender being accepted.

With the fate of the *North Head* in limbo, a bit of political persuasion was applied to Mr Mulock by Labor colleague Neil Batt, who was Leader of the Opposition in the Tasmanian Parliament, suggesting surprise the fresh tenders were going to be called and pointing out that the Labor Party in Tasmania could do with some inspiration and support from its big brothers in the major States.

So ends the story of the *North Head*, sold out of the harbour she graced for so many years to end her life as a floating restaurant in Hobart.

Her long-time companion, the *Baragoola*, never really made it as a floating university. After lingering in Rozelle Bay for long enough to give the Maritime Services Board constant jitters, fearing that she would sink at any time, the academics awoke from their dream of turning her into a university and sold the vessel to Mr David Ashton, who had waterfront interests around Balmain.

In more than two years lying around the upper harbour backwaters, the *Baragoola* had become a pathetic sight. Her engines idle and impotent, she had been towed down the harbour a couple of times, once for some television filming to be done aboard and on another occasion to take a party to watch fireworks from Fort Denison. Most people in the thousands of cars and buses passing the *Baragoola* along Rozelle Bay were not very interested, but those who were saw that for some strange reason the academics had painted the funnel yellow. They were probably more concerned over what could be happening below the waterline. The hull was not in good condition at all and she would leak badly if any of the doubling plates reinforcing weak parts of the hull were to fall off. One did come off and caused some trouble while the *Baragoola* was still in service on borrowed time on an extended certificate helping to keep up the Manly service until the new *Freshwater* was ready to replace her.

But some good fortune was shining at last in the direction of the *South Steyne*, which had been lying at Ballina Slipways for more than a year while Michael Wansey tried to find someone who would buy her or provide the money to finish the restoration work.

The Sydney *Sun* on 4 November 1986, published an article headed '$4 m ferry return idea sinks. Harbour flagship may now go to Melbourne.' The *Sun* said:

Sydney has lost an opportunity to have the SS *South Steyne*—once the flagship of its ferry fleet—back as a harbour attraction. Instead, the grand old steamer may go to Melbourne for a new life as a floating restaurant or Port Phillip Bay. An owner of the *South Steyne*, Newcastle businessman Michael Wansey, claims that the Urban Transit Authority baulked at paying $4 million for the refurbished ferry, despite its initial interest in the scheme. 'She would have been fully refurbished and ready to give another 36 years of service.' he said. Urban Transit Authority spokesman,

The North Head *on her last trip down Sydney Harbour as she left under her own power for Hobart on the morning of 26 March 1987.*

Mr Kevin Price, said Mr Wansey had offered the Authority the *South Steyne* eight months ago. 'We evaluated the whole thing and, bearing in mind the modern craft we are using today, decided against it,' he said.

Michael Wansey told the *Sun*:

It has cost us $2 million to make her seaworthy again. When the Urban Transit Authority plan fell though, we investigated a plan to put the *South Steyne* on Sydney Harbour as a floating restaurant, but another firm has that business well and truly parcelled up, so we looked to Melbourne.

The deal was finalised two days after that story appeared in the *Sun*. Michael Wansey told me on 15 November that on the previous Thursday week the *South Steyne* had become part of a new company, to be called Vintage Travels Incorporated. Not only did he have the only steam ferry left in Australia but he had also acquired a steam train and proposed to operate the two as a tourist project based in Melbourne. The finance came from the Victorian Government Economic Development Corporation, which was providing a $4.7 million loan. From this loan, $2 million was to be spent completing the restoration of the *South Steyne* and in the latter half of 1987 she would steam her way down to Melbourne to take up a new role as a luxury cruise ship on Port Phillip Bay.

Work resumed at Ballina on 17 November 1986. It involved opening the ship out and sandblasting everything in preparation for the major rebuilding work, to begin in January. By August of 1987 it was hoped to light the boilers for the first time in 12 years and take the great ship out again for sea trials. Michael Wansey said:

We hope to get her to Melbourne about 1 September, the interior will be fully carpeted, seats and tables will be in the old-style cane of the P & O ships. The end of the upper deck, which has been open, will be closed in and we will delete the for'ard and after stairs of the promenade deck, using a centre stairway only. This will give us a dance floor and enable us to accommodate 1180 passengers, all with tables and chairs. The steam engines and boilers will be retained intact, but all new electrical equipment and generating plant will be installed. The roof is to come off and she will be rebuilt completely inside.

Mr Wansey was planning, after the roof was replaced, to put on the bridge deck a steam calliope containing a set of tuned ships' whistles. Using steam from the ship's boilers, it would play like one of those old steam organs on the merry-go-rounds of years ago.

How the train comes into the picture is another interesting story, involving, by coincidence, Michael Muter, who headed the original venture to save the *South Steyne* in Sydney in 1975. He had some part in a project known as The Melbourne Limited, launched in Melbourne in 1985 with fanfare and glossy brochures, offering day and weekend tourist trips on Victoria's 5 ft 3 in gauge railway system. The train venture was financed with $1.5 million in loans from the Victorian Economic Development Corporation and the Royal Bank of Canada and was leased to Steam Age Australia Pty Ltd for an annual fee of $140 000. Mr Muter was a director of Steam Age Pty Ltd. The whole thing seems to have been a disaster, collapsing after about 12 months with a train of debts being dragged behind, including $330 000 to the Victorian Railways, $10 000 to Telecom and various large amounts to individuals. The Victorian Economic Development Corporation's interest in getting the train under new management is understandable. It had not made a journey between early 1986 and November, when Michael Wansey took it on, for better or for worse, although he indicated he was quite prepared to unload the train if an unnamed buyer really was interested, although nobody could say Michael Wansey was not interested in transport of all kinds. In addition to the *South Steyne*, he now had not only a train but also a double-decker London bus and Rebel Air, an airline offering flights by DC3 aircraft.

Back in Sydney things were still happening around the harbour. At the end of November 1986, the hydrofoil service was being operated by one boat, the old faithful *Curl Curl*. The two big new foils were both out of action, the *Sydney* for mechanical reasons and the *Manly* with serious injuries sustained by crashing into the stone wall at the Opera House. But life goes on around the waterfront. In October Charlie Usher retired from his job at Manly wharf after fifty years with the ferries. And a sad day it was for him too. Thirty-four years on the wharf at Manly, catching the ropes thrown by the deckhands to tie up the ferries and casting them off again as the ferries departed. It used to be harder than that. In the steam ferry

days Charlie had to carry bags of ashes from the stoke-holds up the gangway and along the wharf to be carted away.

Things do change, but memories last. As I was finishing this chapter the telephone rang behind me in my study. It was Lew Maxwell, now 85. 'I thought you might like to know,' he said. 'Tomorrow it will be 50 years since the fire on the *Bellubera*—16 November 1936.' How could Lew ever forget. He wouldn't have been here 50 years later if he had not put his head through the engine room porthole.

4. Last Journey

Two of the last remaining links with the Port Jackson & Manly Steamship Company departed from Sydney within a week of each other in early 1987. *South Steyne* skipper Harold Gibson died on 18 March, and the *North Head* sailed out of the harbour for the last time on 26 March on her way to Hobart to take up a new life there as a floating restaurant. Quite a few old colleagues went out to Rook-wood Crematorium to attend Harold's funeral service. Although he had retired from the ferry service nearly 17 years before, carrying his kit bag ashore from the *Lady Wakehurst*, still mourning the loss of his beloved *South Steyne*, many of his former workmates remembered him and went along to pay their tribute.

During the same week the sale of the *North Head* was finalised and the new owners began to get her ready for the voyage to Hobart. After the ferry had been given a good cleaning and the decks had been hosed down thoroughly to take up the gaps between the dried-out timbers, they turned to the vessel's power house, to see how that would stand up to such a long journey. The *North Head* had been lying idle at Cockatoo Island for about 14 months and there was some apprehension about the engines. But the auxiliaries started first go and continued to run beautifully, charging the batteries for the main engines, which would need fully charged cells to turn them over. Here, too, there was no trouble and the ship was taken across from Cockatoo Island to the Howard Smith wharf on the opposite shore in Balmain, where she would be fitted out for the trip.

The night before she left, Jim Hickman, managing director of the new Hobart owners, North Head Pty Ltd, and his partners and crew had a dinner party aboard. Cleaned of the grime which had accumulated in more than a year lying alongside Cockatoo Island, and her lights brighter than the dull glimmer which filtered from them during her last days of Manly service, the old ferry put on a brave show for her last night in Sydney Harbour. Guests included the managing director of the Urban Transit

Authority, Mr Kel Edgar; UTA secretary, Mr Laurie Parker; engineering manager of the UTA ferry division, Mr Len Michaels; Manly ferry skipper Ron Hart, and 85-year-old Lew Maxwell, who had installed the diesel-electric engines when *North Head* was converted from steam propulsion. Two people who were closely associated with the *North Head* were unable to attend. Captain Dave Stimson, her principal master for many years, was on duty on his new command, *Freshwater*, and George Marshall had just come home from hospital after an operation.

Lew Maxwell was taken down to the engine room after he came aboard. He made a leisurely tour of inspection, then patted one of the four 7-cylinder diesel engines which drive the ship's electric propulsion motors. 'They'll do,' he said. 'They've been well looked after.' Jim Hickman's son, Captain Roger Hickman, an Australian National Line skipper, was in command for the voyage to Hobart.

Fog almost smothered the harbour next morning when they cast off at Balmain and circled Cockatoo Island to pass the old Mort's Dock site at Woolwich where the *North Head* was built and launched in 1913. John Darroch and I waited in my boat near Kirribilli, John with his cameras ready, not knowing whether the fog would cause the departure to be delayed. The Harbour Bridge was visible only up to the road deck. The arch and its hangers were lost in the clouds. Fog sirens were wailing on Bradleys Head and the Opera House, and the ferries managing to get in and out of Circular Quay added to the dismal din with their tooting. Then the light north-west breeze freshened noticeably and began to chase the fog down harbour. As wisps of cloud thinned out under the Harbour Bridge, the *North Head* suddenly appeared out of the mist, like a ghost ship, gliding slowly towards the bridge in mid-stream. Passing the Opera House, she was given farewell fanfares from every ship's whistle in the vicinity as she continued slow ahead past Fort Denison

and around Bradleys Head, accompanied only by us and one other launch.

It seemed a shame that such a grand old lady of the harbour should be allowed to leave with such apparent unconcern compared with the great farewell accorded the *Baragoola*. *North Head* went off quietly after her last trip in December 1985 and just didn't come back to work again. Now she was leaving almost as quietly. Off Middle Head, the *Lady Wakehurst*, bound for Manly, and the *Freshwater*, going up to town passed, and, the North Head for a brief period, was between them in the back-ground. What emotions it must have aroused for Dave Stimson, blasting a last farewell from the *Freshwater*. The two others paused briefly, then went on their way, their passengers wondering what it was all about. Most of the fog had gone and the sun shone brightly on the *North Head* as she turned near Dobroyd and faced the open sea through The Heads for the last time. She cleared The Heads, her bow rising gracefully to the ground swell, and in no time she was disappearing over the south-east horizon.

Lew Maxwell had declined an invitation after the party at Balmain to accompany John Darroch and me on the harbour next morning. 'I've said my goodbyes tonight,' he said, arriving back at his home in Peters Place, Maroubra. 'It was a great night and I'm proud they asked me.' But in the morning he went and sat on Maroubra Point until he saw the *North Head* coming down from Sydney and he watched her until she was out of sight again off Port Hacking.

The weather was kind to the *North Head* and she arrived in Hobart on the following Sunday, March 29. The only thing that happened was an overheated gearbox when they were off the south coast of New South Wales. So they just turned her around and drove her astern to Hobart, doing about 11 knots. North Head is still in Hobart, doing an occasional cruise trip on the Derwent.

An historic occasion on the morning of 26 March 1987. From left: MV Freshwater *(to Sydney), MV* North Head *(to Hobart) and MV* Lady Wakehurst *(to Manly). The three vessels passed off Middle Head.*

PART IX
THE BIG CATS

1. Unwelcome guests

The biggest change in the long history of the Manly ferries, and perhaps a real indication of things to come, was the letting of tenders in April 1989 for the construction in Cairns of three high speed wave-piercing jet-propelled catamarans to replace the trouble-plagued hydrofoils. Cost of the Jetcats, as they became known, was to be $15.6 million, part of which the Government hoped to obtain from selling the four hydrofoils, the Sydney and Manly, which seated 235, and the Curl Curl and Long Reef, which carried 140 passengers.

State Transit officials promised the public airline style comfort in the Jetcats, designed to take 250 passengers the seven miles between Sydney and Manly in 15 minutes, about the same time as the hydrofoils, but, they promised also, the Jetcats would be much more reliable. The new vessels, to be built with aluminium hulls, were to travel from Cairns to Sydney under their own power. If they proved themselves after a period of service the Government had an option to buy two more.

Some months earlier, in August 1988, a fourth new ferry, the *Collaroy,* had been commissioned with great ceremony by the Minister for Transport, Mr Baird. The new vessel looked very like her sister ships *Freshwater, Queenscliff and Narrabeen,* but there were a few differences, suggesting that she could resume the ocean cruises which had been abandoned since the departure of the *South Steyne.* The upper deck was left open at each end instead of being closed in, giving a better view for travellers who were prepared to brave the wind and the spray, and extensive catering facilities, including a liquor bar, offered more than "the canteen on the upper deck" on the other three new ships. Another feature was the addition of stabilisers, fitted below the waterline amidships, to provide better stability for passenger comfort on ocean cruises. The *Collaroy* was commissioned at Circular Quay on Sunday morning, August 21, 1988, after which invited guests, including the author, were taken outside The Heads for an offshore cruise with morning tea. When the *Collaroy* went into service in October, however, it blotted its copybook the third day out on the run, holding

up commuters at Manly for an hour in the busy part of the morning because the hydraulic gangway could not be retrieved from the wharf. They were stuck until the *Narrabeen* arrived half an hour later. It tied up alongside the *Collaroy,* through which Manly bound passengers had to walk to disembark on the wharf. Some 200 passengers still waiting on the *Collaroy* were then transferred to the *Narrabeen* to travel to the city. A hydraulic hose in the gangway mechanism had broken and when this was fixed the new glamour ferry returned to duty.

But that was nothing compared with the rough debut of the Jetcats. Even before their arrival in Sydney the *Bluefin* and two sister ships under construction at Cairns became the centre of controversy when a Queensland Supreme Court judge found that a similar vessel launched by the same builders was "not of sound design and construction" when it was destroyed by fire off North Queensland three years previously. When fire ravaged the tourist catamaran Reef Link II off Townsville in 1987 the 53 passengers and eight crew had to jump for their lives. State Transit in Sydney, however, said it had set its own quite stringent fire hazard standards for the *Blue Fin* and was monitoring them at Cairns.

By March 1991 all three Jetcats were in service, replacing the hydrofoils on the harbour. The *Sea Eagle,* named by public poll, was commissioned by Mrs Baird, wife of the NSW Minister for Transport, at a ceremony in Farm Cove with the Manly rugby league team (The Sea Eagles) forming a guard of honour. The new Jetcat joined the *Blue Fin* and *Sir David Martin* to complete the fleet of three. Mr Baird was full of praise for the Jetcats, saying they were faster, cleaner and more efficient than the hydrofoils. State Transit chief executive John Brew called the Jetcats a triumph for Australian industry describing them as the best of their kind in the world. The three Jetcats completed the ceremony by cruising up the harbour in formation. During this ceremony Mr Brew said that the Jetcats underlined State Transit's determination to deliver a public transport system second to none with the best high speed maritime transport offered anywhere in the world.

A month later a storm broke with big headlines across page 1 of *The Manly Daily* announcing "Plan to axe Jetcat and ferry services." The story said:

"Harbor ferry services to Manly are likely to be slashed under a State Government plan to cut costs.

"The Government is looking to cancel all Manly ferries and Jetcats after 8 pm and replace them with bus services to and from the city, according to senior ferry personnel.

"The sources said State Transit had already drafted a plan for redundancy and severance pay for some ferry workers."

Mr Baird hastened to deny the claims, saying the Government had no plans to axe Manly services. In Manly there was public anger. Who wanted to spend 45 minutes on a bus trip to or from town instead of 30 minutes in a ferry or 15 minutes in a Jetcat. All this only a month after State Transit talk of providing the best water transport in the world. But the men on the job knew something was going to happen and it soon became obvious what it would be. Another month later, Mr Baird, who had said only a few weeks previously that there were no plans to axe Manly services, revealed that plans were being made to take the big ferries off at night and replace two ferries with one Jetcat, on which passengers would pay only ferry fares, enjoying a much quicker service at no extra cost with the existing

frequency maintained. The Minister blamed an "orchestrated campaign by union workers for attempts to discredit the ferry and Jetcat services".

Another month and there was more trouble, *The Manly Daily* headlines screaming "Service in chaos as Jetcats founder." Remember that fire on a Jetcat in North Queensland? The paper on May 1, 1991, said the harbor Jetcat service was in chaos and the high speed craft were under scrutiny again after a fire on board the *Sir David Martin* a few days earlier. All three Jetcats were out of action while the *Sir David Martin* was being repaired and the *Blue Fin* was having extensive checks on its fuel lines. The *Sea Eagle* was out because of engine problems. To solve such an embarrassing situation they had to get one of the discarded hydrofoils out of retirement temporarily. Cause of the fire on the *Sir David Martin* was a fuel line in the engine room which allowed fuel to leak and ignite. This meant all three vessels had to be taken out of service to ensure it could not happen again.

The year was not over before there was another flare up with maritime unions claiming that State Transit was considering the sale of two Manly ferries in a move which could net the Government more than $20 million. They said replacing night ferries with the faster Jetcats was the first step in a plan to phase out half of the Manly ferry fleet. Naturally the unions were worried at the prospect of the ferries going off at night, taking away penalty rates or overtime for possibly 16 crew in two ferries who were to be replaced with only a few

Jetcat Blue Fin passing Dobroyd on her way to town, The Heads in the background. Blue Fin, the first of the big cats, did not have seating outside on the upper deck, but was modified later.

MV Collaroy, the last of the Freshwater class ferries, shown here on a holiday cruise to the Hawkesbury.

men operating one Jetcat. Maritime unions and the Manly-Warringah Public Transport Coalition (MWPTC) claimed the Jetcats would be dangerous to operate at night at high speed and the unions took the matter to the NSW Industrial Relations Commission.

On December 11, 1991, the Jetcats did not operate because, according to the unions, the seas were too rough. The State Transit Authority maintained that the Jetcats could operate in any weather. The only time they had been stopped previously was when the swell on the harbor was 11.4 metres, too much for the ocean-going ferries. This time the swell was only 2.5 metres and the unions were accused of stopping the Jetcats in an attempt to discredit their safety. The unions claimed that the jets were rated by the Maritime Services Board to operate only in swells of less than 1.5 metres.

Now there was open warfare. A week later ferry and Jetcat staff walked off the job in protest at the plan to replace the two night ferries with one Jetcat. The Merchant Services Guild and the Institute of Marine Power Engineers claimed that under the State Transit's proposed timetable arrangements Jetcat masters would be forced to operate under unsafe conditions. NSW secretary of the Merchant Services Guild, Mr Kevin Pinch, said the proposed

20 minute run between Sydney and Manly was a recipe for disaster. "Safety is a genuine concern with us," he said. "It has nothing to do with loss of time or money." In talks after the crews had walked off the job both sides agreed to test the unions' safety fears with a three weeks trial in January 1992, carried out under various night conditions, at different speeds, with no passengers aboard. The night ferries were to continue until after the trials. Both State Transit and the unions agreed to carry out the trials objectively.

But the battle continued. In the first week the jet masters were running the craft seven knots slower than the daytime scheduled speed of 32 knots, making the night trip five minutes longer than in the day. The unions said some trips had been slowed to 10 knots across The Heads because of the swell. More trials were to be run, this time with passengers, but negotiations broke down, the unions saying the situation was back to square one. Then after more than three and a half hours of talks on January 17 the Firemen and Deckhands Association said its members would refuse to operate night Jetcats alongside the regular Manly ferry service. The wrangling went on through February and March. Jetcats were withdrawn from service in the middle of February

The Baragoola *gliding in to Manly wharf, crammed with nostalgic passengers on her last trip in service on Saturday, 8 January 1983. The author is standing on the starboard edge of the bridge. No ferry had a bigger or better send-off. (John Darroch)*

A familiar sight in Hobart now, the North Head *returning from a cruise to Bruni Island (background), turning out of D'Entrecasteaux Channel between the mainland and the island and overtaking the sailing ship* Eye of the Wind, *also well known in Sydney.*

because the swell was more than 1.5 metres. Then, fed up with what it described as delaying tactics, State Transit, or somebody else close to officialdom, let it be known that the Government might sell the Jetcats to private enterprise unless the unions agreed to the proposed night operations. Who would buy them? the unions argued. They were white elephants. Then there was another engine room fire, this time scaring 200 passengers aboard the *Sea Eagle*, the fourth believed to have been caused by fuel leaks. Eventually the inevitable happened and on March 26, 1992, the first night Jetcats replaced the ferries. State Transit and the unions had agreed finally on conditions.

But the saga was not finished. After only two weeks there was another engineroom fire, this time in the *Sir David Martin*. The Jetcats were all withdrawn and the exiled ferries were back on the night services pending investigations by the Maritime Services Board, State Transit and engineers of BWM Deutz, the German manufacturers of the Jetcat engines. The investigation, expected to take three weeks, took longer than expected and it was two months before the Jetcats were back in business on the harbour. State Transit was satisfied now that any design faults which had been causing the fires were rectified after major redesign work by the German engineers. When this was written in late 1994 the night Jetcat services had operated for more than two years with little apparent trouble.

What has happened with the advent of the big cats may be a pointer to the future, bigger cats still to replace ageing ferries, though many believe this is not practical. The unions are cynical at plans to cut down working staff on the ferries while the onshore bureaucracy has grown enormously. At the time of the Jetcat disputes they pointed out that while the Department was trying to cut ferry crews there was no shortage of "Swiss Admirals" at Circular Quay and on two floors of offices in Pitt Street. Five years previously, they said, there were two superintendent engineers at Circular Quay. Now there were 11. Five years previously the Operations Department consisted of the general manager and two assistants. Now there was a managing director, his executive officer, operations manager with three assistants. By 1994 the onshore establishment had increased considerably, much of it accommodated in even larger premises on the North Shore. They claimed also that the number of wharf staff had more than doubled and in revenue, where there used to be three people at Circular Quay the staff now totalled 12, gatehands and wharfingers had doubled to about 20 and the total bureaucracy had grown to 67.

State Transit maintained its faith in the Jetcats, however, and in November 1991 announced plans to build a $300,000 airport-style commuter lounge at Manly wharf as part of moves to boost passenger numbers for the Jetcat service. The fully-carpeted lounge, with seating for 140 people, was to be built by the middle of 1992. The Minister for Transport, Mr Baird, said State Transit hoped to increase use of the Jetcats by tourists and commuters, especially off-peak. "Jetcat patronage has jumped 11 per cent over the past year," he said. "Jetcat passengers are riding on the most modern and comfortable high speed craft in the world, but the facilities for those waiting to board at Manly are nowhere near as impressive. We intend to change all that with a major facelift providing a fully enclosed lounge and wide windows offering panoramic harbour views." Tenders were to be called later in 1991 for work to begin early 1992.

2. Ferries still tops

Two years later, in 1994, the Jetcat lounge had not been built, although work was starting on much-needed improvements to the wharf as a whole. Jetcat traffic had picked up, though not as much as the ferries were attracting. The figures provided an interesting pattern. Back in 1984 the hydrofoil patronage had declined to 1.58 million from 2.1 million in 1980, but 7.97 million preferred the ferries in that year. In 1992-93 the Manly ferries carried 9,229,000 passengers whereas the jets attracted only 961,000, well down on the earlier hydrofoil figures. For 1993-94 the ferries broke the 10 million mark with 10,012,000 passengers. Jetcats in the same period had passed the million mark to 1,083,000, although this was way behind the hydrofoil patronage of 2.1 million nearly 15 years earlier.

By this time Sydney's road traffic problems were causing some concern and the State Government was trying to entice more people off the roads on to harbour ferries. In the early days of the colony the upper harbour had been the water way to Parramatta, so why not try to bring it back to that use? New sleek craft similar to the Jetcats but longer and designed to travel at high speed with little wash to erode the shores were introduced on a new service to Parramatta, one abandoned many years before the roads became clogged with motor traffic. The Rivercats, as they were called, were an instant success, bringing the overall passenger figures for harbour ferries to a 1993-94 total of 20,618,000. The number of passengers using Sydney ferries went up 15 per cent in the summer of 1994. In December and January alone they carried nearly 1.5 million. A statement issued midway through February disclosed that another 75,000 had used the Rivercat service to Parramatta since it began in early December.

Said Transport Minister Baird: "Growth in patronage is happening right across the harbour as tourists and locals rediscover the pleasures of the harbour in record numbers. Patronage is up by more than 18 per cent on inner harbour services from places like Mosman, Neutral Bay, Balmain and Hunters Hill. Passenger numbers on the big Manly ferries have increased by 17 per cent and Jetcats had 11 per cent more passengers during December and January."

The great success was the Rivercats. So many people were using the service that large numbers could not get on at Parramatta and, in the early days of the service, had to wait for the next boat. This was rectified with the arrival of more Rivercats. Rivercats were introduced then on inner harbour services to Double Bay, Rose Bay and other points and State Transit was considering putting on cross harbour services, even between Manly and the lower North Shore. Mr Baird said more than 6100 trips were taken every week day between Manly and the lower North Shore, 60 per cent of these by car. North Shore ferry services would enable many of these people to leave their cars at home and travel to work by public transport, easing the congestion on main traffic arteries and resulting in better use of the water ways. State Transit was to begin planning for another new type of ferry, not as large as the Rivercats, to provide fast transport on new inner harbour services.

In strange contrast to this Government desire to get people off the roads and into ferry transport came proposals for the construction of road or rail projects between the northern beaches and the city, all of which would take patronage away from the Manly ferries and Jetcats. There seemed to be little awareness of recreating the problem caused years before when the tram services feeding people from Narrabeen on to the ferries at Manly were scrapped and replaced with buses direct to the city.

3. Lost in the fog

To people living at Manly, and beyond, the ferries are always news and what happens to them can usually win a place in the media spotlight. On April 15, 1988, the *Narrabeen* made the headlines when it got lost in a fog during its 6.15 am trip from Manly to the city with 500 passengers. The fog was so thick that the ferry, despite its radar, did not arrive in Sydney Cove until nearly an hour later and then the skipper, thinking he was berth-

ing at Circular Quay, found that he had nudged bow first into a rock wall at Dawes Point, near the Harbour Bridge. The passengers were jolted, but nobody was hurt. The ferry continued on to berth at the Quay, the skipper unaware that the front rudder and propeller blades had been damaged. But, on the return trip to Manly, as the *Narrabeen* rounded Bennelong Point, in front of the Opera House, its front rudder fell off. Back to the Quay went *Narrabeen* to discharge its passengers and have investigators discover what had happened. The ferry was put into dry dock for repairs costing several thousand dollars. An urban Transit official said it was the first time he had heard of a Manly ferry being lost in a fog. Normally they used radar, which, apparently in this case, did not work properly. In the same fog another two Manly ferries collided almost head on in front of the Opera House, stopping only 8 metres apart.

The *Narrabeen* and *Freshwater* made the news on Saturday night November 5, 1988, in the chaos caused on the harbour by crowds trying to get to a big night of entertainment billed as the Sound Cloud Biennial Spectacular. More than 200 passengers staged a sit-in aboard the *Freshwater* at Circular Quay after the ferry was held up and these people did not reach the city in time for the show. They ignored police who were called to get them ashore. *Freshwater* left Manly at 7.30pm, due to berth in town about 8 o'clock, but could not get into Sydney Cove because of the number of spectator craft jamming the area between there and Farm Cove. The ferry was trapped near Fort Denison for about an hour and a half. Water police cleared a path to the Manly wharf at Circular Quay, but when the ferry berthed there 90 minutes late most of the passengers refused to disembark, complaining that they had been deprived of all but the fireworks part of the display and they demanded the right of a return trip to Manly. But there was a problem. The wharf was packed with other people who wanted to go to Manly. Police were called and put several of the mutineers ashore, but gave up when most of those still aboard, including elderly people and young children, refused to move. The gates were opened and the crowd on the wharf was allowed to embark. Some of them had been waiting two hours. They reached Manly about 10.45pm, more than three hours after the ferry had left on its 7.30pm run to town.

There had really been chaos on the harbour that night as ferries and private small craft jostled for vantage positions to see the fireworks and other parts of the show. The Urban Transit Authority, Maritime Services Board and police began an inquiry after the weekend to try to sift through the mass of complaints and allegations, including:

- The *Narrabeen* allegedly hit nearly 50 pleasure boats while trying to make its way through the mess.
- Pleasure craft blocked the movement of ferries and a Japanese car carrier by anchoring in the shipping lanes.
- One man came to blows with crew of the *Narrabeen* after the ferry and his $500,000 motor cruiser collided.

4. Time passes on

Life on the harbour quietened down and apart from a few small things like ferries crashing into the wharves at Manly and the Quay everything ran fairly smoothly. The new ferries gave good service and were popular with the public. By 1994 only one of the old favourites remained in the harbour. Years of painstaking work had failed to produce the required result and the *Baragoola* was reconciled to a static existence at Balmain. *North Head* was still alive in Hobart being used for social functions and cruises on the Derwent estuary and *South Steyne* was leading a busy similar life in Newcastle.

Of the famous skippers and others around the ferries, few familiar faces were to be seen by the middle of 1994. George Marshall died early in the year after a long illness. Eric Gale died in February 1988, aged 94, and Lew Maxwell, 90, died in April 1992. Maxwell, it might be said,

really had two lives. He nearly died 56 years before in 1936, trapped in the engine room as fire gutted the Bellubera. He saved his life by keeping his head out a porthole. Two other men died behind him in the engine room. Lew Maxwell, living in retirement at Maroubra, died peacefully in his sleep 56 years later. Eric Gale was 94. He contributed so much information for this book, but he did not live to see the story in print. He died the day a ship arrived in Sydney, bringing the books from Singapore, where the original edition was printed.

Still at the helm on the harbour were: Roger Smith and Peter Loosemore *(Freshwater)*, Chris Hogan and Max Tadross *(Queenscliff)*, Keith Rosser (Jetcats). In retirement were Alan Hobbs, Noel Heath, Ron Hart, Bill Thomas. Dave Stimson had left the service to become proprietor of a milk run on the Blue Mountains. He and Bill Thomas lived not far from each other at Springwood and Alan Hobbs, whose home was on the North Coast, visited them occasionally. It seems strange that when some men are working on the ferries so many live so far from the harbour. Then, in retirement, some move to the country.

5. Baragoola bows out

Several attempts had been made to give the *Baragoola* a purpose in what life it might have left. At the end of 1983 while she was lying at Cockatoo Island a group calling itself The Eureka

North Head, at home these days in Hobart, where she is a popular cruise ship on the Derwent estuary and is the venue for many social gatherings.

165

Education Foundation bought the vessel, proposing to establish aboard a floating university. Volunteers began restoration work, but the new owners had underestimated the cost of restoration and maintenance and the university was never opened. Three years later the vessel was acquired by Waterview Wharf Workshop Pty Ltd and another plan of restoration was begun. Mr David Ashton, a director of Waterview, was determined that the *Baragoola* should be kept in Sydney and he secured through the National Trust a permanent conservation order on the vessel. Subsequently, the ferry was put into dry dock at Garden Island in 1991 to be prepared for static mooring. Her propellers were removed, the shafts were drawn and stern tubes capped with blanking plates, which were fitted also over other sea water inlets and outlets not needed for emergency or auxiliary functions.

In August 1994 *Baragoola* was towed from Pyrmont to a berth at the Waterview wharf in Balmain, where restoration was to continue pending a decision on her future. "We took Ron Hart along for the ride," David Ashton said. "Also aboard was Wal Tulloch, 94, who worked on the building of the *Baragoola* in 1922 at Mort's Dock, not far from where she is now." David Ashton and his partners had spent more than $200,000 and regarded restoration as about 70 per cent finished, but at that stage there was still no clear perception of what would be done ultimately with the old ship. It could be used as a floating restaurant or perhaps as a centre for conferences or receptions.

6. North Head's new life

Down in Hobart, seven years after buying the *North Head* for $22,500 and getting her under her own power from Sydney to Hobart, Jim Hickman and North Head Pty Ltd had restored the old ship with tender loving care and an immense amount of money, still trying to take the restoration to survey standards. They had done remarkably well with a vessel now 81 years old. In 72 years of ferry service in Sydney she had carried at least 500 million passengers, far more than any other Australian vessel, and now, on Hobart's beautiful Derwent estuary, she was carrying thousands more. Since coming to Hobart *North Head* had made more than 160 cruises on the Derwent with between 60 and 450 guests, functioning as a private yacht with a certificate of seaworthiness. Alongside her berth in Sullivan's Cove she had been the venue for more than 400 weddings, parties, exhibitions, dinners and conferences and had been host vessel for the Sydney to Hobart yacht race and the British Steel Challenge Race. As a

tourist attraction she attracts 100 visitors a day.

Says Jim Hickman: "Our aim has been to restore her as nearly as practicable to her 1951 state and appearance." The amount of work done is considerable. Some 50 square metres of new 8mm plating were welded on the hull after cropping out old plates and sections of 12 frames were replaced. All 234 windows have been repaired and repainted and most other woodwork has been taken back to bare wood and repainted. Virtually the whole ship has been sanded and repainted in the 1951 colours. "The only problem in getting her back into survey is money," Hickman says. "I see her future, with increasing optimism, as a prime historic attraction in survey either on Port Phillip Bay or on Sydney Harbour. If she stays here we should raise about $100,000 by shareholdings and have her in survey by next September, aiming to campaign her in Melbourne at the time of the Melbourne Cup, just 30 years after her first visit there from Sydney and in her 82nd year."

7. The Steyne home at last

In September 1994, news leaked out of an important announcement to be made later by the State Government. The South Steyne was coming home to Sydney. The Government was going to lease the ship for two years and base her in Darling Harbour, where she would be used by the Olympic Committee as an Olympic display and information centre pending construction of a building for the 2000 Olympics, also to be in Darling Harbour. The announcement, coinciding with the first anniversary of Sydney's successful bid for the Olympics, was to have coincided also with a brief visit by the *South Steyne* from Newcastle, where she was being used by restaurateur Brian McDermott as a floating restaurant and function centre, but last minute difficulties intervened and the return to Sydney was postponed until January 2, 1995. The plan was to have the ship berthed on the east side of Cockle Bay, allowing easy public access from the city for people to see a special display designed by the Olympic Committee. The *South Steyne* was to play an important part in Sydney's preparations for the 2000 Olympics and there was a good chance that she would remain in Sydney after the two year lease expired. The possibility of using the *North Head* for the same purpose had been investigated, but she was not in survey and the *South Steyne* had far superior kitchen and catering facilities, which would be important for official functions and possible cruises.

The story has told in part VIII (page 151) how

Newcastle businessman Michael Wansey became a fairy godmother to the *South Steyne* in 1979 when she was lying in Darling Harbour with no future but the hopes of Bob Kentwell that somebody would turn up with some money and the ability to put some action with his money. Wansey had both and the very neglected old ship was towed to Newcastle, put into dock and prepared for a massive restoration program, quoted at $700,000 for the engines, boilers and work on the hull after $40,000 spent already on slipping and repair work on the hull. But she was taken to Ballina, where Ballina Slipways had quoted $100,000 less. At Ballina an immense amount of work was done and by the time she left there more than $2 million had been spent on the restoration program and Wansey was looking for another million to complete his plans, hoping to return her to Sydney as a floating restaurant. But the Urban Transit Authority and vested interests did not want her back in the harbour and in November 1986 Wansey took up a deal with Melbourne based Australian Vintage Travel, becoming a director of the company, which also had a tourist steam train. The deal, financed by a $4.7 million loan from the Victorian Government Economic Development Corporation, provided for $2 million to complete restoration as a luxury cruise ship on Port Phillip Bay.

It was March 1988 before *South Steyne* left Ballina for Melbourne, passing Sydney with her bows bearing the humiliating insignia "South Steyne, Melbourne". But trouble with her condensors forced a slow return from Maroubra to Sydney, where repairs were made. In Melbourne the *Steyne* was the venue for a State reception to Queen Elizabeth and the Duke of Edinburgh early in that year, but only a few months later the ferry was in the news again, tied up under a sheriff's arrest warrant from the Victorian Supreme Court. Ballina Slipway Engineering Company was claiming unpaid fuel bills of $62,364 and $332,686 for repair work and materials.

A month later the tourist train company went into receivership. It had borrowed a massive $15 million from the Victorian State Government. Australian Vintage Travel was not able to meet its loan repayments. Six months later, in February 1989, Starship Enterprises, a Gosford ferry company headed by a Mr Alan Draper, tried to buy the *Steyne* from the receivers and use it for trips between Circular Quay and Manly, but State Transit would not allow the use of its wharves. There was another buyer in the wings, however. Mr Brian McDermott, saw the *South Steyne* as a replacement for his Newcastle restaurant Crackers, wrecked in the disastrous Newcastle earthquake a while previously. He bought the *South Steyne* from the Victorian Economic Development Corporation in July 1990, had work done on the ship over six months in Melbourne and took her to Newcastle in January 1991. There her main use has been as a floating restaurant and reception centre, but she has steamed to Sydney twice for visits, in January 1992 and January 1993. Brian McDermott said he had 400 function bookings for dates between September 1994 and January 1995, when she would be brought to Sydney for two years and, hopefully, the remainder of her life.

When the *South Steyne* visited in 1993, photographed below in Darling Harbour, The Manly Daily asked me for my thoughts. Expressing pleasure at the news, I added: "She should never have left Sydney Harbour. Her demise was a tragedy which should never have occurred."

The Ships and the Men

The Ships

In the space of 138 years, tracing from 1848, when *The Brothers* began the first ferry service to Manly, and 1986, when this story was completed, a total of 52 paddlewheel steamers, screw steamers, motor vessels and hydrofoils, not counting conversions from steam to diesel-electric, have been used in the ferry service between Sydney and Manly.

Some of these were merely part-time operators and little detail is known about them. They spent most of their time as tugs, towing sailing ships, which were not very manoeuvrable in harbour traffic. Here, gathered from various sources, are details of the long line of Manly ferries:

***THE BROTHERS* (1847-86):** Wooden paddle steamer, built in Sydney for John & Joseph Gerard by a builder named Chowney. Dimensions: 67 ft x 10 ft 9 in x 4 ft 9 in, of 23.4 gross tons. Engine of 18 hp. Was the first ferry between Sydney and Manly in 1848, carrying 50 passengers. Hulk broken up at Port Stephens in 1886.

***WARLINGTON* (1851):** This iron paddle steamer was built in England in 1851 and found her way out to Australia. Nearly all that is known about her is that she was plying to Manly with the *Phantom* in 1859.

***HERALD* (1854-84):** Paddlewheel steamer 75 ft long, used as a tug and part-time Manly ferry. Carried 50 passengers. Blew up and sank in 1884 while waiting near The Heads to tow in a sailing ship.

***NORA CREINER* (1854):** Not much is known about the *Nora Creiner* except that she was the first to begin excursions on Sydney Harbour in December 1854, and these trips included Manly. She was an iron paddle steamer.

***THE HUNTRESS* (1854-57):** Newton & Malcolm built this wooden paddle steamer on the Manning River, New South Wales. She seems to have had a short life, but it was an obscure one.

***PLANET* (1855):** Even more obscure. Nothing known.

***EMU 1* (1841):** Captain Manse was the owner of this iron paddle steamer, built in Sydney in 1841 from components made in Scotland and shipped to Australia. She was 94 ft x 14 ft x 6 ft 1 in. In 1855 the *Emu* was doing two trips a day to Manly.

***BLACK SWAN* (1854):** Built in Sydney from frames made in England. Owned by Edye Manning. Iron paddle steamer with dimensions 91 ft x 14 ft 8 in x 6 ft 9 in, 70 tonnes, 40–hp engine. First trip to Manly 25 July 1855.

***PELICAN* (1854):** First trip to Manly on 6 December 1855. Iron paddlewheeler built in Sydney from components shipped from Scotland. Also owned by Edye Manning. Same dimensions as *Black Swan*.

***PHANTOM* (1858-78):** The *Phantom* is the earliest Manly ferry about which any great detail has survived. She was the first double-ended paddle steamer used in the Manly service. *Phantom* was built in Victoria at Williamstown by J.T. Daw & Company with shaped iron components made in England. She was built for Samuel Bowne Skinner, an original partner of Australian shipping owner Captain Howard Smith, for excursions on Port Phillip Bay, but in 1859 Manly pioneer Henry Gilbert Smith bought a share of the vessel from Skinner and brought her to Sydney. *Phantom*, of 63 tons, with a 50–hp engine, was 119 ft 1 in x 13 ft 1 in x 6 ft 8 in. *Phantom*, which became known as 'Puffing Billy' because she puffed out smoke rings, introduced the famous Manly ferry colours—green hull with white band, white superstructure and white funnel with black top—which lasted until 1974, when the New South Wales Government changed them to conform with the blue and cream of the inner harbour ferries and Sydney's government buses.

Smith sold his share in 1860 to Skinner and S.H. Wilson under an agreement which allowed them to continue a regular Sydney-Manly service, which they did for about 10 years. *Phantom* was not the best sea boat because of her narrow beam and shallow draught and her engine was fairly noisy. In 1868 she was sold to Captain Thomas Heselton and T.J. Parker, who, with James Huddart, formed the Australian shipping line of Huddart Parker in 1876. The *Phantom* was retired as a Manly passenger ferry in 1877, but was used between Sydney and Watsons Bay for a few years. Was broken up at Pyrmont in 1886.

***CLOMMEL* (1859-78):** Built at Liverpool, England, as a paddlewheel steamer of 598 tons. No detailed history available.

CULLODEN (1867): Another paddlewheeler with an obscure history.

BREADALBANE (1853-84): A well-known paddlewheeler in the early days of the Manly ferries. She has been described variously as a tug-type iron steamer and a general-purpose vessel, with iron hull and bulwarks and timber superstructure, a clipper bow and a counter stern. *Breadalbane* displaced 161 tons and was 146 ft 4 in x 17 ft 1 in x 8 ft, with an engine of 80 hp. Built in Glasgow by Smith & Rogers, who also built the engine. She was owned originally by D. McMurrish of Glasgow (1853–56), and then went to Melbourne, where she was sold and used as a ferry to Williamstown, also doing duty as a tug for sailing ships in and out of Melbourne. She was bought by a Sydney merchant, Robert Towns, who took her to Brisbane for the up-river trade to Ipswich, but in 1862 she seems to have come to Sydney and on 30 November made her first trip as a Manly ferry. The *Sydney Morning Herald* of 1 December 1862, reported that *Breadalbane* had undergone extensive alterations after being purchased recently for the purpose of running to Manly in conjunction with the *Phantom*. The *Herald* described her as a roomy and fast boat, admirably adapted for passenger traffic. Towns appears to have sold the *Breadalbane* in 1871 to Captain Thomas Heselton and T.J. Parker. Other owners are recorded as John Randal Carey (1875–77), the Port Jackson Steam Boat Company (1877–81) and the Port Jackson Steamship Company (1881–82). With the *Royal Alfred* and the *Phantom*, *Breadalbane* was one of the main carriers in the Manly trade until the *Fairlight* arrived in 1878, when she was retired to towing and relief duties until scrapped in 1882. Her hulk is believed to have been buried under the reclamation of land for Hudson's timber yards at Blackwattle Bay, Glebe.

GOOLWA (1864-1919): *Goolwa*, an iron tug type of vessel, was built at Jarrow-on-Tyne by Palmer Brothers, with a two-cylinder 90–hp steam engine built by J. Thompson & Company, of Newcastle-on-Tyne. It appears the *Goolwa* was ordered originally for an Adelaide tug operation, who sold out before she could be delivered. After arriving in Adelaide in 1867, the *Goolwa* was sold to J.W. Smith and Captain Thomas Heselton, who took her to Sydney, where she was used as a tug and a ferry. In January 1868, Parker and Heselton took over the Manly services and from then until 1873 *Goolwa* did ferry and tug duties with *Phantom* and *Breadalbane*. Superseded by the new passenger boat *Royal Alfred* in 1873, *Goolwa* was sold in January 1876 to the Newcastle Co-operative Steam Tug Company, which used her in a fleet of tugs for towing and excursions in Sydney Harbour

in opposition to the Port Jackson Steam Boat Company for about 20 years, after which the Newcastle company was taken over by the John Brown family interests in 1898. *Goolwa* appears to have been in service until 1905, when she was laid up. She was raised after sinking at her mooring in 1919 and was left on the Hunter River bank near Hexham. The remains of the hull are still there.

COBRA (1871-73): Built in 1849 as an iron tug-boat paddle steamer of 91 tons, 98 ft 8 in x 13 ft 6 in x 8 ft 9 in, *Cobra* operated on the Manly service until 1873, when she was sold to John Dalton for his Newcastle tug business. *Cobra*, renamed *Cobre* in 1888, was a tug in Newcastle for another 43 years before being scrapped and broken up in 1917. She had been around for 67 years.

ROYAL ALFRED (1873-85): This was the first big passenger ferry in the Manly service. With a carrying capacity of 750 people, she provided something more than the part tug, part ferries which worked the run part-time on weekends and holidays. *Royal Alfred* was 132 ft 3 in long, with a beam of 19 ft 4 in and draught of 8 ft 3 in and a 60–hp engine to drive her 141 tons. She was built in 1868 by George Beddoes, of Auckland, New Zealand, and spent some time as a ferry in Auckland before coming to Sydney in 1873 to become, with *Breadalbane*, the basis of the Manly passenger service. *Royal Alfred* continued as a passenger ferry until the big new *Brighton* took her place in 1883. She was the last single-ended ferry in the regular Manly service until the first hydrofoil, *Manly*, in 1965. She was broken up at Berrys Bay in 1892.

MYSTERY (1874-93): Built by Money, Wigram & Company at Northam, England, in 1852, with 60–hp, two-cylinder engines by G. Butchard, of London, *Mystery* was a tug-passenger vessel of 105 tons, 96 ft 1 in x 16 ft 8 in x 10 ft 4 in. Her hull and superstructure were of wood and she had a clipper bow with a bowsprit and a counter stern. *Mystery* was used as a tug in Port Phillip Bay and as a ferry between Melbourne and Geelong from 1867 until joining the Manly service in 1874 with the Heselton-Parker partnership. Between 1877 and 1893 she was registered with the Port Jackson Steam Boat Company. In August 1899 her engine was removed and she finished life as a punt.

MANLY I (1874-79): Wooden hull, screw steamer built by Bower & Drake at Pyrmont in 1874 of 89 tons, 101 ft 4 in x 17 ft 7 in x 8 ft 2 in. Used mainly for towing and weekend and holiday excursions. This first vessel to be named after some part of Manly-Warringah did not last long as a ferry and was sold in 1879. *Manly* was owned by the AUSN company between 1887 and 1906, when she was broken up.

BRIGHTSIDE (1877-1908): Double-ended passenger ferry, iron hull with wooden superstructure, 269 tons, 170 ft 8 in x 22 ft 1 in x 5 ft 8 in, two-cylinder steam engine of 70 hp. *Brightside*, named originally *Emu II*, was an iron paddle steamer built by A. & J. Inglis, of Glasgow, Scotland, shipped to Australia in sections and assembled at Kangaroo Point, Brisbane, for the Brisbane-Ipswich trade of the Queensland Steam Navigation Company Ltd, which she served until the opening of the Brisbane-Ipswich railway in 1876. The Port Jackson Steam Boat Company bought her then and took her to Sydney for the Manly service, in which she was one of the main carriers for some years, but by 1891 she was being used only as a spare boat. In 1897 she sank at her mooring in Neutral Bay. In 1902 she was relegated to the role of a cargo carrier until 1908, when she was gutted by fire. The following year she was broken up and the engines were sold to operate a sawmill on the south coast of New South Wales. *Brightside* was a slow boat compared with *Fairlight* and *Brighton* and her shallow draught was more suited to the Brisbane River than the crossing of Sydney Heads.

COMMODORE (1878-98): An iron· paddle steamer built by J.T. Eltringham, of South Shields, England, as the first new vessel for the Port Jackson Steam Boat Company Ltd. Of 187 tons, she had a two-cylinder, 95–hp engine, a length of 130 ft 9 in, beam 20 ft 8 in and drew 10 ft 3 in. *Commodore* was used mainly as a tug to tow ships in and out of Sydney and as a weekend ferry and spare boat between Sydney and Manly. Sold to J. & A. Brown of Newcastle in 1898, she worked as a tug in Newcastle and Sydney until the late 1920s, being probably Australia's last ocean-going paddle tug. She was scuttled off Newcastle in 1931, ending her life of 53 years, 50 of them in active service.

FAIRLIGHT ˙(1878-1912): Built in 1878 by Thomas Wingate & Company, of Glasgow, for the Port Jackson Steam Boat Company Ltd at a cost of £7600, *Fairlight* had a registered tonnage of 315, she was 171 ft 4 in long, with a beam of 22 ft 2 in, drew 10 ft 1 in and had a·two-cylinder, compound diagonal steam engine of 130 hp driving the paddlewheels to produce a speed of 14 knots. *Fairlight* introduced luxury travelling to the Manly ferry service, replacing wooden benches with cushioned seats, comfortable saloons instead of open decks and carpeted floors in place of wooden decks. She could carry 950 passengers and operated successfully as a good sea boat for 30 years between Sydney and Manly. *Fairlight* was sold out of the service by the Port Jackson & Manly Steamship Company in 1912 and two years later was towed to Brisbane, where her hull was made into two lighters.

GLENELG (1882-91): Another iron tug with wooden superstructure, built by Aitken & Mansel, of Glasgow, Scotland, in 1875 for T. Elder and R.B. Smith, of Port Adelaide. Dimensions: 218 tons, 135 ft 8 in x 21 ft 1 in x 11 ft 3 in. Engine by Rait & Lindsay, of Glasgow, 80 hp driving twin screws. Brought to Sydney by Thomas Heselton and partners in 1882, *Glenelg* operated as a tug and Manly excursion boat for them and the Port Jackson Steamship Company Ltd between 1882 and 1891, when she was sold to Hobart interests. *Glenelg* foundered in Bass Strait in 1900.

IRRESISTIBLE (1884-96): An iron screw steamer of 136 tons, built in London for a Mr Halstead. Used as a tug during the week and for Manly excursions at weekends and holidays. Dimensions: 109 ft x 21 ft x 9 ft. Sold to J. & A. Brown tugs in 1898.

PORT JACKSON (1883-98): An iron screw steamer on the lines of *Irresistible* and used similarly. Built by R.S. Sparrow & Company in Dunedin, New Zealand, in 1883 for the Port Jackson Steamship Company. Data: 108 tons, 103 ft 9 in x 17 ft 5 in x 7 ft 7 in; engine by builders, 38 hp; two masts, schooner rigged. *Port Jackson* was one of the last vessels built for multi-purpose use, towing in the harbour and excursion work to Manly. *Port Jackson* was one of three tugs sold to Browns of Newcastle in 1898—the others were *Commodore* and *Irresistible* —and with the exception of a period under charter to Huddart Parker in Melbourne in October 1889, she worked in Sydney and Newcastle until 20 November 1910, when she was wrecked near Catherine Hill Bay on her way from Newcastle to Sydney.

BRIGHTON (1883-1916): This magnificent big paddlewheeler was really the forerunner of the big Manly ferries. In fact, she was almost as big as the greatest of them all—the *South Steyne*. *Brighton*, built at Rutherglen, Scotland, by T.B. Seath & Company, was launched on 14 December 1882. She was said to have been designed by James Richmond, manager of the Port Jackson Steamship Company, for whom the vessel was built. Data: 417 tons, 220 ft 2 in x 23 ft x 10 ft 7 in. Engine: two-cylinder, compound diagonal oscillating surface condensing steam engine, driving two paddlewheels; 160 hp, increased later to 230; four horizontal coal-burning boilers, in pairs in two stokeholds; two funnels. Engine built by A. Campbell & Sons, Glasgow. *Brighton* was a double-ended iron and steel hull with wooden superstructure and decks. A promenade deck was on the roof of the main deck. It was open under canvas awnings with a smoking cabin amidships under the navigation bridge, which originally was open under a canvas awning. The main deck had three saloons, including a ladies' cabin. Outside seating consisted of wooden benches, but velvet-covered upholstered lounges were inside the cabins and saloons. The *Brighton* came to Sydney under sail and steam, leaving Glasgow on 2 June 1883, and arriving in Sydney Harbour on 1 September. Normally the *Brighton* did not have masts. Two masts and schooner rig were used to assist her steam propulsion on the voyage out from Scotland. *Brighton* operated as a Manly ferry for 32 years and was largely responsible for boosting the tourist traffic to the seaside resort. She was sold out of service in 1916 and her hulk was used by Burns Philp & Company as a store ship for many years in Salamander Bay, Port Stephens.

NARRABEEN I (1886-1917): The first of eight Manly ferries to be built over a period of 36 years by Mort's Dock and Engineering Company, *Narrabeen I* was the last of the Port Jackson Steamship Company's double-ended paddlewheelers. Data: 239 tons, 160 ft x 22 ft x 9 ft 2 in, engine two-cylinder, compound surface condensing steam engine driving two paddlewheels, 65 hp, also built by Mort's at Balmain. Although this vessel spent 24 years as a passenger carrier, she was not quite big enough for the growing passenger traffic. From 1911 she was used to take cargo to Manly until sold in 1917. Of some interest, she was the last paddlewheel vessel acquired for the Manly ferry service and the last paddlewheeler to be withdrawn. Hulked in 1917.

NARRABEEN II (1923-28): A single-ended screw steamer, built by David Drake, of Balmain, for the Port Jackson & Manly Steamship Company's cargo service before the Spit Bridge was built. She was also used to take fishing parties outside the harbour. Sold to the Westernport Steamship Company in 1928, after the Spit Bridge was opened and the cargo service discontinued, and went to Victoria.

MANLY II (1896-1924): This vessel brought something new to ferry design as the first by naval architect Walter Reeks who introduced the double-ended screw steamers. She was built by Young, Son & Fletcher at Balmain, and had wooden hull and superstructure, two decks with turtle-backed bows, between which a promenade deck stretched over the main deck. There were two wheelhouses immediately fore and aft of the single funnel. Dimensions: 229 gross tons, 147 ft x 26 ft x 10 ft 5 in. The engine, built by Fawcett, Preston & Company, of Liverpool, England, was also the first triple-expansion steam engine in the Manly ferries. It produced 100 hp to drive a three-bladed gunmetal propeller at each end and give the ferry a speed of more than 14 knots. The *Manly*

was fast, although not popular because of vibration from her three-cylinder engines, and her small size was also against her, providing accommodation for only 820 passengers. The Port Jackson & Manly Steamship Company took her over with other rival assets when it became the supreme company in 1907 and fitted her with four-bladed propellers. The *Manly* was nearly wrecked when she broke down between The Heads in 1901 and had to be towed to safety from Old Man's Hat by the *Brighton*. The *Manly* gave 30 years of service before she was sold for £600 in 1924. Two years later her engines and boilers were taken out and refitted in the island trader SS *Madal*.

KURING-GAI (1901-28): This vessel was another step forward in design by Walter Reeks. *Kuring-gai* was built for the Port Jackson Co-operative Steamship Company Ltd by Mort's Dock & Engineering Company Ltd at Balmain in 1901, and was the shape of things to come in what was to be regarded as the typical Manly ferry. Data: double-ended steel and iron hull, wooden superstructure, two wheelhouses facing fore and aft each side of the funnel and, for the first time, gangway exits on the promenade as well as the main deck, two lifeboats on twin davits, 497 gross tons, length 175 ft, beam 31 ft, depth 13 ft 3 in, draught 10 ft 6 in, *Kuring-gai* had three-cylinder, triple-expansion steam engines driving a single propeller at each end, one pulling, the other pushing. These engines, of 85 hp, fed with steam from two Navy-type boilers, gave the *Kuring-gai* a speed of 15.66 knots on her trials. Her certificate was for 1221 passengers in good weather and 744 if it was rough. *Kuring-gai* cost £23 789 to build. She gave her original owner and the Port Jackson & Manly Steamship Company, which acquired her in 1907, a total of 27 years of good service until the arrival of the big new *Curl Curl* and *Dee Why* in 1928 phased her out. Sold to Newcastle Ferries Company Ltd for £8000, she carried passengers to and from Newcastle's Walsh Island Dockyard for some time and did other trips up the Hunter River to Raymond Terrace and made excursions to Broughton Island and Port Stephens. The United States forces bought her as a hulk in World War II and towed her to New Guinea for use as a store ship. When the war ended *Kuring-gai* was towed back to Newcastle and moored near the Hunter River bridge at Hexham, were she eventually sank into the mud. The rusted remains are still there.

BINNGARRA (1905-30): The first of the double-ended screw vessels to be developed from Walter Reeks' design of the *Kuring-gai* into what became the traditional Manly ferry type. Built by Mort's Dock & Engineering Company Ltd at Woolwich in 1905. Five others of similar design followed between then and

1922—*Burra Bra* (1908), *Bellubera* (1910), *Balgowlah* (1912), *Barrenjoey* (1913) and *Baragoola* (1922). The *Binngarra* was the first to have the wheelhouse placed fore and aft instead of on each side of the single funnel, a practice which ended with the *Kuring-gai*. The engines, of 133 hp, also built by Mort's Dock, were a considerable increase over the 85/800 hp of the *Kuring-gai*. Yet neither of these vessels, with top speeds of only about 13 knots, were really fast enough for the growing Manly traffic. *Binngarra* carried 1372 passengers. In 25 years of service she was reputed to have carried more than 30 million passengers in 98 279 trips to Manly. She was yard No. 31 at Mort's, official number 121108. Dimensions: 190.5 ft x 31.7 ft x 11.5 ft. Tonnage 442 gross/301 net. Sold in 1933, *Binngarra*'s engines were taken out and the hull was taken to Port Stephens for use as a timber store ship. During World War II the US Navy acquired the *Binngarra* and had her towed to New Guinea to be used there as a store ship. She was returned after the war and was eventually scuttled in the graveyard of ships south-east of Sydney Heads in 1946.

BURRA BRA (1908-42): The second of the *Binngarra* type built by Mort's Dock at Woolwich as yard No. 33, official number 121175, launched in 1908. Dimensions: 195.3 ft x 31.7 ft x 13.5 ft. Engines, also built by Mort's, 105/1200 hp. Passengers 1448. Speed 13.5 knots. Sold out of service in 1942, *Burra Bra* became, as HMAS *Burra Bra*, a torpedo target vessel for the RAAF at Jervis Bay. A 12-pounder gun was mounted on the after end of the upper deck. She had two Vickers machine guns on the bridge and carried four depth charges. Broken up in Sydney in 1950.

BELLUBERA (1910-73): Double-ended passenger ferry, steel hull, wooden superstructure, built with steam engines for the Port Jackson & Manly Steamship Company. Built at Woolwich by Mort's Dock & Engineering Company Ltd, who also built the engines. Dimensions: 210 ft x 32.2 ft x 14.1 ft. Draught 12 ft 2 in. Engines: three-cylinder, triple-expansion, driving a propeller at each end of vessel. Horsepower: nominal 123, indicated 1350. Gross tons 499, net tons 340. Speed 15 knots. Passengers 1529. Converted to diesel-electric propulsion in 1936 with four 5-cylinder diesel engines driving electric motors to single screws at each end of vessel. Engines built in Glasgow by Harland & Wolff under licence from Burmeister & Wain, of Copenhagen. Each developed up to 450 hp at 600 rpm. Speed after conversion, 16 knots. After being gutted by fire at the Kurraba Point works in 1936, the *Bellubera* was rebuilt at Cockatoo Dock in Sydney. In 1954 she was taken to the State Dockyard in

Newcastle, where some replating was done on the hull and the Burmeister & Wain diesels were replaced with three 7-cylinder diesel engines and electric motors by the British Thompson-Houston Company Ltd, of Glasgow, and the English Electric Company, of Rugby, England. *Bellubera*, built originally with open promenade deck, had this area enclosed later, except for a portion fore and aft. Her one long funnel was replaced with two short funnels after conversion to diesel-electric, one of the funnels being a dummy, just for appearance. *Bellubera* was taken out of service in November 1973, and after lying in Sydney Harbour for years was scuttled off Long Reef on 1 August 1980.

BALGOWLAH (1912-51): Almost identical ship to *Bellubera*. Same dimensions. Same builders at Woolwich. Launched 18 June 1912. In 40 years of service *Balgowlah* made 110 000 trips to Manly, covering 715 000 miles and averaging 17 440 miles a year. Taken out of service on 27 February 1951, laid up until sold to Stride's shipbreakers at Glebe in August 1953. The last coal burner in the fleet.

BARRENJOEY (1913-48): The *Barrenjoey* was rebuilt and re-engined between 1948 and 1951 and, renamed *North Head*, was still in service as a spare boat until 1986. The *Barrenjoey* was the last of three identical sister ships built by Mort's Dock & Engineering Company Ltd at Woolwich in Sydney. The other two were the *Balgowlah* and *Bellubera*. Their dimensions have been listed as: length 210 ft, beam 32.2 ft, depth 14.1 ft, draught 12.2 ft. The only difference seems to have been that *Barrenjoey* was credited with 500 gross tons, just one ton more than the other two, which were registered with 499. All had three-cylinder, triple-expansion steam engines built by Mort's at Balmain with nominal horsepower of 123, indicated 1400, driving a single screw at each end of the steel-hull vessels. The two boilers were of the Navy water-tube type, 19 ft 6 in long and 11 ft 8 in internal diameter, and each boiler was fired by three 18–in diameter corrugated furnaces. These were grand looking ships in their day with their single, long, white, black-banded funnel belching smoke as they churned up the harbour at 15 knots. Like the others, *Barrenjoey* had a passenger capacity of more than 1500 in fair weather, although it was supposed to be reduced to 978 in rough conditions. The promenade (top) deck of these three vessels was closed in during the 1930s to give greater passenger comfort, still leaving open portions at each end. *Barrenjoey* was launched 8 May 1913, the last of six vessels built by Mort's for the Manly ferry service between 1901 and 1913.

NORTH HEAD (Ex *Barrenjoey*) (1951-85): The *North Head* took shape at Mort's Dock, Balmain, between 1948 and 1951, during which time her steam engines were taken out and replaced with four 4–stroke, seven-cylinder diesel generators to supply current to four 500–bhp electric motors in pairs at each end of the vessel. These electric motors were to drive short propeller shafts through 5:1 reduction gearing. The new ferry had 2000 hp and speed up to 16 knots. The engines were built by the British Thompson-Houston Company Ltd and the English Electric Company. They were controlled direct from the bridge, the system replacing the Chadburn engine room telegraph system between the captain and the engineer. The steam-assisted steering with chains was replaced by electro-hydraulic steering. The external appearance and lines of the ship were changed considerably, too, giving the *North Head* a look somewhat like the *South Steyne*—two short funnels instead of a single long one and the hull built up above the sponson at each end into flared bows and stern. The wooden superstructure of the promenade deck was rebuilt in steel, and extended to enclose the open portions. Considerable replating and other work was done to the hull, no doubt the reason why the *North Head* lasted so long and gave such good service. Her hull was still considered to be in good condition in 1985—72 years after her launching as the *Barrenjoey* in May 1913. The conversion work cost a total of £275 000—quite a difference to the £32 000 the *Barrenjoey* cost to build in 1913. *North Head* entered service under her new name on 7 May 1951. Midway through 1985 *North Head* was being given an extensive refit, which, the Urban Transit Authority hoped, would keep her going for another few years as a spare boat to fill in while the *Freshwater, Queenscliff* and *Narrabeen* were in for their refits. Taken out of service in December 1985. Sold to Hobart interests in March 1987.

BEN BOLT (1912-24): Wooden cargo vessel built on the Bellingen River, New South Wales, in 1912 for the Port Jackson & Manly Steamship Company's flourishing Manly cargo trade. Length 91 ft 6 in, breadth 22 ft 7 in, depth 5 ft 1 in, 83 gross tons. Steam engine, 15 hp, driving a single screw. Sold after the opening of the Spit Bridge to Harbour Land and Transport Company Ltd. Believed to have been broken up in 1932.

BARAGOOLA (1922-83): The last of the one-funnel ships built by Mort's Dock for the Port Jackson & Manly Steamship Company, the *Baragoola* was launched at Balmain on 14 February 1922, and entered service on 3 September the same year. She was the last of the Binngarra class and the last Manly ferry built by Mort's. There were slight differences between her dimensions and those of her three predecessors. She was shorter, wider and slower. But she was a good sea boat and very popular with the public, as evidenced by the emotional farewell she was given on her retirement in 1983 after 61 years of good service. *Baragoola* was the only one of the Binngarra class built at Balmain. The others were built at Woolwich. The original gross tonnage of 498.04 was approximately one ton less than the *Balgowlah* and *Bellubera* and two tons less than the *Barrenjoey*. Her dimensions were: length 199.5 ft, beam 34.1 ft, depth 14 ft, draught 12.2 ft. Thus, she was 10.5 ft shorter than the *Barrenjoey*, but was 1.9 ft wider. The three-cylinder, triple-expansion steam engine, built by Mort's at Balmain, was of 112 nominal and 1300 indicated horsepower—not quite as powerful as the *Barrenjoey*, *Bellubera* or *Balgowlah*—and her speed was only 15 knots. Steam was supplied from two Navy water-tube type boilers. In the early 1930s pulverised coal was tried as furnace fuel, but the experiment was abandoned because the ship became covered with coal dust. During 1939 the *Baragoola* was converted to burn tar, but when tar became difficult to obtain during World War II the *Baragoola* returned to burning coal. She operated as a steamer for the last time in December 1958, when she was taken out of service and work began at Mort's Balmain works to convert her to diesel-electric propulsion with four English Electric seven-cylinder diesel generators driving electric motors at each end, similar to the plant in *North Head*, controlled direct from the bridge instead of via the Chadburn engine room telegraphs. The new equipment pushed her speed up to 16 knots. Otherwise, the main external difference was a short single funnel instead of the long steamer stack. She re-entered service as MV *Baragoola* in January 1961, and carried on until her retirement on 8 January 1983. In July 1985, the *Baragoola* was lying in Rozelle Bay, where a group of academics were restoring the vessel for possible use as a floating university. The project was abandoned in 1986 and the Baragoola was sold to Balmain interests.

DEE WHY (1928-68): *Dee Why* and *Curl Curl* were identical sister ships, built for the Port Jackson & Manly Steamship Company by Napier & Miller, of Old Kilpatrick, Scotland, to a design by naval architect E.H. Mitchell, suggested by W.L. Dendy, general manager of the Port Jackson & Manly Steamship Company. Both were double-ended, steel hull, passenger ferries with two long funnels set slightly for'ard of amidships. They were faster and more comfortable than earlier vessels, with a speed of more than 17 knots. Dimensions: gross tonnage 799.44, length 220 ft, breadth 35 ft 11 in, depth 14 ft 8 in, draught 12 ft 6 in. Engines built by David and William Henderson & Company Ltd, Glasgow, Scotland, inverted, direct-acting, four-crank, triple-expansion steam, driving a single screw at each end of the vessel. Horsepower: nominal 389, indicated 3200. Boilers: four single-ended Scotch type, back to back in pairs in two stokeholds, 11 ft 6 in long, 12 ft internal diameter. Two furnaces to each boiler, 3 ft 8 in internal diameter. Propellers: bronze, 9 ft 3 in diameter. Steering: steam assisted with chains. Chadburn engine room telegraphs. Boilers used coal, tar or oil fuel. Both *Dee Why* and *Curl Curl* left Scotland for their voyages to Australia with a Lloyds 100A1 certificate and Board of Trade steam 4 and 5 certificates. *Dee Why* was withdrawn from service and sold to Stride's shipbreakers at Glebe in July 1968, having given 40 years service on the harbour. Eight years later, on 25 May 1976, she was scuttled to form an artificial reef for fish north-east of Long Reef, not far from Dee Why, after which she was named.

CURL CURL (1928-60):

Details the same as for *Dee Why*. Arrived in Sydney from Scotland on 25 October 1928, and entered service 6 December. *Curl Curl* was probably the fastest of all the steam ferries. On her official trials in the Firth of Clyde on 24 May 1928, she did 17.561 knots, and on trials in Sydney Harbour on 11 November after arrival from Scotland she clocked 17.75 knots. On 26 January 1936 (Anniversary Day holiday), *Curl Curl*, with a full load of passengers, covered the seven nautical miles between Sydney and Manly in 22 minutes, which is better than 18 knots. This equalled the 22-minute record set by the first double-ended screw steamer, Manly, in 1912. *Curl Curl* was retired from service on 25 October 1960, and tied up, having become too costly to operate. Sold to Stride's shipbreakers in July 1963, *Curl Curl* was towed out and scuttled in the ship's graveyard south-east of The Heads in August 1969.

SOUTH STEYNE (1938-74):

The *South Steyne* finished her life as a Manly ferry after a fire gutted her at the Balmain ferry depot on 25 August 1974. The *South Steyne* was the vision of Port Jackson's general manager, W.L. Dendy, and was built by Henry Robb Ltd, of Leith, Scotland, from designs by Robb's chief draftsman, J. Ashcroft, in collaboration with Dendy. When launched on 1 April 1938 she was regarded as the biggest and fastest ferry boat in the British Empire, although actually she was not quite as fast as the *Curl Curl*. She was 1203.37 gross tons. Dimensions: length 220 ft, beam 38 ft, depth 14 ft 9 in, draught 12 ft 6 in. Engine: built by Harland & Wolff Ltd, Belfast, inverted direct action triple-expansion steam, driving a single propeller at each end of vessel. Horsepower: nominal 410; indicated 3250. Boilers: four single-ended, Scotch-type, oil burning, in pairs in one stokehold, 11 ft 6 in long with 12 ft internal diameter. Two

furnaces to each boiler, 3 ft 8 in internal diameter. Steam hydraulic steering controlled by a telemotor. Chadburn engine room telegraphs. Double-ended steel hull of riveted construction. Seven watertight bulkheads. Two funnels, one a dummy containing a water tank. Eight gangway exits on each of the main and promenade decks. Speed: official trials Firth of Forth 23 June 1938: 17.105 knots ahead, 17.23 knots astern. Sydney Harbour 21 October 1938: 17.1 knots. Certificates on leaving Scotland: Lloyds 100A1. Board of Trade steam certificates 4 and 5. Propellers: bronze 9 ft 3 in diameter. Passenger certificates: normal 1781, rough weather 1398, ocean cruises 998. After the retirement of the *Dee Why* in 1968, *South Steyne* was the only steam ferry on the harbour. Nearly 10 years after the fire ended her career as a Manly ferry, the *South Steyne* was towed to Newcastle and subsequently to Ballina, where more than $2 million was spent restoring her to top-class condition to enter a new life in Victoria as a cruise ship on Port Phillip Bay.

LADY WAKEHURST (1974-):

Built by Carrington Slipways, Tomago, Hunter River, near Newcastle, New South Wales, for the Public Transport Commission of New South Wales. Double-ended steel passenger ferry of 366 gross tons. Length 143 ft 8 in, breadth 33 ft 11 in, depth 10 ft 9 in, draught 7 ft 3 in. Diesel engines built by Mirrlees Blackstone Ltd, Stamford, England, two 4–stroke single-acting six-cylinder driving a single propeller at each end of vessel. Brake horsepower 810. Engines controlled from bridge. Speed 13 knots. Passengers 800. When built in October 1974, the *Lady Wakehurst* cost $750 000. Although designed for the inner harbour service, principally Mosman, the *Lady Wakehurst* went straight into relief duty on the Manly run, replacing *North Head* and *Baragoola* while they were given a repaint and refit, but a few months later, in January 1975, she was loaned to the Tasmanian Government for use as a Hobart harbour ferry after the collapse of the Derwent River bridge. *Lady Wakehurst* is the only Manly ferry to do commuter work in another capital city. While she was in Tasmania, a sister ship, *Lady Northcott*, was used as a relief boat on the Manly service. *Lady Wakehurst* returned from Tasmania in November 1977, and after an overhaul was added to the Manly service in January 1978, to provide a three-boat timetable for a three-month trial period. The service proved itself and until the arrival of the new Freshwater class ferries the *Lady Wakehurst* and *Lady Northcott* spent much of their time as Manly ferries. This was a job for which they were never designed, but foresight in modifying the height of the bows to handle heavy weather and providing extra gangway exits enabled them to fill in satisfactorily. In 1984 the *Wakehurst* was given two small drawbridge

In disgrace. The Freshwater, *hard and fast on the beach at Manly after failing to stop at the wharf. (John Darroch)*

The North Head *berthing at Circular Quay. (Bill Allen)*

MV Queenscliff *being launched at the State Dockyard, Newcastle, 4 December 1982. (John Darroch)*

gangways similar to those of the Freshwater class vessels.

LADY NORTHCOTT (1975-): Same statistics as *Lady Wakehurst*. Same builder. Spare boat on Manly service 1975-84. Mosman ferry since.

The Freshwater class

FRESHWATER (December 19, 1982), *QUEENSCLIFF* (July, 1983), *NARRABEEN III* (August 19, 1984), *COLLAROY* (August 22, 1988). Basically these are identical ships, *Freshwater* and *Queenscliff* built at the State Dockyards, Newcastle, and the *Narrabeen* and *Collaroy* built at Carrington Slipways, Tomago. They have a crew of seven and carry 1100 passengers on the harbour, 750 on ocean cruises. Length overall is 70.03 metres, breadth 13.06 metres, moulded depth 5.52 metres, draft 3.35 metres, displacement 1140 tonnes fully laden; speed 15 knots single engine, 18 knots both engines. All except *Collaroy* have two Diahatsu 8DSM-32 diesel engines rated at 2200 kw driving two lips controllable pitch propellers. *Collaroy* has two Diahatsu BDSM-32 diesels rated at 1940 kw. Because of this lower power, she does 14 knots on one engine and 17 on both. All vessels are a double ended single hull of welded steel construction. The upper cabin is of aluminium. All have radio and radar. *Collaroy* has features not common on her three sister ships which include:
● Open areas on the upper deck for better view.
● Stabilisers below waterline amidships for better passenger comfort on ocean cruises.
● A bar galley and food servery to provide meals on ocean cruises or charters.

The hydrofoils

The hydrofoils were of three types——PT-20 *(Manly I)*, PT-50 *(Fairlight, Palm Beach, Long Reef, Dee Why)*, RHS 140 *(Curl Curl)*, RHS

160F *(Manly II, Sydney)*. All except *Manly I*, which came from Hitachi Shipbuilding & Engineering in Japan, were built by Rodriquez Cantiere Navale, Sicily.

MANLY I (1965-80) Length 18.59m (61ft), 32 tonnes, 75 passengers. Engines one MTU 12V 493 DB rated 1350 bhp, speed 30 knots.

FAIRLIGHT (1966-84), *PALM BEACH* (1965-85), *DEE WHY* (1970-84), *CURL CURL* (1973) and *LONG REEF* (1978) were identical. Length 28.96m (95ft), 64 tonnes, 140 passengers. Twin propellers. Engines two MTU 12V 493DB rated 1350 BHP. Speed 35 knots. Dimensions of two other identical craft—*(MANLY II* and *SYDNEY)* were: Length 31.2m (102ft 4in), 90 tonnes, 235 passengers, twin propellers. Engines two MTU MB 16V 396TB83, each 1400 kw. Speed 38 knots.

The Jetcats

The three Jetcats in service up to October 1994 were:

BLUE FIN (July 16, 1990).

SIR DAVID MARTIN (December 21, 1990).

SEA EAGLE (March 1991).
Each, built in Cairns at a cost of $5.3 million, were designed to carry 280 passengers and a crew of four. Dimensions: Length overall 34.8 metres, breadth 10 metres, draft 1 metre, displacement 91 tonnes (Blue Fin 108), speed 30 knots. They are twin hull catamaran craft of welded aluminium construction and the cabin is of aluminium. Machinery: Two MWM TBD 604BV 16 engines developing 1675 kw, rated 2230HP, two Kamewa waterjets, one 40 KVA Stamford UCM coupled to a MWM D226B. All are equipped with radio and 32 mile radius radar.

The Captains

Although a good deal has been recorded about the ships of the Manly ferry service, very little is to be found about the men who manned them, which is a great tragedy because there must have been some colourful characters. This seems to have been true of much maritime history. We know a great deal about the voyages of Captain James Cook—but it is difficult to get any extensive picture of Cook himself because little was written about him personally. We are faced with a similar situation here. Even the staff records of the Port Jackson & Manly Steamship Company seem to have disappeared and with them has gone the names of people and their service details. From what sources are available have come a few clues. For instance, one captain of *The Brothers*. We know who he was, but nothing else about him. There are big gaps at various stages, so any attempt at a complete record is futile. However, here is the story, or what there is of it.

Captain J. Yuell is mentioned as master of *The Brothers*, no date given, and in 1876 **Captain J. Tyrrell** was master. Others in that early period include:

Captain J. Manse (*Emu I*) 1855.

Captain Molland (*The Phantom*) 1859-78.

Captain J. Wardlaine (*Breadalbane*) 1876.

Captain Pettit (*Goolwa*) 1871, (*Mystery*) 1876.

Captain A. Morton (*Mystery*) 1874, (*Royal Alfred*) 1876.

Captain J.H. Cork (*Manly I*) 1876.

Captain Roderick brought the paddlewheel ferry *Fairlight* out from Scotland in 1878 and also commanded the paddlewheeler *Brighton* on her voyage out in 1883, but Captain Roderick left the vessel at Malta and the rest of the voyage was taken over by the first officer, James Japp.

Captain Neil Meikleson was master of the PS *Fairlight* from when she went into service in 1878. Was in command when the ferry ran down a sailing boat off Middle Head in 1882, killing a boy in the boat.

Captain Sutherland (*Goolwa*) 1879.

Captain James Drewette, who died on 13 February 1928, was the master with the longest continuous service with the Port Jackson & Manly Steamship Company. He joined the service in 1891 and was the commodore skipper when he died. Reporting his death, the *Daily Telegraph* said:

His record was a splendid one and he was popular with all. It was while he was master of the *Brighton* in July 1901, that he showed sterling seamanship. During a heavy southerly gale, the steamer *Manly* met with a mishap to her machinery when between The Heads at night and was lying helpless. Captain Drewette came along in the *Brighton* and managed to get a line aboard the *Manly* just in time to tow her clear of Smedleys Point. For this performance, the Insurance Company presented Captain Drewette with a piece of plate. His comrades and all those associated with the company sincerely regret the loss of so fine an officer. His last ship was the *Barrenjoey*.

This was a sloppy piece of reporting. The *Manly* was saved by the *Brighton* at Old Man's Hat, not Smedleys Point. Nor did the 'Insurance Company' make the presentation. It was the Sydney Underwriters' Association.

Captain Percy Davies (*Manly II*) 1896. He was master of the *Manly II* when she broke down in 1901 and had to be rescued by the *Brighton* off Old Man's Hat.

Captain G.H. Goldie retired in June 1922, after 20 years' service and was presented with a gold watch and chain on behalf of the employees and a letter of thanks and a cheque from the Directors. Reporting the event, the *Sydney Morning Herald* said:

Through storm and calm for 20 years, Captain G.H. Goldie has been on the bridge of Manly steamers. Now, though a comparatively young man, he has resigned to go and live in Tasmania. During the time he was in command of Manly steamers he made 110 560 trips between the Village and the Quay, travelling about 780 000 miles. Millions of people have crossed The Heads under his care and no vessel commanded by him has figured in any kind of accident. During his time on the harbour, Captain Goldie has seen many changes. Fine houses have made their appearance where formerly there was only virgin bush and Manly has grown from a little village to one of the finest seaside resorts south of the line. The captain smiled at the recollection of the time when the Manly steamers running at night were guided to the village pier by a man with a red lantern. Having regard to their size, Captain Goldie asserts that the Manly steamers are the finest sea boats in the world. They could go anywhere with perfect safety, he says.

Captain Harold Gibson was one of the best known of the Manly skippers. He retired in November 1974, with nearly 30 years' service, mainly in the *South Steyne*. Harold Gibson was almost as famous on the harbour as his famous ship. It was a sad day for him when she was put out of service after the fire at Balmain, leaving him with little inducement to remain in the service, even if he had not passed retiring age some time before the government took over the Port Jackson & Manly Steamship Company—

without its last steamship. He came ashore finally on 29 November 1974, carrying his kit bag from the wheelhouse of the *Lady Wakehurst*. Harold Gibson was known unofficially as 'The Commodore', although there had been no official commodore since the position was discontinued in 1951.

He came to the Manly ferries from New Zealand, where he was born in 1899. He went to sea in the New Zealand training ship *Wakatere* when he was 15 and sailed in the crews of Pacific troop ships during World War I. His father, who lived to 92, had been to sea 'before the mast', as they said in those days. When Harold Gibson arrived in Sydney he had a New Zealand coastal master's ticket, which the then Sydney Harbour Trust would not accept, so he sat for a coastal ticket in Sydney and got it. Most Manly ferry skippers have a harbours and rivers ticket, which is all they need.

The steam ferries were Harold Gibson's life, especially the *South Steyne*. 'She was a real ship', he said in a newspaper interview the day he retired. 'Yes, she was a real ship—not just a ferry like these new diesel jobs.' Harold Gibson carried nearly 7 million passengers and was happy to say he had never lost one, even those who jumped overboard. One of his closest friends was George Marshall, who looked after the old skipper when he became very ill in later years. Of him, George said: 'One of the best captains we ever had. He was never in any accident, he was always very careful and very thorough. He was a gentleman and one of the most loved by all.'

Harold Gibson died at Marrickville on 17 March 1987. He was 87 years old.

Captain Keith Rosser was on the way to holding two records when this story was written, the youngest master in the fleet when he got his master's certificate and one of the longest with service as a captain. Keith Rosser joined the Port Jackson & Manly Steamship Company in 1949 as a yard boy, 14 years old and just out of school. He was soon a deck boy in the *Dee Why*, under a tough tutor in Captain Norman 'Scupper' Smith and had his master's ticket by the time he was 23—the youngest in 100 years of Manly ferries. He remained in the *Dee Why* as one of its masters for 10 years until it was retired to Stride's shipbreaking yards at Balmain in 1968. Keith Rosser had the sad task of taking the *Dee Why* on its last trip as a ferry. He served in most of the other ferries and, in later times, as one of the hydrofoil skippers, commanding the hydrofoil *Dee Why* for several years. In 1985 he went back to the ferries as one of the skippers of *Queenscliff*. The following year he became one of the longest serving captains, with 37 years in the Manly ferry service from yard boy to deck boy and then as one of the captains. If the line had a commodore up to his retirement it would have been Keith Rosser by virtue of service. He spent some of

his earlier years in the *Dee Why* under the last official commodore, Captain Harold Liley. Keith Rosser is one of the many who came up through the ranks, as it were, with the Port Jackson company in the days when they had to polish every bit of brass in the ship before they could think of becoming a master.

Captain Ron Hart was determined when he left school in 1954 that he would never work in a closed environment, so he took a deck job with Charlie Rossman's ferry service to Balmain from the Erskine Street wharf at the foot of King Street. He spent two years in the famous old pilot steamer *Captain Cook*, then, when he became 18, turned to the Manly ferries, like Keith Rosser, starting in the *Dee Why* with Captain Norman Smith. That was in 1956. Ron's long love affair with the *Baragoola* began in the 1950s when she was still a steamer, being used as the spare boat when one of the others was off. He worked in those days with men in the crews who had been deckhands for 30 years or more and Ron was a deckhand himself for several years before he crewed with Captain Russell Jones. Ron recalls:

If Rus had a deckhand who showed a bit of promise he would give him a hand to get his ticket. I did all my studying with him, under his guidance. I felt like turning it up a few times, but he encouraged me and I succeeded first time when I went for the test in March 1963.

Most men with new certificates had to wait years for their first command, but Ron Hart was lucky. A vacancy came up a few months later and he was given the *Bellubera*. How did it feel?

I remember the first trip very well. On the *Baragoola* I would practise berthing with Captain Jones looking over my shoulder, but when I went to berth the *Bellubera* for the first time on my own there was the dread realisation that nobody was there and I was all alone.

Ron Hart spent two years with the hydrofoil *Manly I* from 1965 to 1967 and then, in 1968, a permanent berth became available in the *Baragoola*, which was to be his ship for 15 years until it was taken out of service in January 1983. He was appointed to the *Queenscliff* after leaving the *Baragoola*.

Captain Russell Jones retired in 1986 as superintendent of operations after 35 years with the Manly ferries. His was not a case of boyhood ambition. He served his time as a metal moulder in a Sydney foundry. George Marshall gave him a start as a deckhand and three years later he got his ticket and became a relieving master in 1955. The following year Rus Jones was given a permanent appointment to the *Dee Why*, where he remained until 1965, when he was the first captain appointed to the hydrofoil service. After nine years of piloting the early hydrofoils, he came ashore in 1974 to the position of superintendent of operations—virtually the same position from which George Marshall had just retired as traffic manager.

Russell Jones is another who thinks the days of steam were the best. He served in the *Dee Why*, *Curl Curl*, *Bellubera*, *South Steyne*, *Baragoola* and *North Head* as well as the hydrofoils and several present-day skippers trained with him as deckhands. These include Ron Hart, Keith Rosser, David Stimson and Roger Smith. Captain Jones' career was long but uneventful in that he never had an accident, either in the ferries or hydrofoils.

Captain Alan Victor Hobbs, born in Bristol, England, went to sea when he was 15 and has been at sea ever since. He started in tug boats in the Bristol Channel in 1944 and while the war was still making life at sea hazardous he signed on old tramp steamers operated by Smiths out of Cardiff. Arriving in Australia in 1954 in a ship called the *Windsor*, Alan Hobbs came ashore and took a job with Nicholson Bros, later Stannards, working in tugs towing small ships up the Parramatta River. Eighteen years later, in 1972, he joined the Port Jackson & Manly Steamship Company and has been one of the captains ever since, nowadays in the *Freshwater*. His first Manly ferry was the *Baragoola*, then the *North Head* and the *South Steyne*. He also did some time in hydrofoils, but they are not his first love, for very good reason. Allan Hobbs had two bad days on the harbour. The worst day in his life he vows was in the *South Steyne* the day the Queen opened the Sydney Opera House, with the dense water traffic and a westerly gale making conditions very unpleasant. The other was the day he rounded Bradleys Head in the hydrofoil *Curl Curl* and smashed a catamaran sailing boat to pieces. That was his only collision in 12 years. Nowadays he prefers ferries to hydrofoils.

Captain David Stimson, well-known on the harbour as one of the senior Manly ferry captains, nowadays in the *Freshwater*, he was for years in the *North Head* as much a part of that ship as Ron Hart was of the *Baragoola*. He became a ferry master by chance. His original ambition was that of many boys—to be a train driver—and when he left school in the Sydney suburb of Leichhardt, where he grew up, he applied to the then Department of Railways for a job which would lead ultimately to driving trains. Dave Stimson was heartbroken when he was eliminated in tests for the railways. A slight eyesight defect in telling shades of pink was enough to eliminate him in those days. So, settling for an office job near Circular Quay, he spent his lunchtime watching the Manly ferries and one day he walked into the offices of the Port Jackson

& Manly Steamship Company to see whether there might be any vacancies for deck boys. To his surprise, Traffic Manager George Marshall told him to start as soon as possible. That was in 1962. After a couple of years working with young skippers like Keith Rosser and then Ron Hart, he decided that was the life for him. But deck boys had to wait until they were 21 to become deckhands and then serve three years as a deckhand before they could sit for a master's certificate—unless they went to sea, in which case the time spent on deck on the coast would count as time served for a ferry master's certificate. In 1965 Dave Stimson left the Manly company and went to sea in coastal ships—to New Guinea with Burns Philp, to Fiji with CSR, to Tasmania and the Northern Territory. He rejoined the Manly company in February 1970, and in June that year obtained his harbours and rivers ticket and, only 22 years of age, was appointed to the *North Head* as master, the youngest in the service. In 1977, as representative of the captains' union, the Merchant Service Guild, he was invited to discuss with the general manager of the Urban Transit Authority ferries division, Mr Tom Gibson, preliminary plans for a new style of ferry to replace the existing fleet and he and other captains contributed a good deal to the plans. Captain Stimson brought the three new ferries from Newcastle to Sydney on their delivery voyages and formally accepted the first of them—the *Freshwater*—in an official ceremony on behalf of the Urban Transit Authority. Although he spent so much time in the *North Head*, his favourite ferry was the *Bellubera*. Nowadays he has no regrets about that train-driving job. The ferries are his life.

Captain Ron Dickson, a deckhand on the *Bellubera*, was helmsman the night the *Bellubera* ran down the launch *Sydbridge* off Bennelong Point, killing its driver, Sidney Rose. He never got over the horror of that accident and although he went on and got his master's certificate and was regarded as a good skipper, the accident preyed on his mind. Eventually he resigned command and went back to work as a deckhand until 1976, when he retired and died soon after. To the day he died the memory of that launch rolling over under the bows of the *Bellubera* haunted him.

Captain Roger Smith comes from a long line of Manly ferry men, but he is the only one of the family to wear the captain's cap. His paternal and maternal grandfathers, his father and three uncles worked on the ferries. His mother's father, Jim Leonarda, had been a deckhand for 40 years when, aged 65, he retired. His own father was a deckhand for a long time—just how long Roger can't remember. Three uncles started with the Port Jackson & Manly Steamship Company as change boys—women do that job now, selling ferry turnstile tokens and hydrofoil tickets—and all the uncles graduated to become deckhands. Roger's father was the late Owen Smith. Roger's career began in 1956, when he joined the company as a deck boy. Five years later he became a deckhand and in 1967 he received his ferry master's certificate. His first command was the *North Head* and up to 1969 he had the *South Steyne, Dee Why, Bellubera* and *Baragoola*. Since 1969 Roger Smith has been a hydrofoil man, starting with the original little *Manly I* and working in all the hydrofoils to the big *Manly II* and the *Sydney*. In 1986 he had been 30 years in the Manly ferry service.

Captain Christopher Francis Hogan is another well-known figure on the ferries and, like Ron Hart, had a great affection for the *Baragoola*, in which he served most of his time on the Manly run, although he was occasionally on the *North Head*. When this was written he was one of the three skippers in charge of the *Queenscliff*. Chris Hogan was attracted to the ferry life during travel to and from Manly in his younger years. He became a ferry master in the inner harbour service of Sydney Harbour Ferries Pty Ltd after three years as a deckhand from 1969, and in 1974 transferred to the Port Jackson & Manly Steamship Company, which was then operating the inner harbour ferries for the State Government. Captain Hogan had only two months with the company before it, too, was taken over by the government in 1974.

Three people tried to commit suicide by jumping from the *Baragoola* while Captain Hogan was on the bridge. One succeeded. The other two were recovered alive. Chris Hogan feels that his job has been very satisfying, despite the problems of berthing at Manly in strong winds, the odd morning fog and the weekend sailing boat races, in which some risk their lives by going across the bows of ferries rather than give up their position in the race. Like all the others, he appreciates the modern comforts of amenities and accommodation aboard the Freshwater class ferries. But in bad weather he preferred the deeper draft of the *Baragoola*. 'She carried less leeway', which, in landlubber's terms, means the sideways drift of a vessel caused by wind and sea.

Captain Dick Kirkwood is a hydrofoil man whose life on the harbour goes back to the early 1950s, when he was a deckhand. In 1968 he went to Queensland, where he worked on charter boats in the Barrier Reef and gained a master's ticket. In 1983 he returned to Sydney and the Manly ferries and has been with them and the hydrofoils ever since. Captain Kirkwood became interested in the ferries when, as a boy, living in Hunters Hill, he travelled on the inner harbour vessels serving that route up river. Nowadays, like several other skippers, he lives a long way from the harbour, travelling to and from Berowra every day to work.

Of the big hydrofoils *Manly* and *Sydney* he says: 'They are fine vessels and I enjoy being with them.'

Captain Max Barton has spent all his Manly service since 1979 with hydrofoils. Previously, he was nine years with the inner harbour ferries in the *Lady Edeline* and *Lady Woodward*. He had a background of experience in small ships and trawlers—with the American small ships after the war, in a steam schooner which carried lumber to New Guinea and through the Pacific and the Philippines. For some years he skippered large private motor yachts for a Sydney hotel owner. Max Barton has been a hydrofoil skipper exclusively and has led a comparatively uneventful life in the Manly service, not having been involved in some of the colourful incidents of the ferry men. The only thing that happened to him was when he was taking the inner harbour veteran *Lady Edeline* up river under the Harbour Bridge one night and an Italian prawn trawler ran under his bows.

Captain Peter Loosemore made maritime history when he berthed the *Lady Wakehurst* at Manly wharf on Monday 11 January 1978, according to the *Manly Daily* of the following day, which said:

He would be one of the few captains to be given a hero's welcome on his first day in command of a vessel. It was to the cheers of a big crowd and the music of a jazz band that the 26-year-old captain stepped ashore to a mayoral welcome and garlands of flowers from a bevy of beach belles. It was only his third trip in charge and he admitted that it was a nerve-racking experience manoeuvring the ferry into position with several thousand sightseers looking on.

It was an important occasion because the *Lady Wakehurst*, back from three years on loan to Hobart while the Tasman Bridge was repaired, was being added to the Manly ferry service, which since 1974 had languished as a two-boat service. The whole town turned out to welcome her, as it were, and Peter Loosemore, on his first day as a captain, was certainly a hero. Peter Loosemore had graduated through the ranks as a deckhand up to Christmas 1977, but he had also been to sea for eight years in the British Merchant Navy. When this was written, Captain Loosemore was attached to the hydrofoil service.

Captain Bill Thomas, yet another of the hydrofoil skippers, served also in the Manly ferries. An Englishman, native of Liverpool, he joined the Port Jackson & Manly Steamship Company in 1962 with a foreign-going master's certificate after some years at sea and was for two years an assistant master to Captain Harold Gibson in the *South Steyne*. Having handled ocean-going cargo ships, the *Steyne* made him feel quite at home, but in 1964, for family reasons, he returned to England. In 1970 the company had need of a skipper with his experience in the *South Steyne*, and George Marshall induced Bill Thomas to return to Sydney and help with the ocean cruises in the *South Steyne* to Broken Bay. Of him, George Marshall says:

> He was an excellent master. One of the best. On the ocean cruises he would mingle with the passengers and chat to them and make them feel as if they were on an ocean liner. He was always a thorough gentleman.

Captain Thomas has another quality of which few would be aware. He is a very talented artist and has done some beautiful paintings of the Manly ferries, hydrofoils and ships in the harbour.

Because records of the Port Jackson & Manly Steamship Company have been lost since the transfer of the Manly ferries to the State Government—first the Public Transport Commission and later the Urban Transit Authority—it has not been possible to get detailed information about the many fine masters who have been in the service. It must be emphasised that the space given to those mentioned from here on does not indicate any degree of importance compared with others. A bit more information was available about some. That is all. Here is the record as far as it was available:

Captain John Hart was the first master of the *Balgowlah* when she was commissioned in 1912 and first master of the *Baragoola* when she was added to the fleet in 1922. No relation to Captain Ron Hart, master of the *Baragoola* until she was retired in 1983. Captain John Hart started with the Manly ferries back in the 1890s. He was master of the ferry *Manly II* in 1896.

Captain Harold Liley was the last official commodore of the Port Jackson & Manly Steamship Company. He served mainly in the *Curl Curl* and the *Dee Why*, which he commanded for many years. Captain Lyley was involved in several incidents—principally a collision with the harbour ferry *Kirrule* off Kirribilli Point, and another clash in the same area with the tug *Himma*. Captain Lyley was one of the best known masters on the harbour over a long period.

Captain Alex McIntosh was one of the masters of the *South Steyne* before he retired. He was in charge when the *Steyne* went through the harbour pool at Manly.

Captain Tom Thornton served for many years. In his later years he stepped down from the bridge at his own request and finished his time as a wharfinger at Manly.

Captain Bill Chapple is remembered as one of the old brigade. According to George Marshall, Bill Chapple knew the roster of every man in the company and could give it to you verbatim at any time.

Captain J. Clarke was master of the *Baragoola* in 1926.

Captain George Clark was skipper of the *Curl Curl* in the late 1930s.

Captain Charles McKinnon was opposite number in the *South Steyne* to Harold Gibson for many years. He was with the Australian National Shipping Line previously and had a foreign-going ticket. When the *South Steyne* was put out of service Charles McKinnon transferred to the *North Head* until he retired in 1982. He died in 1984.

Captain Fred Tocchini served his time as a deckhand and became a skipper. He retired in the late 1950s and went to live in Queensland. He had a sea-going foreign ticket.

Captain Frank Farrugia spent 41 years in the Manly ferry service, during which time he estimated he made 85 000 crossings of the harbour, without an accident. After he retired, Frank Farrugia went to live at Narooma, on the south coast of New South Wales. He died at Batemans Bay on 28 March 1986, aged 76.

Captain Alfred Rowlings was sent to England to come out with the *South Steyne* as mate on the delivery voyage from Scotland and stayed on as a captain in Sydney. He had a foreign-going ticket. Captain Rowlings was the first to take the *South Steyne* on the ocean cruises and continued with her until he died.

Captain Laurie Bruce spent years on the *South Steyne*, first as a deckhand and later as master.

Captain John Brew obtained his master's ticket with the Port Jackson company and later left to work with the Maritime Services Board.

Captain Norman Smith, a real Manly identity in his day, started with the company about 1913 and was a deckhand until he enlisted in the Army in March 1916, and went to France. Discharged in July 1918, Norman Smith returned to the Manly ferries, serving again as a deckhand until 1921, when he gained his master's ticket. Ron Hart, who served with Captain Smith as a deckhand, still has the receipt for Smith's examination fee of $1 10s 0d, dated 29 June 1921. Ron Hart and Keith Rosser both served their time with Smith, known as 'Scupper Smith', although nobody seems to know why. Ron Hart recalls:

> The facilities were quite grim in those days. There was only cold water in the captain's cabin behind the wheelhouse and when we finished the last run at night he would put a tub of water on the stove, strip off and have a hot wash.

Norman Smith retired in 1957, having served with the Port Jackson & Manly Steamship Company a total of 42 years, deducting the two years he was at World War I.

Captain Jack Mann served for many years in the *Bellubera* until he had eyesight problems. He came ashore then and worked until retirement as a gate hand at Circular Quay.

Captain V. Nixon was master of the *Bellubera* in 1914. In 1936 he was in command of the *Curl Curl* when she encountered fog and ran aground at Bradleys Head.

Captain Bill Harris was in the service for many years, principally on the *Dee Why* and the *Bellubera*. He was in command of the *Bellubera* in 1941 on the night it ran down the launch *Sydbridge* off Bennelong Point, killing its driver, Sidney Rose. He was also skipper of the *Dee Why* when it went aground in Obelisk Bay on Christmas night, 1946, in an unseasonal fog bank. Eric Gale said Bill Harris was one of the best skippers he knew when he was in the ferries as an engineer, mainly because his berthings were so good that he never hit the wharf. It was said that W.L. Dendy gave him an extra pound a week because of what he saved the company in damage to sponsons, wharves and ropes.

Captain Jack Hickey, a former tug man, did not stay long with the ferries.

Captain Robert Walker, ex-RAN, had a foreign-going certificate. He did not serve long with the ferries.

Captain George Cladinbowl was one of the youngest to get his master's ticket after working as a deckhand. He served in the ferries during the World War II years.

Captain Arthur Lucas, came from the Middle East. No long period of service.

Captain Richard Litt served his time as a deckhand and went through to get his master's ticket. His last ship was the *South Steyne*.

Captain Frank Walker was a foreign-going certificated master who went to an administrative position.

Captain Daryl Hatch was in the *South Steyne* and left the service to work with the Maritime Services Board.

Captain Ted Cochrane came to Sydney after working in the *North Head* during her excursions in Port Phillip Bay in Melbourne in 1967. He left after a short stay with the Sydney ferries.

Captain Noel Heath is still in the service, mainly on MV *Freshwater*.

Captain Garry O'Connell worked his way from deckhand to master.

Captain Ray Cox left the Manly ferries to go to CSR.

Captain Geoff Hayward left the ferries to go with the 60-miler colliers working between Sydney and Newcastle.

Captain Laurie Inkster came from the Shetland Islands and was with the Manly ferries from 1946 until the early 1950s.

Captain Tony Slattery. No long service.

Captain Max Tadross is still in the service, mainly on the hydrofoils.

Captain B. Brown served his time with the Manly ferries, and is still there, on the hydrofoils.

Captain William Mitchelmore was master of the *Binngarra* in 1927 when she collided with the interstate ship *Lady Isobel* near Bradleys Head.

Captain Ken Martin served only a couple of years.

Captain Walter Henry Dohrn the older of two Captain Dohrn, father and son, who were both well-known in the Manly ferry service. Wally Dohrn senior collapsed and died on the bridge of the *Bellubera* crossing The Heads going to Manly on 6 February 1945.

Captain Wally Dohrn (Jnr), the son of Walter Henry Dohrn was also well-known in the Manly service. Left the ferries in the 1970s for a position with the Maritime Services Board.

Captain Tim Aitchinson came to the ferries with a coastal master's certificate, and was on the *South Steyne* for a while.

Captain Keith Ridgeway worked through the company for his master's ticket and eventually went to Queensland.

Captain Bill Benecke was with the Port Jackson & Manly Steamship Company between 1947 and 1969, mainly in the *North Head*.

Captain Jim Shimeld started as a deckhand in 1955 and got his master's certificate about 1958. He was mainly in the *Dee Why* and *North Head*. Captain Shimeld retired in 1972 and went to Warwick in Queensland, where he died a few years later.

Captain Norman Gordon worked for a brief time after 1965 in the *Dee Why*.

Captain Fred Pocock served 35 years with the Port Jackson & Manly Steamship Company, starting as a deckhand. His main service was with the *Bellubera* and *North Head*.

Captain Albert 'Digger' Villiers was with the Port Jackson company before World War I, in which he fought in France. During his war service he was affected by gas. Captain Villiers returned to the Manly ferries after the war and served for about 43 years. In 1961, a few months before he was due to retire, he collapsed and died on the bridge while taking the *Bellubera* from Circular Quay to Kurraba Point for refuelling.

Captain Jack Parsons came through as a deckhand and got his master's ticket in 1955, but left to go into business ashore for 10 years. He came back in 1965 and was relieving skipper under Ron Hart in the *Baragoola* and the hydrofoil *Manly I*. He retired in 1968.

Captain Peter Grant came from the east coast of England, and had two short periods of service in the *South Steyne* up to 1965. He left to work with dredges in New Guinea.

Twenty-six captains came through the Port Jackson &

Manly Steamship Company from deckhands to masters. They are Captains Dickson, Harris, Ridgeway, Brew, Inkster, Thornton, Chapple, Norman Smith, Roger Smith, Brown, Tocchini, Farrugia, Bruce, Litt, Stimson, Rosser, Mann, Shimeld, Benecke, Ron Hart, Jones, George Cladinbowl, Peter Loosemore, Garry O'Connell, Pocock and Parsons.

On Shore

Ships don't move only by the work of the men who crew them. Behind their operations are those on shore who manage the business side of things and, as has to be done with ships like the Manly ferries, berth the vessels and keep them running. Here is part of the story—as much as can be gathered—about some of the people who managed the ships and kept them going.

Management

F. J. Doran was general manager of the Port Jackson & Manly Steamship Company in its early days when some of its most famous ships were built at Mort's Dock. He was there through the building of the *Balgowlah*, *Bellubera*, *Barrenjoey* and *Baragoola*. Mr Doran was general manager until 1925.

Walter L. Dendy was the man who built the Port Jackson & Manly Steamship Company to the peak of its long reign on Sydney Harbour. He was general manager from 1925, later managing director up to 1948, when he died, but his association with the company went back longer than 1925. Walter Dendy was born in South Australia in 1876. When he was 14 he ran away from home and went to sea, serving 'before the mast' until he was 20. Then he joined the Manly ferry company in Sydney in 1897 as a junior clerk.

Dendy had the right background to take charge of administration, having served his time at sea and through the company's offices ashore. As much as is known about him is told in the first chapter of Part IV, A New Star is Born. For a man who was so much in the public eye in his day, little was written about him when he died. 'He was a big man, a tall man, a strong man—both in physique and in mind,' according to Brian Verey, who knew Dendy for many years. 'He was a man of a few words who demanded respect and good manners from everyone'—and got it. He often clocked ferries in and out of the wharf. They had to run on time, a tradition which remains. Long after W.L. Dendy has gone, the Manly ferries keep their timetable better than any other public transport in Sydney.

His was the hand behind the design of the big steam ferries *Dee Why* and *Curl Curl* and—the greatest of them all—the *South Steyne*. His dream for developing tourism in Broken Bay and the Hawkesbury River never material-

ised, but the concept was good and others are taking it up nowadays. Walter Dendy was a leader and everyone in the company gave him loyalty. To them, W.L. Dendy was the Port Jackson & Manly Steamship Company and when he died it began to die, too. But times have changed and nearly 40 years after Dendy's death the Manly ferries are coming into their own again. New ships have been built and more are planned. The tradition that grew up with Dendy will remain, despite the ascendancy of industrial might over passengers' rights.

Claude Ewen Cameron, generally known as Brigadier Cameron, succeeded W. L. Dendy as general manager after Dendy died in 1948. Although Cameron was not as colourful a figure as Dendy, he played a very important part in control of the ferries at a very difficult time. Cameron took over in the post-war years when the ferries were beginning to be affected by the end of petrol rationing and the introduction of direct bus services from the northern beaches to the city. Cameron had been secretary of Sydney Ferries Ltd before the war and Dendy noted and appreciated his ability, so much so that when Cameron returned from the war in 1945, he was appointed general manager of the Port Jackson company and remained in that position under Dendy as managing director until 1948, when he became managing director. Those who worked with Cameron said he inspired great loyalty in the whole staff. He knew every man in the company. The employees, in their turn, would do almost anything for him. He had few industrial problems. Brigadier Cameron retired from the Port Jackson & Manly Steamship Company in 1964 when it was taken over by the Needham group.

J. C. Needham. In 1964 a group of businessmen bought the controlling interest in the Port Jackson & Manly Steamship Company and replaced the old management and Board of Directors. The new owners were two solicitors, W.G. Hoyle and R.E. Martin; Neil Barrell, an accountant, and Bjarne Halvorsen, of Halvorsen boats. With them came J.C. Needham as managing director. Needham had some experience with small inner harbour ferries, including the Hegarty 'Star' ferries to Kirribilli and Lavender Bay. He carried on after the Public Transport Commission took over the ferries for the New South Wales Government in 1974 until succeeded by Captain Tom Gibson. Mr Needham died on 11 December 1986.

Reginald Dyer was the last manager of the Port Jackson & Manly Steamship Company. He had been secretary of the company until the take-over by Brambles in 1971, after which he was working between the ferry company and Brambles. He became manager of the Port Jackson assets left with Brambles after the Public Transport Commission took over the ferries. He wound up the ferry company's affairs and retired in 1974. This ended more than 100 years of the Manly ferries under what was virtually the one company, although its name changed slightly a few times. The company had a bank account at the Bank of New South Wales Royal Exchange branch in Pitt Street all that time.

Arthur Roy Butterfield was one of the company secretaries under Walter Dendy. When it looked as if the Needham group would succeed in its take-over bid for the Port Jackson company, Cameron had Butterfield transferred to the Sydney Harbour Transport Board as general manager of the inner harbour ferries, which the Port Jackson & Manly Steamship Company was managing for the State Government. Butterfield was in that position until Phillip Shirley came into the Public Transport Commission as commissioner.

Traffic and Engineering

Most ferry travellers on the inner harbour think of deck-hands as the fellows who lasso wharf bollards with a rope, tie up the ferry and push a little gangway on to the wharf to let passengers disembark. On the much bigger Manly vessels, where the ropes have to be hauled on to the wharf by men who catch a smaller rope thrown to them by the deckhands on the ferry, their conception of a wharfinger is the fellow who catches the small rope, hauls the big rope on shore and puts its noose over the wharf bollard. Actually, the wharfinger is far more important than that. In the Port Jackson days the wharfinger could tell the captain what to do and he controlled ticket sellers, gate staff, and was responsible for replacing ferry crew in emergencies. If somebody was off sick, he had to find somebody else in a hurry. It is still more or less like that. The wharfinger has to see that the vessels are berthed properly and the passengers are disembarked and embarked safely.

George Marshall was overseer of all these operations and more. He was traffic manager for nearly 30 years, first with the Port Jackson & Manly Steamship Company and for four years before his retirement with the government control of the ferries.

George had grown up with boats and boatbuilding in the Palm Beach boatshed of the famous Goddard family. They were also operators of the Pittwater ferries, which W.L. Dendy bought for the Port Jackson company in 1942. George Marshall remained with the Port Jackson company until he went into the Army and when he returned in 1946 he was transferred to Sydney and worked on the wharf at Circular Quay with Bill Little, who was then traffic manager. Little had replaced Arthur Kiss, who was the first traffic manager. George Marshall was the third and last. After his retirement the position was retitled superintendent of operations after it had become superintendent of terminals when the government control began.

Like Dendy, George Marshall knew his job and the men with whom he worked. It worked, he said, because he had the best crew in the world. He said:

These people—masters, engineers, wharfingers—had been there for years. They had been taught their jobs properly and knew what they were doing. During the years I was there they gave a service second to none.

William Little was traffic manager before George Marshall. He had previously been in charge of the cargo service from Woolloomooloo to Manly in the days before the Spit Bridge. Of him, George Marshall said:

When I came back from the war in 1946 I was put on the wharf at Sydney and given to a fellow named Bill Little who had been with the company all his working life and who knew more about ferries than any man I have ever known.

Allen Arthur Conwell. Quite a few families have had more than one generation working with the Manly ferries through their working lives. Three generations of the Conwell family gave a total of 146 years. Allen retired in 1984 only six weeks short of 50 years, some of it as a deckhand, but mostly as a wharfman at Circular Quay. His father, George Conwell, had 44 years' service and his grandfather, John Conwell, worked with the ferries for 52 years.

These were the men who worked in the days when things were really tough. Crew slept in a corner of the foc'sl. There were no such things as individual cabins for each deckhand and hot and cold showers. Captain Wally Dohrn collapsed and died in the arms of Allen's father, George, on the bridge of the *Bellubera* as they crossed The Heads and George, who was helmsman, took the ferry into Manly. Allen's workmate, Tom Hancock, died in his arms on No. 3 wharf at Circular Quay. Allen Conwell started as a change boy, giving change for the turnstiles at Circular Quay, worked as a deckhand and later a wharfinger under four general managers—Dendy, Cameron and Needham (Port Jackson) as well as Tom Gibson (Urban Transit Authority).

Charles Usher came from another Manly ferry family. Charlie Usher was 50 years with the Manly ferries on 2 October 1985, and of that 50 years he had spent 33 years on the wharf at Manly. His father was a wharfinger with Sydney Ferries for 48 years at Milsons Point, McMahons Point and Lavender Bay. Charlie's grandfather was a skipper on the old 'horse punts', the common name in the old days for the vehicular ferries between Fort Macquarie, where the Opera House is now, and Milsons Point. Two uncles were skippers in the inner harbour ferries—Sid Green and Bill Thomas—another uncle was an engineer and two more were firemen in the steam ferries. The tradition will be carried on. Charlie has a son, Phillip Usher, who is a deckhand on the *Freshwater* with Captain Alan Hobbs.

As a boy, Charlie used to play on the 'horse punts'. He worked for some years as a deckhand on the *Burra Bra* and later the *Dee Why*. Like Allen Conwell and others who have spent much time on the ferry wharves, Charlie Usher saw many aspects of human tragedy. He saw two people die—one jumping off a ferry and the other trying to jump on. He was a deckhand on *Burra Bra* one morning in 1938 and as it moved in alongside the wharf at Circular Quay a schoolboy jumped off. The boy missed the jump and went down between the wharf and the ferry, right in front of where Usher was standing. Horrified, he grabbed the boy's head, which was the only part of him visible above the sponson. The head was all Usher had when the ferry moved out enough to leave a gap.

One night he was deckhand on the *Dee Why*, going into Circular Quay for the last trip to Manly. A man ran down the wharf, obviously thinking the ferry was going out instead of coming in, and tried to jump aboard. He hit his head on a bollard and fell into the water. He was dead when they fished him out. These were horrifying experiences.

Charlie Usher has some memories, too, of thankless rescues. One cold winter morning in June he dived overboard from the *Dee Why* and rescued a fellow who had jumped in as they crossed The Heads. A week later the fellow made sure of it. This time he cut his throat.

George McNamara another of the old brigade, retired in 1974 after 49 years' service with the Port Jackson & Manly Steamship Company, the Public Transport Commission and the Urban Transit Authority. George started in 1925 as a change boy and worked on the manual turnstiles until the company automated them after the Harbour Bridge opened. Then he worked at the Kurraba Point depot until 1940, when he returned to the Quay on gate duty. He spent four and a half years in the Army during the war.

Frank Conroy worked on the gates at Circular Quay for 33 years until bad health forced his early retirement. He died in December 1984.

Other wharf staff include: **George Rochester** who was with the company for more than 20 years at Sydney; **Arnold Smith**, wharfinger at Sydney for many years and an uncle of hydrofoil captain Roger Smith; **George Bradshaw**, wharfinger at Manly and Sydney after being a deckhand in the fleet for many years; **Fred Hancock**, one of four brothers who worked for the Port Jackson & Manly Steamship Company, he lived at Manly and worked there and at Circular Quay; **Bob Basham**, a fireman in the steam ferries who came ashore when diesel replaced steam and spent some years as a wharfinger at Sydney and Manly; **Frank Barker**, wharfinger at Manly, known as 'The Count' because of his fastidious dress; **Geoff Miller**, retired after many years as a wharfinger at Sydney; **Billy Field**, wharfinger at Manly; **Jim Turley**, wharfinger at Manly; **Kevin Campbell** had his master's ticket, but never used it, worked as a wharfinger at Manly for some years and then went to work with the Maritime Services Board; **Ron Roberts**, wharfinger at Manly; **Vincent Spiteri**, well-known figure on the gate at Circular Quay.

The captains have all the glamour, but without these men on the wharves the ferry service would not operate. And the job must be worthwhile. The evidence is in the numbers from the same families who have made it their life's work and the long years they have stayed in the job.

An essential part of the team was the engineering and works depot at Kurraba Point in the Port Jackson days. Nowadays this work is done in the Urban Transit Authority depot at Balmain, formerly the workshops of the old Sydney Ferries Ltd. Balmain, union-dominated in the government set-up, is plagued by strikes and work bans which frequently keep ferries and hydrofoils out of service for incredibly long periods. George Marshall tells of the contrast:

At Kurraba Point we had absolutely the best group of tradesmen around the waterfront in those days—shipwrights, boilermakers, blacksmiths, joiners, fitters and turners and a reserve of firemen and deckhands. In the whole time I was with the company there was never a stoppage or even a stop-work meeting at Kurraba Point. Some of them had served their time as apprentices with us and spent all their working lives there without a stoppage until the works was transferred to Balmain.

In charge at Kurraba was **Duncan McMillan**. He was Dendy's right-hand man. He was an outstanding engineer and played a big part as adviser in the building of the *South Steyne*. His assistant was Eric Gale. Eric never moved unless he ran. He and McMillan were a wonderful pair and between them and the staff they had at Kurraba Point they really made the place work. Their main object was not to miss a trip.

An example of this was the night when, at about 10 pm, the *Dee Why* overshot in berthing at Manly and went through the tourist bureau on the back part of the wharf. The *Dee Why* came to a stop with a couple of tonnes of smashed concrete in the steerage and a hole in the port bow through which a man could walk. The ferry was taken back to the works and she reappeared on one of the earliest trips in the morning with a plate over the hole, painted green to match the hull colour. The concrete was still there. They got it out later. But the *Dee Why* did not miss any of the morning peak trips, mainly because of the organisation at the Kurraba works. A ferry sent to Balmain after a similar accident today certainly would not be back on the run next morning.

Eric Gale, born in 1893, had a first-class foreign-going engineer's ticket when he applied for a job with the Port Jackson & Manly Steamship Company in 1933, having served his time in the Colonial Sugar Refining Company's SS *Fiona*, travelling between Sydney, Newcastle and Fiji. Ashore in the depression year of 1933 with no job and a wife and four children, Eric applied to the Port Jackson company without any success. As he was leaving the Kurraba depot, looking rather gloomy, one of the workmen stopped him and after hearing his story told him to come back on the following Monday morning, when the *Baragoola* was coming in for a complete overhaul. 'I know there is a job here for a turner,' the man said. 'Go and see McMillan and tell him you want the turner's job and don't tell him anything unless he asks you a question.' Eric did as he was told and got the job. Not long after that an engineer was wanted for an excursion with the *Burra Bra* and Eric confessed that he held a first-class foreign-going ticket.

Nowadays the annual refit of a Manly ferry at Balmain takes at least six weeks. Eric said:

We would send a vessel up to the dock one morning, she would come back the next day with the bottom done and we would have her back in service as good as new within a week.

Eric Gale had as his assistant **Andrew Faulds** and then **Bill McCubbay**, who became works supervisor when Gale retired in 1955. Eric Gale had a top engineer in **Lew Maxwell**, still living in Sydney at this time. Lew was lucky to be alive. He nearly died in the *Bellubera* fire in 1936. Dendy sent Maxwell to England to select diesel-electric engines for the *Bellubera*, *Barrenjoey* and *Balgowlah*, but the *Balgowlah* never got the diesel-electric machinery which went instead to the *Baragoola*, and the *Balgowlah* finished her days as a steamer—the last coal-fired ship in the fleet. One of her engineers was **Bill Irvine** who says he spent five of the happiest years of his life between 1944 and 1949 with the ferries in the Port Jackson days. Bill was a steam man with a long back-ground of the sea when he became chief engineer in the *Balgowlah*. He went to sea first in 1937 with the Port Line in the flagship, *Port Wellington*, as second refrigeration engineer in charge of 10 000 tons of frozen meat around Cape Horn, where 10 firemen had to try to keep their feet while shovelling 10 tons of coal a day each, as the coal-burning ship rode what Bill says were 70-ft waves.

Back in Sydney in 1940, Bill Irvine found a berth as a junior engineer among the 80 engineer officers of the *Queen Mary*, in Sydney Harbour to transport troops to Suez—5000 at a time. Later, the *Queen Mary*, built to carry 1000 passengers, was ferrying 15 000 American troops across the Atlantic to Europe, the largest number of people ever to be transported in one ship. He was in the engine room of the *Queen Mary* in 1942 when, in convoy off Northern Ireland, she sliced through the HMS *Curacao*, killing 300 of the 400 in the British warship's crew. The *Queen Mary*, with 10 000 American troops aboard, dared not stop in that submarine alley and just had to keep going.

When Bill left the *Queen Mary* in Sydney in 1944 to join the *Balgowlah* as chief engineer, it was, as he says, going from the sublime to the ridiculous, leaving the greatest ship in the world to go to the engine room of an old coal-burning ferry. But they were happy years and he had no regrets, although he could see the end of the steam days approaching and left in 1949 to go back to sea in the coastal passenger ship, MV *Duntroon*, to get his diesel qualification. That done, Bill Irvine came ashore and retired eventually from a position with the Shell oil company as a diesel engine consultant.

These are only a few of the men who have kept the ships going, sharing little of the glamour of the upper decks, where the Port Jackson company made the masters all wear gold-braided uniforms and caps. Eric Gale recalls:

They insisted that the fellows below deck were smart, too. We had to wear white overalls, which was ridiculous. I worked all one night converting a tar burner to a coal burner and came up next morning covered in black as the first passengers were embarking. A couple of women screamed and one almost fainted.

To Eric Gale, Lew Maxwell, Harold Gibson, George Marshall and many other old-timers of the Port Jackson & Manly Steamship Company, this book is dedicated. They left a tradition.

Acknowledgements

No book is ever written without the help of many who know things the author does not know, especially a book of this kind, where the story depends on those who can tell what happened or who knew the ships and the men involved. I acknowledge gratefully the help I have received from so many who, like me, love the Manly ferries and want to see their romantic record kept for posterity. The Manly ferries deserve a prominent place in the history of Australia. Not only are they an important part of Sydney's public transport system, but they are also well-known in other parts of Australia—even other parts of the world—because of the thousands of interstate and overseas visitors who see Sydney's famous harbour by taking a trip to Manly.

There is no order of precedence in thanking those who helped, although some have had more to give than others, particularly George Marshall, who was for many years traffic manager of the Port Jackson & Manly Steamship Company through some of its most colourful times, and Eric Gale, aged 92 when he told of his days as an engineer in the steam ferries and later works superintendent at the company's Kurraba Point depot and workshops.

The array of interesting pictures, most of them showing action and drama rather than mere static history, has come from several sources, including John Darroch, a ferry enthusiast and photographer for more than 30 years and a veritable encyclopaedia on harbour history; ferry crew member Robert Needham, who takes some great pictures of passing ferries in rough weather; former colleagues at the *Manly Daily*, where I received tremendous co-operation from chief executives Michael Utting and Laurie Coughlan; editors Murray White and Garry McGay, business manager Ian Muddle and photographers Ken James and John Van Loendersloot; George Marshall again, for some of the Port Jackson company's photographs; Brambles Industries Ltd, for access to the John Allcot paintings; and Captain Tom Gibson, former general manager of the Urban Transit Authority's ferry division, for that graphic Fred Elliott watercolour of the *Barrenjoey* on the cover of this book as well as other valuable assistance.

Others who have contributed greatly are ferry and hydrofoil captains David Stimson, Ron Hart, Keith Rosser, Max Barton and Bill Thomas, and former wharfinger Allen Conwell. Brian Verey had a wealth of reminiscences, particularly of the legendary W. L. Dendy, the man who built the Port Jackson & Manly Steamship Company to its peak of prominence. Brian and John Darroch were active with me in the early efforts to save the *South Steyne*. Then, later, came Newcastle businessman Michael Wansey, who provided the money to bring this great ship back to life. Finally, there was my wife, Vaila, who read each page for literals and things which could be 'better said', especially if the expressions used might not be understood and appreciated as much by the average reader as by the ferry enthusiasts and the ferry crews. She also spent countless hours with me winding the Public Library's microfilm files of old newspapers, reducing considerably what otherwise would have been a long and lonely chore. To everyone, again I say thank you. I think it has all been very worthwhile.

Tom Mead
Manly
30 June 1987

The Paintings

Several paintings by famous Australian marine artist **John Allcot**, OBE, FRAS, have been reproduced in this book by kind permission of Brambles Industries Limited, Rodney Allcot, a son of the artist, and the Allcot Trust. Most of them are part of a commission by the Port Jackson & Manly Steamship Company in which John Allcot did thirty-two paintings of the Manly ferries ranging from the first little paddlewheeler, *The Brothers* (1848), to the *South Steyne* (1938). These were acquired by Brambles Industries Limited when that company took over the Port Jackson & Manly Steamship Company in 1972.

John Allcot painted landscapes, still life and portraits as well as ships and the sea, but his paintings of ships and the sea rate with those of the leading marine artists of all time. They are sought eagerly today as collectors' pieces. He painted ships, clouds and sea so beautifully and authentically because he knew these things intimately, having been to sea himself, sailing before the mast in tall ships.

The sea was in his blood. He was born at West Derby, England, on 13 November 1888, the son of master mariner Captain George Allcot. When he was sixteen John ran away to sea and served eight years before the mast in sailing ships as cabin boy, cook and able seaman. At sea he would scrounge sail cloth and ship's paint and augment his meagre earnings by selling his paintings to the ships' officers. In Sydney in 1912 John Allcot left the sea to spend the next sixty years painting it and the ships that sailed upon it. It was said he had the ability to give a ship body and soul with his brush strokes.

John Allcot was made a Fellow of the Royal Art Society and in 1970 he was awarded an OBE for his services to the arts. He died in Sydney in 1973, but he and his work will never be forgotten by those who love the sea and ships, particularly those who are fortunate enough to have any of his wonderful paintings.

Fred Elliott was another famous Australian artist whose work included ships and the sea. The *Barrenjoey* crossing The Heads in a 60-mile-an-hour gale on Easter Sunday, 1927, is one of his paintings. The original is in the office of the general manager of the Urban Transit Authority's ferries division, by whose permission it is reproduced.

INDEX